TRUST ME

Written By

Richard Rashke

Cover photographs by
Thomas Radcliffe
Point of View Studio
Takoma Park, Maryland

Some of the names in this book have been changed in order to protect the identities of certain individuals.

Published by Narco, L.L.C.
P.O. Box 5153
Laytonsville, Maryland 20882
Direct Inquiries and/or orders to the above address.

ISBN: 0-9706825-0-6

Library of Congress Control Number: 2001094629

Printed in the United States by:
Morris Publishing
3212 East Highway 30
Kearney, NE 68847
1-800-650-7888

Sparshott's Acknowledgements:

There are so many people I would like to thank for their unselfish help in making this project become a reality.

To my wife, Pamela, from the first minute you walked into my life your constant love, support and encouragement have accomplished more than you will ever know ("22"). You contributed countless hours in preparing the book for print, even though you have a full-time job of making our house a loving home. You are a devoted mother to our son, Jake, and a wonderful friend to my daughter, Morgan. Your other dependents are our cats, the fish, and Woodie, our dog. There are times when I know you take time away from your favorite hobby of planning what flower or bush to plant in your wonderful garden in order to take care of us.

To Richard and Virginia Sparshott, my parents, for their constant support in my early years when I could have easily gone to the dark side. They taught me right from wrong and my Dad, a Special Agent with the Department of State, put "the Cop" in my blood.

To my co-workers: Detective June Boyle, whose friendship started this whole case. Sgt. Scott Hammond, a great partner and friend; I couldn't have done it without you. Agents Jerry McCready and Billy Campbell for being great friends; I am dyslexic and without their help, I would never have made it through all the federal red tape and the mountains of paperwork would have surely done me in. Tom Roberts and Bob Bonsip, two excellent prosecutors. Steve and Mike, two law enforcement officers with whom I did not always see eye-to-eye, but without them the case would never had made it off the ground and come to its successful conclusion. Chief Ronald Ricucci for believing in my undercover abilities.

To the members of the following agencies: Montgomery County Police Department, Prince Georges County Police Department, Fairfax County Police Department, the IRS and the FBI.

To Muriel Nellis for introducing me to Richard Rashke, and to Paula Kaufman, Richard's wife, whose hours of editing were greatly appreciated. Thanks to Lisa Townsend; her patience and computer skills were invaluable to the completion of this book. And, finally, to Mike Buchanan, WUSA Channel 9 News in Washington D.C., for giving me the push I needed to start this project in the first place.

April 1983

A cab pulls into the parking lot of Powder Mill Village. It's dark, just before eight, and Laurie sits in the back seat with Alfredo. She's in her early twenties, slim, attractive, except for the slightly swollen jaw Alfredo gave her earlier and her hands and feet are as cold as winter sheets.

"One more time, bitch," Alfredo says like a movie director. "Twice in the head, then grab the money and the shit. Fifteen minutes is all you get. I'll let it ring once, hang up. Then I'll call again." He hands her a small .32 Saturday night special, an automatic with a pearl handle that looks like a dime store toy. She slips the gun into her vest pocket, afraid to leave the car but more afraid of what he'll do if she doesn't.

Alfredo opens the door and pushes her. It's chilly outside, she stumbles, she click-clicks across the parking lot in her high heels, rings the bell at 201. The April night air has already crept up her skirt into her panty hose, only fifteen minutes, thank you Jesus the place is deserted. Raul lets her in. He's tall like Alfredo with light brown Cuban skin that reminds her of coffee with too much cream. She likes him, maybe even loves him a little but not more than white powder or as much as she fears Alfredo. Laurie has known Raul for five years since when they were teenagers and fucked and ran the streets together, sniffing, smoking, dealing an ounce here, an ounce there. In the beginning she did it with him for fun and because she liked his creamy brown body. But he got her hooked on cocaine and then she laid him for the shit, his friends too, two or three at a time, anyone, anything, anywhere, anytime. What the hell, Raul wasn't possessive, he liked to share her. She'd come to his stash pad—actually his cousin's apartment—when she needed a fix or he wanted to ball her. Sometimes he took pictures and sometimes he laid his friend while his friend laid her, everybody high, eyes as big as saucers, blood pounding, it didn't make much difference to her who was poking what where as long as she got high and went home with a few grams snug inside a leak-proof snow seal, for later.

It's a nice apartment, middle-class like, new furniture, not too expensive except for all the art on the walls. Raul collects the stuff and likes to talk to her about it, she listens but what the hell does she know or care. That Gene Davis shit with candy stripe lines any kid can draw, and Rebecca Davenport who needs painting lessons bad, and that Spanish shit that doesn't look like anything. Raul likes to go to all those art auctions and bids and buys, just like in the movies, sometimes with a gay friend like that Andy Warhol creep who was always after Raul's coffee-colored cock.

Raul leads her into the dining room where little baggies of joy powder line the table next to a scale and white plastic bottles of lactose, all cut, weighed, and ready to go, looks like half a kilo. She knows he has more, that black bitch Chicky was in town, at least a "key," maybe two if he had the front money.

She takes off her vest and drapes it over a chair at the end of the table far away from Raul as if it were mink. It feels like it has a lead lining and sags to one side, sweet Jesus I hope he doesn't notice.

Raul lights a roach, takes a hit, his eyes are already big and glassy, he doesn't do coke just weed, and gives it to her. She takes a long hit, her lungs are ready to burst, her mouth is dry, she's scared, she needs a real fix so bad she'd suck all the pricks in Powder Mill Village for it. Another deep hit and thirteen minutes to go.

Laurie stands behind Raul, runs her hands under his shirt and over his purple nipples, she can feel the heat rising. I need you, baby, she says. Christ, she just can't pull a gun, say "surprise!" and shoot poor Raul, she needs to lower his guard and raise his flag.

Raul leads her into the bedroom, lights low, wallet on the

dresser, the only phone in the place on the night table, bed made, as stack of porn magazines on the floor nearby. Raul likes to look at pictures, and take them too with that cheap little Polaroid of his, Christ he has pictures of her doing it to everyone but lady cops.

Raul takes off his shirt and shoes, a gold cross on a chain around his neck, some Cuban Catholic rabbit's foot, well Jesus won't do you no good now, baby, this is your last fuckin' fuck, make it fast and make it good like when we were kids. He takes another hit. She does too, sweet Jesus don't let it make me shoot crooked, ten minutes, she hopes he isn't so high she'll have to work hard at getting him, you know, ready. Alfredo didn't count on that, that Raul would be high and soft.

She slips out of her blouse, her nipples are still hard from the cold, she isn't wearing a bra, can't waste time, have to make it easy, make sure she doesn't leave anything behind, Alfredo warned her, the meter's running and he's waiting and he's mean when he's mad. She pulls off her skirt and strips off her pantyhose, she's not wearing panties, Alfredo told her not to, she has to get dressed in a hurry afterwards and get the hell out of there in case someone hears the shot and calls the cops. She's naked, she saved a minute, ready for work.

Laurie walks over to the bed, she doesn't feel sexy, she doesn't want to fuck, she doesn't feel like a killer, she feels numb with guilt and fear. She pulls off his pants, he's wearing red briefs, no crotch, Cuban macho shit, he's too high, Christ, this will take all night.

She kisses him the way she knows he likes it, wet and searching, his body warms her like a water bottle, she strokes him, she tries every trick she's learned from every man she was ever with and it's beginning to work, he's getting there, but not quite, not yet.

Raul reaches over the side of the bed and picks up the porn magazines, boys and girls, and pages through them with her. Six minutes. The men seem to excite him more than the women, what the hell, no time to be sensitive, as long as it works, everything you ever wanted in porn, big black cocks, big white cocks, pussies air brushed and styled, tangled and glistening, everybody doing it every which way, nothing she hasn't done before herself. Nothing turns her on, she's uptight, dry, anxious to stuff him inside her and coax him into climax, then shoot him and split with the shit.

Raul's getting as big as his eyes, it's about time, she'll make him come before he can say "Jack shit" but he's stubborn and won't, usually it's just the opposite, the luck of the Cuban, damn, she's running out of time.

The phone rings, now what, she panics. It stops before he can pick it up, it rings again, he grabs it, "Hello?" he says, he waits then hangs up. "Must be a wrong number," he tells her. What's Alfredo going to do now, will he leave her there, should she still shoot him?

Raul's soft again. She tells him, you know, how big he is, how good he feels against her, she needs him so much, she moans, she whimpers a little, he's getting excited now, he stops talking, he stops breathing for a second, then he begins to breathe heavier and faster, she loves the sound of him puffing like a toy train, she sneaks a look, his eyes are closed, it won't take long now, just one more little whimper and "oh baby, yes, yes," and it'll be over.

"Get me a drink," he says after he pushes himself off her, flexing his biceps. He rolls over the porn magazines and reaches for the phone and dials. She hurries out to the gun, it feels warm like it was sitting in the sun, it fits snugly in her tiny hand, not too big or too small. She stands in the bedroom doorway, naked, some of him running down her leg, the pearl handle behind her back. She doesn't want to kill him, she likes him, maybe even loves him a little, but shit is shit, he has it, she doesn't, that's his problem, and Alfredo is Alfredo, that's her problem, he'll slice up her mother, father, and brother one by one while she watches, then her if she doesn't do it.

When Alfredo found out a couple of months ago that she was balling Raul for toot, she thought he would kill her, but he told her hey baby, just keep humpin' away. He wanted to know everything about Raul, how much money he carried, where he hid the stash, how much weight he dealt, where he got the Mojo from. He made her tell him when Chicky was in town with her big black bodyguards. He made her phone Raul earlier that evening and tell him she wanted to come over and, you know, and then buy four ounces. She called but when Raul asked her to drop by later, her will turned to water and she said she couldn't make it, she was busy, her mother was sick. Alfredo slugged her in the jaw when he found out, then dragged her back to the phone, Christ her arm was sore, and stood right over her with those hammy fists of his while she called Raul a second time and told him she'd be over around eight, she needed him so bad she just couldn't wait. On the drive to Powder Mill, Alfredo told his friend the cab driver to pull over next to some dark woods. He pushed her into the trees and pulled out the small .32 with the pearl handle that gleamed in the darkness. She was ready to meet Jesus, amazing grace, she thought this was it, after all that she had seen and done in her twenty-four years, to rot in some stinking woods in Maryland until some kids found her body. But Alfredo handed her the gun and told her to fire it so she could hear how loud it was and wouldn't get scared after she shot the Cuban who had all that shit. For a small gun it made a lot of noise she thought, and Alfredo told her to shoot through a pillow or a towel to muffle the sound.

Laurie watches Raul talk into the phone from the bedroom doorway. "Roberto there?" he asks. "Put him on . . . hey man, come get me in twenty minutes. I'm at the apartment."

There's no time for a towel or a pillow, the gun suddenly has turned to ice, heavy as an ingot, she enters the bedroom. Raul is still stretched out on his stomach in his devil-red shorts surrounded by dirty pictures. All she has to do is wait until he hangs up, then squeeze the trigger, slowly like Alfredo showed her, before Raul can turn around, she can't look him in the eyes and kill him like he's some kind of stranger. She moves closer to the bed, points the pearls at the back of his head, he hangs up and she fires and the gun sounds like a cherry bomb, and Raul slides forward, his torso still on the bed, his head on the floor under the night table. She knows she's supposed to shoot him again, Alfredo told her to, twice he said, in the head he said, but she can't, not Raul, maybe some stranger, but not Raul.

She dresses quickly, glad that Alfredo told her not to wear panties or a bra, she snatches Raul's wallet from the dresser and drops it in her purse without even looking inside to see how much he has, she races into the dining room and scoops the baggies into her purse next to the still warm gun, she knows there must be more shit around but there's no time to look for it, some nosy sonofabitch is probably doing a 911 already.

The phone in the bedroom rings once, then stops, she rushes to it and waits, it rings again next to Raul's twisted neck, he looks dead, no need to bang him a second time, she picks up the receiver. I did it, I got it, she says. Come by and pick me up. She hangs up, grabs a pair of scissors with orange handles from the dresser top and cuts the phone cord like Alfredo told her, like a Hitchcock, all done, ready to split with the shit before . . .

She hears a whisper, "Help me!" Oh shit, she almost drops her purse. It can't be, she shot him, he's dead like Alfredo said, that was the plan. "Help me!" Raul whispers again.

Laurie stares down at him, he still looks dead, he isn't moving, still bent like a pretzel, but his eyes are open, puzzled and pleading. She can't shoot him again, he's dying anyway, it's only a matter of minutes, she can't risk another shot, there's no time, Alfredo's waiting, she needs a hit so bad she's shaking.

"What happened?" Raul's voice is stronger now. She doesn't answer, she panics, she likes Raul, maybe even loves him a little, but she has $15,000 worth of shit, enough to keep high for, who the fuck can count.

"Kill me!" Raul pleads. "Don't leave me like this." He's looking at her, his eyes are scared and hurt, she can't look him in the face and fire, sorry Raul, this isn't the way it was supposed to be, baby. A whole *pound* of shit, $15K, not bad for a single fuck, Alfredo'll be happy.

She runs to the door, she's in a hurry now, Roberto will be there soon, the cops are coming, no sirens yet, still time, she has to split, she closes the door but there's no time to pull it tight and check to see if it's locked, it doesn't make any difference anyway, he's dying, the Jesus call, you can see it in his eyes and smell it.

"What the fuck took you so long, bitch?" Alfredo says when she gets to the cab. "Got the shit?" She pats her purse and he opens the door, she's anxious to crawl into the warmth of the back seat, speed home and get a fix. But he snatches her bag, pushes her with his foot. She is still half in the cab, trying to hold on to the door when he tells the driver to go. It almost jerks her arm off.

Laurie stands and brushes off the parking lot dirt and looks around to make sure no one saw her, shit she says. She's stuck in Beltsville ten miles from Washington in high heels, eight thirty at night, in the dark, no money, no ID, the cold fingers of wind playing with her pussy, no nose candy, and Raul dying on the floor back there.

She takes off her shoes and walks quickly to a gas station on Powder Mill Road, praying to sweet Jesus that Raul will be dead when the cops break in, that no one saw her, wishing to god above she had shot him a second time. She begins thumbing her way home ready to pay with the only thing she's still got even if it is wet with Raul and cold.

□ □ □

Roberto doesn't mind picking up his older brother, Raul has the shit and always gives him some, never enough, just a snort or two, maybe a gram to take along. Raul doesn't trust him because he has the habit bad, and besides Raul is jealous because he's got a college degree and Raul doesn't. Roberto hangs up, feels a sharp pain in the back of his head, and faints. He's out for a flash and when the room stops spinning he knows something happened to Raul, a vision of intense light that looks inviting but feels bad.

Roberto races over to Raul's stash pad about fifteen minutes away, parks in the lot, and runs to 201, the bedroom and dining room lights are on, he rings the bell, then pounds on the door, he knows Raul is there, he just talked to him, he knows he's in trouble, he can feel it, where the shit is he, taking a shower maybe, in bed with somebody and doesn't want to come to the door. Roberto tries the knob, the door is locked, he peeps in a window and sees the scale on the dining room table, he puts his ear to the door, it's quiet. Then he hears, "Help me, help me," weak but clear, he gives the door a kick and it flies open.

Roberto runs through the dining room past the table with a film of white powder on it so he knows Raul didn't finish cleaning up, but where's the shit? He bursts into the bedroom and finds Raul half on and half off the bed but there's no blood, he doesn't know what's wrong, did Raul have a stroke or what?

Raul looks up at Roberto, his body twisted around the night table, red crotchless bikinis, gold cross on his bare chest. His eyes roll back, he's gone, looks dead, orange-handled scissors on the carpet, phone cord cut.

Roberto bends over to lift his brother onto the bed, sees the blood-stained carpet under his head, and knows he's been shot, call 911 is all he can think of, 911. He runs out of the apartment and beats on the door next to Raul's but no one answers he tries the next door down, there's a light on inside, he pounds and shouts, "It's an emergency, someone's dying, I need your phone!" A woman comes to the door, "Just a minute," she says, "I'm on long distance."

Fuck it, lady. Roberto pushes his way past her into the apartment and grabs the phone, disconnects her call and dials 911, "My brother's been shot," he yells at the dispatcher, he gives her the address, then calls Raul's wife Lolita, no time to ease it to her, "Raul's been shot," he blurts. Lolita starts screaming so he knows she got the message, he hangs up and races back to help Raul, save his life, the ambulance and the cops are on the way.

Roberto runs past the dining room table, stops on a dime, turns and comes back, what the hell, can't waste the shit. He brushes the white residue into a neat little pile, cleanliness is next to godliness his mother always told him and snorts, then he goes back to Raul to see if he needs help, to wait for the rush, the explosion in the head, the calm, he knows Raul understands.

Raul is still out, dead probably, no way to tell, and he's not interested in playing doctor, taking a pulse, shoving a mirror under his nose or putting his ear to his chest, like on TV. He collects all the porn magazines from the bed and stashes them in a closet, that's no way to die, to have the stretcher guys and the cops see him with all those pictures, what will they think? His brain explodes, good shit, thank you Raul, then he lifts the body back onto the bed so his brother'll look nice, fuck all that cop shit about not disturbing the evidence, if they want to see how he was shot there's plenty of blood stains on the rug under the night table.

Roberto waits a minute, he's feeling pretty good now, proud of himself, mellow and confident, fuck the cops, then he hears the sirens, faint at first, then louder. He knows Raul has more shit around the place, he's tempted to look for it, it wouldn't be good for the cops to find it, would it? Then he sees the red lights flashing through the bedroom window, spinning shadows on the wall. Hey Raul, he says, they're here big brother, hang in there, you'll be okay.

But Raul doesn't move, his eyes don't open, he doesn't seem to be interested.

PART ONE

The Trail
Spring 1986

ONE

June Boyle had the little prick by the balls. His name was Curtis and he had just sold her a quarter ounce of coke for the third time and faced five years for possession with intent. She offered to drop a couple charges if he'd roll over, but he decided to play tough. Hey, no way he's gonna snitch to some fucking narc with big tits.

Boyle squeezed. "Okay, Curtis, babe, let's make it *real* simple. You help me and stay male . . . or . . . you do five and come out female."

Curtis blurted, "I buy from Mick."

Hey, at least the guy's smart enough to know that little 22-year-old white boys are jailhouse hors d'oeuvres.

"Where's he live?"

"Somewhere in Maryland."

"What's he do?"

"Some kind of computer shit. He hangs with rock bands."

"Good goin', Curtis." Boyle smiled, even white teeth, disarming and sexy. "You set me up, I'll blow your fuckin' head off."

Boyle had just taken Curtis down in the parking lot of the Howard Johnson's south of Old Town Alexandria. Every narc has a favorite place for buys and busts, a kind of undercover good luck charm, and HoJo's was hers, a perfect spot. All the bad guys had to do was roll down the ramp of the beltway that ties Washington to Virginia and Maryland, look up, and there it was—a blue and orange gingerbread chalet set in cement. The food was mediocre but the parking lot was wonderful. Plenty of open space for surveillance, good access in case of trouble, one way in and one way out, about as safe as they come for a late night shootout. Boyle had made at least thirty buy-busts there in her nine months as an undercover narcotics officer with the Fairfax County Police.

Although she loved her work so much she couldn't dream of life without it, Boyle had to pay for her shield. It began her first day on the job with, "Don't think you're coming on to break up marriages!" and came to an ugly head one day when she was still a patrol officer. The guys grabbed her in the squad room, handcuffed her to a bench, then unzipped her trousers and unbuttoned her shirt while her supervisor stood by and watched. The boys in blue stopped short of feeling her up but she was outraged that her colleagues—six to one—would dare drool over the curve of her crotch right in the squad room and in front of brass. "What are you going to do about this?" she demanded of her supervisor when someone finally uncuffed her. "Nothing," he said. Christ, it was worse than having every Curtis in Fairfax itching to get into your pants.

Boyle filed a sexual harassment complaint, internal affairs investigated, the incident died in the files. When she threatened to go public, her superiors threatened to expose a private sexual indiscretion of a married friend. There were no rules, precedents, or old-girl networks back in those dark ages before Anita Hill let the skeleton out of the closet for its debut on national television. Boyle gave in to the blackmail but never forgave herself for the cowardice. Now, as the only woman on a twenty-five man narc squad, she had to produce three times as much as the boys just to be considered average and she ended up doing more weird Pagan-biker and PCP shit than any other narc. "You're better at it because you're a woman," the men had told her. Sure, guys! It took her six months to figure out they shoved the dangerous assignments at her because they were too scared to take them themselves, so much for brave-talking, iron-pumping, big-prick men . . .

Three minutes after busting Curtis, Boyle had sensed that he was the kind of wimp who'd roll on his mother to reduce jail time, so she processed him as quickly as a burger before anyone he knew spotted him in the station and before the press could get curious, not that she thought he was worth even a graf in the *Alexandria Gazette,* but it was a slow April night and narcs survive on caution. If this Mick ever got wind of Curtis's arrest, he'd smell a setup and Boyle would have to settle for the little prick after all. What the hell, in the narc business you take what you can get and move on.

Spinning two-bit bad guys is every county cop's M-16 in the war on drugs. "Locals" as the Feds call them—they don't even try to hide their contempt—can't do all the Hoover G-men shit you see in the movies. In June Boyle's world, you make a contact in a bar or a 7-Eleven, buy a couple Gees of powdered coke, maybe even an eightball for $500. You set up a second buy for, say, a quarter at $850 if your boss feels generous and the narcotics budget still has money. Ounces at $2,200 are out of the question, hell, you can cop four eightballs for that, and kilo buys are the stuff that a county narc's wet dreams are made of. Without money to flash and time to kill, you sometimes get lucky and nail a street user-dealer like Mick, rarely his bagman who swaddles himself in more layers of protection than a snow goose has feathers. It's not that the big bad guys are so smart. It just costs more than taxpayers are willing to spend to catch them. So narcs like Boyle settle for little pricks, play stickball instead of hardball, and try to spin every little scumbag they catch.

"Listen real good, Curtis." It was the opening line of Boyle's Snitch 101 spiel. "My name is Rene . . . You don't know me well . . . My boyfriend holds the bread . . . That's all you need to know. One, two, three. Got it? Now you call Mick, tell him I'm looking for weight, say, a quarter pound to begin with. Ask him if he can do it. Then set up a meet at Denny's."

Denny's Restaurant, another Boyle favorite, is a quarter mile down from Howie J's on the strip, the stretch of U.S. Route 1 between the beltway and Fort Belvoir, seven miles south of the White House, the crotch of Fairfax County, number one in robberies, rapes, stolen cars, narcotics, bar fights, prostitution. Pagans in leather jackets sell "green" and "crank" in the topless bars there where their chicks make up eight out of ten tits twirling pasties—Fairfax believes in modesty. Prostitutes who have raised the blow-job-while-you-drive to an art parade across the road from HoJo's. Johns glide down the beltway ramp and stop long enough to get a price and a peek down cleavage lane. By the time they reach the last bus stop on the strip, they have smiles on their faces and towelette-wiped dicks. The prostitutes then hop a bus back to HoJo's smirking all the way. Nine out of ten are men in drag, so much for truth in advertising.

Denny's was a logical choice for a first meet with Mick. His buddy Curtis lived a few blocks away in Belle Haven Towers along Route 1 between Howie Johnson's and the restaurant. An introduction in a public place near Curtis's would lull Mick into a false sense of security. Boyle couldn't count the number of snitches and dirtballs she had met in the restaurant and bar or the number of buys she had made inside and out. On one Denny's undercover assignment, she spent several nights on a stool recording a gambling operation which used the bar phone for contacts. But that was in her pre-narc days when she played an occasional vice squad moll or a rape decoy.

Curtis made the call to Mick. Boyle could just see the guy nearly creaming in his pants—a buyer who wanted four ounces, $8,000 worth of powder-shit for openers, mentally calculating how much he could skim off the top, praying that his source would front the blow, saying of course he could deal a quarter pound, what did Curtis think he was, some schoolyard pusher?

When Boyle pulled into Denny's a few days later, Mick and Curtis were already there, wedged in a horseshoe-shaped, green vinyl booth, the kind that farts every time you move. She parked and studied them from a distance.

Curtis was sitting up close to the table as if he was afraid he'd stick to the backrest and kept folding and unfolding his hands like an old lady. Mick was a Geraldo look-alike, droopy mustache and all, five-ten, one-sixty, soft mouth, reedy hands, an all-American wimp.

Boyle knew she could take both guys down faster than they could snort a line, but her heart still pounded so hard—it always did before a buy—she was certain Mick would see it fluttering against her shirt. She patted the .38 special in her purse, pure reflex, this meet was as safe as they come in the u.c. trade. She already knew Curtis, Denny's was home to her, it was broad daylight and the place was public. But she had no backup and wasn't wearing a wire. Christ, anything could go wrong anytime. She could blow her lines, Mick might know her, Curtis could make a slip. If Mick was juiced, he could freak out. It had happened before.

Boyle once bought a tin of green—PCP sprayed on parsley leaves and wrapped in tinfoil—from a young woman not long after becoming a narc. She offered to let the woman work off the charges as an informant and the woman agreed and introduced Boyle to her supplier, a stringy-haired blond biker who lived in a one-room shack in Falls Church, Virginia, ten miles west of the Kennedy Center. Boyle could smell the pungent hospital odor of PCP as soon as she stepped into the shack, once you whiff the stuff your nose never forgets it. Blondie's wild eyes and dirty fingernails told her he was a PCP hophead, a genuine green bean. She bought a can for $50, then got the hell out of the tiny dump before someone changed a mind, if there was one present.

Boyle returned a week later for a second buy. She wasn't wired and didn't have a gun just in case Blondie decided to search her. His green-bean girlfriend let her in. Blondie himself was stupored out on the sleep sofa that took up three quarters of the room. The girlfriend pulled down a five-pound Folger's coffee can from a wall shelf next to a bow and a quiver of hunting arrows, pried open the can, dipped out a spoonful of parsley, and put it into an empty 35mm film canister. Boyle gave her the fifty and was half out the door when Blondie popped up like a mummy in an Abbott and Costello movie and pinned her to the doorframe with his foot. "Fuckin' narc," he screamed. "Goddamned fuckin' narc!"

Keeping her nailed to the doorframe, one breast in and one out, Blondie pulled her shirt out of her jeans and ran his hands up and down her legs, then around her bare waist. She slapped his paws with her one free hand before they found her breasts. Blondie leaned back, lit up a PCP cigarette the size of a big firecracker, puffed it into a glow. "You're gonna smoke this fuckin' cigar," he said.

"Fuck you," Boyle yelled back. "I'm splittin' . . . gotta pick up my kid."

The word "kid" sent Blondie's girlfriend straight into PCP land. "Kids are baby goats," she sang. "Kids are baby goats." Then ba-a-a-ing like a billy goat, she grabbed the bow and an arrow from the wall and aimed it at Boyle while Blondie said, "She's gonna kill you if you don't smoke this whole thing!"

At that point, Boyle's partner waiting in an undercover car fifty yards away tooted the horn, no one had to tell her she was in green-bean shit. "Your partner too," Blondie said.

She'd have laughed if she wasn't so fucking scared. Great timing, partner, why not just blow a bugle and send in the cavalry. Christ she'd smoke all the green in Falls Church if it would help. Fuck the undercover rules, better fired for sampling and alive, than nailed to the door like a possum skin.

Blondie leaned forward to hand her the cigarette and when he did, he relaxed his foot long enough for Boyle to squeeze through the door. She caught her jacket on a nail, left a piece of denim behind, better than a piece of tit, and raced to the car with Blondie's girlfriend chasing after her still making like a goat, half expecting an arrow up her narco ass any second.

The green beans taught Boyle three lessons: any deal can go sour anytime, fear is the only undercover bullet-proof vest you can count on, and death is just a ba-a-a away.

With those lessons in mind, Boyle took a deep breath, opened the door and walked into Denny's.

2:15 P.M.

She slides into the booth next to Curtis and across from Mick so she can watch his face. She is dressed in jeans and a blouse that hints at the round of her breasts. "How's it goin," she says to Curtis. Her heart has stopped pounding as it always does once she begins the undercover seduction. She feels Mick's eyes on her and knows exactly what he's thinking: "Is this bitch setting me up or what?" quickly followed by "Is she a good lay?" She watches the two thoughts wrestle. "Good lay" wins by a length, it always does.

Boyle uses sex in the undercover game like men use biceps. She has this theory that the more bad guys dream about big tits, the more they talk themselves into believing she can't possibly be a cop. Like, hey man, who ever heard of a pig with nice tits. She tested the idea one day on a hinky scumbag who saw a narc on every barstool. Posing as a prostitute, she softened him with a smile, teased him with cleavage, then suggested they do the buy in a motel room. The sucker was drooling down his gold chain when he rapped at the door with four ounces of white. She tested the shit and made the buy, he took the money, then tried to feel her up but she was wired and told him she had to, you know, go get ready. She slipped into the bathroom while he began peeling off his clothes. SWAT smashed through the door before the horny prick had his shoes off. He was as hurt as he was stunned. "A fuckin' narc!" he kept saying. "I don't fuckin' believe it, man. I thought you *liked* me."

Back at Denny's, Boyle plays vulnerable to make Mick feel macho. Her name is Rene, she tells him with no attempt to disguise her Boston twang. She wants to buy a couple ounces. If the shit is good, maybe a pound, if it's Lipton Tea, goodbye Marco, baby. Her boyfriend David owns a small construction company, mostly asphalt parking lots, nothing big. She runs all his shitface errands and makes the small buys, a few Gees here, an eightball there. David makes the big buys, the sonofabitch doesn't trust her with the money. She keeps her daughter in daycare while she's working.

Woven from fact and fiction, everything in Boyle's cover story has a purpose. She once dated a guy named David who owned a small construction company so she knows enough about asphalt to hold her own. The twang makes her an unlikely Fairfax narc. The girl Friday role gives her the excuse to drive around northern Virginia at odd hours in everything from a sports car to a pickup truck with a beeper in her pocket and enough cash to buy an eightball. The daughter-in-day-care bit provides a quick out—"gotta get my kid"—when a deal starts to turn sour or a bad guy starts insisting on a blow job for the coke.

Mick buys the cover and starts playing smartass in a squeaky rapid-fire as if he's wired. He'll help her out, he offers like a big-shit philanthropist. He's seen a kilo or two sitting around his source's place, a Cuban hombre. But the buy will have to go down in Maryland near Aspen Hill, no way he's gonna let that much shit walk into Virginia, what does she think he is, some kind of sucker?

Right on, baby!

As she listens to Mick puff, Boyle carefully sifts through the bullshit for leads and inconsistencies. Aspen Hill is an upper middle class enclave in Montgomery County—the fifth richest county in the country—on the Maryland side of the Potomac. Mick's Cuban supplier must live there otherwise Mick wouldn't drop the name, and Mick's insistence on doing business there makes perfect dope-logic: Street dealers prefer to sell on their own turf in case the deal goes south and they have to run. Unless they have front money, and most don't, their sources don't trust them with the shit longer than ten minutes, an edgy ten minutes at that. And buyers like "Rene" don't want to wait an hour for their man to come back with the fix. In, zap, out, and on their way to a grand old high.

But Boyle knows if she crosses the Potomac she'll have to work with Montgomery County narcs and she isn't thrilled with the idea. *She* nailed Curtis, *she* flipped him and set up the buy with Mick. If the Cuban source really deals kilos—dirtballs lie more than they tell the truth—it will be a big case for suburban Washington. Coke is just beginning to powder the area. Ounces are the rule, pounds the exception, kilos a species native to south Florida. She wants the stat on her own scorecard, she wants to run her own case not play the dick-whipped girlfriend of another narc, and later she wants to savor the knowledge that she, June "Rene" Boyle, the only woman on the Fairfax County uncle squad, made what may turn out to be the biggest hand-to-hand buy in the Washington area. But if she wants Mick and his Cuban supplier, she has no choice but to cross the river.

"No problem," she tells Mick, "but David comes with me."

Mick shifts in his green vinyl seat and his voice rises a note higher. "Hey, no fuckin' boyfriend," he says. "Shit, I ain't gonna get ripped. Curtis said *you* wanted to do the buy."

Boyle holds her ground. "You want Maryland, you deal with me *and* David. No fuckin' way I'm goin' in alone, man." She knows that bad guys prefer to deal vulnerable women rather than men, cokies who'll suck or fuck for a snort, and she can feel Mick struggling with greed, her best undercover partner in a buy. Street dealer-users sell for a cut of the shit and she gambles on them taking big, even stupid risks, to feed their habit.

Mick gives in. "All right, but I'm gonna check you out in case you're a fuckin' cop. Gimme the name of the company, the phone number, and your number. I'll call if everything's cool."

Boyle's company, "R&R," is her private joke. It stands for "rags-to-riches" and has its own answering machine in the narc office to field her calls. R&R is also listed with the telephone company in case anyone phones the operator to check it out.

"You're mine, Marco baby," Boyle promises herself. She knows exactly who she wants to play her boyfriend David. "I'm gonna tie your little coke balls in a knot."

TWO

Tracy Sparshott bounced into the squad room like a frisky St. Bernard. It was early evening, the time of day when the bad guys are just beginning to stretch and he was ready for them. Leather boots, cap, and vest over a Harley tee shirt which barely hid a hand-tooled belt with a big Harley buckle. Thirtyish with shoulder-length fine brown hair and a bushy beard covering his pebble-smooth face. Six feet, 240 pounds, mostly iron-pumped muscle, a hint of flab. He had gentle brown eyes except when he was excited, then they sparked, or mad, then they burned, one of his best weapons as an undercover cop. Women loved them, snitches found them understanding, bad guys trusted them until he turned the anger on, then he scared the stink right out of the pieces of shit. In a word, Tracy Sparshott was the kind of guy dirtballs respect.

"Anything going on?" he asked no one in particular.

"A couple of possibles," no one in particular answered.

Eight other narcs sat at or on desks cluttered with files, phones, scales, and a curious assortment of bongs, pipes, snorting bullets, and Deering kits—trophies of busts gone by. Their desks formed a square in the living room of a townhouse on Stone Street in Rockville, Maryland, the undercover headquarters of the narcotics division of the Montgomery County Police, fifteen miles north of the White House and halfway around the beltway from Howie Johnson's on Route 1. They were an odd-looking bunch. All men, mostly in jeans, tee shirts, a couple of beards, a mustache or two, one "Joe Preppy" in designer shoes, and one "Black Dude" smelling of aftershave. They counted money for a buy, weighed dope for a sale, caught up on the endless stream of paperwork as they waited for the first curtain call of the evening.

Sparshott waved to his supervisor insulated behind a Plexiglas window, then sat down behind his own desk. He was about to return a beeper call from Hewey, a snitch he had groomed like a fucking poodle, hey, what would a narc do without them, when his phone rang. It was June Boyle.

"Doin' anything tonight, Trace?" she asked.

"Christ, give me five minutes will ya, June? I just got in. What's up?"

"The deal came together, you know, the one with Mick."

Boyle had called Tracy right after she met Mick and he had agreed to work with her, no way he was gonna pass up a chance to pop someone who deals weight. Ten years in and out of Montgomery County sewers and the guy still thinks police work is a ringside seat at the greatest show on earth, two thumbs up.

"The meet's at ten tonight."

"Super! Where's the buy going down?"

"Around Aspen Hill. Mick'll beep me later to get the location. You gonna have a problem?"

Tracy had liked June Boyle from the moment she grabbed the mike at the Green Turtle in Ocean City, Maryland, where the Washington Council of Governments was holding a narc weekend, jumped on a table, and started singing, "I Fought the Law and the Law Won." She was only a rookie u.c. cop then, but quickly turned into a bust-driven narc who could improvise as well as she acted. Every narc in the area knew her pussy story. She was posing as a prostitute one night and making a buy from a sly, hinky dealer no other narc in Fairfax could get close to. She sat in the front seat of her car, wired; he was in the back, armed. He handed her a quarter ounce. She opened the plastic zip-lock bag, stabbed it with her index finger and was about to "test" it on her gums with her pointing finger when the scumbag leaned forward and caught her faking it. She knew she was dead meat. "Ah shit," she told him. "I gotta put it where it's *really* gonna do some good." She jumped out of the car, faced the creep, then shoved her hand down the front of her tight leather skirt into her crotch and rubbed slowly. "A-a-ah," she sighed. Quality coke numbs sensitive skin. "Good shit." The jerk got as excited as a tomcat and the surveillance guys watching her through binoculars and listening to her wire went crazy. "I'm just a working girl," she said. "I gotta take *real good* care of it." It was a beautiful buy, a work of narc art, and Sparshott always thought she should have been voted Narc of the Year for that performance. He had hoisted a few beers with her that Ocean City weekend and looked forward to working with her some day.

"No problem, June," Tracy said. "But you know we gotta get something out of this."

Boyle knew and accepted the unwritten rules of the fiercely competitive narc game: If a Fairfax deal goes down in another county which fronts the buy, then that county gets to stage the raid, bag the stat, and keep the drug money it seizes. However, if a Fairfax deal goes down in another county and *Fairfax* fronts the money, then Fairfax can negotiate a share of the booty. But Boyle knew that the mere thought of spending a couple grand *inside* Fairfax sent shivers through the county budget. As far as Fairfax—the sixth richest county in the country—was concerned, Maryland might as well be Canada and it sure as hell wasn't going to risk its narc money there.

"Okay, Trace . . . what do you want?" Boyle asked.

"The paper . . . and we want to bang the house." Sparshott wasn't bashful.

Boyle agreed. If she didn't, Tracy's boss would say, "We a fuckin' bank or something?" Besides, she had wanted to work with Tracy Sparshott ever since fellow narcs from the thirty departments in and around Washington voted him Narc of the Year for cracking a major dope ring. It had begun with a threadbare lead from a narc in a neighboring county . . . Hey, Trace, how's it going, buddy, got something for you, a former D.C. cop, a real douchebag, doing coke and PCP in your yard, no name, no address, but the snitch says the guy drives a '65 Vette with "Maylo" on the plate . . . It ended seven months later with Sparshott making major back-to-back cocaine and PCP buys on the same night followed by a string of raids in and around Washington, three police departments and the DEA involved, not a shot fired, eight arrests and convictions, $1.3 million worth of dope, the biggest PCP seizure in Washington's history, two gallons of liquid shit, a million hits. It takes a narc to appreciate the beauty and balls of it all . . . And after he accepted his Narc of the Year award, Sparshott had thanked each of the brothers who helped on the case by name, then asked them to join him on stage. He blew the cork off his bottle of Dom Perignon, theatrically of course, like a fucking cannon, then shared the champagne with them.

"Got a buy for ten tonight," Sparshott shouted to the undercover cops in the squad room after Boyle hung up. He loved to be first and that day he was the first narc in the squad to line up a buy. "Who's free?" Just about everyone volunteered.

"Anyone on overtime?" Sparshott asked. Two narcs said yes. Sparshott picked them and three others. Cops didn't make a hell of a lot of money and he liked to give his buddies a break every chance he got. Fuck the taxpayers who dump on cops until they really need them, then it's, "911, officer help, please help!"

Sparshott filled out a Narcotics Enforcement Fund request for $1,500, explained the deal to his supervisor, then pitched to the boss' greed with, "Hey, the bad guy deals weight." The greater the volume, the better the odds of seizing drug money, the greater the probability that the bust will do more than pay for itself, the latest in law enforcement usury.

Montgomery County was the envy of nearly every other police force in the country in 1986. It was one of a handful of jurisdictions and the only one around Washington that allowed its narcotics division to use all the money it seized on busts and raids for drug enforcement. Every other ball-busting cop had to dump the loot in the county's general operating budget to make the politicians look good, only to come begging each fiscal year for more buy-money, extra training, safer equipment. Just one more form of legalized cop abuse, but what the hell, as the old saying goes, don't piss on the hand that feeds you.

Sparshott watched the super take the money from the safe and count it. Then he strolled over to the copy machine, photocopied the bills for later use as evidence—in the Al Capone days they wrote the serial numbers down one by one—and called Boyle back. "All set . . . how many people can you spare?"

"Four or five," she said.

"Okay, let's meet at the Wheaton substation. Have your people there by nine . . . tell the bad guy we'll see him in the parking lot of the Baptist church, you know, right off the beltway ramp at Georgia."

Sparshott believed in risk, not chance. He chose the church lot to make it easy for Mick, who lived in Greenbelt, Maryland, a few minutes east of the Georgia Avenue beltway exit. All the scumbag had to do was coast down the ramp, up Georgia Avenue a few hundred feet, and turn right. The church lot was empty, dark, and secluded at night which made it look safe, but it was lit by beltway spill lights and wide open which made it ideal for surveillance. There were plenty of side streets to hide eight to nine undercover cars. Georgia Avenue itself was a four-lane artery pumping cars in and out of Washington day and night which made it easy for undercover cars to blend with traffic. And Aspen Hill was six miles north of the church, straight up Georgia.

There was a low ripple of excitement when the Fairfax and Montgomery undercover teams met in the substation squad room just off Georgia on Randolph Road halfway between the church and Aspen Hill. Bulletin boards, a couple of tables, TV, soda and snack machines, blackboard. Ten backup narcs, two supervisors, and two undercovers. It was critical to a safe and smooth buy for everyone to meet, see what Sparshott and Boyle looked like in particular, and understand what was going down, when and where.

Boyle began the briefing since it was her case . . . The unwitting is Mark Megerer, five-ten, 155 pounds, a Caucasian in his late twenties, wavy shoulder-length hair, mustache, brown eyes. He lives at 9250 Edmonston Road in Greenbelt and owns a 1980 red Chevy Monza, Maryland registration CXY 377. He may be driving another car. He has no priors and we don't know if he'll be armed.

His source is a Cuban. We believe he deals weight. He lives in or near Aspen Hill where we think the deal will go down.

Sparshott laid out the buy-strategy since he was the lead undercover and Aspen Hill was his turf . . . This is just a first buy, brothers, not a buy-bust. Our goal is to cop a quarter ounce directly from the source, the Cuban himself. He may be new, we have no intelligence on him. If I can't get an introduction, Mark will get the dope and bring it back to me. A Montgomery County surveillance car will follow him . . . sorry Fairfax guys, we know the area better than you . . . Now listen up! We can bust Mark anytime. It's his man we're after. So we *have* to get a fix on the Cuban's residence or the whole fucking buy's a waste . . . If the bad guy leads us north on Georgia like we think he's gonna do, we want *loose* surveillance. He may have counter surveillance and we don't want to blow the deal just because somebody gets burned . . . All we need is *one* car to follow us. Save the others in case the bad guy gets nervous and starts making turns to shake surveillance. You guys work it out . . . If it looks like everything's goin' real good, I might decide to make *two* quarter buys tonight to save time. Whatever—I'll let you know when I get what I need, then we'll all meet back here.

Communication is the most critical factor for any safe buy. Unfortunately, the two counties were using different radios that night because Montgomery didn't have enough extras to go around, the usual budget shit. A bad break and dangerous, but what the hell, undercover cops learn to make do.

Sparshott continued . . . Fairfax and Montgomery supervisors will share the command car. Each surveillance team will communicate by radio with its respective supervisor. Each super will hear the other's radio chatter and will pass important information down the line . . . The meet is set for ten, everybody should be in place no later than nine fifteen, so get your sodas and a bite to eat now. I'll raise you on the radio just before we pull into the lot around nine thirty . . . Everybody, get a good look at each other's cars. June and I'll be in her blue Charger. Check it out before you leave. She'll take the wheel . . . You guys from Fairfax, follow one of our cars down to the church. Everyone, spread out and stay back. Once you're in place, let your supervisor know where you're sitting . . . Don't be late. And listen up to the radio.

Sparshott didn't have to say half of what he did, there wasn't a rookie in the room, and each man could work out the square root of first-buy surveillance in his head. But there were ten cars from two different police forces and Sparshott was a perfectionist who lived by the first rule of undercover work: plan as if your life depends on it, then expect the unexpected as if planning doesn't count. He knew there would be surprises, there always were, and that's what made the job so much fucking fun.

The squad room emptied quickly. Sparshott and Boyle climbed into her Charger, drove across Randolph Road to Country Boy Market for a six-pack of Bud, the street-dealer's beer of choice. Sparshott knew the owner and his crotchety old man and liked to shove as much county business their way as he could.

Sparshott squeezed back into the Charger next to Boyle and they drove south down Georgia past Hardee's, Dunkin' Donuts, and a string of mini-marts to Montgomery Hills Baptist Church where they parked in a moon shadow. They were aware that bad guys had murdered a Montgomery County narc during a u.c. buy in the Silver Spring Holiday Inn a mile south from where they sat, but they were confident. Between them, they had made more than a thousand buys without ever getting anyone killed.

As they waited for Mark, they watched for counter surveillance. Bad guys sometimes send a car on ahead to see where the buyer is coming from and whether he or she has surveillance. If Sparshott or Boyle spotted a suspicious car, they'd radio a description and the tag number if they could read it. Someone would then run a make to see who owned it.

Sparshott tore open a can of Bud and passed it to Boyle who was wearing her usual jeans and a straining tank top, a Smith & Wesson model 10 in her purse. Usually, she bought dope alone from armed men in dark places and risked rape every time she did, which was why she was the only woman on the Fairfax narc squad. But tonight she had 240 pounds of beef sitting next to her and her heart wasn't pounding.

Sparshott opened a beer for himself and took a gulp to get the smell on his breath. If this were a dangerous buy-bust instead of a safer first buy, he'd gargle the stuff like Listerine. He took another gulp. Hey, the County's paying for the six-pack, no use wasting more taxpayers' money. He packed a two-inch Smith-Wesson with slip-free Pachmyre grips in his left boot and a switchblade in his leather vest. He carried no ID in case Mark pulled a gun and searched him. A radio kept his crotch company. To Boyle, he appeared Bud-cool but under the veneer of suds he was as excited as a kid on a third date. He had backed into police work in the summer of '75. He was working his way through his first year of college as a security guard and planned to join his father in the Foreign Service some day. There were a couple of last minute openings in the police academy and the department offered one to him. He was twenty-one and to him, three more years slouching in a classroom and guarding gates was more of a sentence than an opportunity. Fuck the foreign service dream, he became a local, spent five years on patrol, three more on a special Assignment Team, then on to narcotics. He took to undercover work like a retriever to water, loved tip-toeing along the edge, the higher the better, and became the biggest producer on his squad. He developed an allergy to paper and quickly learned to live with the fucked up revolving door that eggheads call the "legal justice system." In just a few minutes, he'd become David, a role he had never played before, with a partner he had never worked with before. He'd meet a bad guy for the first time, and get to con him, set him up, and take him down. Hey, is there a God or isn't there?

He went over the cover one last time. He doesn't want to make the tiniest slip even if Mark fails to notice it. Facts about David and his relationship to Rene are the threads from which he'll weave an identity to scam Mark, keep him from getting hinky, and lure him back for more buys until they don't need him anymore. Then he'll pop him, Mark will pull jail time, another dirtball will snatch his place on the street. But Tracy doesn't worry about that, he worries about a perfect scam, a clean bust, and catching the Cuban:

I'm your boyfriend, my name is David, we've been living together for five years, none of that hello young lovers shit. I own a construction company, asphalt mostly, I do some work in Montgomery County. I always hold the money, I treat you like shit, I do my own big buys and like to deal with the man himself. I'm into bikes, an all around badass, that's it, nothing more. If the bad guy asks any questions, let *me* handle him. If I tell you to shut the fuck up, I'm not mad at you, I'm just showing the wimp I'm in charge and it's none of his fucking business, play along.

It was a few minutes past ten. The radio crackled: "I just saw a silver Torino with two guys drive by twice. It could be the car. You copy?"

"We copy," Sparshott said. The surprises are beginning. A different car, a pair of bad guys, a two-fer.

The radio crackled again, a different voice: "A silver Torino with two guys is parking behind the church on Forest Glen . . . one guy's getting out . . . he's running behind the church . . . he's coming toward you . . . Lost him."

"Got him," Sparshott said into the radio. He could see Mark jogging through the shadow of the white church and into the spill of the beltway lights. "We're closing down."

THREE

10:00 P.M.

Mark jogs over to Sparshott's side of the Charger, leans down, and says into the open window: "Follow me and my partner, we're parked around the corner." It is more nervous invitation than command. Then like a dog-race pacer, he leads the Charger, headlights out, back behind the church to the silver Torino waiting on Forest Glen Road and climbs in. The Torino makes a u-turn back to Georgia, then turns right toward Aspen Hill.

Sparshott pulls the radio out from under the seat and sets it in his lap where it can't be seen but where it can easily pick up his voice. If anyone's watching, it will look as if he's talking to Boyle. He says: "This is it. The bad guys are here and you're right . . . it *is* the silver Torino, Maryland registration John-Frank-Paul 174 . . . we're following it north on Georgia, somebody get a listing."

Sparshott wants to know who owns the car and where he lives. The more he knows the better he can play his undercover David role, the safer he and Boyle are, the better the odds that they'll catch the bad guys. Who knows, maybe he'll get lucky. Maybe the driver of the Torino is the actual owner of the car. Maybe the Torino is stolen. The radio crackles: "The tag is listed to a John Brent Friedberg, nine-three-four-eight Cherry Hill Road, number three-oh-seven . . . College Park."

College Park, the home of the University of Maryland, is just east of Greenbelt where Mark lives. The address is important in case Mark tries a rip-and-run or in case Sparshott wants to do surveillance on the place between buys. But he doesn't risk writing the address down because the bad guys might be running counter surveillance and see him taking notes.

"You all getting the times?" Sparshott says to his lap. He's thinking ahead. He'll need exact surveillance times later in order to get a search and seizure warrant for the Cuban's house.

"We got 'em," someone answers as three surveillance cars cruise by the Charger. Sparshott points them out to Boyle who is concentrating on the Torino in front of her. They pass Mark's car and pull on ahead, part of a classical leap-frog maneuver, a ballet through heavy traffic nearly impossible to detect:

Two cars hightail it straight to Aspen Hill to watch for counter surveillance. One becomes the Torino eyeball car. It pulls in front of the Torino and keeps it constantly in sight in the rearview mirror. If Boyle has to stop for a red light after the Torino crosses an intersection or Mark makes a turn and she loses him in the traffic, the eyeball will help her find him again. The other surveillance cars follow her and Sparshott in a broken line at discreet distances. The car closest to the Charger is *their* eyeball. Its job is to keep them in sight until it's relieved. After about half a mile, it either switches lanes and falls back to the end of the line, or turns off Georgia and rejoins the end of the line as soon as it can. The second car then moves to the eyeball position for the next half-mile before it too drops out. The leap-frog continues until Sparshott and Boyle reach the buy location where the surveillance cars spread out and position themselves to watch both undercovers and to be ready to follow the bad guys whichever way they go.

Tonight the leap-frog is as smooth as a ballroom dance. "I'll pick them up at Dennis then cut them loose at Windham Lane," the second car in line radios the eyeball.

"I got them at Windham," the third car tells the second. "I'll cut them loose at University."

"Got them at University," the fourth car says. Sparshott and Boyle find the radio chatter comforting, the heartbeat of teammates they can't see, calm, cool, experienced.

There is a moment of radio silence, then a surveillance car behind Sparshott: "Hey, we want to drive on up and have a look at the silver Torino."

"Okay, why don't you *all* just drive on by and have a good look," Sparshott suggests. It's a calculated risk. He wants every cop on the team to have a close look at Mark's car so they won't lose it later on the winding and wooded roads of the Aspen Hill developments, but he doesn't want anyone to get burned and blow the deal. He takes the gamble because he's been reading the Torino ever since it left the church for any of the usual tics of bad-guy nervousness: alternate from fast to slow, pull over suddenly and park, speed uphill then coast downhill, make a last-second turn into a side street. He's reasonably certain that Mark feels safe.

Sparshott has also been examining the spoors of traffic patterns for signs of counter surveillance. If he spots any, he'll radio his team which is also scanning the traffic. They'll work out an instant plan to take the counter out of the game: Encourage it to speed, then flash a red light, pull it over and ticket it. Zip one car in front of it, zap another on its rear, box it in and slow it down. Or stall a car on the road ahead, hood up, to snarl traffic to a crawl. But Sparshott doesn't notice any suspicious cars on his tail or in front of Mark.

The Torino leads Sparshott and Boyle past Dick Stevens Chevrolet and the sprawl of Wheaton Plaza, across University Boulevard, the heart of Wheaton, across Randolph Road past the substation where the clutter of Amocos, McDonalds, and 7-Elevens gradually ends and a two-mile stretch of lovely green dotted with suburban homes and apartments begins. The Torino moves into Aspen Hill, crosses Connecticut Avenue, another major artery leading to the White House fifteen miles south, and passes the two surveillance cars who radio its position. Mark turns right on Bel Pre, then takes another quick right into Manor Apartments, and parks.

Manor Apartments are three-story garden jobs sitting on a former pasture where cows grazed not too long ago, suburban-clean and well-lit, surrounded on three sides by miles of townhouses, duplexes, and storybook homes carved out of Maryland woods and farms. After nine miles of almost uninterrupted neon and plastic which began at the District-Maryland line, the Aspen Hill neighborhood feels like a foreign country filled with people who have fled near-metropolitan Washington to escape drugs, crime and violence.

The apartment parking lot is perfect for undercover surveillance with easy access, plenty of traffic, and open space. Sparshott now knows that the Cuban lives a mile or two away, five minutes at most, bad guys deal close to the stash. He doesn't bother to radio his new position, the eyeball's been telling the other surveillance cars his every move.

Mark pops out of the Torino and jogs over to the Charger while the Torino cautiously pulls out of the lot and turns right on Bel Pre away from Georgia. As it does so, Sparshott gets a make on the driver—Caucasian, early twenties, bushy dark hair, ear length, short beard and mustache, boozy looking face, flabby, an easy guy to take down.

Sparshott is certain that the driver of the Torino is on his way to check with his source about an introduction—something he was hoping Mark had done in advance—but he's not unhappy. A surveillance car is on the Torino's tail and will get a fix on the Cuban's house. Then if Sparshott gets an introduction later that night, it will be easy to cover him while he's inside the house. They don't come more dangerous than a first-time buy in a bagman's house.

"Wait here," Mark tells Sparshott when he reaches the Charger, "My partner'll be right back . . . So how's it goin'? Who are you anyway?"

"What the fuck's this?" Sparshott says to Boyle. It's a fine blend of question and piss.

"Hey, you tell me, David!" Boyle plays along.

Sparshott is pleased. He now knows their cover story is beginning to stick. Mark accepts David as the badass boss and gives him the chance to use his number one rule of undercover strategy: get the bad guy on the defensive as soon as you can and keep him there as long as you can so he doesn't have time to think narc.

Sparshott turns to Mark: "Who I am is none of your fucking business, pal. Rene says you got good stuff. I got good money. That's all you need to know."

"Okay, okay, man," Mark squeaks. He puts up his hands as if to stop a train.

"And why the fuck are we sitting in a parking lot while your buddy drives off?" Sparshott jabs. "I don't like being jerked off."

Mark is anxious to keep David calm. "J.B.'s just gonna make sure everything's okay with our man. Then you can come, you know, and get your stuff."

Sparshott concludes that Mark isn't very bright. He gave him the name of his partner, J.B., who is most probably John Brent Friedberg and confirmed his suspicion that J.B. is leading a surveillance car right to the candy man. Sparshott also concludes that Mark is scared, but not scared enough to try something stupid, and that Mark believes he's edgy because he's on *Mark's* turf. The wimp is following the script perfectly.

"In the back, pal," Sparshott orders. "We're gonna find J.B . . . if you're setting us up—"

Without a car and outnumbered two to one, Mark has no choice and obeys like a trained terrier. When he climbs inside, Boyle backs up the Charger and points it toward the Bel Pre exit, but before she can pull out of the lot, J.B. glides back in. Mark is so glad to see him he leaps out of the car and trots over to the Torino as if he's a hostage and this is a big ransom instead of a simple drug buy.

Sparshott still feels uncomfortable with the way the deal's going down. He doesn't know a thing about the new player J.B. or the Cuban, and he's not in total control yet. Until he is, he views Mark and J.B. as two dangerous amateurs.

Mark trots back to the Charger. "Hey, our man doesn't want to meet anybody." He seems more nervous than when he jumped out of the car. "Gimme the money and we'll go get your stuff."

"Fuck you, pal," Sparshott says. "You think I'm fuckin' stupid? I'm not gonna give you shit. Just because the broad knows you, doesn't mean *I* know you. Well, it ain't her money, pal. The deal was, we were goin' to the house. If that's not the deal, we're out of here."

"But my guy doesn't want to meet anybody," Mark almost pleads. "Why don't—"

"When you get it together, pal, you let Rene know!" Boyle starts the car.

Sparshott wants Mark to understand from the first meet that he is a man of his word who doesn't go for last minute seller jitters, and he wants to reinforce Mark's belief that David is worried about a ripoff. He senses that Mark is desperate for the sale so he can get his fix and split back to his lair in Greenbelt. And since all indications are that the wimp bought the Rene-David line right down to the last "fuck-you-pal," why rush the deal? Impatience kills more buys than caution.

Boyle pulls out of the lot, leaving Mark standing under a light like a jilted boyfriend, turns left onto Bel Pre, then left onto Georgia. Sparshott gets on the radio: "It's a shut down, a no go . . . meet back at Wheaton."

☐ ☐ ☐

Sparshott grinned to himself as Boyle headed back toward town. He had gotten half of what he wanted and didn't spend a dime. Even though the introduction to Mark's source fell through—intros are always a longshot—he at least knew where the guy lived. He'd work on matching a name with the house in the morning, then shadow the place to see who lived there, who came and went, and who drove what. He'd cruise around to get a feel of the neighborhood, dope out all entrances and exits, one-way streets and cul de sacs and make a composite of the neighbors. He couldn't lose. If Mark came back—and the greedy shithead would but only if Sparshott had convinced him that he, Mark, blew it—he'd know more about Mark's man than Mark did. Then, he would make a couple of quick buys from Mark and J.B., bust them, and bang the Cuban's house while the buy money was still warm. Three bad guys, hopefully a stash of coke and a pile of drug cash, maybe an address book with the names and phone numbers of customers. Then, he'd flip the Cuban like Boyle flipped Curtis.

If Mark didn't come back, who gives a fuck, he knew where the shithead's connection lived. The rest was just time and patience. Either way, the taxpayer won. And if Sparshott still believed anything after ten years on the force, it was that the line between anarchy and order is thin and blue.

Everyone was laughing and joking when Sparshott and Boyle walked into the station. It was like the locker room after a good game. A decisive victory and no injuries. "You got the times and locations?" Sparshott asked. Several Montgomery County u.c. cops said yes.

"Great . . . Okay, who followed the Torino to the house?"

"We did, Trace," one Montgomery County cop said.

"Great . . . "

"We got it in the neighborhood—"

"Super . . . "

"But then we lost it."

"Lost it! How the fuck—"

The squad room grew as still as an Aspen Hill back road while the two teams waited for Sparshott to erupt. The cops who had worked with him before knew he was an undercover perfectionist with a short fuse and extra-large lungs.

But Sparshott didn't explode. He was more embarrassed than pissed. Shit, even pros lose cars on dark roads with no traffic. You gotta hang way back so you don't get burned. If the bad guy makes a quick turn at the bottom of a hill or around a curve, he's gone, like a gopher in his hole. But it was his own guys who had lost J.B. and he was sure the Fairfax cops were chuckling under their bulletproof vests.

"Fucking bad break," Sparshott said like a disappointed coach. "Next time, brothers!"

The truth is, Sparshott was even more embarrassed because

after nearly five years on the narc squad he had made a dangerous rookie-mistake. He had read the scene right. Bad guys are as superstitious as medicine men. They'll back out of a deal even as they test the shit because something doesn't *feel* right. Bad guys also know narcs are eager to deal, don't negotiate hard enough, overpay, itch to split, and that real users like David hide their eagerness like the clap. So turning Mark down made flawless dope-logic and Sparshott sensed he played the scene convincingly. But his decision to walk was also based on an assumption—surveillance had a make on the source's house. Assumptions are like bullets. They kill cases and cops.

It was easy for Sparshott to say, "Fucking bad break . . . Next time, brothers." But what if he hadn't acted as well as he thought he had? What if Mark didn't come back? What if there was no next time?

FOUR

Mark beeped Rene a week later. Boyle was so pleased she could hug the little prick. It was like waiting seven days for the first review to appear. Mark said: Hey man, if you wanna, you know, try again, meet me in front of Crown Books in Aspen Hill at ten tonight. A rave review and Boyle couldn't wait to call Tracy. For him, copping from Mark was no longer a routine buy or a chance to earn stats, his undercover junk food. After the last goof, nailing the shithead was a matter of pride. Hey, if an undercover doesn't have that he shouldn't be in the fucking game, man.

When he hung up on Boyle, Sparshott was so confident he told himself what every narc does at some point in a good case—"Gotcha, dumbfuck." Then he cleared the buy with his supervisor and called a briefing in the Wheaton substation for nine.

Sparshott and Boyle took great pains to field the same two surveillance teams for the second meet. Everybody knew Mark and J.B., each other, Aspen Hill, and the fucked up radio communication system. They also understood that the deal would not go down at Crown Books which was only the meeting place. Nor would it happen in the parking lot of Manor Apartments. Bad guys worry so much about ripoff, they rarely use the same place twice. But it would go down *near* Manor Apartments unless the bad guys had the dope with them, which was unlikely since they didn't last time and didn't know how much David wanted to buy.

Sparshott had cased the area where J.B. vanished like a ghost last time and had diagrammed it on the squad room blackboard. He opened the briefing:

The bad guys might be driving Mark's red Chevy Monza, Maryland registration Charlie-X-Ray-Yankee 377 instead of the silver Torino. Heads up, everyone. They surprised us last time so maybe they'll be using a third car this time . . . I still want an introduction to the Cuban. If I can't get one, I'll give J.B. $500 for a quarter ounce and keep Mark with me for insurance while J.B. gets the shit. When he comes back, I'll either go for a second buy right away or set him up for a buy-bust later . . . We want what we wanted last time—a fix on the source's house. So this time *two* cars will be waiting inside the development where we lost the Torino. It's called "Aquarius" and it's on Homecrest Road a mile from the Manor Apartments—here. It has two entrances—here on Aquarius Drive and here on Hydrus Drive. A third car will still follow J.B. just in case Aquarius isn't the right development.

After the briefing, Boyle, Sparshott, and a six-pack of Bud headed north on Georgia Avenue to Aspen Manor, a small shopping mall halfway between the Wheaton substation and the place where the team had lost J.B. last time.

God designed the mall for undercover cops. Aspen Hill apartments flanked it on the south and the Gate of Heaven Cemetery on the north. A row of five small brick houses lined the other side of Georgia Avenue. Crown Books itself was sandwiched between a liquor store and Gotta Dance, a theatrical supply store, how appropriate. A pizza parlor, Dairy Queen, laundromat and all-night drugstore kept the place hopping late into the night but not so busy that surveillance could lose Mark and J.B. in traffic. There were only two entrances to cover, and the parking lot, which could easily swallow 200 cars, stretched along Georgia, making it easy for surveillance to blend in. A median strip divided Georgia Avenue so that if Mark and J.B. made a dash, they either had to speed north past Gate of Heaven where a surveillance car would be waiting or race south against the traffic into the grill of another surveillance car. Finally, Aspen Manor was a sea of asphalt so the eyeball wouldn't have any trouble keeping Boyle's blue Charger in sight. From these lookouts, surveillance could watch the bad guys approach, cover both mall exits, protect Sparshott and Boyle, and slip into Georgia Avenue traffic unnoticed when the bad guys left. Thank you, Marco baby.

Ten minutes after Sparshott and Boyle parked in front of Crown Books, the eyeball spotted Mark and J.B. coasting into the parking lot. "We got 'em," it radioed. "They're *not* in the silver Torino . . . they're in the red Chevy Monza, Maryland registration Charlie-X-Ray-Yankee 377."

"Got it," Sparshott radioed back. "We're closing down now." He shoved the black box under the seat just before the red Monza eased up alongside him.

10:06 P.M.

Mark climbs out of the Monza and walks over to Sparshott. "We're going to a tennis club." He oozes confidence, the kind of bravado a toot of coke gives you. "I know a guy who works there. It's a good place, close to the man's house. Follow me." He hops back into the Monza which glides onto Georgia Avenue and heads north toward Bel Pre.

Sparshott slips the radio back out from under the seat. "Heads up . . . we're on our way to the racket club on Homecrest," he announces. During the briefing, he pointed out the club on the blackboard map for the benefit of the Fairfax narcs, a quarter mile down Homecrest Road from Aquarius. He knows the area around the Aspen Hill Racquet Club and Fitness Center better than his own backyard.

A few years earlier, he helped trap the "Aspen Hill Rapist" who stalked teenage girls in the new developments near the club. The creep had assaulted thirteen and the Montgomery County Police Chief was getting a bleeding ulcer from the townhouse communities along Homecrest. Sparshott got a description of the rapist's car from a victim, followed a hunch, and found it. Then he and four other u.c. cops shadowed the owner around the clock for three weeks watching him watch girls. The guy was about to attack number fourteen in her house—Sparshott had a gun beaded on him from next door, he had never killed anyone before but he was fucking ready to blow this piece of shit away—when her father came home. The creep slithered back into the sewer. Vice decided to arrest the guy anyway—it didn't want to risk another rape—and Sparshott and his search-team found a desk drawer full of panties and the credit card of one of the victims which earned the weirdo so many life sentences he'd be seven hundred years old when he finally got paroled. Fuck, Sparshott knows every willow oak and silver maple in the neighborhood.

Tonight, the Fairfax and Montgomery county teams send half their cars on ahead to stake out Homecrest Road and the racquet club. They deploy the remaining cars in the same leap-frog surveillance as last time. Since they know exactly where the bad guys are going and it's nearby, they are more relaxed, there's less radio chatter. Sparshott and Boyle are more relaxed too. They know J.B. and Mark this time, where the bad guys are taking them, and approximately where the Cuban lives. Surveillance will already be in place when they get to the racquet club. Given the goof last time out, they're determined to make tonight's performance perfect—as if the bad guys would know the difference—no mistakes, no ambiguity, with probable cause coming out their ass.

Sparshott and Boyle follow Mark and J.B. past the Manor Apartments on Bel Pre for a mile, then left on Homecrest and into a deserted asphalt parking lot. Mark pops out of the Monza and hurries over to the Charger. Sparshott and Boyle get out to meet him.

A row of closely planted pines guards the Aspen Hill Racquet Club and Fitness Center from people without money and makes the place so isolated that you'd drive right by if you didn't know it was there. The L-shaped lot has two entrances off Homecrest Road and is designed for about eighty cars. But only one leg of the "L" is paved and the outdoor courts are still under construction. The clubhouse, which houses the indoor courts and gym, is nearly finished and already open for business. But it's after ten, the club is closed for the evening.

Sparshott will do the negotiating, Boyle will be his extra set of eyes and will cover his ass while he's conning Mark. She holds her purse, she's a fast draw, a good shot. Mark no longer oozes self-confidence. He's close to the coke now, wants to hurry up, get it over with, pocket his cut, and get the hell out. He's tense. He thinks ripoff and narc. The only way he'll know for sure is to show the shit, hold his breath, and see what happens. Hey, it's not easy being a good bad guy.

"How much do you want?" Mark asks Sparshott.

"A quarter ounce."

"You mean a quarter pound!" Mark fidgets. "I thought you were gonna do, you know, a couple of ounces!"

"Not until I test the shit, pal," Sparshott says. He knows that Mark knows that most first buys are small, that David doesn't trust him, and that David wants quality coke not flea powder. Besides, why waste a whole worm when you can catch a toady fish on a small piece? Hey, narcs have standards, too.

J.B. is watching the negotiation from his car twenty feet away, and although he can't hear the conversation between Mark and David, he can sense something is wrong. He lumbers out of the Monza like an arthritic bear and walks over to the Charger. If there is a problem, it's obvious he doesn't trust bubblehead to solve it.

Sparshott and Boyle size J.B. up quickly. This is the *first* time they've seen him close up, outside a car. They look for the bulge of a gun and wild eyes, so they can be mentally prepared to jump or shoot him if he makes a move. They listen for mistrust between the two bad guys so they can exploit it later. They know J.B. is in charge but they need to know whether he considers Mark his flunky or his partner so they can play Mark against him.

"What's wrong?" J.B. asks Sparshott. He seems more miffed at the delay than alarmed.

"I'm not gonna let a lot of money walk the *first* time," Sparshott says. "I only wanna do a quarter ounce. If I like it, I'll do another buy right away."

"My guy's in the hospital," J.B. says. "The woman's doin' his business tonight. She'll only let me in *once*."

Sparshott's thinking fast now, revising the plan, building on what he knows: Buy the quarter ounce, test the shit, then insist on another quarter right away, it's not his problem the shithead can't go back again, twist the knife, keep the bad guys on the defensive, set them up for the buy-bust.

J.B. and Sparshott haggle over price then settle on $500 for the quarter ounce, a fair street price. Sparshott peels the bills from his wad, mostly twenties, and hands them to J.B. who refuses to take them. Mark snatches them instead, then gives them to his partner.

Fucking scumbags like J.B. watch a lot of TV and think that if they don't take the money directly from a buyer who turns out to be a narc, they can't get popped. Well, "Miami Vice" ain't Harvard Law School, pal.

J.B. pockets the money, orders Mark to stay put, then squeezes his belly back behind the steering wheel of the Monza. "Hey, don't fuck with us," Sparshott warns. "You're not back here, it's your buddy's ass." J.B. pulls out of the second parking lot exit, turns right, and heads toward Aquarius less than a mile away where two surveillance cars are waiting, lights out, heads down.

As soon as the red glow of J.B.'s taillights disappears around a curve on Homecrest, Sparshott turns to Mark. "See the size of these arms?" He flexes his biceps, even Boyle is impressed. "If your buddy rips us, I'll wring your scrawny neck!"

"Hey, man," Mark squeaks to the 240-pound, badass biker. "He'll be right back . . . be cool, man."

Sparshott is as pleased as a cat after dinner. The bad guys are scared, he's in charge and calling the shots, he now knows the Cuban is working with a woman, another two-fer, no mistakes so far, everything falling into place, going down good.

An unidentified car, lights out, cruises into the lot and glides straight for Sparshott and Boyle who are still standing outside the Charger. When they see it, they quickly slip into sync like undercover twins. Neither knows who's in the car which they can't identify in the dark. Neither is wired. They smell a setup which always spells guns, sometimes shootout, sometimes car chase, and if the bad guys manage to stage a ripoff, it's as embarrassing as a bare ass. What are you gonna tell your fucking supervisor? "Hey, boss, I'm really sorry but two bad guys robbed me?"

Boyle hugs her purse, flap open. The eyeball is out there somewhere, but shit, it'll take at least a minute for it to reach her. It could all be over by then. And Sparshott knows he has just seconds to decide how to play the scene. Curtain up . . . the driver of the car could be a bad guy, or Mark's friend who works there, or a club security guard sneaking up on trespassers. Footlights low . . . one thing is certain—the driver sure in hell isn't looking for directions to a fucking subdivision. Then . . .

"Hey, who the fuck's this?" Sparshott shouts at Mark.

Boyle picks up the cue and slaps Mark in the face, like hard, man, no love tap. "What the fuck's goin' on here?" she yells.

"I don't know," Mark stammers. He looks stunned, confused. "I don't know man."

Sparshott and Boyle believe Mark. He sounds convincing, no stage shit, he's not that bright, not quick on his feet. If it's not a setup, they ask themselves in sync, what the fuck *is* going on as the darkened car pulls alongside the Charger? The driver lowers his window and sticks his head out.

Even if she couldn't see the guy, Boyle would recognize the voice. Her mouth turns dry . . . Christ it's Donny . . . what the fuck's he doing, he should know better, stay out of sight until the deal is over or the bust goes down.

"Are the bad guys here yet?" Donny asks Boyle. Then, he notices her pissed face, sees Mark, shoots out of the lot like a racer from a pit stop. It's save-your-ass-time.

Sparshott and Boyle are on Mark like hornets. She screams: "Waddaya *mean* you don't know, you little shit! Who the fuck *is* that, huh?" At the same time, Sparshott grabs him by the throat with his beefy paw and slams him against the Charger, damn near knocks the wind out of the wimp . . . what was that Fairfax dumbfuck thinking about . . . Sparshott whips the switchblade from his vest . . . fucking stupid, he should know better . . . Sparshott springs the blade.

"What the fuck *is* this, pal?" Sparshott is standing two inches from Mark's face, close enough for the guy to feel his spit, teeth clenched like Stallone and knife at Mark's throat. "You said you knew someone at this fuckin' place. That's why we came here, right? That's him, right?"

"Hey man, I swear I don't know—" Mark rapid-fires. His voice is real high now.

"I can't fuckin' believe it. One of your friends drives up and wants to know if the bad guys are here yet," Sparshott hammers away, won't let up, not just yet, blade pressing so hard on the guy's throat that if he swallows, it will hurt. "Well, I'm no bad guy, pal. If your buddy comes back with the cops . . . I'll fuckin' deny everything, then I'll cut you later . . . got it?" Mark nods yes. His eyes are bulging just like they do in TV cop shows.

Sparshott and Boyle relax a little. The strategy is working. They know Mark is now thinking, hey, it's dark, maybe it *was* my friend. It's a good beginning.

"If you're setting up my boyfriend, we're gonna kill you," Boyle says. She punctuates the threat with a rap in the face Mark will never forget, a perfect play off Sparshott's lead. "Count on it!"

Mark counts on it so much he now *needs* to believe it was his friend. "I don't know why he came up," he stammers.

Boyle reads him perfectly. She helps build on his fear, gives him an out, hopes he's bright enough to take it. She turns to Sparshott and softens: "Hey David, maybe the guy *was* a security guard."

"You're probably right!" Sparshott relaxes his grip on Mark's neck, good cop, bad cop, just like Stallone would have done it, and tucks the knife away as the Monza pulls back into the empty lot.

When J.B. gets out of the car holding a plastic bag, Sparshott turns up the heat. "Hey pal," he shouts to J.B., "your little prick buddy here had one of his friends check on us . . . well, we don't like it . . . we don't wanna deal this way no more."

"What's goin' on?" J.B. asks Mark, a can't-you-do-anything-right kind of question.

"Some guy just pulled up and asked what we're doin' here," Mark says. He's changed the story so he doesn't look so bad and now is *certain* the guy was a racket club security dick who saw mean-looking David and ran.

Sparshott decides not to push Mark and reaches for the bag of coke chunks in J.B.'s hand, but J.B. pulls it back and sets it on the hood of the Charger. "No way man," he says. "Just in case you're a cop . . . I don't want a hand-to-hand buy."

Mark picks the dope off the hood, more Abbott and Costello shit, then hands it to Sparshott who slips the knife back out of his vest and dips the tip of the blade into the bag. He rubs the powder sticking to the blade between his fingers to warm it up—smooth and oily is good, grainy and dry is "Lipton Tea"—the shit is oily. Sparshott nods okay.

"You want more?" Mark asks.

Sparshott decides to call it a night. No-balls Mark is so scared now he can't even remember that his partner said he can't go back to the Cuban's house, the woman is in charge, one trip no more, hell, she sounds smarter than both wimps put together. Mark is so dumb and greedy—Sparshott is counting on both—that he'll call Rene for another meet. If he doesn't, fuck it, with one clean buy and a make on the source's house he has enough probable cause for a search and seizure warrant from a friendly judge to bang the Cuban. As for J.B. and Mark, hell, he can pick them off any time.

Sparshott tells Mark: "Not now, not in this fuckin' place. But I'm willing to buy four or five ounces next time . . . if this shit's any good. We'll be in touch."

Sparshott and Boyle climb into the Charger and drive out of the lot, turn left and head back to Georgia Avenue. "The buy went down," Sparshott says into the radio as soon as it's safe. He can't wait to slap Donny's dick. "We'll meet at the Wheaton station."

FIVE

Everyone joined the Donny roast even though they knew the poor guy had gotten everything second-hand over his Fairfax radio, a Fred Flintstone way to catch bad guys, but still, lame excuse, he was no rookie, he should have known better. They didn't let up until Donny felt like snailshit and started getting mad.

"Okay . . . who got the car?" Sparshott asked. He was still so pissed he wanted to shove Donny's badge right up his ass but he kept his mouth shut. He liked working with the narcs from other jurisdictions, especially Fairfax, they were good folks and he made it a point to hoist beers and arm wrestle with them on Friday nights at the Fairfax Police Association Club. He didn't want any burrs under the saddle of cooperation. Hey, fuckin' locals need to work together if they're gonna survive. Cuz if they don't, fuck, forget the bad guys, who's gonna protect them from all those good guys in fed city who think "War on Drugs" is a new video game.

"Who got the car?" Sparshott asked again.

"We did," a Montgomery County narc said. "We saw it pull up to a duplex."

"Great."

"But the doors are in the rear, Tracy . . . we couldn't see which one the asshole entered."

It wasn't just Sparshott who moaned, shit, not again.

"Anyway . . . we got a make on a Chevy wagon parked out front . . . Maryland registration Henry-Paul-Bennie 450."

Hey brothers, heads up, sometimes you gotta lose a couple to win.

One look at the Cuban's u-shaped duplex and Sparshott knew that close surveillance on J.B. had been an impossible assignment. The beige house with brown shutters and trim sat just inside the Aquarius complex, second on the right. Two garages—one for each unit—formed the arms of its "u" which concealed both entrances. To make bad worse, the duplex was the *only* one of a hundred look-alikes with its rear facing the street.

On that first night, J.B. was already parked, lights off, in the duplex driveway when the surveillance car turned off Homecrest Road onto Hydrus Drive. Tough break. J.B. would have had to be standing on the sidewalk waving his flabby arms for surveillance to spot him. On the second night, surveillance watched him pull into Aquarius, glide into the driveway, and walk toward the duplex. But the garage closest to the street blocked surveillance's view and it couldn't see which of the two units J.B. entered. Tough break. Surveillance would have had to be sitting in the woods separating Aquarius from the next development to note which door J.B. had entered.

Sparshott returned to the office and ran a check on the red wagon, Maryland registration HPB 450, the only car parked in front of the beige duplex. Small dirtball world . . . the wagon belonged to Victoria Lopez. He remembered her from a fed case he worked in 1980, six years ago, and pulled the record to refresh his memory. It was just after he finished working late-night burglary detail at Wheaton Plaza, around the corner from the station, where a gang of thieves had been ripping off stores. An inside job, forty bad guys caught with their dicks in their hands, how could he forget?

The captain had been having a problem with a sergeant on that burglary detail, a real tick up his ass, and he knew how Sparshott loved a good prank. Trace, the captain says one night, it sure would be nice if somebody'd go fuck with this guy. Hey, is that an order or what!

Sparshott knew the sergeant was afraid of heights but

wouldn't admit it, so he assigned the guy to the plaza roof on a slow night, then began teasing him from below. "Hey Sarge, I saw someone in the doorway of the liquor store," he radioes and the guy runs across the roof, peeks over the edge and gets dizzy. "I saw someone in the doorway of Woodies," he says and the sergeant races back to the other side, looks down and gets even dizzier.

Fucking fun, man. Bored with that game, Sparshott had dressed a manikin and laid it in an alley running behind the plaza. "Hey Sarge, there's someone in the alley," he radioes and the asshole trots to the other side of the roof in time to see Sparshott speed down the alley, hit the fucking manikin, brake, and jump out. The sergeant watches in shit-shock as Sparshott drags the body to the trunk, opens it, stuffs the stiff inside like it weighed two-hundred, then speeds away. The guy kept running around the roof like a kid just off a merry-go-round. Fuck yes, the captain loved it.

Then a team of FBI clones came marching into the station and asked for a couple of F.L.'s to stake out a two-bit fencer called Pedro Lopez. The captain assigned Sparshott and his partner, Rick Gibbins, to go make the feds happy. The captain knew that the Bureau was only interested in Lopez' hot goods because some of it was government office shit like, gee wiz captain, what can be more important than an Uncle Sam typewriter?

Pedro "Lucky" Lopez wore a huge gold star on a chain around his neck, a glazier by day, when he wasn't too hung over, an aftershave-doused scumbag by night. Two kids and a wife, Victoria, whom he beat when he was drunk and that was most of the time. A loser who fled Cuba in the mid-sixties and moved up from Miami in the mid-seventies looking for work and finding a bunch of fast-snorting fellow Cubans. The membranes in his nose were already gone and he bled like a hemophiliac.

Lucky had a nightly routine: Leave his house just off Georgia Avenue in Silver Spring which borders Washington on the north, hair greased down and shirt open to the navel, fifteen minutes before the Maryland lottery closes. Buy 200-300 tickets at a local drugstore. Wait for the winning numbers to be announced, then pitch the stubs . . . Lucky never wins. Eat scampi at a seafood restaurant a few blocks from his house, a gathering place for local pimps and pushers, then hit the strip for women and booze.

Back in 1980, the last two blocks of the D.C. side of Georgia Avenue were little more than a string of bathhouses, porn shops, and nightclubs with dancers who enjoyed artistic freedom, no pasties or g-strings, what you see is what you get if you can afford it. Lucky Lopez could. He'd drop a hundred or two buying drinks for the call girls and dancers in the Shepherd Park Restaurant or in his back blow-job booth at Chances R across the street, take one across the Maryland line to the Georgetown Motor Inn, then go home high, drunk, and spent.

Night after night, Sparshott and Gibbins watched a stream of scum seep into Lucky's house with cameras, typewriters, TVs, and stereos, and ooze out empty-handed. They smelled drugs, and even though their assignment was fencing surveillance, they began sniffing for narcotics. One night they spotted Lucky slipping a bag of white powder into the window of a black limo parked outside Chances R. Gotcha, dumbfuck. But the Feds weren't interested in cocaine, no way they were gonna let locals fuck up their typewriter investigation, not that Sparshott and Gibbins were surprised. Hey, every local knows the FBI guys take a special vow of conformity. That's why they call themselves special agents.

Sparshott and Gibbins continued to work fencing for the Feds and drugs for their own narc squad on the sly and soon spotted a tall, young Hispanic guy loaded with gold and dressed straight out of GQ pull up to Lucky's house in a new white El Dorado. Hey, what good's drug dealing if you can't flash! The Caddy was registered to a Raul Tabares.

When SWAT finally banged Pedro's place, search teams found $13,000 worth of hot goods in the attic and $10K in cash hidden behind a ceiling panel—which gave the FBI their jollies—and several ounces of coke under floorboards and a rabbit hutch filled with marijuana in the basement—which gave the narcs a rush.

Victoria Lopez, it turned out, was Raul's mother through a previous marriage which made Pedro Raul's stepfather, typical drug incest. Pedro was getting his herb from Miami and his coke from his stepson through a New York courier named Chicky. The narcs offered Pedro a deal to flip, but his mouth was as tight as a mouse's ass. He pulled five, did three. Victoria walked. Raul slipped through the cracks.

□ □ □

Once Sparshott linked the red wagon parked outside the duplex to Victoria Tabares-Lopez, he was ready to bet his shield that J.B. had slipped into Victoria's door. He asked central records to pull the criminal file of Raul Tabares to see what kind of trouble the kid had gotten into during the six years since his stepfather got busted and learned that in April 1983, just about the time Lucky was getting out of jail, a hooker called Laurie had shot Raul in the head during a cocaine ripoff. Medically speaking, he should have died but the narcotics in his system had slowed his bleeding and pulse just enough to keep him alive. The bullet to the head had severed his spinal cord and left him a quadriplegic. The U.S. Attorney had declined to prosecute him for possession with intent because the guy was already locked in his personal prison. A jail hospital would be a ridiculous burden on the taxpayer. Raul told the police that Laurie had shot him. She fingered her boyfriend Alfredo, then pleaded guilty to attempted murder and pulled ten years. Alfredo was tried and convicted of conspiracy to commit murder—twenty years. Raul had refused to roll on his source or to implicate his cousin, the lessee of the Beltsville apartment where he was shot.

At two the next morning, after his shift, Sparshott drove by Victoria's duplex and got lucky. Her green garbage bags sat on the curb which was county property instead of in her yard which wasn't. To lift them from private property Sparshott would have needed a warrant . . . more probable cause, more paperwork, more delay.

Sparshott cruised around Aquarius looking for another set of heavy-duty, green garbage bags on a curb, but all the sacks he saw were either white or brown. So he crawled through the other developments along Homecrest Road until he spotted two look-alikes and snatched them. He crept back to Victoria's house, lights out, made the switch, then drove home, leaving the trash in the trunk of his undercover car, and went to bed. The next afternoon, he walked into narc headquarters toting the two bags.

"Christ not again," Dad groaned. "Here comes the trash man."

The narcs called Jerry Boone "Dad" because he held the double title of old man and rookie, a recent transfer from homicide where he had been an ace investigator for years. Dad liked to call Tracy "trash man" because of Sparshott's blind faith in garbage which, unlike people, never lies. "Show me your fucking garbage," he'd say, "and I'll tell you who you are."

It was garbage that had nailed the crooked ex-cop and won Sparshott the Narc of the Year title and a medal. In one week, he had found: Seven empty bottles of Dom Perignon . . . not bad for a former cop . . . bank deposit slips . . . a lot of extra income there . . . phone numbers and name-doodles . . . great leads . . . drug calculations like "RB—$240" and nose tissues spotted with blood . . . the dirtball's a sniffer . . . empty bottles of lactose and a bunch of empty freezer bag boxes . . . signs of distribution . . . snow seals which tested positive for cocaine. Enough probable cause to get the court to order a Dial Number recorder placed on the ex-cop's phone which led to the guy's girlfriend-dealer and a PCP operation, a Best Western motel and the New York kingpin. So who gives a dealer's damn if Dad calls him "trash man."

Sparshott spread a piece of plastic on the floor inside the square formed by the squad room desks, wheeled in a large trash barrel, and slit open the green bags with the blade he had used on Mark. The smell was overpowering and Dad's ribbing more intense than usual. Sparshott didn't care. Garbage picking is the most neglected tool in the undercover cop's kit.

The Lopez garbage was another mother load: letters addressed to Victoria Lopez, medical assistance envelopes addressed to Raul Tabares, a prescription bottle in his name from the drugstore in Aspen Manor where Sparshott and Boyle had met Mark and J.B., paper scraps with drug calculations, the butt of a marijuana roach, and two plastic baggies and several snow seals that tested positive for cocaine.

Sparshott also found something lumpy inside a wad of paper that smelled like rotting chicken skin. He opened the package to Dad's "oh no . . . leave it alone Trace . . . hey, take it outside, come on . . . " It was a colostomy bag.

"Christ, Tracy," Dad moaned.

"Hey brother, all in a day's work." The pieces began to fit—Raul Tabares, quadriplegic, medical assistance checks, prescription bottle, colostomy bag, coke and grass, and J.B. saying that his source wasn't home because he had to see the doctor. So . . . the dirtball was living with his mother, still smoking grass, and still selling shit. But *how*, if he's a quad? And who's his source?

Sparshott tossed the colostomy bag in the trash barrel and went to the bathroom to wash his hands. While he was gone, Dad pulled a Snickers bar from his desk drawer, ripped the wrapper off, and took a big bite. Then he set the bar on a piece of clean paper and placed it next to the garbage Sparshott hadn't examined yet.

Sparshott found Dad rummaging through the garbage bag when he returned. The squad room was quiet and all the cops seemed busy for a change. Dad suddenly pointed to the half-eaten candy bar. "Hot damn, isn't that a Snickers?" He scooped the candy up and stuffed it in his mouth like a kid.

Sparshott was ready to heave when Dad and the other cops broke out laughing. "Hey brother," Dad said. "All in a day's work."

Sparshott was shocked at first that anyone could slip a fast one by him. "You got me, Dad, you sonofabitch," he said. Then he roared. The gag was so fucking good he couldn't wait to pull it on someone else.

One bright afternoon a few days later, Sparshott slowly drove by the Lopez-Tabares duplex to see if there was any activity. He saw a man sunning himself on the patio in a medical chair, his feet pointing to the sky like jack rabbit ears. He was wearing a Redskin knit hat, a table-tray locked him in place. On the tray were a book, telephone, and special pencil-like instrument with a mouthpiece.

The scene made a deep impression on Sparshott. The last time he had seen Raul Tabares the guy was tooling around Silver Spring in a new El Dorado and strutting in and out of Lucky's house as if he had the world by the balls and every woman in it by the ass. Now? Stretched out in a hospital chair, feet silhouetted against the sun, sentenced to life with a colostomy bag he couldn't even change himself. What a waste! He wished he could take a picture of that scene to remind himself during the lonely hours of surveillance how drugs fuck up lives.

As he drove on by Victoria's house so Raul wouldn't burn him, Sparshott saw Raul take the pencil between his teeth and begin dialing the phone. "So that's how you do it, douchebag," he said to himself. "Well, I'm gonna get you. You can bet your fuckin' pencil on that!" Hell, he already had enough p.c. to make any judge in the county wet the bench even without a second buy.

Back in the squad room, Sparshott sat down at the computer, called up his boilerplate warrant and filled in the blanks. He made the paper good for fifteen days—standard procedure—and left the date open in case Mark called Boyle again. It had been two weeks since he and Boyle made the meet with Mark and J.B. But they had scared the shitheads so badly that he wasn't sure they'd try to score again.

Whatever, Sparshott didn't need another buy to pop the bad guys and bang the Lopez-Tabares duplex. But to do it after a *second* buy would be better and a lot more fun. Two buys would keep the scum off the street a little longer. And if he was lucky, the buy money would still be in the house when he searched it—another link in the chain of evidence.

The phone rang. It was June Boyle. "Mark called," she said. "He's ready to deal again."

"Great!" Sparshott was ready too. "Let's do it tonight."

SIX

June Boyle called Mark back to set time and place. It was late morning and Mark sounded like he was already coasting. She played him like a grifter.

"Who's this?"

"It's Rene."

"Hey Rene, where do you want to meet?"

"Where we met last time, you know, Crown Books," she says.

"That same shopping center?"

"Same spot. Dave's supposed to be home around eight. How about ten-fifteen, ten-thirty?"

"Perfect," Mark says. "What car?"

"Mine. Dave doesn't want to take his Benz."

"He has a Mercedes?"

"Sure he does," Rene says. It's important to impress dirtballs. "He likes driving it but not when, you know, when this is going on."

"Really?" the dumbfuck says.

Boyle called Sparshott. "All set, Trace . . . between ten-fifteen and ten-thirty . . . same place."

Sparshott shifted into overdrive. He cleared the buy-bust with his supervisor who, in turn, notified SWAT to make sure a six-man team was available. It was.

Sparshott called up the draft warrant on the computer. The paper would give him the right to seize any evidence he could find to prove possession, intent, or conspiracy: drugs, drug paraphernalia, drug money, drug records, pocket phone books, bank statements, phone bills, credit card receipts and so on. The law is generous for a change.

Sparshott keyed in the last remaining paragraph in the warrant: "Police Officer III Tracy C. Sparshott personally appeared before me, a Judge of the District Court for Montgomery County, Maryland, on this 20th day of May, 1986, and made oath in due form of law that the contents of this six-page application are true and correct to the best of his knowledge, information and belief."

Next, Sparshott phoned his friend, Judge Donald T. Mates, and made an appointment to get the warrant signed that evening after the judge got home from court. Sparshott had dated the daughter of another judge who introduced him to Mates, an easygoing jurist always willing to help put the bad guys away day or night. Hey, you gotta have a friend on the bench to keep a step ahead of the dirtballs. That done, Sparshott ran down the buy-bust-bang checklist:

Contact the communications supervisor, tell him about the raid, and give him the time and the address of the Lopez-Tabares home in case there's a shootout. To prevent a leak, the communications coordinator will be the only other person besides Sparshott and Boyle to know the details well in advance. Inform the head of the narc division and the Night Hawk, the captain or lieutenant in charge of after-hours operations, in case of an emergency. Notify the commanding officer of the five districts that make up the Montgomery County police department in case his teams need extra help.

Finally, Sparshott briefed the SWAT supervisor whose team would take down Mark and J.B., then raid Raul's house. It's a buy-bust, he told him, two bad guys and a raid on a duplex with a quadriplegic and maybe four other unwittings inside. He's a multi-kilo dealer and it could be dangerous. A full all-team briefing at the Wheaton substation at eight.

The thirty-cop team was in place by ten o'clock, the warrants signed and sealed. Boyle and Sparshott sat in the Charger in front of Crown Books. Bill O'Toole was hiding in the bushes behind Raul's house where he could easily watch who came and went. Surveillance cars were strategically spread out between the Aspen Manor parking lot and Raul's place. Two uniformed officers were all set to transport Mark and J.B. to jail in a squad car. A black SWAT van waited nearby.

Sparshott got on the radio. "Any activity at the house?" he asked O'Toole in the bushes.

"No one's come or gone. There's a light on in the living room and bedroom. Everything's quiet."

O'Toole cursed Sparshott. The sonofabitch was sitting in a dry car with a sexy woman and a six-pack while he was up to his neck in leaves and feeling miserable. It had just stopped raining, it was hot under his slicker, he hadn't eaten dinner yet, and like him, the mosquitoes were working overtime. Just like the time Sparshott was feeding the face of a bad guy at the Seaport Inn in Old Town Alexandria.

Of course, it had been a first class joint, a block from the city's historic waterfront. Naturally Tracy hadn't cleared the dinner with his supervisor who would piss paperclips when he saw the tab. Those two guys never could see undercover the same way. Tracy thought like a dope dealer, his super thought like a desk-jock cop. One went with the flow, the other stuck by the book. Oil and water every time. It was one of those humid August nights. O'Toole had just come on duty without eating, something Tracy knew damn well, and was badge-deep in intimate restaurants tucked away in charming old townhouses. Tracy was wired so O'Toole could hear every slurp and crunch, which Tracy also knew damn well and couldn't resist playing to . . . Hey Julio, great Dom Perignon, here have some more. My lobster's super, how's your steak, buddy? You find it chilly in here? Waiter, would you please show us the dessert cart. How about an after dinner drink, Julio? . . . The sonofabitch kept rubbing it in all night and afterwards he says, hey Billy, all in a night's work, brother.

But mosquitoes aside, O'Toole liked backing Sparshott. The guy knew what it was like to sit for hours dying to take a piss or jog around the block and he made it a point to take care of his buddies whenever he could. Like the time he gave a bad guy from New York the ride of his life on the DEA yacht fitted with video cameras and moored at the Gangplank on the Washington wharf just off Maine Avenue. Of course, Tracy had stocked the boat beforehand with the best booze fed money could buy, Johnnie Walker Black, Captain Morgan's rum, Beefeater's, Heineken, enough to water a whole drug family. Afterwards, he invited all the backups on board to party. Hey, no use pollutin' the Potomac with all this good piss. Or the time he took the same bad guy to M Street, heart of Washington's legal district, to see the barepussy strippers. He knew backups *had* to follow him inside where they *had* to watch the show, knock off a few beers, maybe wolf down burgers, so they wouldn't get burned. Then, when he came back out with the scumbag, he said, pretty fuckin' good, man, there's another one next door, let's go do it. Tracy just wanted to give the other backups a peep and a brew.

10:15 P.M.

The radio crackles: "Two guys in a Pontiac Firebird, black over red, are pulling in . . . it looks like them."

Sparshott spots the car. "I see them," he says. "So far it looks like a go . . . keep on your toes . . . we'll be back as soon as we know something."

The Firebird pulls up next to the Charger. Mark eases out and walks over to Sparshott. "Hey, how's it goin'?" he asks.

"You're not gonna jerk us around like you did last time, are you pal?" Sparshott says, keeping Mark off balance, on edge, defensive. "I don't have a lot of time to waste."

"No way, man."

"I got the money," Sparshott says. "Don't put us on the spot like you did last time."

"No way. Let's move on up to K-Mart."

The K-Mart store is in K-Mart Plaza, a small mall with a huge lot, less than a mile up Georgia Avenue, across the road from the Manor Apartments and five minutes from Raul's place. It's a perfect spot for a buy-bust. A lot of open space, some traffic but not heavy, easy to watch, and as safe as it ever gets for a SWAT team takedown. Georgia and Connecticut Avenues, which border the plaza, are a little slick from the drizzle which could cause a problem stopping the Firebird. Otherwise, a clear, warm night.

Sparshott gets back on the radio as Mark and J.B. pull out of Aspen Manor onto Georgia. "It's still a go," he says. "We're following them to K-Mart. J.B. will get the dope. Mark will stay with us. If the dope is good, we'll let both bad guys leave. Then, we'll give you the 'go' signal. Pop them as soon as you can."

The Charger pulls into K-Mart Plaza and parks. The place is nearly empty since the big store is already closed for the night. Sparshott and Boyle can see the black SWAT van parked in easy reach of the exits.

Mark trots over to Sparshott's window. "I want an ounce," Sparshott tells him. "If it's good, I'll want more." He gives Mark $2,100—the price they agreed on earlier.

As Mark takes the cash to J.B., Sparshott keeps one hand on the radio under the seat just in case they try a rip-and-run. If they do, the SWAT team will nail them before they can count the first hundred dollars.

J.B. drives off. Mark joins Boyle and Sparshott as they had agreed earlier. If he's worried about being held hostage, he doesn't show it, a sign that he expects J.B. to return with the dope. "J.B.'s gonna be right back," he tells Sparshott.

"Then get in the back," Sparshott orders. Mark climbs in as if he's expecting the order. Sparshott offers him a Bud which he takes and they make small talk and wait.

J.B. returns in just under ten minutes and parks next to the Charger but stays in the car, his window down. Boyle, Sparshott, and Mark climb out of Boyle's car and stroll over. Sparshott bends down, looks in the window, and sees J.B. holding a plastic bag with the dope. He reaches for it, but the dirtball still plays the game and pulls the bag out of Sparshott's reach, "No way," he says. "I don't need a distribution."

Mark snatches the bag and sets it on the hood of the Firebird. Sparshott hefts it. He's so used to handling shit he can tell if it's light. He knows that J.B. pinched a few grams . . . even shitheads have to be paid . . . but he must have recut it because it still feels like an ounce.

Sparshott and Boyle climb back into the Charger to be closer to the radio. They'll have to move quickly once the buy is over to make sure the bust is safe for their team and any civilians on the road. Sparshott opens the plastic bag while Mark and J.B. watch from their car. He rubs white powder between his fingers, the shit feels oily.

"It's good," Sparshott tells Mark.

Mark and J.B. don't wait around to say good-bye. They make straight for the nearest parking lot exit, turn right onto Connecticut, and drive toward the traffic signal at Georgia a block away.

Sparshott grabs the radio. "The buy went," he says. Then he settles back to listen to the chatter and enjoy the ringside seat.

This is the moment he lives for as a cop even if it is over in a flash. It's payday. The sound of a buzzer at the end of a game you're winning. The one thing that makes all the bureaucratic bullshit worthwhile, especially to a narc. In other police jobs, you investigate a crime *after* it's over, try to find the bad guy and if you do, wait months or years for a trial which is at best a toss-up, heads or tails depending on county politics, personal ambitions, judicial personalities, court calendars, and most importantly the temperature in Tierra del Fuego. In narcotics—how sweet it is—you catch the bad guys with their pricks still dripping . . .

□ □ □

"Okay, let's take them down at the light . . . I got the rear . . . I got the front . . . I got the driver."

Three Special Investigation Team cars come out of nowhere as if on cue and hem the Firebird in at the light. One blocks Connecticut Avenue so it can't go forward. One blocks the driver's side, hanging back a little so it won't be an easy target in case J.B. jumps out and tries to run for it. One covers the rear so the Firebird can't back up . . . Tires squeal . . . brake lights pop on all around like giant red fireflies.

The SWAT van screeches to a halt behind the Firebird . . . the door slides open . . . six cops wearing blue crash helmets and bullet-proof vests and toting MP5 machine guns with thirty rounds of ammo, and flashlights mounted on the barrels jump out like Marines . . . Two cops look into the back window to make sure no one is hiding in the back seat.

"Hands out the window," someone shouts. "Get your fucking hands out the window." Mark and J.B. obey.

"Turn off the ignition . . . now . . . turn it off." J.B. obeys. Two SWATs cover the Firebird's front door. One yanks Mark out. Two SWATs cover the driver's door. One grabs J.B. . . . They slam both bad guys to the ground and cuff them.

"All clear . . . got them both," the radio crackles.

□ □ □

Sixty seconds tops and it was all over . . . thirty cops . . . perfectly coordinated, flawlessly executed . . . a thing of beauty, a work of art . . . no car crashes, no gunshots, no one hurt.

Sparshott and Boyle were laughing when they pulled up to the traffic light. They got out. Sparshott stood over Mark, cuffed on the road face down, and nudged him with his badass biker's boot.

"Hey Mark," he said, "are the bad guys here yet?"

SEVEN

The SWAT team leader began the ritual chant as the black van rolled down Homecrest Road past the Aspen Hill Racquet and Fitness Center:

"Does everyone have a badge on?"

"Are your weapons loaded?"

"Finger off the trigger unless you're on a shootable target."

"'Police . . . Search warrant' once the door opens."

It was ten-thirty now. Mark and J.B. were already at the Wheaton substation being fingerprinted. Sparshott and Boyle were hiding in the bushes outside Raul's house with Bill O'Toole. Unmarked police cars discreetly lined Hydrus Road and plainclothes officers had the patio doors to Raul's house covered. Radios were eerie-quiet as everyone waited for Act Two to begin.

The six men inside the van sat on a u-shaped, padded bench, tense like commandos about to storm a fort. They held six-pound MP5 machine guns attached to shoulder straps which would free their hands to smash doors, slam prisoners to the floor, or do anything else that called for mitts. They packed .38 special Ruger revolvers with extra speed-loaders as well as spare thirty round magazines for their MP5s.

They called themselves the elite. Most waited up to eight years for an opening on the two-team squad and once on SWAT, no one wanted to quit. Other officers called them "the kids" because they were so enthusiastic about their jobs and loved to play with their cop-toys.

A ninety-pound, three-and-a-half-foot long steel ram with

two handles sat at their feet on the carpeted floor of the van. The front handle had a guard to protect the first hand to smash through the door.

Chain cutters and a hydraulic doorframe spreader were tucked away under a seat. SWAT called the spreader a "rabbit" because its long teeth bite the doorframe, forcing it to buckle and the lock to pop. A Montgomery County firefighter designed the gadget which is especially useful on stubborn metal doors with metal frames and bolt-action locks.

Tonight, SWAT would ram its way into 14936 Hydrus Road because, although the door was metal, it was attached to a *wooden* frame. One or two bangs and the wood would splinter like kindling. Although it could stop a platoon, Montgomery County SWAT rarely fired a weapon. It relied on teamwork, speed and surprise to handcuff drug dealers before they could reach for a gun. It gave itself ten seconds to break into a house, every beat beyond that it considered exponentially dangerous. And like a good undercover cop, it left little to chance.

SWAT had spent several hours that afternoon plying the special investigations people with endless questions: What kind of house does Raul live in? Who would be inside? Do they have arrest records? Will they be armed? Are there kids to worry about? Any pets to get underfoot? Does the house have a dog that could give us away? How many people live in the duplex next to Raul's? Any kids? Do the neighbors have any dogs? How many entrances and exits to Raul's house? Does he use counter-surveillance? How many windows do we have to cover for lookouts and snipers? Do we need to assign more than one team member to a particular room where the dope is kept? What kind of lock does the door have? Is there a screen door to be cut?

Although SWAT knew that the only easy raid is one that's over, it was pleased with the advantages of this night's foray. It had the floor plan of a typical two-bedroom Aquarius home and the team leader had had time to case the house and the neighborhood that afternoon. Raul's duplex had a perfect approach through the woods, no fences, no dogs. There were no windows near the door to worry about. The door itself was unsophisticated. No kids inside to get under foot or shot. And Raul Tabares, the principal suspect, was a quadriplegic who posed no threat.

But there were disadvantages too. Raul dealt kilos. Where there was that much dope, there was money. And where there was dope and money, there were guns. SWAT didn't know what kind of lock was on the door—critical for quick entry—who was inside besides Raul and his mother Victoria, and how badly they were wired. And SWAT would have to convince them in seconds that they were police, not competitors trying to rip them off, or they might open fire.

As the van coasted toward the Hydrus Road entrance to the Aquarius development, the mood inside grew tenser. Each man knew he might have to kill someone or be killed. The ritual chant of assignments began:

"I'm number one man. I got the back bedroom on the right."

"I'm number two man. I'm on the ram. I got the bedroom on the left."

"I'm number three man. I'm on the ram. I have the living room."

"I'm number four man. I got the dining room and kitchen."

"I'm number five man. I have the bathroom."

"I'm number six man, I'm security. Thumbs up for an open door. Thumbs down for a locked door. I have the bedroom on the right. If we have to throw a bang, I throw it."

The team leader had decided earlier in the day to use a flash-bang, an M116-Al military grenade simulator that packed 185 decibels of deafening noise, to rattle the people in Raul's house so they wouldn't think of reaching for guns or flushing the drugs. The security man, number six, carried the three-inch long canister on his belt like a grenade.

The van doused its lights as it turned left on Hydrus Drive into Aquarius and parked just inside the development a hundred feet from Raul's duplex. The van door slid open and SWAT jumped out one by one like paratroopers. They headed single-file, slowly and carefully, into the woods that formed the perimeter of Aquarius, security man first, ram carriers last. They emerged through the bushes behind Raul's house close to where Sparshott, Boyle and O'Toole stood waiting.

Sparshott pointed out the door to the security man to make sure there was no mistake. It wouldn't be the first time SWAT broke into the wrong house. Still single-file, SWAT crept slowly toward 14936. There wasn't a sound and they weren't in a hurry.

The team halted in front of Raul's door in a line. The security man tried the screen door. It was locked. He pulled out a long knife from a sheath on the back of his belt and slit the screen like a surgeon, reached in and unhooked the latch. He ripped off the piece of masking tape he had stuck on his helmet and placed it over the peephole in the door. Then he tried the knob.

The main door was locked too. He gave the thumbs down sign and stepped aside as he held the screen door open. At the same time the two men on the ram, machine guns dangling from their shoulder straps, rushed forward like fullbacks and banged the door. The frame shattered on the second blow. They tossed the ram on the grass and waited.

The security man pulled the flash-bang from his belt and, his finger through the ring of the pin, peeked inside to make sure no one was nearby. The detonator of the M116-Al flies off the canister with the velocity of a bullet when the little fucker explodes and can kill anyone in its path. The foyer was empty. The security man pulled the pin, tossed the grenade inside, and stepped aside once again. The first SWAT man rushed through the door screaming, "Police! Search warrant. Police! Search warrant."

Victoria was asleep on the couch, her face swathed in bandages. Her boyfriend had played rugby all over her and she had more stitches in her body than on the hem of her skirt. She jumped up when the flash-bang exploded and began shouting in Spanish. All she could think of was, "Ripoff, I'm dead." When she saw the SWAT cop standing over her with a machine gun, she was relieved.

"Shut your fucking mouth," the SWAT ordered. "Don't talk. Down, down on the floor." He helped her to the rug, cuffed her, then searched behind and under the cushions of the couch for a gun.

Victoria's daughter darted out of Raul's room like a frightened fish in a tank, screaming and yelling her head off. She ran right into the muzzle of an MP5. The next thing she knew, she was face down on the hallway floor.

Raul was sitting up in his hospital bed, a roach in the ashtray on the night table. He was wearing a burgundy and gold Redskins cap, the TV was blaring. "I'm okay, mom," he shouted in Spanish when a SWAT burst into the room. "I'm okay."

"Shut the fuck up," SWAT ordered.

Sure pig! What you gonna do? Shoot a quad?

"Don't worry, mom. I'm fine."

□ □ □

June Boyle watched SWAT at work with a horrified fascination. No one had told her there would be a flash-bang, and she had never seen one before except in training films. Fairfax County outlawed them. She saw a burst of fire through the partially opened door, then heard an ear-splitting explosion. Windows all around her rattled. Lights popped on in the other duplexes.

"Jesus, Trace, what the fuck was that?" Boyle said. Talk about surprise. If her heart was pounding, imagine what the poor bastards in Raul's house felt like.

"Isn't it great?" Sparshott laughed. He was enjoying all the pyrotechnics, a fucking Fourth of July in May. Why shouldn't the good guys have an advantage for a change?

The smoke detector went off like a delayed burglar alarm. People began screaming in Spanish. SWAT yelled back at them: "Get down, down on the floor. Shut the fuck up. Speak English. Only English."

Sparshott was not as relaxed as he seemed. Even if SWAT

pulled off a perfect raid, everyone cuffed, no one hurt, all guns confiscated, things could still go wrong. Thirty cops were out there, many on overtime, and he had just spent $2,100 of narcotics fund money. He had to score, the pressure was on. It was like betting someone else's money at the track. He remembered the time SWAT had banged the wrong house and walked in on a costume party.

The time he had hit a place just after the dealer made a major sale, the apartment was empty, no dope. The time he had raided a house minutes after his snitch made an intelligence buy, but couldn't find the buy money—his evidence for chrissakes. The time the dealer hadn't liked the way the buy went down, got all hinky and burned the fucking buy money, can you believe it, just before the raid. What if Raul was empty? What if he didn't keep the dope inside? What if they couldn't find the $2,100 he had just paid J.B.? His ass was square on the line and whatever the county paid him, at this moment, it wasn't fucking enough.

The smoke alarm died, someone inside Raul's house opened a window and the patio door to clear out the flash-bang smoke, the night held its breath for a beat, then from inside the duplex:

"Clear, clear, everyone clear."

Sparshott and Boyle went inside. It was Act Three, Sparshott director, Boyle observer. They found Victoria on the couch, hands cuffed behind her back, her daughter still on the hallway floor face down, and Raul in his hospital bed. Sparshott asked SWAT to seat the daughter next to her mother and to leave two officers inside to cover the front door just in case Raul had a visitor while the search team was combing the house.

Four SWAT members climbed back into the van and drove off. They were covered with sweat but pleased. No bullets, no blood, no bodies. The two SWATs who remained inside the house nailed the doorframe back together as best they could so nothing looked suspicious, turned off the porch light, took positions just inside the door and waited. A surveillance car would radio them if a stranger approached the house.

The three-hour search began. Sparshott assigned a room to

each of his four experienced searchers. Take your time, be thorough, he told them, rotate rooms, don't overlook anything.

A classic search pattern. Begin at one wall and examine everything on, or against it. Then go to the next wall. If the paint or screws around light plates, outlets, and door hinges are scratched or the paint seal is broken, take a close look. Check the frame around doors for stress marks, there may be a pocket under it. Check the top of the door for plugs. Rub your hands over the walls to see if anyone has plastered over it. Take each picture frame apart. Remove the backs from TVs, stereos, radios, and take all telephones apart. Check the tops and bottoms of window shades and Venetian blinds, and remove the caps on both ends.

After the walls, go to the center of the room and begin with the furniture. Turn each piece over to see if anything is taped to the bottom. If the piece is upholstered, make sure the staples are intact and all material matches. Shine a flashlight through the bottom to see if anything is taped to the springs. Remove cushions from zippered covers. Roll back rugs and check floorboards for suspicious marks.

Take special care in the bathroom. Look for traps in laundry baskets and under sinks and watertight containers floating inside flush tanks. Open every prescription medicine bottle. When in doubt, seize it.

Be on the lookout for special hiding places: books, gloves, hatbands, shoes, dolls, flashlights, flowerpots, fuse boxes, record albums, salt and pepper shakers.

All the rooms were clean except Raul's which turned out to be narc heaven. Within three minutes, a searcher found the first Ziploc baggie of coke. "Bingo," he shouted. Everyone, especially Sparshott, began to relax. The searcher placed a white three by five inch card in front of the bag, Sparshott wrote "#1" on it, the photographer snapped a shot of it, the recorder entered the description of the item and where it was found on the "Evidence Inventory" form, Sparshott signed it, the evidence collector bagged it. By the time searchers finished the room, Sparshott had more than enough to prove both possession with intent to distribute and conspiracy to distribute several kilos of coke:

A container of Inosital, a vitamin B supplement used to cut cocaine, and a strainer, grinder and scale. Papers with drug calculations ("$1,650 + $150 + $2,500 = $4,300," said one), an address book with the names of fifteen to twenty buyers, baggies with cocaine residue, two small packages of marijuana, three ounces of coke worth $6,000. Also—$4,000 in tens, twenties and hundreds in a blue bag on the closet floor, in the pockets of a bathrobe, behind picture frames, in a shoebox. And Sparshott's buy money inside a tan boot in the closet. Not bad for one night's work. But the two big questions still remained unanswered. Who cut, weighed, packaged, hid and sold the shit for Raul, and who supplied him?

At first, Raul wouldn't even admit there was dope in the house. "Why the fuck you here, pigs?" he shouted at the narcs. "You tell me. I didn't do nothin'. I can't even move my fuckin' arms and legs! Pigs . . . pigs . . . fuckin' pi-i-igs!"

When the searcher found the first baggie of coke, Raul turned arrogant. "Hey, what you gonna do, pig?" he taunted Sparshott. He rolled his head back and forth on the pillow in a helpless rage, like a beached flounder Sparshott thought. "Shoot me? Well, go ahead, pig-shit. Shoot me. Shoot me. I'm no good. I got nothin' to live for. I'd rather be dead."

When searchers found the second piece of evidence, it was Sparshott's turn to taunt. "Hey Raul, the price of poker just went up. I hope you got a good attorney . . . Here comes a rent-free room." The more dope and money the searchers found, the angrier he became.

Sparshott made it a point to keep busts impersonal, you know, like a doctor who builds a scalpel-cold wall between him and his patients. It's only a fucking game, he reminded himself when he felt anger or sympathy tugging, sometimes *you* win, sometimes the bad guy wins, cops and robbers, remember? Hey, there's always a next time.

But Raul Tabares was getting to Sparshott. Joy powder's last ride, a paralyzed, broken, useless piece of shit who destroyed his whole family because he thought he was untouchable. Mr. Cocaine Blow, Mr. Toot White, Mr. Nose Candy. You'd think the stupid sonofabitch would have learned his lesson, but he's jokin' about it, he knows he's gonna get away with it, like last time when Laurie popped him, and he's right. Who the fuck is going to send him to jail? He knows everyone knows he's not in it alone and he won't flip. The shriveled little creep thinks he has us by the balls and he's enjoyin' the squeeze.

Sparshott knew he wasn't going to get jack shit out of Raul by playing nice guy. Christ, he had no hold on him. Drop a couple of charges if he flipped? Send the guy to a prison hospital and let the taxpayer pick up the tab? Fuck, the guy was already serving a life sentence for dealing and the U.S. Attorney would probably drop all charges like he did last time. Raul knew it, so why should he talk?

Sparshott began to fuck with Raul's head, maybe the guy would get angry enough to spill something. It happens. He knew he was breaking another of his sacred bust-principles—treat the bad guy like a person, hey, you okay, just doin' my job, man. Sometimes he'd check up on a guy in jail, talk to his girlfriend, you know, stay in contact. Most ex-cons head right for the old shitpile and make great snitches. But not Raul. Raul wasn't goin' anywhere. Raul hated himself and everyone who reminded him he was no longer a man.

Sparshott was angry and his normally gentle brown eyes had turned flinty and mean. He picked up a picture of Raul and a woman, from the time when he was handsome and slim and oozing testosterone, not bloated like now with withered legs and arms. "Hey stud, this you?" Sparshott smashed the glass and tore the picture out of the frame. "Hey guys, take a look at stud here." Sparshott tossed the picture on Raul's bed, then emptied the ashtray with the roach on top of it. The other narcs played along to see who could be the meanest.

Raul wouldn't break. He sneered back at Sparshott as if to say, "Come on and get me, come on, all talk no balls."

Sparshott grabbed Raul's special pencil, his lifeline to the world, and snapped it. "Get someone else to make your phone calls, stud!"

Raul wouldn't break. He called Sparshott a fucking pig.

Sparshott pulled back Raul's blanket. The guy just laid there naked, face red in anger and shame, his colostomy bag in place, spindly white legs and useless prick.

Raul wouldn't break. This time he merely sputtered.

While the search team tore the house apart and put part of it back together again, the radio crackled: "A maroon and silver van is pulling into the driveway . . . a tall, heavyset black suspect is getting out . . . he's walking toward the door."

The two SWATs guarding the front door smiled. Cops always hope for more. Sometimes a user will call during a raid and a narc will answer the phone. He'll disguise his voice and invite the caller over. Sometimes the suckers actually come. Sometimes buyers, mules, and runners come to the door unannounced. SWAT will take them down and the U.S. Attorney will subpoena and immunize them if they'll testify that they had copped from the dealer. Sometimes they sing.

The doorbell rang. The SWATs opened the door, yanked the guy inside like a big sack of potatoes, then flattened him against the wall. "Hey, I'm just a friend of Raul's," the guy said. "I just came by to visit."

Sure you did, dirtball. They searched him for weapons and found a baggie of coke. Rick Gibbins, who worked with Sparshott on the Lucky Lopez case—he wouldn't have missed this bust for all the two-bit crooks in Silver Spring—found a .22 caliber revolver in a blue cloth bag under the seat of the van. An NCIC check advised that the gun had been stolen in Danbury, Connecticut. Two uniformed officers took the scumbag to the station and charged him with possession of cocaine and theft of a firearm.

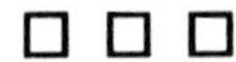

All evening long, June Boyle listened to the locker room nastiness with disgust. Although she understood Sparshott's frustration and anger, she couldn't excuse the cruelty. Even worse, she felt sorry for Raul. She knew he was a bad guy, that he was in the business of destroying lives, but she couldn't help herself. She felt so embarrassed for him that she turned her face away when Sparshott pulled back his blanket. She picked up a family photo. "These your daughters, Raul?" she asked as if to prove to him that some cops are sensitive. "They're beautiful. You must be proud." And she cursed herself as she did it.

While the search wound down, Sparshott sent Boyle and Gibbins through the woods to pay Raul's wife Lolita a visit. She lived in an identical duplex a few hundred yards away with their two daughters. Somebody had to be helping Raul, maybe it was her. Maybe she had a pile of shit stashed in her house.

Lolita let Boyle and Gibbins in and agreed to allow them to search. They did a very superficial job figuring if she had anything to hide, she would have made them go get a warrant. By the time they got back, the shit would be gone. They were gentle so as not to frighten the kids. Boyle was feeling sorry again. Two beautiful, wide-eyed girls, dressed so pretty in nighties, frightened of police with guns invading their home at midnight, a father who couldn't hold them or play with them, lost to drugs. They found nothing and left quickly.

All in all though, Boyle was pleased. It had started three weeks ago in Denny's on the strip. It was her case, she set it up. It netted Mark, J.B., a gun thief, Raul, a wad of cash, a few bags of dope, and some nice stats—for Montgomery County, of course. Raul wouldn't talk, but what the hell, it happens. His supplier would turn up sooner or later, they always do, maybe *she* wouldn't catch him but someone else would. She hated getting pulled off the case before it was over but that's how it goes in the real world. At least she learned something. Tracy loved sharing his undercover tricks and strategy with other narcs and had dissected his every move for her. She had fun. Playing Rene to his David, especially in the racket club parking lot, was something she'd always remember. And she appreciated how Tracy had treated her like, well, just like another brother, none of that big-tit sexist shit she had to put up with in her own department.

While Boyle went back to Fairfax, Sparshott began the hunt for Raul's source. It didn't take long for the cards to flip and street sources to talk. He quickly learned that the supplier's name was Roberto, a old Cuban. But before he could get a last name to match the first, Sparshott walked into a murder-for-hire conspiracy and had to put the Tabares case on hold. Hey! Montgomery County ain't Hollywood, man, where a cop solves a crime every hour with time off for commercials. And fucking locals aren't fatass feds who get to stick with a case until it's closed. F.L.'s are the mules of the crime biz. They begin one case, top priority, then get pulled off for another hot-shit priority, then get their balls squeezed for dragging their asses on the first one. Fucking yo-yoville, man, watch your back. If the bad guys don't get you, the bureaucracy will.

PART TWO

The Stalk
Spring-Summer 1986

EIGHT

Marty Preston waited outside a brick rambler eight miles east of the White House. Down the street, two dark vans watched and listened for his signal to begin the raid. It was a ball-chilling night two months before Sparshott busted Raul Tabares, nearly the witching hour and so quiet Preston's undercover radio sounded like gunfire. He didn't know how many drug dealers were inside the house and until he did, he wasn't about to bang the place.

A cautious cop in his late twenties but as intense as a Redskin quarterback, he had shoulder-length brown hair, green eyes, and a compact wrestler-body. Born and raised in PG and a county cop for six years, he had worked his way up to narcotics through patrol and plainclothes investigations. Before that, he was a security cop at Andrews Air Force Base and a uniformed Secret Service Agent who walked the White House and Embassy Row beat along Massachusetts Avenue.

Preston had learned caution the painful way. As a young patrolman long before he became a narc, he covered the back door of a large apartment building during a drug raid. Inside, a dealer had barricaded himself in one of the apartments with a shotgun and revolver. When the SWAT team couldn't coax him out, it charged the door. The dealer answered with gunfire, SWAT shouted back with shotgun blasts. An officer went down. Then as Preston peeked around the corner of the building, the bad guy fired from the window. Red brick chips splattered, close but no cop. The wounded SWAT officer inside wasn't so lucky. He died on the way to the hospital. The shootout taught Patrolman Marty Preston a lesson he'd carry with him on every future raid: when it comes to drugs, never underestimate what's behind a closed door.

Like Sparshott, Preston turned out to be one of the highest producers on his narc squad and, like Sparshott, he loved everything about undercover work, the chase, the edge, the high stakes. But unlike Sparshott, he wasn't impulsive, didn't limbo under the rules, and was as reserved as a New Englander by comparison. Tonight, he was a nervous cop as well. Besides the two emergency service teams waiting with him, there were nine vice officers, two agents from the Bureau of Alcohol, Tobacco and Firearms, and one K-9. A heck of a lot of manpower swinging on a single, slim thread.

Two days earlier, an anonymous snitch had called the Bowie substation, the undercover headquarters of the Prince George's County Police. The small town of Bowie hugs the eastern edge of PG, as everyone calls the county—halfway between Washington and Annapolis, just far enough away from the county crime belt to discourage bad guys from driving by and copying the license numbers of the u.c. cars parked in the lot. Cops don't like to admit it publicly, but crooks are as lazy as housecats.

It was eight in the morning and Preston, who had just begun his day-shift, grabbed the phone. IT, as cops call confidential sources to shield their butts, told him that two men and a woman—Josie, her boyfriend Jimmy, and his brother Walt—were dealing powder cocaine and PCP from a rambler in District Heights, a middle-class Washington suburb.

Preston pressed the receiver closer to his ear to filter out squad room chatter. It sometimes happens that way in the drug business. You dig, you squeeze, you sit outside a house for hours pumped full of coffee and dying to take a pee, and you come up dry. Then one phone call and you just may have the biggest case of your career served up on a scumbag platter.

Fuckin' heavy-weight she-e-it, IT said. The blow comes from a geezer called Roberto. He deals keys, man, and can't even speak fuckin' English. A guy called Davis delivers the Juice. He's one of those Phantom fuckers that brews his own cocktail. But you gotta be careful, man, the place's one fuckin' arsenal, I mean, shotguns, semi-automatics, M-16s, couple a Uzis.

Preston gulped back his excitement. PCP and the Phantoms Motorcycle Club were his specialty. The bikers were just starting to rise from the ashes of the last big burn and White was just beginning to dust the county like a February flurry. The snitch was pissed and hell-bent on revenge, the safest motive as far as a narc is concerned, and if only half of what IT said was true . . .

□ □ □

PCP or Angel Dust (try *p*henyl*c*yclohexane*p*iperidine) is sometimes known as Hinkley since John Hinkley was supposedly on a trip when he shot Ronald Reagan and James Brady. Sold as liquid, it's called Juice and Rocket Fuel. Sprayed on parsley it's known as Green, Flakes, and Lovely. Served on marijuana, it goes as Boat, Loveboat, and Killer Weed. Low doses treat smokers to visions, voices, gibberish, weightlessness and alienation. Heavy doses send them into orbit and they rarely come back with all their marbles.

Inner-city Washington is the biggest PCP market in the world and its suburbs used to be the biggest PCP lab until PG, Montgomery, and Fairfax counties began knocking them off like six-packs. Now most Washington PCP comes from Los Angeles, courtesy of the Hell's Angels who have precisely what it takes to brew the shit—three buckets, two balls, and one gram of brains. A bucketful costs a couple hundred to make and sells for just over 100 thou on the street, that buys a lot of Harley power, man.

The outlaw Phantoms are a local gang of twenty-five to thirty with maybe two hundred associates—wannabes who party with the big boys and girls but can't go to "church" when they talk biker business. They have their hands in the topless bars along Branch Avenue and at Silver Hill near Andrews Air Force Base. And they pimp, heist cars, rob liquor stores, brew Juice, sell Green, Boat and Crank, and blow people away now and then.

The U.S. Attorney in Baltimore targeted the Phantoms and

a rival gang, the Pagans, in mid 1980, figuring that if he boxed them, he'd solve half the crime along the Baltimore-Washington corridor. Since Phantoms hung out in PG and neighboring Charles County, the U.S. Attorney asked Preston to hunt them down. They were easy to find—they played in an after-hours place ironically called "Touch of Class"—but difficult to nail because no one dared to swear on a Bible against them. So Preston slipped underground as "Marty" and apprenticed himself to a PCP meisterbrauer:

Just watch me, man, it's like makin' bread. Mix water in a bucket with cyclohexanone (a dry cleaning fluid), then add a dash of sodium bisulphate; in another bucket, mix water with piperidine (a controlled substance used in glues and plastics) but don't let Big John catch you, then add a dash of sodium cyanide; combine both buckets into a third, then brew phenylmagnesium bromide out of bromobenzene, magnesium turnings, iodine crystals and ether; gently, ever so gently, add the bromide to the cocktail, stir, and serve cold. Don't smoke or whistle while you work. The stuff is cock-crazy until you blend it.

Amazing grace, what people will smoke, snort, shoot, and swallow for a high! Preston ended up busting fifteen to twenty Phantoms. The rest of the gang went underground only to crawl back out the following spring like groundhogs. The U.S. Attorney reopened the investigation and once again asked Preston to keep his nose downwind.

As far as coke was concerned, well, when Preston joined the narc squad in '83, about the same time Sparshott signed up, he found mostly PCP and marijuana on drug raids, sometimes heroin or a little Crank, a variety of speed native to the east coast. But lately like Sparshott, he had been finding a "G" of powder here, an eightball there, rarely anything as large as a whole "O." None of the PG narcs knew where the toot was coming from. And now . . . IT was talking about *kilos* which wholesaled at 36 thou per key. It looked like a brand new drug game had just come to town. Who wouldn't get a narc erection?

Preston wanted to bang Josie's place the same night IT had called, hey, drugs are like homemade fudge, they don't sit around long. Like Sparshott, he had a friendly judge who gave him a search and seizure based on IT's anonymous report, a few hours of surveillance on his part, and a crime computer check on the suspects. The Navy had an APB out on Uzi-Walt for desertion, and PCP-Davis had thirteen priors. But EST—that's what PG calls its SWAT unit—was already ramrod-deep in raids, so Preston had to book them for the following night.

Unfortunately, IT called again to say, tough break, man, Josie had a blowout with Walt over all the fuckin' in and out of the basement where, you know, he dealt. She was purple-shit scared the neighbors would call the cops so she told him to scram. Walt took his stash and most of the bang-bang with him. But hey man, don't worry, Josie and her skinny-prick boyfriend Jimmy still have plenty of blow, herb, and juice upstairs.

Preston was disappointed but, what the heck, that's how it goes in the drug trade. You get a sizzling lead one minute, then watch it freebase into smoke the next.

Shortly after midnight, Preston watched the front door of the rambler open and Josie walk out. She was one of those fiftyish women who passes for forty, like her drug of choice was formaldehyde, and she wore tattoos like medals. She climbed into a Chevy pickup parked in front of the garage, then backed onto Benson Lane. Preston radioed two undercover cars to follow her—he preferred five but he was short-handed—then to wait for his signal to take her down. As soon as he found any drugs in her house, he had probable cause.

As far as Preston could tell, Josie was the only one home. Walt's car was nowhere in sight, Jimmy's truck was gone, no one's shadow passed the lighted windows for the two hours Preston had been watching the place, but still, you never know, it's healthy to be cautious.

"Okay," he radioed the EST vans. "Let's go do it."

Preston was lead man on the front door ram, not that he was eager. But it was PG policy in '86 to make the narc in charge bang the door himself so he couldn't bitch afterwards if the bad guys had time to flush their drugs. Josie's door was a piece of EST cake, wood on wood, and the frame snapped on the second rap. Simultaneously, the second EST team broke through the basement door. Preston had requested two units even though Josie's kitchen had a door leading down to the basement. Heck, no use taking a chance, a stairwell is a death-tunnel, easy for bad guys to see into and difficult for good guys to see out of.

Excited but as calm as a casino dealer, Preston waited outside until EST and K-9 secured the place—no one was home. Then he made straight for the refrigerator where IT had told him he'd find a Coke bottle filled with PCP. Warm rocket fuel loses much of its pungency and green beans mistakenly believe the stronger the smell, the bigger the blastoff. Preston found the bottle with two ounces of liquid strong enough to clear his sinuses and satisfy any PG judge, thank you IT, at least he didn't look bareass foolish. He radioed surveillance to bust Josie who happened to be sitting in a shopping mall parking lot with a guy who happened to have an H&R .22 Saturday night special tucked under the seat of his pickup. Another twofer.

Preston nailed the doorframe back in place and turned off the porch light. Josie's boyfriend Jimmy worked the four-to-midnight shift in the maintenance department of the metro transit system and Preston wanted to shout "surprise" when the guy came home. Then he began to search the place, show and tell time, the egg-on-your-face hour, a special narc hell. What if IT was wrong? What if IT was setting him up to embarrass him? Bad guys have such a sick sense of humor.

Even without Walt's drug stash, Preston scored big—$19,000 worth of coke, PCP, and marijuana, and about $6,000 in cash, most of it taped under the bathroom sink. Several semiautomatic rifles and revolvers. A CO2 bomb with a fuse which he handed over to the bomb unit of the Fire Department. The dope was everywhere—hall and broom closets, attic, refrigerator, garage, living room. In vases, jars, plastic bags, cookie tins, bongs, briefcases. Some of the PCP was liquid, the rest sprayed on parsley and stored in plastic bags ready to sell—in tinfoil as a "tin" or "dime" for $10, in 35mm plastic film containers as a "can" for $50.

Preston also found more than enough evidence to make *distribution* charges against Josie, Jimmy and Walt stick. A Triple Beam scale tucked away on a bottom shelf in the kitchen—"Triple Beam" is the brand name of a lab scale popular with dealers, accurate down to a tenth of a gram and easy to buy in lab supply stores. A Deering kit—"Deering" is the brand name of a sifter system which consists of a grinder to pulverize coke rocks or cakes, several screens ranging from fine to coarse, and a cup to catch the powder. Ten bottles of McCormick parsley—the most popular brand in the county for making Flakes. A dozen brown vanilla extract bottles with PCP residue—light causes the liquid to change color and look weak. A contact beeper, an "owe" sheet with the names of customers and amount of money they owed, and two dealer phone books, one in the basement belonging to Walt, and the other upstairs belonging to Josie. A photo of Walt with an M-16 in his hands and a kilo bag of coke in his mouth like a happy puppy. Nice bunch of people. Preston was so happy he could kiss Josie's tattoos.

The drug paraphernalia added up to a well-organized drug operation capable of distributing a key of coke and a half-gallon of PCP to forty or fifty customers every two weeks. A little drugstore worth $50,000 if it was worth a dime. And if that wasn't enough narc pleasure for one night, Jimmy pulled into the driveway at 3:30, got out of his truck, and walked into the arms of the narcs freezing the hair off their balls while Benson Lane snuggled under quilts. In his pickup, they found a can of PCP and a photo of Jimmy sitting in front of a mirror with a line drawn in white powder. Can you believe how vain these guys are?

No legal doubt about it, Preston had Josie and Jimmy cold—three counts of possession each and three counts of intent to sell coke, PCP, and marijuana. The lovebirds wisely pleaded guilty to one count of possession with intent in exchange for what they knew:

Walt buys keys of coke wrapped in silver duct tape from a guy called Roberto, a Hispanic in his late fifties, who lives around the beltway in Maryland and travels with an armed interpreter. They help Walt package and sell the shit. The guy is mucho peligroso, man. Walt told them that if they ever breathe the name "Roberto," even in their fuckin' sleep, they are muerto, man . . . and not from an overdose.

Preston set Josie and Jimmy free on their own recognizance and got a warrant for Walt. He wasn't really worried that the creep would disappear, turds like Walt always float back to the surface. Over the next few days, Preston plied snitches and sources for a handle on a Hispanic named Roberto who dealt keys, but came up empty. Then, during a lull about a week after the raid on Josie's house, he began sifting through the box of evidence he had collected during the search. He knew from experience that the box would contain a wealth of intelligence. Of special interest were the two dealer phone books in which he expected to find the names of losers he had already busted and the names of users begging to be busted, maybe even a few newcomers with ice-cream habits.

Preston found the entry "R" in Josie's book and a Hyattsville, Maryland, phone number behind it. He found the name "Roberto" in Walt's book with three Hyattsville numbers behind it—one the same as Josie's—then called the operator. Two of the numbers were disconnected, the third was current but unlisted. He wasn't surprised. Drug dealers use unlisted numbers and change them like underwear whenever they get scared. From his desk drawer, Preston pulled out the form for subpoenaing the name and address that goes with an unlisted phone number and brought it to his favorite judge. Then he returned to the father-son-daughter case he had been tracking for weeks, one of those family-that-snorts-together-stays-together cases. Heck, you become a cop and end up a fireman. Put out little blazes night after night. You can't solve the problem, so you contain the damage like a spin doctor. Wouldn't it be a narc-hoot if the new guy Roberto supplied this little family of snorters too?

NINE

It was ten-thirty, twenty degrees, and snowing. Preston and a seven-man Special Op Division team—EST's bang card was filled for the night—passed Warehouse Liquors, an open-air drug market and a hangout for local bikers, and turned onto Pumphrey Drive lined with pickup and panel trucks with "roofing" and "plumbing" painted on them. Mick Jones's place was the last World War II bungalow on the street seven miles southeast down Pennsylvania Avenue from the White House, a red brick bungalow on a small wooded lot. Preston knew the house because neighbors had complained about the number of cars coming and going all hours of the night, but he had been so busy banging other houses, sometimes three a night, that he hadn't had the time to sit with a cup of coffee and watch this one. A snitch had made a buy for Preston from the house earlier that week.

IT was your typical junkie-snitch who drank, popped, and shot anything he could beg, borrow or steal—uppers, downers, heroin, coke, grass, speed, crank, PCP, alcohol. Like every pro worth snitch money, he'd rollover on a newborn to stay high, not much different from lab monkeys who kill themselves trying to get the coke they're addicted to. A good slimeball kind of guy who could ooze in and out of anywhere without arousing suspicions, the nose of an aardvark, sniff until he found out who had what, and where, then drop by. If there was a party, he'd beg for a snort. If he couldn't get a freebie, he'd try to borrow half a G, hey come on, man, pay you later, you fuckin' well know I'm good for it. If no one would front him and he had money, he'd reluctantly buy, then, bent on revenge, report back to his narc control what he saw and heard in the hopes of landing a freelance assignment and maybe stiffing the county for the buy money he just blew. The kind of guy who was smart enough to know that if he lied or exaggerated too much, hey, narcs expect a little hype, he'd be out of a job, but as loyal as a valet. "Hook a snitch," as they say, "and you got a snitch for life."

Unlike Sparshott, Preston preferred to use the snitch rather than make his own undercover buys even though he loved the thrill of the hand-to-hand. He was convinced that a controlled buy was a better deal for the taxpayer—faster, safer, and cheaper, and that if you did it by the book, bad guys pleaded guilty just as fast. Sparshott believed that although the hand-to-hand took longer to set up, it paid better odds—more dope, more intelligence, more introductions, more arrests.

The raid on Mick Jones's place was an emergency and Preston was praying the guy still had some coke left and that it had Roberto's name on it. He had planned to bang the house later in the week, after IT verified that the Joneses had bought a fresh supply. But the case had taken an ironic twist that very afternoon when another narc walked into the squad room with a street user-dealer in tow.

The guy turned out to be Mick Jones's partner and housemate which meant Mick would probably hear about the arrest before the night was out—news of busts spreads like AIDS—and hide the dope. The narc had gotten a snitch-call earlier that day: A little shit called Rick is gonna walk out of Mickey's place with an "O" at four this afternoon . . . he's gonna be drivin' an orange Cutlass you can't miss, man.

Every narc on the squad, especially Preston who had made a couple of intelligence buys there, knew Mickey's house in Landover along the Baltimore-Washington Parkway just outside D.C. A regular warren of petty dealers and cocaine whores, you know, blow for blow kind of hopheads. The narc got a quickie search and seizure for Rick's car and sat outside Mickey's house. Sure enough, the orange Cutlass pulled up at four-ten. Rick got out and went inside, then came out a few minutes later with two young women and a teenager sniffing after him. They all piled into Rick's car for what looked like an all-night party at some motel. The narc let them ride for a mile or so, then radioed uniformed officers to pull them over . . . An ounce of coke in Rick's jacket and a prescription bottle with a gram and a half on the dash.

Preston had no choice but to raid the Joneses that night—first Mick, then his father—a gamble all around. Fifty-fifty Mick wasn't waiting for Rick that afternoon and therefore wouldn't get suspicious if he didn't return. Fifty-fifty there was still some dope in both places. Fifty-fifty Frank Jones wouldn't learn his son got busted before Preston could bang his place. Hey, narcs live by the roll of the dice and good ones like Preston knew how to play the odds.

The wood-on-wood door of Mick's house broke like an orange crate and Preston's first gamble paid off. He found a plastic bag of white powder tucked under Mick's balls, a favorite stash in a pinch since most cops don't like looking there. Preston took a vial of pink liquid from his Ferguson Test Kit, a plastic container the size of a wide matchbox, broke the vial in half, stabbed the tip of a bent paperclip into the powder, then dipped the clip into the vial. The liquid turned robin-egg blue, definitely cocaine. He also found an "owe" sheet in Mick's pocket with names and amounts as well as a phone book. Small dirtball world, wouldn't you know, "Roberto" again, Mr. Everywhere, and the same current Hyattsville phone number next to his name.

Preston did only a cursory search of Mick's house, he was in a hurry to raid the guy's old man and sister who lived with her father. Even so, he found plenty of evidence for possession with intent: a tin of green and two ounces of cocaine (about $5,000 worth) ready to go in small zip-locks or in wax-coated snow seals; Triple Beam scale, fourteen small baggies, cutting mirror with coke dust—all adding up to another distribution operation with thirty to forty customers. Preston left a couple of men to watch Mick's house, he'd return for a more thorough search later.

Frank Jones lived a few miles from his son in Fernwood

Trailer Park, a deceptively clean-looking place without a fern or a wood in sight, just rows of trailers on cement blocks separated by patches of grass just large enough for a picnic table and grill. A soft blanket of fresh snow which sparkled in the streetlights like pure cocaine carpeted the place when Preston pulled in, a beautiful sight, we're happy tonight, a real winter wonderland. Surveillance and backup was already in place.

PG cops knew Fernwood for its trove of stolen and abandoned cars. Narcs knew it as a place where drug busts never went down easy. The trailers, which lined treeless streets like metal sardines, posed security problems for everyone, good guys, bad guys, neighbors. And the trailer doors—metal on metal—opened outward making them nearly ram-proof. IT had made another controlled buy from the Jones trailer earlier that week, which was enough probable cause to bang the place.

As Preston and the SOD team piled out of the van, the trailer door opened and a man stepped out. Backup pinned him before he could say, "Hey Frank, visitors," and stuffed him into an unmarked car. He had an eightball in his pocket so Preston knew there must be dope inside, sleigh bells ring, are you listening. The SOD team rammed the steel door but it wouldn't give.

Frank Jones and the four women inside—Frank's daughter, his girlfriend, Mick's girlfriend who was pregnant, and a guest snorter, all in their early twenties and white—froze as they waited for the gunshots that signaled a ripoff. When the trailer shook with a second bang, the guest snorter shouted, "It's a bust . . . it's a bust." Like a fire drill, they all knew what to do.

The guest snorter quickly hid her coke in a pile of clothes sitting near a suitcase on the floor. If the narcs found the shit, she could always play dumb. The pregnant woman, who was in the bathroom cooking coke on tinfoil with an alcohol torch, flushed her drugs down the toilet, bolted out the back door, and hid behind two oil drums a few trailers down. Bad break, kid. Two undercover cops tracked her down. Frank opened the door as cool as the snow in the lane glistening. Hell, Frank's not afraid of narcs. They're only doin' their job, nothing personal mind you, just don't resist, be civil, give them a little of what they want so they won't get pissed, then bide your time. You can always jerk off the court later.

It turned out to be a respectable haul and enough for possession with intent: around $3,000 worth of coke in Frank's shirt pocket, under the couch, in a kitchen cabinet, in Ziplocs, in snow seals. A can of green, a small baggie of grass, a vanilla bottle with traces of PCP, a tinfoil package with coke residue. An owe sheet and a thousand in cash. And oh yes . . . ten rifles and pistols spread all over the place. Frank, it turned out, was a gun collector, a minor detail the snitch had forgotten to mention. Hey, good thing the guy wasn't a green bean or he might have blown a few heads off and not remembered a thing the next day.

Preston charged dad and mother-to-be with possession and intent. He wrote up the other three kids as suspects and let them go—until next time. Back at the Bowie substation, Frank pleaded guilty to simple possession but not to intent to distribute. He knew that with a little bit of judicial luck, he'd never have to face a jury of his peers. Rick, Mick, and Mick's pregnant girlfriend agreed to plead guilty to one charge of possession with intent and to cooperate if Preston dropped all other charges. He learned:

Mick is the kingpin of the dope ring. Rick and Mick's father help him distribute. He buys half-key bricks of cocaine cakes from Roberto, same day delivery. Roberto exchanges the dope either at a 7-Eleven store on New Hampshire Avenue in PG just inside the beltway or at a Bob's Big Boy down the road in Montgomery County just outside the beltway and one of Sparshott's favorite buy-spots.

Knowing how dealers like to sell close to home, Preston figured that Roberto must live in one of the apartment buildings near the 7-Eleven. And based on Mick's description of the coke he had bought, Preston knew that Roberto was peddling cocaine hydrochloride, a white crystalline cake that sparkles like diamonds, in its purest form 89 percent coke and 11 percent hydrochloride. Leech away the hydrochloride and you get pure cocaine, fluffy flakes that gleam like pure white snow. By the time the coke reached the street as Powder, Flake or Snow, it was between 15 and

18 percent pure. The rest was white adulterant such as Lidocaine (a local anesthetic), Mannitol (a mild baby laxative), Lactose, Inositol, or Quinine. Buyers like Mick preferred crystalline cakes to powder because they believed the cakier the coke the purer.

In one week, without warning, like a blizzard: Josie and Jimmy with forty to fifty customers; the Jones family with thirty to forty customers; Jimmy's brother Walt on the lam, probably selling dope in another corner of the county; Mickey's house full of snorters, smokers and whores; all white and all connected to this Hispanic guy Roberto with an armed interpreter and coke pressed into tidy half-key cakes, a major dealer who sold in bulk or ounce baggies but without a face.

Well not exactly. Baby Bell came through a few days after the Jones family bust. Roberto now had a last name, middle initial, and address.

TEN

Preston had never heard of the guy before. His name was Roberto Tabares and he lived in apartment #1210 at Presidential Towers, pissing distance from the 7-Eleven where he dealt. He actually had two telephones in his apartment and six previous numbers, all changed in the past few months.

Preston quickly checked the Washington metropolitan white pages and found three other Tabares listed: Raul who lived in Aspen Hill, Roy in Columbia, Maryland, and Roberto, Jr., in northwest Washington near the District line. Criminal records had nothing on Roberto, Jr., or Roy but it had plenty on Raul. A multi-kilo cocaine dealer, Cuban, busted but never prosecuted, a quadriplegic with a hole in his head.

Raul and Roberto, same last name, two drug pushers, both coke, another probable drug incest. This sucker was big and Preston didn't know how the heck he was going to handle it . . . by himself . . . between cases . . . when it looked like the whole county was snorting Roberto's stuff. What's a narc to do?

Preston had learned early in his narcotics career that you can blow more cases by snapping on the cuffs too soon than by waiting too long. And he knew from experience that he would probably need a court-ordered wiretap to identify the entire Tabares organization, and that the courts demanded a thorough and patterned police investigation before they granted one. So he cautiously and methodically began to weave three separate but interrelated investigative threads—Dial Number Recorders on Roberto's phones to see whom he called and how often; spot surveillance to profile the man and his activity; and a dead-mail cover to see who wrote to him.

Like most apartment buildings, the twin Presidential Towers had a phone room in the basement. To hook up the DNR or pen register which nestled in a metal box with a roll of paper attached to it like a supermarket tape was a fifteen minute job if you knew what you were doing, forget it if you didn't. With more than 300 phones and a four by eight foot telephone box filled with rows of wires, you could be there all day: check the log book in the phone room which lists the wire code for each apartment in the building; using the code, find the two lines to #1210 in the phone box; clip the DNR wires to the lines and plug the box into the wall outlet; call the operator and ask which apartment the DNRs are tapped into; then call the numbers and watch the little sucker write away; come back every few days to pick up the goodies, like collecting eggs.

The two pen registers soon told Preston that Roberto placed forty to fifty calls to the three other Tabares in the phone book, to Frank Jones (dad) who was out on bail waiting trial, to a new guy called "Danny" who was listed in both Josie's and Walt's drug book, and to an unlisted number in Adams Morgan, the Latino section of Washington. There were few incoming calls. The wiretap judge would love the telephone traffic pattern. The high volume of outgoing calls to at least three known or suspected drug dealers pointed to a probable conspiracy to distribute cocaine. And the dearth of incoming calls suggested a telephone beeper, the dealer's indispensable tap-proof toy.

Between buys, busts and raids, Preston had little time to sit and watch Presidential Towers and no partner to help with surveillance, so he crawled under Roberto's car early one morning after his shift and attached a bird dog tracking device nice and tight. PG has a heart of stone, you lose the bird dog you pay for it, all $2,500 worth, a comfort if you're a taxpayer but a big risk if you're a cop. Then Preston watched and followed Roberto around town every chance he could, especially on his days off. He liked developing a case alone and, frankly, he enjoyed his own company.

All that back-slapping, arm-wrestling, beer drinking macho stuff Sparshott loved didn't appeal to him. Not that he minded having a drink with the guys now and then.

A shadow of the dealer soon began to emerge: Roberto Tabares was short, pudgy, late fifties, and nearly bald. He liked to wear a light-colored suit, usually gray, a shirt open at the collar, and elevated shoes like Alan Ladd. He parked his car in the lower lot of Presidential Towers—Preston spied from the upper lot—walked up a set of cement stairs, and entered the building through a side door, then took the elevator up to the twelfth floor and walked a few doors down to 1210. He had a friend on the fourteenth floor of the other twin tower, a Cuban called Saulo Hernandez. They used each other's cars, exchanged packages, and swapped women.

Other than Hernandez and the three men with the same last name as his, Roberto had few friends in Washington but plenty of women. They tramped in and out of his apartment, some black, some white, and stayed too long for a simple drug transaction. He also kept a room at the Georgetown Motor Inn on Georgia Avenue (Lucky Lopez' old playpen), stocked it with liquor, and brought women there. He visited an apartment building in Adams Morgan—the unlisted phone was probably in one of the apartments there—and exchanged packages with several different people in the parking lot of Bob's Big Boy on New Hampshire just north of Presidential Towers and the 7-Eleven.

One day about a week after Preston started spot surveillance, the car with the bird dog disappeared and the DNRs went dead. Preston felt the old narc rat gnawing at his gut, the one that always gets hungry when a deal begins to turn sour. He panicked, bye bye birdie, adios amigo. Roberto must know by this time that several of his customers—Josie, Jimmy, Rick, Mick, and Frank—had been busted. Did one of them also warn the Cuban? Was there a leak at the federal courthouse? Did Roberto move or skip town for good, case over, nice try, Preston?

Then late one night, ten depressing days after Roberto had disappeared, the bird dog detector in Preston's u.c. car began chirping again as he approached Presidential Towers for his daily check. Preston was so happy he began to sing along. He parked and crawled back under Roberto's car to make sure the bird dog was still securely fastened and found the gadget filled with sand. He cleaned it, then checked the DNRs in the telephone room—the front desk held the key—and noted a string of calls, like fresh droppings, to Frank Jones, the new guy Danny, and the phone in Adams Morgan.

No narc wants to be accused of jumping to conclusions, but come on now! A Cuban cocaine dealer without many friends in Washington sneaks out of town for ten days, returns with sand under his car only to make a string of calls to his best customers? Of course, he went to Miami for a fresh load of cocaine. Heck, half of being a good narc is trusting your instincts.

Right after Roberto returned with the sand, the court approved the dead-mail cover and instructed Roberto's post office to give Preston the names and addresses which appeared on the outside of all envelopes addressed to him for one month. Dead mail is pot luck, and Preston got lucky twice: an envelope from National Car Rental at Washington's National Airport; and what looked like a bill from Multi-Com in Chevy Chase, Maryland, just outside the District. Multi-Com specializes in beepers.

A visit to National's rental office confirmed that Roberto had rented a car and paid with American Express. No big surprise, nervous dealers like to use rented cars which they change frequently to confuse the feds and to give them less to seize if it ever comes down to that. Heck, every dealer knows that narcs get a hard on for expensive cars. A check with American Express led to a home address on South West 25th Terrace in Miami's Little Havana and a phone number which had already appeared on the pen register every now and then. A subpoena to Multi-Com produced two beeper numbers registered to Roberto Tabares. Nice to know in case you run across them in some bad guy's phone book and important to establish probable cause for a wiretap.

In the middle of Preston's investigation, while Sparshott was a whisker away from finding the last name to go with Roberto, Bob Bonsib stopped in the Bowie substation to chat. He had spent nine years as a PG County prosecutor in Upper Marlboro, the county seat, where he quickly learned that the system was more creative in finding ways to shit on local cops than it was in prosecuting bad guys. So he made it a point early in his career to understand what drove narcs and to get close to them, part business, part friendship. The more he worked with them, the more he came to respect how much they accomplished with so little. Hell, who would he have to prosecute without them?

When he moved on to Baltimore as a U.S. Attorney, Bonsib kept an experienced eye open for promising cases that locals like Sparshott and Preston couldn't handle because they spilled over into other counties and states where they didn't have jurisdiction, or became legally too complex for inexperienced county prosecutors, or required more officers and equipment than county police could spare. His grand jury investigation of outlaw motorcycle gangs was just such a case, and Preston was his nose. Besides admiring the guy's quiet tenacity, Bonsib knew that whatever scum Preston managed to skim off the county cesspool would stick in court like Elmer's. "How's it going, Marty," Bonsib asked. "You got anything?"

Come to think of it, Preston did. He told Bonsib about the biker Davis and the PCP in Josie's, Mick's, and Frank's places and said he felt certain the Phantoms had supplied most of it. Bonsib was so tickled he promised to draw up subpoenas in the morning, if Preston would serve them, no easy task since druggies are nomads by necessity.

Preston debated whether to tell Bonsib about Roberto. If the case kept snowballing, he'd have to make an important decision soon: either give it to a county or state prosecutor who would move quickly and insure Preston investigative control, but who would narrow the focus of the probe to Roberto himself and eventually win only a slap on the wrist; or take the case to a U.S. Attorney like Bonsib who would broaden it to include Roberto's entire organization and eventually win respectable jail time, but who would probably take the investigation away from Preston and toss him a bit part like a bone.

It was a short debate. To take down Roberto's whole organization—source, mules, muscle, lieutenants, principal buyers, money launderers, and assets so they couldn't deal from jail—was the cop-smart thing to do even if Preston had to play fourth fiddle, and the case could turn out to be the biggest of his short career as a narc. Who better to work with than Bob Bonsib who swam through the federal bureaucracy like a snail darter. And what better time to do it than now while the case was still filled with surprises. So Preston, who prided himself on doing the cop-smart thing even if it was less fun, calmly told Bonsib what he knew about Roberto, it was hard to be calm, was Bonsib interested?

"I think we can do something with this," Bonsib said. It was hard to be calm, *kilos* of coke in the Washington-Baltimore corridor are, pardon the pun, nothing to sniff at. "A friend of mine at the FBI is looking for drug stuff. This could be Presidential Task Force, Marty."

□ □ □

President Reagan created the Presidential Task Force in 1982. It was to be his howitzer in the war on drugs, the government's answer to the biggest problem in narcotics enforcement: rivalry among the generals who prefer scrapping in bureaucratic gutters over money and stats than talking to each other. Suggested by the Justice Department, the idea was to create a simple and effective way to get enforcement branches to swallow their pride, forget past insults, and work *together*: city and county police departments, state bureaus of investigation, and federal agencies like the U.S. Coast Guard, Immigration and Naturalization Service, Customs Service, Drug Enforcement Administration, U.S. Marshals Service, Bureau of Alcohol, Tobacco, and Firearms, IRS, U.S. Attorneys, and FBI.

To tie the FBI closely to the Task Force, Congress authorized the Bureau to help the DEA enforce national drug laws, thus enlisting the most powerful and wealthiest federal enforcement agency in the drug war. The resulting Organized

Crime Drug Enforcement Task Force (OCDETF) was the loosest and least bureaucratic institution Washington ever created. Money became the carrot *and* the stick:

Congress would approve block grants for each federal enforcement agency pro rated, in part, on the arrest and prosecution record of the previous year. But the agencies wouldn't be able to spend the money until regional Task Force coordinators cut it loose after making sure there were at least *two* agencies on each case and that the target of the investigation was a major player not just street scum. After the bad guys were arrested, U.S. Marshals would seize their money and sell their houses, boats, airplanes, cars, jewelry, and businesses. The Justice Department would skim a 15 percent administrative fee off the top (more if the case went to trial), and the cooperating agencies would divvy up the rest of the loot depending on how much time and personnel each devoted to the case.

If locals like Sparshott and Preston were involved in the case, Federal Marshals would deputize them so they could work across county and state lines. The Task Force would reimburse their departments for their overtime and give them a fair share of the booty. The system worked. On winning drug convictions with jail time, the Task Force was batting over .800. With a stat like that, how could the good guys lose?

□ □ □

As impressed as he was with Preston's one-man investigation, Bonsib knew that the Tabares case would not impress Task Force coordinators because it was still more smoke and mirrors than substance. Frankly, Preston needed something to convince them that Roberto Tabares was worth the money.

In mid-May, two months after Preston first stumbled on the name Roberto, he and Bonsib attended the monthly Council of Governments narc meeting at the Prince George's County Country Club. Preston never missed. Bonsib tried to get there every month if he wasn't in court . . . Tracy Sparshott co-chaired the meeting.

ELEVEN

It was a voluntary, narcs-only Council of Governments lunch closed even to country club waiters. It drew from thirty-two police departments, usually around fifty people came, and as far as co-chair Tracy Sparshott was concerned that was a dead shame because information saves lives. They all got to meet the new crop of narc rookies. And they shared whatever they had—part swap, part gripe. Department problems and policies, their cases, the latest fashions in drug enforcement and smuggling, what's new on the street. Personally, Sparshott made it a point to keep up to date. Like a disciple at the feet of a master, he frequently took time with a snitch or a newly-cuffed bad guy just to listen to them shoot the shit. Drug language changes quickly on the street and as the old saying goes, "A narc who talks like yesterday goes bye-bye baby today." The big issue at this May meeting was the PCP/biker blight and the startling amount of cocaine fluttering down over quiet county lanes and roads.

Sparshott took the mike and told his fellow narcs about the Tabares case, how it began with June Boyle over in Fairfax who called Montgomery for an assist, the setup, the buy-bust, and the bang. How much coke they had found and how they had arrested three dirtballs then skidded to a quadriplegic dead-end. He praised Boyle and said, "Come on brothers, cooperation between departments really works!" Not that they hadn't heard Sparshott say that a hundred times before.

Bob Bonsib sat at a table with Marty Preston and several other PG narcs and listened to Sparshott talk about Raul Tabares.

He would have pounded his fist on the table and said "gotcha Roberto" if he weren't a poised U.S. Attorney, clean shaven, manicured, and well groomed, so unlike the hairy apes around him. Sparshott had just given him a new link to the Cuban and it looked like he and Preston had stepped on a whole nest of dealers with a ten-year family history, more than Bonsib needed to seduce federal funds from the Presidential Task Force.

Bonsib called Sparshott over to his table—Tracy had worked with the attorney before and thought he was cool—and said you guys are onto something, why don't you get together, pool what you have, then get back to me.

Bonsib knew that what narcs kept in their heads was more important than what they put on paper, and that most narcs were paranoid about sharing unless the prosecutor, the Man, insisted on it. It was the nature of the game. Undercover cops are quarterbacks, loners by nature but team players by necessity, two never take the field at the same time. They like to call their own plays, but when they can't, they read the field and try to make the coach's play work. They anticipate and scheme, psych out the enemy and take calculated risks, they look for weaknesses to exploit and feel invincible under the oxygen of competition. They live for the thrill of the pass caught, the goal line crossed, the game won, the super bowl dream. In the heat of battle, they sometimes forget the game is a team effort, and they fear the bench as much as an old man fears a wheelchair.

Bonsib recognized two quarterbacks in Sparshott and Preston, and only one could start. He understood that each believed the Tabares case was his and that they would eventually have to settle their differences, no matter what the coach decided, or lose the game.

Sparshott understood all this as well. He had briefly worked with Preston once before and he knew him by reputation as a meticulous and tireless investigator and a good undercover. Given a choice, Sparshott would prefer to work the Tabares case alone. Without a choice, he was determined to be starting quarterback, no matter how much work Preston had already done.

He felt he had more undercover experience than Preston, and that his experience was broader and deeper.

Sparshott also knew something else that he wasn't sure Preston completely understood. If the Tabares case went federal as Bonsib wanted it to—it would make no difference whether the FBI or the DEA stepped in—both he *and* Preston would be just fucking locals. The feds would try their bureaucratic damnedest to muscle them out as they did on Sparshott's Narc-of-the-Year case. Hey, the assholes gotta save the investigation from bungling F.L.'s even if it means putting the u.c. at risk, after all he's only a fucking local, dime a dozen with a long line waiting to get into the academy. Well, the undercover DEA agent assigned to that case almost blew it. The fucking institutional arrogance of it all!

Like a good quarterback, Sparshott was already six plays ahead. His only protection against the feds—forget the bad guys, they're fucking pushovers—was to make himself indispensable. And the first step to becoming indispensable was to pool what he and Preston knew and become an expert on the Tabares organization.

So Sparshott welcomed Bonsib's suggestion which surprised the prosecutor, then he and Preston got together between drug cases. Preston brought a suitcase full of surveillance reports, DNR tapes, and drug organization flow charts to the meeting. Sparshott, who was allergic to paper, carried what he knew in his head. Neither was thrilled with the prospect of working together. Their personalities and undercover styles were as different as coffee and tea, and each wanted to call the undercover shots. They knew there would be sparks, maybe even a fire, but they were determined to make the arranged marriage work. Without voicing their misgivings, they compared notes, went back to massage their snitches, then pooled what they had learned:

As soon as he heard his son Raul had stopped a bullet with his head, Roberto Tabares had rushed to Washington from Miami.

He had known for years that Raul sold drugs and always disapproved, like a good father, with drugs-are-wrong and it's-blood-money lectures. He even spurned Raul's offers to buy him a yacht or set him up with a Cuban restaurant of his own. To Roberto, his son's drug money was as tempting as perky tits but he convinced himself that it was better to scrape along the bottom than live high off other people's misery. Other than cheating on his wife, which didn't count since it was expected, or so he told himself, he was proud of being an honest man who believed in family, hard work, and honor.

But Roberto had troubling second thoughts when he came to Washington after the murder attempt and saw how Raul had lived before drugs froze his body from the neck down. A huge house in Rockville with expensive art on the walls, a new El Dorado and a yacht, beautiful clothes, gold and diamond jewelry, business investments. Ease, flash, comfort, all the things Roberto had once enjoyed, had lost, but still craved.

Roberto had been wealthy back then, in Cuba, before Fidel Castro. His father owned ranches and stockyards and a string of butcher shops, a big home in Havana, and a seaside villa with servants and a pleasure boat. When Roberto married Victoria, a sixteen-year-old, light-skinned village beauty, his father gave him a butcher shop and a house as a wedding present. Raul came a year later, then Roberto, Jr., then a younger woman. Victoria kept Raul, Roberto took junior, Fidel took most of the rest, including the family yacht. El General gave it to the poor villagers who gutted it for a fishing boat.

Roberto was an easy-going man, not especially known around Havana for passion or daring, except when it came to women. So he surprised everyone in the summer of '65 when he and a team of commandos pirated the old family yacht and sailed the Caribbean to Mexico along with his son Roberto, Jr., his second wife, their two children, and thirty other relatives. From Mexico to America, my country 'tis of thee, land of opportunity.

It was the first and last poetic moment in the otherwise drab life of Roberto Tabares. Everything he touched after the pilot's wheel turned to red ink—a gas station in Florida, a supermarket in Texas, a string of mom and pop convenience stores in Puerto Rico—the money spent on young women and tired horses.

Roberto may have been a loser but he wasn't stupid. He looked at what his son Raul had and what he didn't. He looked at his two beautiful, innocent granddaughters, and felt very sad. Who will take care of them, these little ones. They are family, my responsibility now.

Raul's cousin and partner watched his uncle and thought he could hear the worm of indecision gnawing at Roberto. Uncle, he told the old man, your son Raul spent years building a good business here. He can no longer run it, I have contacts, I know the market like my own wallet, how much to pay, how to cut, where to sell for how much, and I can smell cops like buried shit. If we don't move soon our customers will drift away, go someplace else to buy, our runners will join other organizations, we'll lose everything. What do you say, Tio Roberto? You run the show from Miami, I'll manage the market in Washington.

Roberto agreed. What choice did he have? He was the head of Raul's family now, he didn't ask for the responsibility, God and a bitch's bullet gave it to him, and it would be a goddamn shame to let the house that Raul built crumble like a sandcastle.

But the old man was cautious, wanted to move slowly, learn the business from the ground up, and didn't completely trust his nephew. Didn't Raul get shot in an apartment leased to his cousin? Wasn't there money and dope missing from it? Maybe he set Raul up. So Tio Roberto decided that as soon as he learned the business and made his own contacts, he would build his own house.

Okay nephew, the old man said, we're in business, they shook. The son was out. The patriarch was in. And the nephew? He'd soon learn he'd been dealt a joker and it wasn't wild.

Roberto began slowly at first, selling only marijuana, not the coke that Raul used to buy from the black bitch Chicky from New York. What Roberto couldn't see, he didn't trust. His operation was simple. He'd buy a bale of grass in Miami, toss it in the trunk of a rented car, drive to Silver Spring and take two rooms at the Georgetown Motor Inn on Georgia Avenue just across the District line where Lucky Lopez used to snort and fuck. One room for himself and one for a young woman with perky tits. He'd sell the grass to the nephew's contacts, make a few of his own, study the market, then go back home to his wife.

It didn't take Roberto long to figure out he could make five times more carrying small packages of coke into the shadows of the nation's capital where the growing powder market was open to anyone with money. He contacted the relative of a relative, a big-shit candy man who bought directly from Colombia and sold hundreds of keys a month, and backed into the cocaine business like his son before him, but without the nephew. He fronted his son Raul, who now lived with his mother in a duplex on Hydrus Road, enough dope to sell so his daughter-in-law and grandchildren could live in reasonable comfort, and then began building his own network in and around Washington.

Roberto's man in Little Havana also supplied another Miami Cuban, Saulo Hernandez, who had a fourteenth-floor condo at Presidential Towers. Roberto moved into the twin tower next door. When Roberto ran out of coke, Saulo loaned him some from his stash. When Saulo needed an extra key, Roberto supplied him. Hey, compadre, metro Washington is so bi-i-ig there's no need for all that cut-throat turf shi-i-it you see in the movies.

For the second time in his life, Roberto became a swashbuckler. Sometimes he'd tote-bag or shoe-box a couple of keys right on Pan Am or Eastern or rent a car and drive it up to Washington from Miami. Sometimes he'd share Saulo Hernandez' mule who'd deliver shit to Presidential Towers for both men or hire his own mule in Miami to drive it up in a rented car. Sometimes the dope would come to Washington first and he'd follow. Sometimes he'd come first and the coke would follow. All sleights of hand to keep the narcs guessing.

One of Roberto's first and best customers was Nelson, a Cuban who lived in Adams Morgan and specialized in heroin but did some coke just to keep his people happy. He lived in a first floor apartment and stashed his dope in another apartment in the same building. Two of his best customers—Walt and Mick—met Roberto there. When Nelson left the room to go to his stash pad, the old man lured them away with offers of cheaper and better crystal-cakes. Poor old Nelson was arrested for heroin distribution before he could object.

But Roberto was having a tough time sinking roots in Washington in spite of the capital area's growing appetite for cocaine. He spoke only broken English, didn't know the city or its Maryland suburbs, wouldn't move from Miami because of family, and had no local muscle he could trust to collect for him. Losers like Walt and Mick began ripping him off, then hiding in the cracks of PG and neighboring Charles County where Roberto and his broken English couldn't find them.

In desperate need of a Washington manager, the old man turned to his son Roberto, Jr. On the positive side, a smart kid with several years of college who spoke perfect English and knew his way around town. On the negative, a hopeless cocaine junkie, a fact which somehow eluded his father. The old man gave Roberto, Jr., a key to the stash pad in Presidential Towers, asked him to take deliveries when he wasn't there and continue to distribute the dope when he returned to Miami.

Nose Candy paradise, thank you Papa, who said God was dead? Junior began helping himself to an ounce at a time, no one's gonna miss a bag here or there. He snorted so much that he OD'ed and almost died, then turned as paranoid as an old spook. He began seeing narcs everywhere, in the headlights glaring in his rearview mirror, standing on the street corner by his house on Arkansas Avenue near Walter Reed Hospital in Washington, in the bars where he partied with friends. He'd hide the Snow in crazy places, then forget where, he'd toss packets out the car window when he thought he was being followed or flush some shit down a nightclub toilet when he thought he smelled a narc nearby. He'd call the old man in the middle of the night and cry "the narcs are coming, the narcs are coming," tell him to quick, move the shit, change cars, get a new phone number.

At first, the old man listened to his college-educated son who spoke perfect English and knew Washington. But Roberto, Jr. cried narc once too often and the old man, who was as blind as most fathers but not dumb, finally pieced it all together. He took back the apartment key, hid the stash, and wouldn't allow coke and his son in the same room together. Then out of paternal weakness, he supplied Roberto, Jr., just enough toot to keep him alive.

Like addicts everywhere, Roberto, Jr., found a hundred ways to rip his father off. His favorite: bring the old man a customer, a fellow junkie, tell him the guy wanted an ounce on consignment, but stop short of vouching for the guy's integrity, con the old man into giving the junkie the ounce, join the guy and party until, whiff, up the nose and feeling like a Norseman again.

Then one day, a narc busted Josie and Jimmy and the whole Jones family, and two other narcs smashed Raul's operation. Roberto could hear cops breathing all around him like obscene phone callers and hid in Miami for most of May and June. When things seemed to quiet down, he returned to Washington with a carload of dope. Preston was waiting . . .

□ □ □

By early July, the DNRs began humming again, forty to fifty outgoing calls a day, a new number with a Charles County exchange not listed in the Haines Directory which gives an address to go with every listed phone number. Preston knew that Roberto was finally back. He subpoenaed the new number, but before the telephone company could respond, Detective Rex Coffee of the Charles County sheriff's department called.

"Hey Marty, you got anything on a guy called Danny?"

Preston grinned. Danny was one of the names in both Josie's and Walt's private phone book. It never failed, sooner or later the creeps crawl out of the sewer like rats. He'd bet his pension, well part of it anyway, that good old Walt wasn't far away, and Preston wanted Walt. So did everyone else, Fairfax for possession, Prince George's for possession with intent, the feds for desertion from the Navy, and Roberto for a lot of money. Coffee told Preston what he had on Danny:

A snitch saw a bag of coke in a townhouse on Holly Tree Lane rented to a guy called Danny, Caucasian, mid-twenties, five feet five, and a lean 140. He drives an antique panel truck, a hand painted job that looks like a small hearse except it's white. The toy stands out like an aging painted woman. On its sides, a knight, sword drawn, attacking a monster clutching a screaming girl, giant vampires guarding a castle on a hill, the word "Deathstalker" in red and yellow . . . Danny just signed a lease on a townhouse in Holly Station, a new development off Highway 301 between Waldorf and La Plata, where Preston lived, forty minutes from Washington down Branch Avenue, through Anacostia, across Prince George's into Charles County, PG's poor neighbor to the south.

Preston told Coffee what he knew about Danny and his former supplier, Walt. "By the way, what's Danny's phone number. over there?" Preston had a hunch.

Small dirtball world, the number matched the one that Preston kept finding on Roberto's DNR, and suddenly it all made sense. Ever since he first hooked up the pen register, Preston had detected a strange pattern. A string of calls to a cheap motel along Highway 301, a room registered to a woman, occupants gone by the time he got there, sheets still warm, then a string of calls to another cheap motel, same woman, room empty. Preston suspected that Danny and his wife rented the rooms, were buying dope directly from Roberto now and fronting Walt Rogers who, sources had told Preston, owed the Cuban nearly $40K. Poor sneaky Walt. When Danny moved into Holly Station and Roberto returned to town, the Cuban began calling there, ten times a day between July 1 and July 9. The last call before the pen register went dead was to Pan Am. That meant Roberto was in Miami hustling a fresh supply of coke.

Preston offered Coffee a deal he couldn't resist. Preston would monitor the DNR and tell Coffee when Tabares returned, Coffee would draw up the search and seizure warrant for Danny's townhouse and have it ready for a judge to sign. Preston would tell Coffee when the phone traffic between Roberto and Danny got heavy, Coffee would invite Preston to the raid . . . Coffee would get the stat, Preston would get to pull the noose around Roberto's neck a little tighter. Coffee would get the drug money, Preston would serve up another witness for Bonsib's grand jury. Coffee would look good, Preston would get one more reason for the Presidential Task Force to fund the Tabares case and a judge to sign a wiretap order. And if he was lucky, Preston would get Walt as a bonus.

Coffee began the ritual dance of probable cause to add to what Preston and the snitch had already given him. First, he watched Danny's place and noted: Two convicted users dropped by for a few suspicious minutes. Danny appeared at the window eight times in a one-hour stretch, peeking through the curtains, all the lights burning, the usual paranoid drug-dealer-user behavior.

Danny lit a pipe with a flame big enough to singe his hair, probably Green, the ether in the PCP flares like a torch.

Next, Coffee sent his snitch inside to nose around. Danny was dry, the snitch reported back, he was waiting for his man to return with a fresh supply of shit—around the middle of July. A guy by the name of Walt had just moved into the townhouse with a woman called Joy.

Coffee then wrote up the warrant and sat on it. When the time came, no judge in the county would turn him down. Hell, he had a reliable snitch who had seen coke in Danny's house and his truck, two convicted users who had gone in and out, a suspect whom he, Coffee, had seen smoking what appeared to be dope, the usual thick cloud of drug paranoia over the suspect's house, a wanted drug dealer as a roommate, Preston's informants who had fingered Danny as a distributor to whom they sold coke, and Danny's phone number appearing on court-ordered DNRs attached to the phones of a big cocaine distributor from Miami.

On July 14, the pen registers began writing again. Tabares was back and Coffee rushed the warrant to a judge for a signature, then waited. Roberto called Danny nine times on July 16. Coffee and Preston hit the townhouse the next day.

The timing was perfect, it sometimes happens that way. As they pulled up, Danny walked out the front door leaving it wide open for the cops, no door to break down, no time for the bad guys to grab guns or flush drugs, just step inside the townhouse and cuff whoever's there. They grabbed Danny before he reached the Deathstalker parked out front and marched him right back inside where they found everything they hoped for, except Danny's wife and Walt.

Nearly a quarter pound of coke, most of it packaged in eightballs, hidden under a coffee table without legs. "Bought it last night in dogpatch," Danny joked, relaxed like being busted happens every day, these guys never cease to amaze you. About $2,000 in cash in Danny's wallet which made Coffee happy, Charles County got to keep it. A Remington 12-gauge shotgun in Walt's room, sawed-off, illegal in Maryland and stolen to boot. "I told him to throw that fuckin' gun in the woods," Danny said, a little nervous now. And the usual drug paraphernalia pointing to a distribution network of thirty to forty customers.

Jar of Inosital, pipe with PCP residue, v-shaped snorting straw with coke residue, freebase coke pipe, Deering kit, snow seals with coke residue, beeper, film canisters with PCP residue, red phone book belonging to Walt and green book belonging to Danny with Roberto's phone numbers inside, photo of Danny holding a key of coke, another photo of Walt freebasing heroin and coke. Enough to make a wiretap judge weep.

To complete a perfect day, Walt pulled up during the search. Undercovers grabbed him. They found two ounces of coke in the glove compartment and a snorting bullet filled with coke in his pocket. The sure-shot snorter has a lever which releases the exact amount of coke you want into a chamber. You put the bullet in your nose and snort, very efficient, nothing wasted, what will they think of next.

Poor Walt! Coffee and Preston had him three ways to the wind. Added to the charges he already had against him was possession with intent in Charles County and possession of an illegal, stolen gun. They also had Danny and his wife on possession with intent and Walt's girlfriend on simple possession charges. They waited for a couple hours for Danny's wife. When she didn't show, they issued a warrant for her arrest and folded their surveillance tents. She had to come up for a snort sooner or later and when she did, they'd grab her. Preston couldn't wait to tell Bonsib about the latest Roberto Tabares connection.

TWELVE

One thing was certain. Bob Bonsib now had enough on Roberto Tabares to put him away for a long time. Josie and her boyfriend Jimmy, Mick and his roommate-partner Rick, had already testified about Roberto before the Baltimore grand jury investigating biker gangs in exchange for fewer charges against them. Walt and Danny had agreed to do the same, and Danny's wife had just turned herself in to her cousin, a Maryland state trooper. Bonsib was sure she'd flip too, she was only twenty-one, why ruin what was left of her life for a dealer she barely knew. Add to their eyewitness testimony what he already knew about the Tabares family and Bonsib had a solid case:

Raul Tabares started dealing one to three kilos of coke a week in '76; his stepfather-distributor, Pedro Lucky Lopez, got busted in '80; Raul himself got nailed in '83 after Laurie popped him; Roberto took over the organization the same year and set up his son Raul as a distributor; Sparshott and Boyle busted Raul a second time just two months ago. Ten uninterrupted years of family business, two kilos a week on the low average, more than a *ton* of coke sprinkled on metro Washington, steady snow flurries with no clearing in sight.

All Bonsib had to do was ask the grand jury to indict Roberto and it would. But then he'd find himself shackled to a lengthy, expensive trial because Roberto would only plead guilty if he were actually caught with powder on his fingers. When the jury found Roberto guilty, and there was little doubt that it would, he would be the only fish flapping in the net. Like Sparshott and

Preston, Bonsib wanted the whole drug organization and its candy man, the big Miami connection. Jail time all around, shut the Tabares family down for good, one battle in the war on drugs won, on to the next.

But Tracy Sparshott could never deliver the whole Tabares organization, and Marty Preston couldn't either. Nor could they do it together as a team, even though they were crack undercover cops and investigators, even if Bonsib deputized them as federal agents, and he would, even if their superiors sprung them both, fat chance, to work the Tabares case fulltime. Where would they get the backup they needed to pull it off? The surveillance equipment? The money?

Bonsib had a plan. He had already prosecuted a dozen Task Force cases, mostly IRS and FBI, some DEA, and he considered it the best game in town. To win its fiscal blessing on the Tabares case, he would need a federal sponsor which had experience in narcotics investigations and the resources to get the job done. That spelled either DEA or FBI.

Bonsib picked the Bureau even though it was only a buck private in the war on drugs. A purely pragmatic decision. The FBI had more money than the DEA—hey, in drugs as in life, it always boils down to money—field agents in every city, the latest surveillance toys, undercover cars and boats and airplanes, and a big budget. True, it had a bureaucracy as thick as a castle wall. But it had the staying power of a porn-stud. True, it guarded its image and turf like a drug lord. But it had the patience of a spider and brought in solid cases that rarely crumbled in court, and when the smoke of appeals cleared, that won impressive jail time.

Next, Bonsib would give Tabares to FBI Special Agent William Campbell who, like Sparshott, was a slightly square peg in a round hole. They would sell Campbell on the case, easy since he loved catching crooks as much as they did, and he in turn would sell it to his superiors in Baltimore, not easy since the FBI moved about as swiftly as a sloth.

After the FBI adopted the case, and it could take months, Bonsib would add an IRS criminal investigator to the team, he had an ace in mind, then help Campbell present the case to the Task Force regional coordinators. Tabares clearly met all Task Force criteria: His organization was a major cocaine supplier in metropolitan Washington with a Miami connection that was even bigger; the case involved more than one jurisdiction—Montgomery and Prince George's Counties in Maryland, and Dade County in Florida; the investigation would team up more than one agency—two county police departments, the FBI, and the IRS for openers; and the Tabares organization was destroying the fabric of quiet Maryland communities. Just ask Preston.

Bonsib was certain Task Force coordinators would rubberstamp the case and, when they did, he would help the team from the sidelines. Get the court-ordered wiretap, mediate turf wars (and they would be vicious, they always were), soothe institutional hurt feelings, select criminal targets from the list of suspects, evaluate the evidence the team brought him, secure a raft of arrest and search and seizure warrants, negotiate pleas and bargains, and mop up what was left over in the courts.

It was a good plan.

□ □ □

Bill Campbell looked like a typical FBI agent, a trim, wiry, all-American type with dark hair and even white teeth. But he thought more like a drug dealer than a son of Hoover and that made him different. He hadn't always been that way.

Campbell's father was an FBI agent stationed in Montgomery County and it was understood in the Campbell family that Bill would follow his father to FBI boot camp at Quantico. After earning an accounting degree and hanging out his CPA shingle for awhile—Hoover had a sweet tooth for accountants and lawyers—he bided his time as an IRS agent until he was old enough to apply to the Bureau. He spent his rookie year on a white-collar crime team in Baltimore chasing con artists and embezzlers down endless paper trails. But he soon discovered he was a thrill junkie like Sparshott and Preston, not a desk jock, so he asked his superiors for a more exciting street job. They turned him loose on bank robbers and fugitives, and he loved it.

When the FBI moved into narcotics enforcement in 1982 to show the DEA how the pros do it, Campbell's superiors in Baltimore called him and a dozen special agents into a tidy office with an American flag and a picture of J. Edgar and said: "Congratulations and good luck, you're the new drug squad." None of that mythical FBI training shit, just a mandate to go get 'em, win the war on drugs, boys, make us proud and show up the DEA.

Campbell began hanging out with the Baltimore City cops, something he learned from his father. They liked him, he wasn't the usual asshole know-it-all fed, and he didn't treat them like they were too dumb to pass the FBI test. He rode with the narcs, helped on surveillance, got in on their busts and bangs, learned about drugs and dealers, and when a promising case began to develop, asked if the FBI could help. He brought his first drug case to the Baltimore U.S. Attorney who had handled most of his previous white-collar investigations.

"I'm not familiar with drugs," the attorney had said.

"Can you recommend someone who is?"

"Try Bob Bonsib, he did a lot of drug cases down in PG."

It was a good marriage. Prosecutors can be real shits, second-guess every move, play Monday morning quarterback Tuesday through Saturday, too busy to help but never too busy to piss on the evidence investigators bring them, trained parrots with a limited vocabulary, "Need more evidence, need more evidence," who turn down perfectly good cases because of a mere hint of a slight possibility of maybe losing.

Not Bonsib. Having worked with understaffed and undertrained narcs for nine years, he knew what they faced on the street every day and how elusive drug evidence could be. The kind of prosecutor who'd make suggestions, not demands. "Did you try this? Maybe look at it this way." In the end, he'd take a case into the pit even if it wasn't perfect, and he'd win.

When a slot opened in the FBI Silver Spring Resident Agency, a Baltimore satellite office with a desk in the Montgomery

County Police substation there, Campbell asked for it, more freedom and variety, less bureaucracy. The Montgomery cops were glad to have him. They had dubbed his predecessor, a feet-on-the-desk kind of fed, "The Maytag Repair Man."

Two months later, the neighboring FBI Resident Agency in Hyattsville drafted Campbell to work on a drug wiretap case. He moved into the basement of a decaying high-rise just off the Baltimore-Washington Parkway on Route 450, the road to Annapolis, near Mickey's cocaine whorehouse where PG narcs had nabbed Rick and his party girls with an ounce of "C." Campbell had just finished the wiretap, exhausted from the endless stream of paperwork and eager to hit the streets again, when Bonsib brought him the Tabares case, a gift from cocaine heaven.

Bureau "creds" in Washington—that's what fucking locals call special agents who feel positively naked without their gilded credentials clipped to their jacket or shirt—had just changed the FBI's national drug strategy without asking narcs like Campbell what he thought of it. Forget about middle-level dealers, the creds ordered, go for the balls of the organization, grab the big pricks from the top Mafia and Colombian families, they said, the Gambinis and Trafficanas, the major cartels called Medellin, Cali, Bogota and North Atlantic Coast.

The Justice Department was proud of its new Jiminy Cricket, wish-upon-a-star strategy. President Reagan thought it was the best thing since talking pictures. Congress said it was about time somebody had the military courage to go after drug generals instead of lieutenants. But Bill Campbell knew it was a serious mistake, the kind that Washington creds make because the only thing they know about drugs is what they read in the *Post.*

Big cases begin on little barstools, in Howie Johnson's, Denny's, and 7-Eleven, with June Boyle, Tracy Sparshott, and Marty Preston. They begin with dirtballs like Mick, Walt, and Danny. You want big, you work with local narcs who find cases under rocks and in sewers, you win their respect and confidence, you treat them like equals. Then maybe they'll let you in on a case that has tentacles in Miami and Bogotá and Panama City.

Campbell also knew that the Washington creds could never see it that way, not when they call the Sparshotts and the Prestons "fucking locals," not when they support a system that jacks the locals off for leads then shits on them because they didn't graduate from Quantico.

Campbell knew exactly what the new drug strategy would do. Cut the feds off from the locals who dig up the potentially big cases and rekindle all their old resentments. It was like telling them once again: "Hey guys, get off your butts, roll up your sleeves, do all the dirty work. Then when you stumble onto something big, you know, after a year or so of overtime and day-off investigation, give us a call. We'll solve the case for you." Sure, and grab the stat, and seize the assets, and stand in the camera lights. Who are they kidding?

Campbell saw through the PR fog. The new drug strategy was tired FBI hype that had more to do with humiliating the DEA and making headlines than with winning the war on drugs . . . or maybe the war itself was hype. One thing was certain—the new strategy would put Campbell out of business. Where the hell would he and other Bureau foot soldiers find cases that met the new criteria? If the Washington creds wanted Colombian drug families, they should open a Resident Agency in Bogotá.

So when Bob Bonsib told him about Roberto Tabares—"I have something good going with Marty Preston, maybe it will fit your new strategy"—Campbell couldn't believe his luck. I got one, he told himself. I actually got one!

It was mid August, two months after Sparshott had met Bonsib and Preston at the narc meeting at the Prince George's County Country Club. Campbell grabbed the Tabares case like a Sumo wrestler. He met with Preston, whom he already knew. Earlier that year, Preston had asked Campbell for an assist on the Len Bias cocaine case. He had been looking for a car that figured in the overdose death of the University of Maryland basketball star and Campbell had helped him find it. Preston found Campbell easy to work with and almost as sly as Bonsib in pushing paper through the bureaucracy. A good agent who knew what he was doing and when he didn't, said so. Campbell reviewed Preston's notes and flow charts and was impressed with the cop's careful, methodical investigation. He left Preston convinced that the Tabares case would meet the Bureau's new criteria.

Next, Campbell talked to Sparshott whom he had known from narc meetings and had come to appreciate as the best bull-shitting undercover cop around, the kind of narc who could talk his way right out of cement shoes. They had just finished a surveillance case together, and although it never went anywhere, they hit it off famously. Sparshott told Campbell that he was certain he could get his toe inside the Tabares organization if he had enough time, backup, and money. This one can go all the way, he said, right into fuckin' downtown Bogotá itself.

By now Campbell was as excited as an astronomer with a new galaxy, a drug nova exploding over the nation's capital, an organization with a ten-year history and a big Miami connection. He wasted no time presenting the case to Special Agent William Tucker, the FBI Task Force coordinator in Baltimore. But Tucker wasn't impressed. The case didn't fit the Bureau's new criteria, he told Campbell. Roberto was a Cuban, not a Mafioso, and Tabares was not the name of a major Colombian drug family, Bonsib's pleading and Preston's flow charts to the contrary. Bring back someone *big* with the right last name and you got it, Billy Boy.

Campbell was as mad as a dealer who has just been ripped off but Bonsib wasn't ruffled. He knew how badly the Bureau suffered from the xenophobia J. Edgar had bred into it to keep morale high and bloodlines pure. Any case that began outside the FBI was automatically suspect until proven special. So Bonsib told Sparshott, Preston and Campbell to sit tight, it was only round one.

THIRTEEN

Bob Bonsib had just finished working a big PCP case with Gerard T. Macready, a burly IRS criminal investigator with thin red hair, a bushy red beard, and a red face, an expert on money laundering, a fire range instructor, and the best T-man in the Baltimore-Washington area. The kind of guy who thought catching crooks was more fun than sunning by the pool with a Tequila Sunrise. Macready had handed a gang of Rocket Fuelers to Bonsib cuffed in their own tax returns. They had spent, he proved, thousands of dollars on houses, cars, jewelry, and travel, while declaring only hundreds in income. Where did all the money come from if not from the sale of drugs?

It was only logical for Bonsib to offer Macready the Tabares case without telling him, of course, that he had given the FBI the first crack. No use making the guy feel like a second stringer, the IRS already suffered from a bad inferiority complex. And it was also only logical that Macready, a rainmaker who shared Bonsib's allergy to bureaucracy, would run with the case as hard as Bill Campbell had, but without Campbell's sea of red-tape shit to wade through.

First, Macready opened an IRS criminal investigation into the finances of the Tabares organization. Then, at Bonsib's suggestion, he asked the DEA to cosponsor. Macready had been around long enough to know that what made the Task Force pass out money was an undercover drug sting which would earn stiff sentences, not money laundering which was only a white-collar sleight-of-hand. Everyone knows how the system coddles white-collar crooks, hell, America was built by them and to put them all away would be to destroy the very fabric of society. The DEA accepted Macready's offer.

Next, Macready wrote a memo outlining the history of the case, the scope of the proposed investigation, and how much he thought it would cost, then sent it to Don Semeski, the IRS Task Force Coordinator in Baltimore. Unlike his FBI counterpart Tucker, Semeski was impressed with the potential of the Tabares case. He circulated the funding request to each of the eight Task Force member-agencies to see if anyone else wanted to join the IRS probe and if anyone already had Tabares under investigation or had a confidential source placed inside his organization. It happens more often than those in the drug biz want to admit that one agency opens an investigation only to learn that another agency is already on the case or has a valuable inside-snitch who would be killed if the bad guys felt the feds breathing on them. No one else wanted in and no one had ever heard of Roberto Tabares, so Semeski pitched the case at the weekly Task Force Coordinators' meeting chaired by U.S. Attorney Harvey Eisenberg who ran his weekly coordinators' meeting like a trial judge: keep it relevant, keep it moving, any questions, yes or no, on to the next case. Tabares sailed through the committee with unanimous approval.

Sly Bob Bonsib sat back and grinned—and waited for the final arm-wrestle. He knew that the FBI and the DEA didn't like each other, especially after all the serious talk in Washington about merging the two agencies, then eliminating the DEA. As far as the drug agency was concerned, the FBI still couldn't tell the difference between a coke crystal and rock candy. As for the Tabares case, well, the DEA wanted in though not badly while the FBI, which didn't want in, rankled at the idea that the DEA did. Games, the whole war on drugs boiled down to Narco Checkers. On his cynical days, Bonsib thought the best way to win the war would be to have undercover agents inject the drug families with the bureaucracy virus, then the good guys could just videotape the bad guys strangling themselves in reels of red tape.

Two weeks after the Task Force coordinators approved the

Tabares case, FBI agent Tucker came to see IRS coordinator Semeski as Bonsib knew he would. "We've reconsidered," Tucker confessed without admitting, of course, that the Bureau was more interested in keeping the DEA out of the case than horning in on it themselves. "We really want to get into this," Tucker said as Bonsib knew he would. In the end, Bonsib got what he wanted and it had only taken two months. The FBI would sponsor the case—there was no doubt that the FBI would take it over, it always did, which was fine with Jerry Macready and the IRS. And four drug game veterans would lead the offense—Sparshott and Preston, Campbell and Macready—with Campbell doubling as coach. Bad guys look out!

Campbell quickly chose three lines of attack: place a wiretap on Roberto's phones as soon as possible, do an undercover buy from the Tabares organization, and begin a silent hunt for the Tabares family assets. Any single strategy, if it worked, had enough legal teeth to bite the head off the Tabares organization; together they were a legal flash-bang; any one gone awry could kill the others.

A wiretap is deadly when it works, a noose woven from the bad guy's own words, but it doesn't always work and it's as tedious as counting sheep. To get the court to order one, you have to write a fifty-page affidavit which outlines the case and proves that you have already walked down every other investigative lane without success, which takes months. Once the tap is in place, there are no guarantees. Dealers don't always say incriminating things on telephones, sometimes they speak in codes which you may or may not be able to crack, and sometimes they get so suspicious they switch to pay phones before you have the goods on them. It's not unheard of to tap a phone for a year and come up dry.

Undercover investigations are a whole other ballgame. At their best, they can be works of theatrical art. Caught with their pants down and coke on their dicks, dealers are inclined to cop a plea. If they don't, undercover cops, who make colorful witnesses, can charm the jury and the judge into a guilty verdict with a stiff sentence. But the odds are against undercover cops—outsiders to a targeted drug family—penetrating the organization without help from someone already on the inside. If they defy averages and bluff their way in while phones are tapped, they run the risk of blowing the tap if the bad guy gets suspicious. End of case, maybe end of undercover cops.

A financial investigation to prove tax fraud or money laundering is a convincing if limited weapon. After all, it put away crooks like Al Capone, didn't it? But it almost always ends in lengthy trials and, although it's relatively easy to nail *someone*, it's impossible to get everyone. The resulting convictions carry lighter sentences than drug conspiracy or distribution charges. When tax fraud and money laundering probes run parallel to an undercover drug investigation, they pose risks. IRS criminal investigators can't subpoena records and have to be careful not to ask too many questions or get too close to launderers and their assets or they become suspicious that their phones are tapped. End of investigation, maybe end of undercover cops.

Whatever the risks of his three-prong offense, Bill Campbell didn't waste a day. He rented a listening post, which Preston found in an apartment building facing Presidential Towers, and staffed it with an FBI surveillance team armed with cameras and binoculars. Setting up a listening post, even if it doesn't produce usable leads, is an important step in convincing the court to order a wiretap.

Next, Campbell got Preston working on the first draft of the wiretap affidavit since Preston knew more about Roberto's day-to-day Washington operation than anyone else on the team. Campbell's Hyattsville office would write the second draft, Bonsib would review it and ask for a rewrite, the third draft would go to FBI coordinator Bill Tucker, also an attorney, who would review it and ask for a rewrite, the fourth draft would simultaneously go to the Justice Department and to an agent lawyer on the cocaine desk at FBI headquarters in Washington, a fifth or sixth draft would be necessary before the request was submitted to a federal judge.

Next, Campbell asked Bonsib to renew the court order for the pen registers on Tabares' phones until the wiretap was in place.

And at the same time, he asked Bonsib to get a judge to order Multi-Com to furnish clones of Roberto's two beepers so that every time someone beeped him and left a callback number, the clone would simultaneously beep and record the same number. Another little legal trick to keep the dealers on their toes.

Finally, while he waited for the wiretap affidavit to wend its way through the system, Campbell asked for a budget . . . and waited. He asked for permission to rent surveillance cars so his team wouldn't have to use the same cars every day, risky because Roberto could burn them . . . and waited. He asked the Bureau to furnish them with the undercover credentials they requested . . . and waited.

Hey, Roberto he no mind, you take time, amigo. But Sparshott and Preston have no time. The shit's everywhere, man . . .

Preston gets a call from the assistant manager of the Red Roof Inn in Lanham, just down the street from Campbell's new FBI office on the road to Annapolis. She thinks a guest is dealing cocaine from his room where a maid saw a freebase pipe and a pile of white powder that looked like cocaine sitting on a table. Talk about dumb, coke makes you feel invincible!

Preston, another narc, and two uniforms rap on the door of the "Sleep Cheap." A guy opens it, a woman is sitting in a chair next to a table only three feet away cooking a spoon of coke. She sees Preston but is so intent on a fix, poor dumb hooked kid, she looks about twenty-five, that her hand doesn't even flinch and she continues cooking. On the table next to her are two glass pipes, a bottle of grain alcohol, several pieces of coat hanger dressed with cotton tips. Addicts like to melt cocaine hydrochloride into cocaine base, stuff it into a pipe, light it with a hanger-torch dipped in alcohol, then freebase to a glorious high.

What's a cop to do? If Preston barges into the room and searches the place, a judge might toss the case out because he didn't have the renter's permission to enter. But if he arrests someone first, assuming he has probable cause, then he can search the room for weapons and evidence, but only close to where the arrest took place, mind you. Heck, you need a law degree to be a cop these days. Might as well take a leap into the fine print and let the courts sort it out later. He arrests the guy in the doorway, there are drugs in sight, plenty of probable cause.

Preston finds eightballs and snow seals to go—$3,500 worth—and plenty of extra snow seal paper, "Pyramid" brand made especially for drugs and sold over the counter, slick like a magazine so it doesn't absorb precious powder. Also boxes of cotton, snorting straws, pipes, razorblade and mirror for cutting, a regular little "Sleep Cheap" cottage industry. The woman with the pipe tells him that the coke came from some Cuban guy in Presidential Towers . . .

□ □ □

Sparshott and his wife are having a party at their house. It's his day off, it's around nine, things are just warming up. A party with friends—many of them cops with their wives or girlfriends and lots of shop talk—is about as close as Sparshott comes to relaxing. Other than fishing, which is a real passion with many cops, and working with the contractor who is building his new house in order to save money, it's usually a couple of Captain Morgan rum and cokes after his shift, a replay of the day's work, and some planning and scheming for the next day, his beeper at his side like a pet rock. He might not return a personal call but, hey, there's no fucking way he's gonna hide from the office.

Sparshott's beeper goes off in the middle of the party, it's the office, he gets on the kitchen phone, learns that the manager of the Climat de France Hotel not far from his house in Gaithersburg wants to talk to a narcotics officer. Fuck the day off, fuck the party, Sparshott calls the hotel manager who says:

A maid overheard a man say as he left room #203: "The coke is *real* good." The room is rented to a guy who claims to be, can you believe it, officer, a fashion designer from New York. He's been calling room #115 all day.

What would narcs do without hotel and motel managers.

They see in the dark, hear through doors, and try to stop trouble before it begins. Without telling his wife where he is going, why, or when he expects to be back, Sparshott pulls his partner, Scott "Scooter" Hammond, away from the party, and heads for Climat de France. He believes it's healthier for both of them if his wife doesn't know what he's doing. The more she knows, the more she worries and the more he worries that she's worried.

Sparshott positions Scooter in the parking lot and sets himself up in a room across from #203 where he can peephole the hallway. Just before midnight, Sparshott sees a man enter #203 empty-handed and come out with a brown trash bag. The guy leaves the hotel through a side door and climbs into a black Toyota. Scooter radios for backup, follows the car, and stops it . . . a couple of triple beam scales and a bottle of Inositol in the trash bag, and enough coke on the dirtball to arrest him for possession.

Meanwhile, Sparshott assigns two surveillance teams to watch rooms #203 and #115 while he rousts a judge and a SWAT team.

It's six the next morning when SWAT raids the rooms during a freebase party, six kids in their twenties, the men so high they can't find their cocks, the women so strung out they couldn't care less . . . a key of coke, semi-automatic rifle and a .357 magnum revolver, a pile of herb, $12,000 cash, and the usual drug packaging-tooting-snorting-smoking shit. Six more arrests. It's nine o'clock at night by the time Sparshott finishes the paperwork. Twenty-four straight hours without a break . . .

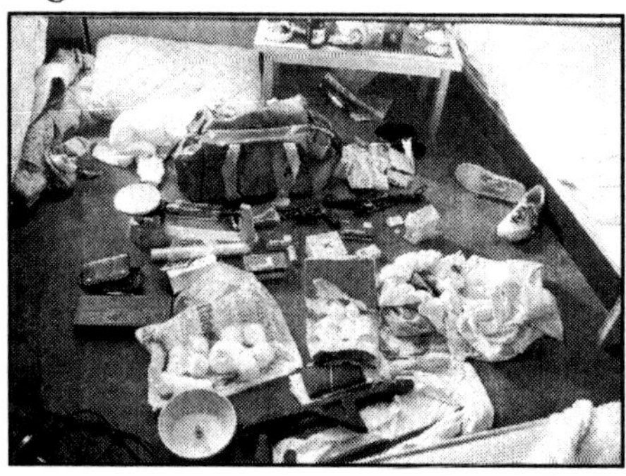

1. Seized from the Climat de France motel

Sparshott and Scooter are on their way to do some surveillance in a cocaine case. Sparshott spots a new car with a Jamaican flag covering a window and two black men with dreadlocks inside. It's clear the driver doesn't know the neighborhood and that makes Sparshott curious. Jamaicans are one of the major marijuana suppliers in the Washington area. Sparshott runs a make on the car which takes less than a minute these days. The car's a rental. Fuck the cocaine case. A rented car, suspicious movement, two Jamaicans—classic drug profile.

Sparshott follows the rental into Prince George's County to a small house on a quiet street near the University of Maryland. The Jamaicans get out, pop open the trunk, and lift out two large boxes which they carry into the house. Fuck man, it's getting better by the minute. Sparshott alerts PG vice and sits tight. Two hours later, the Jamaicans leave the house with only *one* box. PG cops take them down a mile away . . . Sixteen pounds of herb.

Meanwhile, Sparshott continues to watch the house. A man and a woman leave toting a large bag, get into a van parked out front, then drive off. PG cops pick them up a mile away and EST bangs the house . . . Eleven more pounds of marijuana, more than $56,000 in cash, and a letter of commendation from PG for Sparshott and Hammond who return to their cocaine surveillance case. Hey brothers, plenty of work to go around . . .

A snitch calls Preston to say Mickey just got a new batch of coke, around half a key, and hasn't sold it yet to his fifty or sixty customers, all white and under thirty. Since Preston already made undercover buys from Mickey's house, he knows that the guy packs a .38 in his belt and is nuts enough to shoot a cop. The tattooed druggies who share the house with him and his bevy of cocaine whores are also armed and drug-loony. Customers drift in and out all day, there is no telling how many bodies might be inside at any given time, Christ the place is a combination drugstore, cocaine den, and cathouse. PCP, grass, crank, toot, acid, pills. They smoke, shoot, snort, fuck and watch others fuck, men with women, women with women, until the dope they buy there and share with the whores runs out, then they float home. The neighbors are angry and scared.

Preston, an EST team, and two vice squads raid the place at nine-thirty at night to the cheers of neighbors who stand on their look-alike stoops and watch. It takes just twenty seconds to cuff the twelve people upstairs—Marty and another hophead draw pistols but don't shoot, there is a fistfight but only one bad guy gets a bent nose—bodies on the floor stacked on top of each other, four men, eight women, among them a mother-daughter fucking machine, legs everywhere you look. The usual haul of baggies, vials, and snow seals. Mirrors, razorblades, triple beam scales, pocket phone books. Inositol to dilute, syringes to shoot, straws to snort, spoons to cook, grain alcohol and coat hanger-torches to light, glass pipes to freebase. And a small arsenal.

One item sitting on a bookcase next to the front door catches Preston's eye, a printed sign in a cheap picture frame which sums up the quiet, suburban house rules:

DRUG STORE

Grass .... $20 an ounce
Acid .... $4 per tab
Bennies.................................. $1 per 5
The Pill............................ $3 a month
Cocaine .... $30 a spoon

"Request for smack and Meth must be accompanied by a note from your parent or legal guardian. We do not accept credit cards."

Josie and Jimmy, Danny and his wife, Walt and his

girlfriend, the Jones family and friends, the "Sleep Cheap" crowd, the boys and girls at Climat de France, Mickey's place, the Jamaicans. And keys more where their shit came from. Hey feds, shake the lead out of your creds, there's only so much two fucking locals can do out here.

FOURTEEN

Tracy Sparshott had the shortest fuse on the Task Force team and he was running out of patience. It had been six months since he gave Bonsib a hard-on for the Tabares case during the COG narc meeting at the PG Country Club and, as far as he was concerned, what little had happened since then happened too slowly. He knew that the FBI had only weaseled into the case because it was afraid the DEA might make something out of it, and that once the Bureau finally stooped to work with county cops it did nothing but drag its sorry ass.

Where were the rented undercover cars they needed? It's hard enough to tail someone, one on one, without worrying about getting made because the bad guy recognizes your car.

And where the fuck were the undercover credentials it promised him and Preston? The guy in charge of u.c. operations in Baltimore was so white-toothy nice, like icing on a seven-dollar birthday cake, it was hard to take him seriously:

Whatever you need officers, golly gee.

Social Security card? Of course, please fill out the form.

Wallet stuffers? Naturally.

Check cashing card? Now that's original, it'll fool them every time. Don't forget driver's license . . . I see, you already have one.

A *real* criminal record? Now that's a new one.

Narcotics violation, I suppose? Oh, you want credit card theft.

You're afraid that if you got busted for drugs the criminals might think you flipped. What an interesting theory, that.

□ □ □

Christ, two minutes with this undercover "expert" and you know he'd never last ten minutes on the street. Campbell told Sparshott not to take the insults personally, the Bureau prides itself on insulting everyone, even its own, it's just adolescent testosterone, but Sparshott didn't believe him for a rat-fart second. Fuck, the first thing the FBI did when it took over the case was to try to muscle in one of its own agents as lead undercover. The fact that he had expected it didn't stop him from erupting. Luckily, Campbell had argued against the switch. No FBI undercovers could possibly know what Sparshott and Preston did about the Tabares organization, and no FBI agent understood drugs and the county turf as well as they did, in fact, a new guy this late in the undercover game could blow it for everyone. Campbell won the argument—not that any of the Baltimore creds knew what the hell he was talking about—but the very idea of an outside lead undercover had left Sparshott's mouth tasting of fed shit and he wasn't a bit surprised when he later learned that some FBI asshole in Baltimore had actually called him and Preston "fucking locals" which only proved his point that if he had been an FBI agent instead of a county cop, he'd be treated with respect. He'd love to meet that little fed prick on a dark undercover boat on the Potomac, just him, the cred, and bare knuckles, and he'd teach the guy what local fucking is all about.

There was another reason why Sparshott twitched with impatience. He was on loan to the Task Force from Montgomery County, and his bosses were on him every day, like deerflies on sweat, even though the Task Force was paying his overtime. "Hey Tracy, when's something going to happen? When you gonna *do* something? When you gonna bust somebody, Trace?"

Bust somebody? Shit, we don't even know who the fuck they *are* yet. Well, welcome to the world of big business, brothers, get off your asses, drop somebody and take their money, but leave the cars and houses and all that shit for the feds, cash only if you please. And make it snappy. There's gold in them thar snowy hills.

Sparshott couldn't blame the brass. If he was out chasing Roberto in PG, he wasn't busting dealers in Montgomery County and wasn't adding their money to the stash in the narcotics division safe. That's opportunity lost, and he had long accepted the fact that he served two masters—the system and the public. Forget that the narc division stood to make a tidy profit if and when the Task Force took Roberto down, sifted his assets for every cent of loose change, and delivered the Tabares businesses, houses, boats and cars to the U.S. Marshals for auction and distribution to the Task Force team members. Local narcs were trained to think *now* and *small* in line with their budgets and departmental politics. Make a quick buy, take the bad guys down fast, pick their pockets clean, hand them over to the uniforms, chalk up the stat, on to the next bust.

As far as Sparshott and his bosses were concerned, the FBI was a dinosaur stuck in the tar bed of its own hype. Big deal they had the latest surveillance crap in a listening post apartment the Montgomery County narcs could never afford. The cameras were eyeballing a fucking parking lot. Big deal they had clones that ratted on everyone who beeped Roberto and DNRs that burned everyone he called on his apartment phones. They didn't have a running-fuck clue about who said what to whom and why. Big deal they knew the bars, nightclubs, restaurants and homes Roberto visited when he was in town. They didn't know what the fuck he did there except fuck which was good for exactly one slap on the dick.

Sparshott tried to keep his supervisor off his back by making as many nightly drug busts as he could when he wasn't following Roberto, but he felt like a tea kettle on a low burner and didn't know how long he could take the heat without blowing. Then, just when he thought his boss might pull him off the Tabares case, he picked up an important tip that might lead him to someone inside the Tabares organization. Roberto's mule, he learned, a guy called Gustavo, would be driving up from Miami on November 10 with several keys of coke. The mule would arrive on the twelfth and Roberto would be in Washington to take the delivery. The timing was perfect. Sparshott and the rest of the team had sensed a radical change in Roberto's business behavior—shorter visits to D.C., fewer phone calls from fewer people, less moving around town—suggesting that he had recruited someone to manage his Washington operation. Sparshott sensed that "someone" was his ticket into the family drug game. All he had to do was follow Roberto, watch the DNRs, and listen to the beepers. Once Roberto led him to his new man, he'd find a way to make a buy—he had little choice, the clock was ticking—win the guy's confidence and get an introduction to Roberto himself, fuck the FBI and all their high tech shit which could never match the street smarts of a good undercover F.L. Miami . . . Panama City . . . Bogota, watch your ass!

□ □ □

Gustavo sat in the bedroom of the Little Havana bungalow he called home—the house belonged to Roberto Tabares—and wrapped three plastic bags of coke-cakes with brown tape to make them moisture, air, and puncture proof. A careful man who didn't believe in taking any more chances than he had to, especially now that he was a new father, he tightly wound a second layer of red duct tape around the packages to give them added strength. Then he labeled each package "M" with a magic marker, swaddled them in a red towel and placed them in a nylon zipper bag. His boss Roberto was still shopping for the purest and cheapest cocaine in town and the magic marker code reminded him which wholesaler had sold him the dope, just in case his customers complained.

Gustavo set the bag on the floor behind the driver's seat of the new black Pontiac he had rented from National Car Rental and pointed the car north toward Washington where his father-in-law

Roberto was waiting. Around half past three the next morning, November 11, he passed Savannah, Georgia, on 1-95 traveling 50 miles an hour, no faster. Yes, he was anxious to make the delivery and get paid, but no, he didn't want to break a traffic law, the last thing he wanted to see was a fuckin' pig trained to check driver profiles—if you're Hispanic you must deal drugs. He had seen the inside of an American jail in 1982 after he got caught smuggling 2,800 pounds of marijuana into Key West and, although he thought it was a country club compared to Cuban jails, he wasn't eager for a second visit. Gustavo was so tired he could barely keep his eyes open but, rather than check into a motel, he kept muling along the asphalt trail.

A Georgia State Trooper just happened to be cruising north behind Gustavo but at a faster speed. When he saw the big black four-door weaving and drifting, he slowed to fifty miles an hour and watched. The Pontiac crossed the white line once again which meant, in the trooper's mind, that the guy was drunk, high, sleepy or any combination thereof.

The trooper pulled the Pontiac over and took a quick look into the car to see if anyone was hiding in the back seat or if any weapons were visible, then explained why he had stopped the car.

"May I see your driver's permit, please," he asked.

Gustavo was wide-awake now. He handed the trooper the laminated card. He was on his way from Miami to New York, he volunteered apologetically in thick English, you know, to visit relatives, and he just got sleepy. He was a truck driver by trade and the car was a rental.

The trooper studied the license, noted that it was valid, caught the name "Gustavo Rodriguez," and got suspicious. He was trained to spot profiles and this prick fit one as tightly as a condom—Hispanic male from Miami, as smooth as Jamaican rum, driving alone in a rented car heading north on Interstate 95, the mules' highway of choice. Jeez, if he had all the coke that rode down this highway to hophead heaven, he could give Savannah a white Christmas and have some left over for Atlanta.

"Would you please step out of the car, sir?" the trooper

asked, careful not to give the guy any reason to later scream, "abuse, abuse!" Gustavo slid out from behind the wheel.

"Would you please step to the rear, sir?" the trooper asked. If the guy was drunk or high, he wouldn't be able to walk straight. If he was sober and a real mule, he'd pack a mean kick. Better to have the driver outside where he could watch him than inside where he couldn't.

Gustavo walked to the rear of the car holding the rental agreement in his hand. He didn't stumble or reel. "May I see your rental contract, sir?" the trooper asked. Like the license, it was made out to Gustavo Rodriguez. "May I have your permission to search the car, sir?" The trooper didn't have enough probable cause to make the search without Gustavo's okay.

Still as smooth as a Havana, Gustavo agreed and the trooper walked to the cruiser and fetched the search waiver form which profile-spotters use in suspicious cases, then read it to Gustavo nice and slow, he didn't want any of that "Your Judgeship, I no understand, no comprendo" shit later if he found anything.

"Do you understand?" the trooper asked when he finished reading the waiver.

"Yes," Gustavo said.

The trooper checked the front seat, under the dash, in the glove compartment, then opened the back door. He picked up the black and gray bag from the floor, unzipped it, lifted out a package and poked a hole in it. Hell, he didn't have to test the white powder. If it's hidden like dope, wrapped like dope, looks like dope, it probably is dope and no judge in Georgia would fault him for that assumption. "You're under arrest for trafficking in cocaine, sir," he told Gustavo nice and polite like the guy was Robert E. Lee.

"I don't know nothing about that," Gustavo said as cool as a Caribbean breeze. The trooper cuffed him, led him to the patrol car, and called for backup. When it arrived, he read Gustavo his rights which he had to do by law if he intended to ask him questions and he certainly intended to do that. Backup served as his witness.

"Are the cuffs hurting your wrists?" he asked Gustavo just to soften him a bit, a little good cop jig.

"No spe-e-ek English," he said as cool as a banana daiquiri. "No comprendo."

Back at the Chatham County jail, Gustavo told the interpreter who read him his rights in Spanish that he had nothing to say until he talked to his attorney in Miami. He made his one call to Roberto Tabares. The trooper couldn't help but smile, the guy was good, he had to give him that much. He spoke English well enough before the arrest and his answers showed he understood the questions. The business cards he carried in his wallet were all in English, so was the National Car Rental contract. Then when the cuffs snapped shut, a "no comprendo" as cool as Raul Julia, almost as if he had rehearsed the scenario with a slick attorney. A kind of reverse entrapment.

The trooper knew gutsy old Gustavo had outsmarted him, the mule would walk, welcome to America, land of the free. Well at least some dealer somewhere will be out three keys of coke, one small step for mankind, or some such shit.

FIFTEEN

Sparshott was so mad when Gustavo didn't show he could have eaten a DNR. He knew there must have been a change of plans in Miami and went back to his street sources to find out why. He learned that a Georgia trooper had arrested Gustavo several days before with three keys. A call to the Georgia Bureau of Investigation, whose job it was to analyze suspected drugs, confirmed the street report. Gustavo's last name was Rodriguez, GBI said, and he was caught trying to secrete a piece of paper with three phone numbers:

A Maryland number with "Wash" behind it which matched Roberto's phone in Presidential Towers; a Florida number with "Pappi" which matched Roberto's home phone in Miami; and a second Florida number with "Nicky" which turned out to be Gustavo's new home phone number. Nicky was Gustavo's wife and Roberto's daughter by his second marriage.

The new information softened Sparshott's disappointment. Whether Gustavo did time or walked was now irrelevant. Come to think of it, of course the guy would walk, judges are suckers for that "no comprendo" line, christ, it was a legal miracle that the arraignment judge didn't return the three keys of shit along with an apology from the court, in Spanish of course: sorry we took your candy illegally, Senor, please take it back but don't sniff it, don't sell it, and don't drive around with it in your car, amigo, because you might get stopped by a Georgia trooper who speaks Español. What *was* relevant, however, was how Roberto would react to the arrest. Business as usual? Cool it for a while? Find new ways to transport the shit into town? Pull out of Washington for good?

A few days after Gustavo's arrest, Sparshott learned from the street that Roberto would be back in Washington on November 14 with seven keys of coke, and that he was armed and as nervous as a Siamese cat. Sparshott couldn't blame the guy. Hell, Georgia cops just roped his mule, took his coke, and lifted a piece of paper with two of his phone numbers on it. If anything surprised Sparshott, it was that Roberto was willing to show his face at all, but then greed, like the devil, makes people do the damnedest things.

To make sure Roberto didn't sneak in and out of town like a ghost, Campbell drafted ten special agents, some for the listening post and parking lot, the rest for spot checks on the nine Washington area addresses Roberto was known to visit. Sparshott, Preston, and Macready joined the group whenever they had a few hours to spare. Sparshott was working half a dozen drug cases in Montgomery County; Preston was doing surveillance on the Len Bias drug overdose case nearly fulltime; and Macready had a stack of probable tax fraud and money laundering leads to chase down.

But Roberto didn't show up in the usual places and the pen registers in Presidential Towers, the most reliable indicator of Roberto's presence in town, were silent. The beepers twitched now and then but that didn't prove Roberto was anywhere nearby. The team concluded that he had either stayed home because he was afraid or had checked into a motel because he sensed that narcs were watching his apartment. Finally, after two days of spot-checking, an FBI surveillance car found Roberto standing on the lawn of Raul's house chatting with a group of people. But it was too little too late. Roberto left for Miami the next morning, and if he had brought seven keys with him, he managed to spread it around without leaving a powder trace. Hey, sometimes the bad guys score a touchdown, too.

While the team waited for Roberto to return—they knew he would, he had come four days after Gustavo's arrest hadn't he—Campbell continued to work on the draft wiretap affidavit, to build ID kits of suspects like Roberto, Jr., and Saulo Hernandez, and to do surveillance on the people Roberto liked to call from his apartment. It was like working in a snowstorm—slow and only mildly productive, all you ever saw were outlines, but essential to convince a judge that the bad guys were real and that a wiretap would be the only way to catch them.

Then, two weeks after Gustavo lost the three keys of coke, an FBI surveillance car spotted Roberto driving out of Presidential Towers and followed him at a respectable distance north on New Hampshire Avenue. Like Georgia Avenue, New Hampshire is a major Washington-Maryland artery. It begins at the Kennedy Center on the Potomac and slices through the residential northwest section of the city, crosses the District line into Takoma Park, then abruptly turns into a corridor of malls, fast food joints, gas stations, and apartment buildings. It cuts through Langley Park, runs under the beltway past Bob's Big Boy and the Naval Ordinance Laboratory, crosses Georgia, meanders through woods, fields and farms past the new house Sparshott was building, and ends in Damascus, the northern tip of Montgomery County.

Roberto headed straight for Bob's Big Boy where he parked and stepped out of his car. He was wearing his usual gray suit and white shirt without a tie, and he paced up and down on his elevated shoes for ten minutes as if he were waiting for a late date. When he saw a red Datsun 280 ZX pull into the lot across the street and park in front of a Zayre's clothing store, he got back into his own car and coasted across the street to meet the driver. Small scumbag world, it was Frank Jones whose trailer Preston had busted a few months earlier.

□ □ □

Preston knew Frank was out on the street dealing again from two back-to-back snitch calls. First, there was Simpson, a sorry dirtball addicted to alcohol and anything sniffable, shootable, or smokable, eighteen priors for assault and battery, a real the-dope-made-me-do-it kind of guy. He would later die when the car he was fixing slipped off the jack and fell on his chest, not that he ever knew it. Simpson always came sniveling to Preston when he got arrested or when either the cops or his former wife were after him, and Preston helped him with the law, even gave him fifty now and then from his own pocket for back child support. The guy didn't deserve a dime but his kids did. He had made a couple of controlled buys for Preston, brought him a few new cases, but he mostly tried to sell stale information. Preston liked to humor him, you never know when a snitch will score a big one for you.

Simpson told Preston that old Frank had taken over the drug biz from his son. The little sonofabitch was hiding under a rock, he owed the Cuban so fuckin' much money he was afraid of getting his balls blown off. Preston wasn't surprised that Dad was back dealing. The PG State's Attorney's office had accepted the guy's plea of guilty to one count of possession, given him a suspended sentence for intent to distribute, then swept him off the docket and onto the street with a lecture that playing with drugs, like playing with matches, is naughty, naughty. Hey, let the cops worry about the old geezer, it's election time in PG and we have a lot of nest-feathers to collect, you know, so we can protect the electorate from drug dealers, a real kick in Preston's groin but what's a narc to do except double up and go on. Frank wouldn't be the first dealer he had to cuff two or three times before the system took him seriously.

Simpson went on to say that Frank was using his drug profits to pay the attorney fees that kept him out of jail so he could sell more drugs, a kind of money laundering scam which enjoyed the blessing of the system. Hey, don't rap it, attorneys have to eat too. Simpson had no beef with the old Cuban who was just a name and a face. He wanted fuckin' Frank because the sonofabitch got his girlfriend hooked so bad on "C" she lost her head in a car accident, zip, right off as clean as a saber cut. For that, Simpson would do anything to get fuckin' Frank.

Next, Preston got a jail-call from Mick's pregnant girlfriend—the one who had skipped out the back door of the house trailer into the snow. She was in deep-shit trouble again. Forgot to make a court appearance on drug charges, hey man, the judge was pissed, faced up to twenty years, and was scared the judge might toss the book at her. She didn't want to have her baby in jail, she knew a lot about Frank, she knew a lot about Roberto, she wanted out so bad she'd testify before any grand jury anywhere if Preston could get her immunity and convince the court to slap her wrist, after all she's pregnant and the prosecutor should think of her baby, not hanging another scalp on his belt. Could Preston help her? He promised, she spilled:

When Frank took over his son's business, she became Frank's runner. Roberto supplied the dope on consignment and Frank paid the money back four or five thou at a time which she delivered at a second 7-Eleven just off the beltway halfway between Roberto's apartment and the Fernwood trailer park near the Capitol Center, home of the Washington Bullets and the Caps. Sometimes she ran dope, up to a kilo tucked in her panties where narcs would like to look but won't, but not too often because Frank didn't trust her she was hooked so bad, hell, she could now do an ounce a day without overdosing like she used to all the time. Other women usually picked the shit up at Roberto's apartment where the old man treated them to a quarter or half an "O" as a "gift" that she was sure they had to "pay" for, not that she was ever there to watch, mind you. She hadn't seen Frank for a couple of weeks, ever since she and Mick stole an ounce of shit from his new stash behind the bumper of his pickup parked in front of the trailer.

Preston got the woman, she was just a girl really, released on her own recognizance and helped her pull weekends in jail instead of a long stretch, another one of those life-isn't-fair deals. The county lets big dealer Frank go free one day, then nails little pregnant runner the next, a real shame because she wasn't a bad kid and deserved a chance. With help and understanding, she could turn the corner, stay clean, make a new life, heck, maybe even be happy instead of just high.

The FBI watched the two dealers chat for a minute in front

of Zayre's. No one exchanged packages that they could see, then Frank drove off. Roberto followed him for a mile, then stopped at a pay phone outside his favorite 7-Eleven and made a short call. He hung up and took off south down New Hampshire Avenue toward the city but it was five o'clock on a Saturday afternoon and the traffic was heavy with weekend shoppers. The FBI lost him. They looked for him all day Sunday. At Presidential Towers, at Raul's, at Roberto Jr.'s, at the other addresses—but the guy had slipped out of town.

Sparshott didn't take the news calmly, not that he blamed the feds for losing Roberto. One-car surveillance is a joke under any circumstances, and with a hinky bad guy on a busy street it's a disaster. He had hoped to ram his foot in Tabares' door during the November 10 trip but Gustavo's arrest fucked up that chance. Then he had hoped to con his way inside during Roberto's next visit but the FBI lost the old man. When he learned from his street sources that Roberto would be back on or about December 10, Sparshott was ready to swing on the first vine he could grab. Enough of that "Wheel of Fortune" shit. True, the fifty-page wiretap affidavit was finally seeping through the layers of FBI bureaucracy, but who the fuck knew how long it would take for the stack of creds to sign off so it could reach a judge. Listening posts, clone beepers, and DNRs out your ass are all great if you're a fed, but they're a luxury if you're a Montgomery County cop with bosses barking at your balls for results. It was time to take an undercover risk, force a hand, make it happen. The Tabares case was Sparshott's big chance to do what every narc prays to the god of drugs for—the opportunity to play a challenging role on a big stage. His five-year tenure as a narc was running out. It was now or never, and no one was going to stop him. Not the creds, not his bosses, not Preston, not Roberto.

Sparshott joined Preston and Campbell on surveillance at Presidential Towers on the morning of December 10 even though Roberto had not shown up yet. Usually, he waited until the FBI actually made the guy. But today, he had a premonition that something was going to break and he wanted to be part of it.

Unlike most cops, Sparshott liked surveillance work even if it was as boring as a movie in slo-mo. For one thing, he always wanted to see the bad guys for himself, not just read about them in someone else's report, learn more about them than they would ever know about him beyond what he spooned them, study the way they walked, how they dressed, what they did for fun—boys or girls—make them *real* in his mind, then from all those impressions figure out how they thought. You know, like a quarterback studies the game films of the other team. Until he knew how the bad guys thought, he was at risk and would never win the undercover game. For another thing, Sparshott liked to feel in control even if control was only an illusion. If he was tailing someone and got burned or lost the guy in traffic, he wanted to make the mistake himself. If he got bored sitting in a cold car for hours on end, he thought of his baby daughter Morgan, his first child, and how he was making her Montgomery County world safer. Somehow everything was different after her birth. The fun of the chase could no longer fill the off hours or justify the danger. The father-daughter bond had subtly changed police work for Sparshott. Catching bad guys was more personal now, more serious.

When three o'clock ticked by and Roberto hadn't shown, Sparshott called for a lunch break in Preston's customized undercover van called the "Chief's Van" because the PG brass liked to use it—car phone, four captain's chairs, conference table, and sofa bed—great if you're a horny chief, though everyone knew that was a physical impossibility because chiefs lose their balls somewhere on their way to the top.

Sparshott suggested they have pizza for lunch and, hey, let's have it delivered, why waste taxpayers' money by driving to the pizza joint next to Roberto's 7-Eleven, why not make the pizza guy's day and ask him to deliver an extravaganza with extra cheese to a brown van parked on Metzerott across from Presidential Towers. Sparshott liked being first, and as far as he knew, pizza delivery to a surveillance car might just set a new law enforcement trend. Campbell didn't think it was such a good idea but Sparshott convinced him to go for it, hey Billy, loosen up, this isn't FBI headquarters, we gotta have a *little* fun. What the hell . . . Campbell gave in.

While the four of them—Sparshott, Preston, Campbell and Scooter—ate pizza, they discussed where Roberto might be, what he was thinking, what was holding him up, how many keys he might be bringing, whether he had changed his delivery and marketing strategy, whether he was coming at all. And what they should do next since they were running in surveillance circles.

"How are the clones doing?" Sparshott asked Campbell.

To have the two beepers and not know who had the originals was driving Sparshott crazy. Campbell carried the clones with him and recorded every call—time, date, phone number of the caller, and code if there was one—on index cards which he tied with rubber bands, one stack for each beeper, and kept in his shirt pocket. Buyers sometimes punch in a code after their phone number to indicate what kind of drug they want or how much. They might key in "28," for example, "two" for cocaine and "eight" for an eighth of an ounce. That would tell the dealer that the buyer wanted an eightball of toot.

"One's active," Campbell said. "The other's dead."

"Whose beeper is it?" Sparshott figured that maybe Campbell had found out and hadn't told him, but Campbell still didn't know. "Then fuck, why not just call the beeper and find out?" They debated the suggestion:

Whoever answered the beeper call might get suspicious . . . or he might not. The call might blow their cover . . . or it might turn up a lead. They didn't even know if the clone worked . . . so here was a chance to check it out. What did they have to lose . . . everything so why take a chance? Why not take a chance, they sure in hell weren't getting anywhere this way . . . the guy would be stupid to call back cold without an introduction. So maybe he *was* stupid . . . what would we say if he *did* call back?

"Fuck it, just punch in the van phone number, Billy." Sparshott shoved the phone across the captain's table.

"Stupid," someone objected. "The number can be traced.

Then what?"

"Well, we gotta do *something,*" Sparshott said. His gut told him now was the time to take the calculated risk.

Campbell punched in the beeper number on the touch-tone then, after the signal, tapped in the van phone number for the return call while everyone else continued attacking the pepperoni. No one really believed the guy would answer the call. If he did, he was either dumb, new to the drug trade, or very greedy.

The phone rang two minutes later. It surprised everyone, even Sparshott. They all stopped munching for a moment like they just got caught smoking behind the shed and looked at each other like, now what?

"Gimme the phone," Sparshott said. He tossed his pizza back into the box and wiped his mouth with the back of his hand. "Gimme the fuckin' phone!"

Campbell slid it back across the table while it was still ringing. "What are you going to do?"

"Find out who the fuck's calling."

Sparshott picked up the receiver. His mind was racing like a Harley down an empty highway, no idea where he was going or what he was going to say, he cleared his head, forgot he was a cop in a surveillance van with an audience of three. He was a grifter. He had to create an opening, keep the guy on the phone like a hostage negotiator, make the guy talk, then weave a story from the threads of what he heard. Phone-fucking as "Terry Petit," the undercover name he used, was one of his favorite undercover pastimes, like calling bad guys on slow days and offering them a free subscription to *Esquire*, just to hear their voices. He concentrated like a sharpshooter before a target, felt the pressure, and it felt g-o-o-d. A hit or a miss could determine the final score of the game, he told himself, one phone call, that's it, pal. You gotta make it work.

No one in the van was eating and it was so quiet you could hear a butterfly fart. It was golden-horseshoe time and Terry Petit jumped right in.

SIXTEEN

4:00 P.M.

"Hello . . . Is Julie there?"

Sparshott makes his question sound as if he's been waiting for the return call, mildly expectant but not anxious. He doesn't know any Julie but she's as good an excuse as any. She starts to become real in his mind maybe he'll even like her, who knows, maybe score.

"You got a wrong number," the voice says. He speaks with a Hispanic accent and sounds young. Clearly not Roberto.

"No I don't, man," Sparshott says. "I'm supposed to find a *Julie* at this number."

"Well, there's no Julie here."

"Look man, this is the beeper number." He recites the number Campbell slips him but changes one digit to make it look as if the call was an honest mistake to the wrong beeper. He's talking for time now, the door's open a crack, enough to get a glimpse of who's inside, and he needs to keep the guy on the phone until he can find an angle to coax the door wide open. "I'm not from around here. There's a game tonight at the Cap Center and this fuckin' Julie and me are supposed to party afterwards and she's gonna show me a good time."

"Like I say man, you got the—what kind of party?"

Sparshott has the sucker pinned between caution and greed.

If he didn't know better, he'd think the guy was a narc trying to set him up for a buy. It's time to quit fooling around and take charge, don't seem too eager now, keep the guy wondering about how to scam this Julie-character. "Who's this?"

"This is Carlos."

"Look Carlos. I got some people up in Frederick who told me, 'you wanna good time when you come down to D.C., you call this number for Julie.'"

"What you gonna party with, man?"

Sparshott looks up at Preston, Campbell and Scooter for the first time and smiles. He can't believe how well it's going, he already knows the guy's first name, the guy's buying the cover story—the I'm from western Maryland shit and I come to Washington every now and then—and he's beginning a slow sales dance. "You got somethin' for me to party with?"

"I could."

"Shit man, I don't even know you."

Sparshott's got the sonofabitch, he knows it but can't believe it, cold call, no intro, no "hey I know this guy, you can trust him." Carlos is taking one hell of a risk and Sparshott doesn't know or care why, he'll figure that out later. All he knows is that he has to let Carlos' greed do all the talking.

"What you want?" Carlos asks as if programmed.

"Julie."

"Fuck man, you got a wrong number." Carlos sounds impatient.

"Shit, I'm sorry to bother you, man." Sparshott creates the impression he's about to hang up in order to force Carlos to pitch or lose a customer. "I'm just down here looking for, you know—"

"Hey man, I got some stuff that'll give you a real good time."

"Whatcha got?"

"Who's this?"

"Terry!" He wants to appear cautious, like he wants Carlos to make the offer, like he doesn't trust him, like maybe Carlos is one of those sly narcs. He's thinking ahead, laying the groundwork. He weaves another piece of his cover story—his first name—into the conversation, natural like. Terry Petit is a name he's used before, and he has forged ID back at the office to prove it. "What's the deal?"

"You lookin' for, you know, some powder?"

"Yeah, a little blow for the chick."

"What you want?"

"What's it gonna take me to get laid? A G?"

More cover story—Terry doesn't use cocaine himself, the shit is for Julie, and he doesn't know the cocaine market. He senses that it's just a matter of negotiation and feels like Arsenio after a great monologue. But he's also worried. Where's he going to get the money to make a respectable first buy? The team doesn't have a budget. If he agrees to buy, say an ounce, and can't come up with $2,600 fast enough, he'll be slamming the door on Carlos forever. So he suggests a gram which only costs a hundred bucks, fuck, the four of them can pass the hat around.

Carlos laughs. "I don't do Gs."

"What *do* you do?"

"Anything you want. I'm the best around."

"Well if you help me get laid, man, I owe you one." Sparshott now knows that Carlos is no street dealer. If he were, he'd deal a G. He could ask for an eightball or a quarter ounce which the team might be able to afford, but he's afraid that Carlos might not take him seriously if he did and just walk away. "How about half an 'O'?"

Carlos laughs again. "No problem."

"How much?"

"Eight-fifty."

"Eight-fifty's fine."

In fact, eight-fifty is a great price, half an ounce of coke on the street usually goes for $1,200 which only confirms in Sparshott's mind that Carlos is no street punk with a beeper.

"Where you calling from?" Carlos asks.

Sparshott has to make some quick decisions. He can't buy the dope immediately because he needs time to get the money. It's getting close to rush hour, Carlos has a Maryland number so he's probably calling from Maryland. Sparshott can use rush hour traffic to buy time. He likes the van, it has a phone and it's classy, and wants to work Preston into the scam. "In Virginia . . . I'm with my man, Marty . . . in his van."

"Call me back in a few minutes," Carlos says.

"I misdialed and can't remember what fuckin' number I called." Sparshott is trying to be consistent now, make all the pieces he created fit. He's not sure how smart Carlos is, whether he's setting a trap. "Gimme your beeper again."

"Fuck, I can't remember it either, call me on the car phone." Carlos gives Sparshott a new number, then hangs up.

□ □ □

"Got him!"

Sparshott is grinning ear to ear as if he just won an Emmy. In one five-minute phone call, he had made himself and Preston two indispensable F.L.'s. "Let's go make the fucking deal. We need a thousand, Billy. Can you get it?"

When Sparshott first hung up the van phone on Carlos, Campbell was as excited as a safecracker. Although he relied on the slow, safe magic of wiretaps, he preferred the immediacy and decisiveness of an undercover operation. Now here he was, three months into what he believed was a big case, his undercovers ready to make a move, and he still didn't have a budget-pot to pee in. How could he possibly explain that to two hardworking cops like Sparshott and Preston? And how could he tell them that the creds who stand guard at the Bureau coffers don't give a Hoover damn about the pressures of undercover work . . . Dear special agent with your butt on the line, please write a memo explaining what you need and why, get your superior to sign it, then send it to Baltimore where the Assistant Special Agent in Charge (ASAC) will sign it and send it to the cashier who will write you a check for $850 then send it back to the ASAC who will call you to say "your check is ready, come and get it, nine-to-five only, if you please."

Forget the money, all Campbell could possibly manage to scrape together for the first critical buy was one extra backup—

most FBI agents work bankers' hours unless detailed before the clock strikes five and it was already well after four when Carlos returned the beeper call—and possibly Stew Tippett who had done very little surveillance work so far.

Campbell had asked Tippett, a former Texas cop and a new FBI agent in Hyattsville, to help with the Tabares case. Campbell had just finished a long narcotics wiretap and was exhausted from climbing a mountain of paper. The last thing he wanted was to have his badge glued to a word processor on another wiretap. Tippett, who looked good on paper, seemed like a reasonable compromise—a former SWAT team commander and special investigations supervisor responsible for smashing a methamphetamine ring, then a special agent detailed to gambling, fraud, and recently narcotics—not that Campbell was terribly impressed by résumés. He had never worked a case with Tippett, and if Campbell had learned one thing in his seven years as an FBI agent it was: just because you made it through the academy doesn't mean you can survive on the street. But Tippett was free and Campbell needed help, so he had offered Tippett the Case Agent title if he'd baby-sit the wiretap memo and traffic-cop the stream of telexes between Hyattsville and Baltimore and Hyattsville and headquarters. It would be a loose federation. As the Case Agent of record, Tippett would get the big brownie point if the investigation succeeded and the boot in the ass if it failed. As the real Co-Case Agent, Campbell would direct the undercover operation which would get him out of the office, screw the career brownie point. A fair but risky swap.

Campbell's initial excitement in the captain's van soon turned to embarrassment. There is a time to be proud of your FBI shield and a time to be ashamed of it. This was red-face time.

"We don't have that kind of cash in the office, Trace," Campbell said. "If you can get it, we'll reimburse you."

"Okay—I think I can sell it."

Sparshott wasn't happy, he was already planning the details of the buy and didn't need the added money worry, but neither was he surprised. He knew he could save the team's ass this time, but he sure as fucking hell hoped he wasn't getting a sneak preview of things to come.

"But the deal'll have to go down in Montgomery County, Billy."

In the threadbare world of undercover cops, it was a fair compromise—an FBI show on borrowed money which goes down on Montgomery County turf inside a Prince George's County van, with only two hours to set up the buy, unless Montgomery County wouldn't come up with the money, then it's back to the surveillance van boys.

If the bad guys with their beepers and rented cars, semiautomatics and armed bodyguards, boats and airplanes, runners and middlemen only knew! Hey dirtballs, welcome to the *real* war on drugs.

SEVENTEEN

Sparshott's supervisor was pissed. "A thousand? What do you mean? Aren't the feds supposed to cough up for the buy?" His boys had to do a lot of busts and bangs to keep the narcotics enforcement fund flush, and now Sparshott was asking him to turn it into a fucking federal Savings and Loan.

Sparshott explained. A buy out of the blue, late in the day, just a quickie loan. The super agreed, not that he was happy. It was the principle of the thing. Besides needing five agents to do the work of *one* good Montgomery County narc, the Bureau had everything a local cop could dream of—labs, boats, airplanes, specialists, the best weapons, the latest in surveillance gadgets. But it couldn't come up with a piddling thou for a half ounce buy. This is narcotics enforcement?

Sparshott counted and photocopied the money—nine hundreds and two fifties, a little extra for flash—then stepped into the undercover phone booth in a corner of the squad room in Rockville and closed the glass doors. The phone had a recorder attached, which he needed, and the door shielded him from background noises that might give his location away. He turned the tape on and said into the receiver for the record: "This is officer Sparshott . . . ID number 909. It's December ten, 1986 . . . 1800 hours. I'm going to call a subject named Carlos to set up a hand-to-hand buy. The number I'm calling is . . . " Then he dialed Carlos' car phone. The chain of evidence begins.

"Hey man, this is Terry. We still on?"

"Yeah."

"Half ounce . . . eight-fifty. Sounds good. Where ya at?"

"I'll meet you at Kangaroo Kate's."

Kate's bar in Greenbelt, close to where Mick lived before the judge gave him a new address, is dangerous. Not only does Sparshott know the place, he frequently hoists beers there with PG narcs. Any one of three dozen regulars could blow his cover, including Carlos himself. If the guy suggested Kate's, he must have been there, maybe when Sparshott was arm wrestling for drinks.

"I don't know that place," Sparshott says. "Fuck, I'm all the way over in Virginia stuck in traffic, man."

Sparshott has a lot to do before the buy—line up surveillance and backup, brief the players, clean all traces of police shit from the van, set up in advance, suck a beer, and psych up. He needs every minute he can con. "Why don't we meet at Bob's Big Boy on New Hampshire. It's right on the way to the Cap Center and I know it."

Just north of Presidential Towers inside Montgomery County—Kate's is in PG—Bob's is ideal for backup and surveillance. It just happens to be one of Roberto's favorite trading places as well.

"Hey man," Carlos says. "No problem."

7:00 P.M.

Sparshott and Preston pick a spot in the parking lot of Bob's Big Boy where they can see both entrances, the restaurant, and the surveillance cars, then wait. Their guns are tucked behind the cushion they're sitting on and the emergency radio is hidden in the pouch behind the driver's seat covered with the *Washington Post.* If they have to make a run for it or block an exit, they're only feet from the street. As an undercover blind date, Carlos is more dangerous than Mick and J.B. together. No one knows if he has a criminal record, whether he's armed, how much muscle he's likely to bring, and whether he'll use counter surveillance.

The van phone rings. It's five past seven, only three hours since Carlos answered Campbell's beeper call. Sparshott picks it up.

"Terry? Carlos, man. I'm gonna send a guy by. Get in his car and show him the money."

Carlos is challenging Sparshott to a pissing match and showing his dick at the same time. It's normal for a dealer to send a runner with the dope, especially on a first buy, and to insist on seeing the money before the runner shows the shit, even if it's only eight-fifty. But to expect the buyer to show the money inside the seller's car is to signal a possible rip-off.

Sparshott now knows that Carlos is more worried about a setup than a bust, and that either means that the Terry-Marty cover is sticking or that Carlos is taking a big risk out of blind greed. Either way, gotcha, man.

"No fuckin' way," Sparshott says. "You drive on up, you get on the phone, we'll talk . . . your car to my car . . . we'll work something out. If it doesn't feel right, hey, go on and drive off . . . no hard feelings. But I ain't gonna get into your guy's car, no wa-a-ay."

"Okay, okay," Carlos says. "But I'm telling you, man, I'm gonna have a lot of people with me. Anything goes wrong, you got big fuckin' trouble. If everything's cool, shit, I'll make you one rich fucker. I'm waiting for my guy now."

Fifteen minutes pass as slowly as a sermon, then a burgundy Camaro pulls into the lot followed by a white Camaro. Neither car makes Scooter watching from an unmarked car across the street next to a Citizens Bank of Maryland. From there he can race to help Sparshott and Preston if they get in trouble, block the street if Carlos tries a rip and run, or easily slip behind Carlos' car without getting burned if ordered to follow the guy. The white car parks near the van—so far so good—its clone slowly cruises around the lot x-raying everything.

Bill Campbell is sitting in the command car parked far enough away from Sparshott and Preston so as not to appear suspicious—he hopes—but close enough to have a good view of the buy. The burgundy Camaro drives by him without a second look—so far so good—then heads toward Stew Tippett who is parked so close to the van that Sparshott's skin is crawling. He doesn't trust Tippett. True, the guy's friendly, one of those "hey, buddy" types with a Texas drawl. But it takes more than a twang and a smile to catch bad buys and in Sparshott's undercover book, Tippett is a health hazard, one of those special agents who doesn't understand what undercover work is all about but is afraid Hoover would kick his ass from the grave if he admitted it. Fuck, the guy may be the best bank robbery man in the FBI, but Bob's isn't a bank and a buy isn't a robbery, and that makes Tippett more dangerous than Carlos. Sparshott feels for his gun.

The burgundy Camaro slows to a crawl as it passes Tippett, then parks across the lot from its white twin. A Hispanic type in his early twenties wearing a baseball cap with a "C" on it, eases out of the car and, in no apparent hurry, scans the lot like an Indian scout. No one recognizes him from surveillance. He heads straight for Tippett, walks around the car, then bends down. He stares at Tippett for a long moment before strolling over to the pay phone in the entrance to the restaurant. He drops in a quarter and dials.

Tippett is hanging by his balls. When Campbell told him about the buy, he opposed it as too much too soon but didn't have enough time to go over Campbell's head and block it. So he did the next best thing—insisted on backing Sparshott and Preston, you know, to lend an aura of professionalism to the operation. You just can't trust those fucking locals.

"I better get out of here," Tippett says into the radio as he starts the car. "I think the guy burned me."

Sparshott watches the Hispanic on the phone say a few words into the receiver, no doubt telling Carlos the deal smells and he should call it off, then hang up just as Tippett pulls out of the lot into the street. Sparshott fights the urge to chase after the jerk and wring his scrawny little balls. Carlos is so close—only a hundred feet away—that Sparshott can almost hear him breathing. All the months of work to get this far and some know-it-all FBI agent with his eyes up his ass blows it, maybe for good.

The van phone rings. Sparshott lets it go a second time, then grabs it. He expects the worst.

"Where are you, man?" Carlos asks. He doesn't sound angry or scared. He doesn't sound hinky.

"In the brown van." Sparshott gives Marty the thumbs up sign. Fuck Tippett, lucky again, round one for the good guys. "I saw you pull in. I'm here with Marty. He's driving. Come on over and get in."

"Okay, man—but just to talk, man."

"Fuck talk, pal. You told me you're gonna do a deal. Then, get the fuck over here and *deal.*"

"I wanna check you out first, man. I got no dope."

Sparshott watches Carlos hang up, ease out of his white Camaro, and start over to the van, nice and slow like he doesn't have a care in the world, without looking around, his man does that for him, concentrating on the van doors to see if they're going to fly open and if someone will jump out with a gun. His lieutenant, the guy in the baseball cap, also begins to walk toward the van from the pay phone, faster than his boss, he has further to go.

Sparshott is certain the lieutenant is armed but isn't sure Carlos is. He looks younger than he sounds on the phone, early twenties, six one and thin with thick black curly, almost kinky, hair and a medium complexion. A handsome guy, but not as handsome as Raul before Laurie shot him and his body withered in bed, in a dark jacket and white sweatsuit pants, designer quality all around. He and his lieutenant reach the van at the same time. He slides the panel door open and steps inside. "Turn the lights on," he orders.

Round two for the good guys. Marty flips on the overhead. Carlos is wearing the usual dope dealer's shit—gold chain with a gold and diamond bar dangling on the end, a gold and diamond signet ring with the letters "CM" on it, and a gold Rolex with a blue face. Sparshott casually rests his arm on the top of the driver's seat so that Carlos can see the Rolex he's wearing, top of the line, diamond bezel, a fourteen grand gift from his very generous wife.

Carlos checks out the van carefully but doesn't pull the newspapers out of the pouch behind the driver's seat. If he did,

Sparshott would tell him he's using the radio to monitor police chatter, hey man, just in case you're a fuckin' narc.

"What's that?" Carlos points to a radio dangling from the dash.

"A CB to raise trucks," Marty says. "Wanna try it?" He hands the mike to Carlos who looks at it, pushes the transmitter button, then gives it back.

"What if you're a cop?" Carlos asks just like that.

"Then I'd be dead by now," Sparshott says just like that.

Carlos smiles and accepts the answer. "Nice watch. Rolex?"

"Presidential."

"Let me see it. Mine costs twelve thou."

They exchange watches. Carlos wants Terry to know that if he can afford a Rolex, he's good for a lot of blow. He examines Terry's watch carefully to see if it's fake. If it's real, Terry probably isn't a narc, cops are Timex guys.

Carlos gives Sparshott his Rolex back. "Let me see some ID, man."

"Fuck—what are you?" Sparshott asks. "A cop?"

"Fuck no, you a cop?"

It's a critical moment, the kid's spooked, the deal can turn sour just like that, hey, no hard feelings, man, but I gotta go. Have to settle him down, feed him a sugar cube, get his trust for another minute or two.

"Shit man," Sparshott says. He's grinning like Jack Nicholson. "If I were a cop *you'd* be dead by now."

Everyone laughs. The moment passes. Sparshott opens his biker's wallet which is attached to his leather belt by a chain and hands Carlos his Terry Petit Maryland driver's license. Marty, who goes under the cover of Michael Barry, a co-owner of The Tower Company which builds small radio towers and antennae, does the same.

"Now let me see *your* ID," Sparshott says.

Carlos pulls out a Panamanian passport with a driver's license taped inside and passes it to Sparshott who studies both documents for a second. He catches Carlos' last name, "Medina," and feels lucky once again. His father got posted to Panama as a security officer just as he began Montgomery Community College and his sister went to the Canal Zone College in the American sector. He used to go down and visit her whenever he had the chance. "Look at this, Marty . . . Panama."

Sparshott hands the passport to Marty, maybe he'll see something Sparshott missed like date of birth which they will need for a positive ID and criminal check. Marty returns the passport to Carlos who opens the door and says to his lieutenant, "Go get the stuff."

Score another round for the good guys. Sparshott has three things in common with Carlos—dope, jewelry, and Panama. Three foundations to build on, to win Carlos' confidence, to suck him into the scam, maybe even build a friendship. But most important is Sparshott's own background. He grew up around foreigners—second and third grade in Lebanon, fourth and fifth in Ivory Coast, sixth through eighth in Germany, and high school graduation in India. He learned to make new friends quickly, feel at ease in new places, and enjoy the adventure—all essential qualities in a good undercover. His life as the son of a foreign service officer was better preparation for this meet with Carlos Medina than the police academy could ever be, and Sparshott knew it. That knowledge gave him even more confidence.

"I live up north of Frederick," Sparshott tells Carlos while they wait for the dope. He's five con-moves ahead of the guy. "I'm into reefer up there. My man Marty is introducing me to some new business down here."

When he tells Carlos he's dealing marijuana, Sparshott is saying that he's not a competitor but a potential customer if Carlos can convince him to switch to powder. When he sets Marty up as his man in Washington, he's creating a role for Marty in all future buys and scams. And when he makes western Maryland his home base, he's creating an alibi for when he needs to buy time.

"I've been to Panama, man," Sparshott continues. The mindfucking begins. "My dad was a diplomat at the American

Embassy, you know, along the ocean on Aveneida Balboa. Shit, I used to hang out at the Balboa Yacht Club. You know Davis the Jamaican bartender there, a big black sonofabitch?"

The Balboa Yacht Club at the Pacific mouth of the Canal is a rundown but chic open-air watering hole in the basement of the American Legion Building along the causeway that tongues into the ocean. From canalside tables you can see the Bridge of the Americas, a lacy bridal arch that unites the two continents, and Taboga Island, a shimmering dot of gold at sunset. Millionaire yachtsmen and brass from the U.S. military base nearby drink alongside smugglers and dope dealers, old expatriate barflies and wealthy third generation Zonies bend elbows with old time canalers who work the locks and sailors from every port in the world.

Sparshott doubts that Carlos knows Davis or that he's ever been in the club—Panamanians can't get into the American sector unless they're invited guests of Americans with zone passes—but it doesn't make any difference. He has Carlos thinking what he wants him to think, that no fucking cop is going to live in Panama, wear a Rolex with a diamond bezel, and drink Captain Morgan Rum and Coke at the Balboa Yacht Club.

"Fuck, I used to go fishing for Dorado," Sparshott continues, "Deep sea shit, off Las Perlas. You fish?"

"No man," Carlos says.

The Archipelago de Las Perlas is down the Pacific coast from Panama City. It's famous for its oysters with real pearls and its dolphins which run twenty to thirty pounds. Too bad, Sparshott is thinking. He was hoping to use fishing as one more hook into Carlos Medina.

The lieutenant returns, Sparshott rolls down his window, the guy shows him a baggie with rock crystals of cocaine hydrochloride just like the ones he and Boyle bought from Mark and J.D. Sparshott pulls out a roll of bills, peels off eight hundreds and one fifty, and hands the bills to Carlos who quickly counts them and nods. The lieutenant gives the shit to Sparshott who says, "Hey man, it looks okay." He doesn't even fake-rub the dope on his gums or crush it between his fingers, he has to be consistent now, he can't afford a slipup in front of the lieutenant who's probably armed. Terry Petit deals herb not cocaine, and Terry Petit doesn't know about blow.

Carlos says: "We should have lunch and, you know, talk a little."

"Sounds cool. I'll tell you something about my business."

"Call me, man." Carlos steps out of the van and walks back to his white Camaro.

They're inside . . . in spite of Tippett . . . on a fucking big roll . . . in spite of the FBI. They just slipped a ring through Carlos' nose and the guy doesn't even know it. Now all they have to do is con him into leading them to Roberto Tabares. But slowly, step by calculated step.

PART THREE

The Stalk
Winter 1986-1987

EIGHTEEN

When the guy in the baseball cap walked over to Tippett's car and looked in, Bill Campbell knew his FBI partner was burned and the gig was up. And when the guy placed a call to Carlos—Campbell could even see Carlos pick up his car phone—he assumed the guy was warning his boss that the deal was a setup. To salvage what he could from a buy gone sour, Campbell grabbed his radio and was about to tell Scooter sitting across the street to tail the white Camaro, then to tell Tippett to . . . well damn it . . . just keep out of sight. But before he could press the transmission button, Campbell saw Carlos punch in a number on the car phone and he hesitated.

Campbell was confused momentarily when he heard the van phone ring over the receiver in his car, then pleasantly shocked to hear Sparshott and Carlos begin negotiating buy rules without Carlos demanding, "Hey man, who the fuck was that guy in the car?" When Carlos strolled over to the van and got in, Campbell knew for sure that the guy in the baseball cap hadn't burned Tippett and that a buy was still possible.

With a lump in his throat, Campbell heard Carlos ask Sparshott if he was a cop, question the CB, and ask the cop question a second time. He expected to see the van door slide open and Carlos jump out, but instead he heard Sparshott playing the Panama opening Carlos gave him like a flute. Campbell could almost feel Carlos relax, and he thought he heard the subtle strain leave Carlos' voice, almost as if he were begging Terry and Marty to convince him they weren't narcs after all, just two honest bad guys looking for blow. By then Campbell knew that, unless someone goofed in the next few minutes—a possibility he never discounted—the first buy from the Tabares organization was probable.

There was no goof. Everything had gone down as smooth as Southern Comfort. Sparshott and Preston, two fucking locals mind you, had turned in a flawless performance without even a rehearsal. Three hours of seduction, twenty minutes of foreplay, then a quickie with the promise of a more leisurely tryst soon. Suddenly, the Tabares case was no longer just a list of suspects—real, probable, possible—some with faces and some without, who exchange envelopes and packages at Bob's and the 7-Eleven and leave phone doodles on DNRs. Campbell now had a Ziploc of little white rocks of actual cocaine for the creds in Baltimore to fondle, 85 percent pure, and kilos more where they came from. Campbell was never one to underestimate the spell a baggie could cast on purse strings. While he and the rest of the team shivered down cold beers after the buy, it was forty degrees and damp, Campbell could feel ripples of excitement in the voices and laughter around him. He was only sorry that Jerry Macready wasn't with them. There's nothing like victory after a close call to fuse a bunch of distinct egos into a team.

As important as it was, however, the score on Carlos Medina that night raised a series of troubling investigative questions: who the hell was he, who supplied him, whom did he work for, why did he risk selling to someone he didn't know, and who were his major customers? The only thing to link Medina to Tabares was a Multi-Com beeper. That single fact led to three possibilities: Carlos was an independent associate of Roberto's like Saulo Hernandez; Carlos was a major customer of Roberto's like Frank Jones; or Carlos was a new Tabares distributor in metro Washington.

The day after the buy, Campbell asked the Baltimore creds for $850 to reimburse Montgomery County, then he and Tippett sat down and sketched a rough undercover plan and budget. The idea was to link Sparshott to the Tabares organization as a cocaine franchiser who would buy multi-kilo lots first from Roberto, then from Roberto's supplier. In turn, Carlos and Roberto would each get a finder's fee for introducing Sparshott to the mother organization and a royalty on every key he subsequently bought. At the same time, the IRS would send in an undercover mole to penetrate the money-laundering shield of the Tabares organization.

The undercover operation would take four months and cost $700,000, a reasonable amount considering the potential of the case. It wasn't FBI money anyway. It was a chip off the old block grant the Department of Justice awarded the Bureau with congressional approval and earmarked for Task Force investigations.

While the proposed budget snailed around the corners and through the tunnels of the system, Sparshott planned the next five moves of the scam. Over the years, he had learned to fill in the tedious hours of surveillance with dream-scenarios he'd stage one day if he ever woke up cop-rich with money, men, and equipment. The more he planned, the more he realized that as a cop he had never wanted anyone or anything as much as he wanted Tabares. Roberto was his Everest, his Guinness Book, his Olympic gold and nothing was going to stand in his way.

The cornerstone of Sparshott's strategy to nail Tabares was to play hard to get. Besides conning Carlos into buying the cover story, he had to encourage the kid to convince his new acquaintance "Terry" that he could make more money selling coke than reefer, then to trust Terry enough—trust in the drug trade is as rare as pure cocaine—to introduce him to Roberto with avaricious enthusiasm. It was a game of timing. If Sparshott made his move too soon, Carlos would sense Terry's eagerness and use it against him. If he moved too slowly, Carlos would have too much time to replay meetings and buys. Seeds of doubt could take root, maybe even flower into something that could poison the relationship.

To make the strategy click, Sparshott decided to manipulate what he sensed were Medina's greatest weaknesses: drug-dealer curiosity about Terry Petit's reefer business, the need for friendship (a lonely drug-dealing kid in a cold foreign country), and obvious greed. It was Roberto himself who gave Sparshott an opening. The day after the half-ounce buy, both the DNRs and the beepers went berserk. That meant Roberto was back in town. Sparshott checked with his sources on the street and learned that a new shipment of coke—no one knew how much—would soon be arriving at Presidential Towers. Then, at noon on December 12, two days after the buy from Carlos, an FBI surveillance team made Roberto coming out the back door of the apartment building dressed in his usual gray suit and white open-collar shirt. He walked down the cement stairs to the lot, got into a rented blue Toyota Corolla, and headed for the beltway. He cruised up the east ramp, across from Bob's Big Boy, then blended into the heavy four-lane traffic. Surveillance lost him in the snake of weaving cars and trucks.

Roberto pulled back into Presidential Towers three hours later with—it was enough to make a narc's heart flutter—Carlos Medina. The two men entered the back door of the apartment building, then came out half an hour later and got back into the Corolla. This time surveillance didn't lose Roberto. It followed him to a quiet street of neat bungalows in Hyattsville just a few blocks from Campbell's office and Mickey's old place.

The shipment of coke arrived by mule two days later, no one yet knew how much, and Roberto went home the following day which meant he had distributed the shit in less than *one* day. This fact led Sparshott to three working hypotheses: One—Roberto no longer distributed his own coke in the Washington area. Two—he supplied several distributors here, one of whom was Carlos Medina. Three—as a new player in the Tabares organization, Carlos had to prove himself and thus was likely to take more chances and ask fewer questions than an established dealer. The three hypotheses fit the DNR traffic, Roberto's sudden change in business habits, and the wary but risk-taking behavior of Carlos Medina.

Sparshott decided to make another move on Medina right after Roberto left town while Carlos was still flush with dope and feeling self-important. He pitched the Terry-Marty scam to the team which thought it was devilishly creative, perverse beyond any undercover move they had personally made or seen, and cheap. Tippett initially opposed it—no one was surprised—as too risky, too complicated, too showy, too soon, but Campbell talked him into playing along just for the hell of it. There was nothing to lose if Carlos didn't buy the scenario and it made no observable dent in the budget they still didn't have yet.

Sparshott told the team he needed the chief's van—Preston said no problem—and a tape recorder-attaché case to pull the scam off. Campbell volunteered: "I can get the recorder. I've seen two or three sitting in Baltimore."

Sparshott said he needed an airplane, single or twin engine, and two pilots. He had once used a plane on a drug reverse play—delivered two keys of dope to the bad guys in a Maryland State Police airplane to impress them, set them up, and, hey, let's face it, have a little fun. Campbell volunteered: "I think I can arrange it."

Sparshott said he needed a fancy car both to impress Carlos and remain in character, a contradiction of biker-leather and dealer-gold. Macready volunteered: "We got a Mercedes 380 SL convertible all wired and ready to go. I think I can get it."

The IRS had just seized the top-of-the-line sports car in a drug raid in Baltimore and put it into service as an undercover car.

2. Sparshott and Preston in the IRS undercover vehicle used by Sparshott

Technicians had wired it for studio quality sound—a tape recorder in the trunk, tiny mike hidden behind the sun visor, and an on-off slide switch on the side of the driver's seat. No one had yet used the sexy young thing in an undercover operation.

Having missed the first meeting with Carlos Medina, Jerry Macready was especially eager to be part of the second. He had listened to the buy-tape the next day and when he heard "Panama," he saw "money laundering" in red neon. As anyone who read the papers knew, Panama was one of a handful of countries—including Switzerland, the Grand Caymans, South Korea, and England—which shields money launderers behind a legal curtain of banking secrecy. And of course, Panama was the fiefdom of Manuel Noriega whom the feds had long suspected of protecting drug cartel dollars. So Macready had asked himself: "Is it possible that the Tabares organization is laundering drug money in Panama too?" And Macready answered himself: "You're damn right." He had a lot of work waiting for Tracy "Terry Petit" Sparshott.

Sparshott said the scam would take place at the Montgomery Airpark as soon as Macready and Campbell assured him they had what he needed. He had chosen the tiny airport in Gaithersburg for the show because it was in Montgomery County—that would satisfy his boss as well as spring his partner Scooter to help with surveillance. Sparshott also knew the place well—he had taken flying lessons there. Carlos probably didn't even know where the fuck Gaithersburg was—so he'd be on edge where Sparshott wanted to keep him. And the Airpark complemented the Terry-Marty cover story.

When Macready and Campbell came through later that same day, Sparshott called Carlos on the undercover phone in Rockville to set up the meet. He'd be somewhere near Washington in the morning, he said, but wasn't sure exactly where. Would Carlos like to have that business lunch he, Carlos, had suggested? Carlos said, sure man, I got classes at PG Community College in the morning but I'm, you know, free in the afternoon . . . Hey, man, fuck free. As a new dealer in the drug trade, he was drooling.

□ □ □

Like every Panamanian kid with a few Balboas, Carlos Medina wanted to study in the States. He chose Washington because his girlfriend was a Journalism major at the University of Maryland where he planned to enroll. But UM didn't offer courses in English as a second language so he went to Prince George's Community College instead. Of course, he would have preferred George Washington University or American or Georgetown, all private schools and well-respected in Panama, but he couldn't afford the steep tuition and didn't have a green card. To supplement his monthly stipend from his stepfather, he took a job cleaning carpets as an illegal alien.

Carlos soon discovered Cafe Met in Georgetown, a hangout for foreign students, especially Spanish-speaking ones, most of whom attended the universities he couldn't afford and had more spending money than he did which offended his sense of "machismo." His best friend at Cafe Met was Eddy, an outgoing Latino who bought him drinks with the money he made selling grams of coke in the restaurant. Eddy introduced Carlos to the shit and taught him how to snort a line after he caught Carlos faking it.

When the narcs nabbed Eddy, he had a pound of coke stashed away. He asked his user-dealer friends to sell the shit and hire him an attorney. Hey, drug money keeps the wheels of justice turning. They in turn asked Carlos to push an ounce. Just one, for a friend, a piece of cake. Fuck, man, he didn't know a thing about selling shit. Nothing to it, hermano, just watch.

They showed him how to cut and snow-seal the shit, then price it. All they wanted for the ounce after he moved it was $1,400, they said. If he was smart, they said, he could make a few hundred for himself.

"I don't know anybody who uses," Carlos said.

"Ask around," they said.

What the fuck, a friend's a friend.

Carlos had seen a couple of tattooed guys hanging around so he asked one if he, you know, knew anyone who wanted to buy some really good blow. The guy said, yeah man, he could use an eightball. Carlos sold him one for $275 like his friends said to. Not fucking bad, man, $275 times eight eightballs is $2,200 less $1,400 which comes to $800 profit and that sure beats four weeks of cleaning fucking carpets. Old Tattoo kept coming back until the ounce was gone.

"Hey, you need up front money?" he asked when Carlos told him he was empty. "Fuck, I'll give it to you, man."

Carlos took the money and went back for another ounce, 50 percent pure, and became a small-time dealer. A couple of months later, in May 1986 just after Sparshott and Boyle busted Raul Tabares, one of Carlos' customers said, "They're ripping you off, man. I know this Cuban from Miami who'll sell you an ounce of shit for $1,000 and it's pure, man. I'll introduce you to him for a quarter ounce." Carlos couldn't believe it. He was paying $1,400 for shit that was only 50 percent pure. Fuck, he could more than double his profit if he dealt with this Cuban.

Carlos met Roberto Tabares in a restaurant not far from Presidential Towers. He was scared, man, like he was meeting Scarface himself. Shit, he had never met a big drug dealer before and he didn't know what to expect. Roberto confused him. He was fatherly, spoke in a soft, kind voice, came alone, none of that bodyguard shit with Uzis like on TV. He drove a cheap car and wore no flash. Like his customer had said, Roberto offered to sell him an ounce of nice rocky shit for $1K.

"How often can I get one?" Carlos asked.

"Every month."

"Fuck, I move one a *week*, mostly grams."

Sly old Roberto shrugged. Of course, he came to Washington more than once a month, but he wasn't about to tell the kid that. So Carlos put up most of his ready cash and bought twelve ounces to make sure he wouldn't run out. He was so new to the drug trade that he didn't even try to haggle for a bulk discount.

Roberto returned to Washington two weeks later and met Carlos at Carlos' place. He set a kilo of coke tightly wrapped in tape on the table. "I don't want to take this back with me," he said.

"Will you hold it?"

"No way man." Carlos had never seen a whole key before and was scared of getting caught or ripped off. Fuck, this was big time shit.

"Well, I might not be back for awhile," sly old Roberto said. "So why not just sell whatever you can until next time."

"How long do I have to pay?"

"Whenever you have it. Don't worry. I trust you."

Fuck, how could anyone pass up a deal like that? A whole key on consignment, no pressure to sell, pay as you go. Carlos snapped up the deal, then split the shit into packages and asked his people to hold it for him. He was so scared he couldn't sleep. And so it began . . .

By the time Sparshott cold-called Carlos from the chief's van five months later, the kid was moving a key a month. He had spent $10,000 of his profit as a down payment on a modest house, bought a Rolex for flash, and paid his first semester tuition at George Washington University where he would soon begin his junior year as a Business major. Fuck, even his friends at Cafe Met were beginning to look up to him.

But Carlos wasn't dumb, man, he knew he was only an amateur in the drug trade and that there was a lot more money to be made . . . if only someone like Terry Petit would show him how. Fuck, that's what students do, don't they, learn from teachers?

As he waited for a call from Terry with time and place, Carlos reminded himself to be careful and not let on that he was just a fucking ounce-dealer who had never seen more than a kilo of shit in his life. Hey, even drug dealers have pride.

NINETEEN

12:30 P.M.

The cast is in place. Marty Preston sits at a window table in the airport's tiny second-floor restaurant overlooking the entrance to Montgomery Airpark and the parking lot. Scott "Scooter" Hammond waits in the chief's van a hundred feet away with a 35 mm camera and a zoom telephoto lens. There are no obstructions between the camera and the restaurant window. A single-engine Cessna is parked outside the terminal's back door ready to taxi. Bill Campbell mans the command car from a location where he can watch the entire show—the airpark entrance and exit, Preston's window table, and the airplane sitting out back. Jerry Macready and the IRS Mercedes are with Tracy Sparshott. Stew Tippett is back at the office sweating under a mound of paper.

Sparshott calls Carlos. "I'm on my way down to Montgomery Airpark," he says. "I got some business to take care of with Marty. Let's meet there for lunch."

"Good idea, man," Carlos says.

As Sparshott hoped, Medina doesn't know where the airport is, so he gives directions: take the beltway past Bob's Big Boy to 270 north, get off 270 at Gaithersburg Road, turn right, follow the signs.

Sparshott waits a long hour but Carlos doesn't show. Is he lost? Does he have car problems? Has he turned around and gone back home which happens, especially if the dealer is also a user.

Hinky at the slightest unpredictable thing like a restaurant he never heard of and can't find.

But Sparshott doesn't think about a meeting turned sour. He thinks positive. Energy level high and mind focused on the scam, he calls Carlos a second time. Carlos says he's on the way, just getting onto 270 north, be there soon. Sparshott radios the team. It's hard to keep the excitement out of his voice.

"Okay boys . . . he's coming."

Sparshott slides behind the wheel of the Mercedes and drives it in back of a maintenance building where he can watch the airport road. Macready reminds him for the tenth time not to forget to massage Carlos for money laundering leads, then shows him once again how to use the Mercedes' recording system. Sparshott rehearses until flipping the switch on and off feels natural. They wait and watch from their hiding place like kids playing cops and robbers.

When he sees the white Camaro moving down the empty blacktop toward the airport, Sparshott feels the familiar adrenalin rush and steps back behind the building out of sight. He tells himself: "A piece of cake. You're *not* a cop. You're just a fucking drug dealer having lunch with another drug dealer. Nothing to it, brother." Then he grabs the radio.

"He's here . . . it's Showtime."

Carlos parks in front of the terminal—the airpark isn't National or Dulles so there are plenty of places—while Scooter snaps the first pictures for the Medina ID kit from the chief's van. Carlos enters the terminal, follows the restaurant sign up the only set of stairs, and waves to Marty waiting at the window table. If he's nervous, Carlos doesn't show it.

Preston knows what he has to do and plays his part like a pro. He makes sure Carlos takes the seat he chose for him—profile to the camera, say "ch-e-e-se"—so that he can't possibly miss the toy Mercedes when it pulls up to the entrance. He tries to put Carlos at ease, but doesn't explain why they're having lunch in such an odd little restaurant or why Terry is late. And since he isn't wired, he avoids all reference to the dope business so nothing important is lost. Want a drink? How's school going?

Sparshott waits ten minutes, long enough to let Carlos know that he, Terry, is in charge and short enough to keep the kid cool—like good comedy, it's all timing—then drives up the road and parks in the spot under Carlos' window that he chose in advance. He gets out slowly and adjusts his Balboa Yacht Club hat.

"Hey Marty, there's Terry," Carlos says. The Mercedes impresses the kid like, hey wow! Everything perfect so far.

Sparshott walks to the rear of the car, opens the trunk—he can feel Carlos' eyes on him—and carefully pulls out the attaché case. The candid camera in the van snaps a picture—UCA Tracy Sparshott, MCPD, with an attaché case, suspect Carlos Medina looking down from the restaurant, an "Aero Flight, Ltd." sign between them.

3. Sparshott arrives at Montgomery County Airpark. Preston and Carlos can be seen waiting to have lunch in upper right corner of photograph

Sparshott walks into the restaurant like someone straight out of "Mission Impossible," says hi to Carlos, then sits down next to him and across the table from Marty. He places the attaché case at his feet as if it were Venetian glass and slides the name plate under the lock to the right to activate the recorder. He says nothing about the Balboa hat which he knows Carlos noticed.

Sparshott and Preston are about to demand a lot from each other without a dress rehearsal. The plan is to flash their marijuana operation like a bare thigh, let Carlos play voyeur—now you see it, now you don't—then lead him to the conclusions they want without any prompting on their part. They want him to feel that Terry and Marty trust him so much they're not afraid to talk about their reefer business in front of him, and they want to give him an opening to talk about his cocaine business without appearing to pry, give the guy a chance to brag a little, play big shot. To accomplish that, they have to push and lean together like sledders on a luge.

"The guys here?" Sparshott asks Preston.

"Waiting outside."

"Did they get some food?"

"I took care of 'em."

"Everything okay? Talk to the people in Ohio?"

Carlos hangs on every word. He doesn't move a muscle.

"Yeah."

"Okay, then let's eat."

Sparshott senses it's working so he cuts the dialogue short. Carlos has lapped up the shit as fast as he's shoveled it, like when he asked Preston if he'd talked to the people in Ohio yet. He hopes Carlos is asking himself, "I wonder if that fucking attaché case is filled with what I think it is?" If you only knew, sucker! The waitress brings their burgers and Carlos comments on the Balboa Yacht Club hat, the opening Sparshott's been waiting for.

"You ever party on 'Jay' Street?" Sparshott asks.

Carlos laughs. "*Everyone* parties on Jay Street, man."

Lined with tattoo parlors and whorehouses—Five Star, Ovalo, Buffalo, Golden Key—Jay Street is one of Panama's most popular tourist attractions. Sidewalk tables at the Napoli Pizzeria attract Zonies and Panamanians alike who gawk at hookers until the wee hours when the streetwalkers and their pimps take the place over. And the Anchon Inn on the corner of Jay and Fourth of July Avenue with its expensive booze and cheap strippers is a beacon to sailors from around the world. Carlos brags:

"The owner of the Anchor Inn is a friend of mine."

"You're kidding. I wanna go *back*, man."

"I spent so much money in one night there, man. Believe me . . . twenty thousand."

Sparshott feels a sense of satisfaction only he can appreciate. He just pushed the right button. They talk about the Causeway, Panama's lovers' lane, and how the setting sun turns the three islands at its toe into sapphires, Naos, Perico, and Flamenco. About Panama Viejo which Captain Morgan once sacked, and the rows of pushcarts selling snow cones the color of parrot feathers. About the white beach up the coast at Rio Tita and the tanned tits pointing up at the hot blue sky.

Carlos opens up. He tells Terry and Marty that his mother is a TV personality in Panama, a singer with her own talk show, "Anayansi Invita," that his stepfather is a businessman who shits money, man, and that life down there was fuckin' good, man, before his stepfather walked out, a new Mercedes and women, shit, you wouldn't believe it. He says he's going home as soon as the semester is over, for Christmas, and won't be back until January 12.

The more Sparshott and Preston listen, the more impressed they are with Carlos. He's a bright friendly kid with a warm smile that would melt any muchacha's heart, big appetites, and a stepfather who dribbles him money from a spoon. The news about his going home for Christmas is good. It buys time to get the undercover budget approved and set up the next move.

They push their plates away. Terry orders a round of drinks, then abruptly turns the conversation to business. "The shit was good," he announces.

Carlos preens. "My man always gives me good shit . . . the absolute motherfucking best."

"But I gotta be honest with you, the reefer business is good to me." Sparshott challenges Carlos to convince him that he should switch from hemp to coke. "And I'm fuckin' careful who I trust."

"My people used to be in marijuana but they got out." Carlos begins his sales pitch. "It was too hard, you know, to move it around from the Islands, boats and all that shit. They found out there's more fuckin' money in coke, man."

"Maybe . . . but I use planes and I run a tight network in West Virginia, Western Maryland, Ohio and Pennsylvania. Marty takes care of Maryland. My business is fuckin' good. I'm my own boss, man, understand?"

Having distributors in five states again buys time like, "Hey, I'll get back to ya, I gotta check with my people." In the undercover game, time is both an opportunity and a weapon in the hands of a skilled player. The number "five" is critical to Sparshott's cover. It makes Terry a player on the level of Roberto and gives him a reason later to order coke in fives and its multiples—five one-ounce packages, ten pounds, fifteen keys.

Carlos continues his pitch: "I get deliveries every two weeks from Miami. I got two customers who buy by the key. Fuck man, I can get you five to ten keys tomorrow . . . just on a phone call."

Sparshott isn't sure how much of what Carlos said is drug-dealer bullshit. Like snitches, they love to crow. It makes them feel important and secure. "You need a plane? I got one you can use."

Vintage Sparshott, thinking like a drug dealer instead of a cop. Tippett will shit creds when he reads the transcripts. What if Carlos borrows a plane and never comes back? How would Tippett explain that? Holy J. Edgar Hoover, his federal mandate is to seize drug assets not give them away.

Carlos is pleased with the offer. "Thanks, man. My connection takes care of everything."

"How much for a sample key?"

"Thirty-eight thou . . . but you don't want just one."

Sparshott and Preston look at each other and laugh. The price is outrageously high. Carlos is embarrassed. Roberto charges him $36K a key and two thou is a fair profit.

"Well, that's the price *here*, man," Carlos says defensively. "One kilo down there would be about $32 thou."

"Too fuckin' much," Sparshott says. He knows the going rate in Washington is $25-26K and in Miami $20K. He's not sure if the kid is green or playing him for a sucker.

"If you pick up ten kilos yourself in Miami . . . twenty-six, maybe twenty-five."

"No problem, I got planes."

Carlos knows he's in way over his head and he's confused.

If a key in Washington is really as cheap as Terry says it is, then the old man is ripping him off again. If that isn't bad enough, he has no idea what the fuck to charge for a multi-key buy or what the *real* going rate is in Miami. He runs scared.

"I don't wanna sell the shit to you myself, Terry. I want you to go to Miami and meet, you know, my man. I just want a fuckin' commission on whatever you buy, man."

Is this guy a mind reader or what? Sparshott didn't even have to say "take me to your leader." And the guy's offering to set him up in a cocaine franchise. Why hang around any longer?

Sparshott looks at his watch, then pushes his chair away from the table and says, "It's just about time, Marty." He doesn't respond to Carlos' invitation to meet, you know, his man. Let the kid swing in the breeze of doubt over Christmas, make him come back from Panama eager to see Terry and Marty.

They lead Carlos down the stairs and out the back door to the airstrip where forty to fifty planes are battened down, mostly single-engine jobs. A large hangar in the corner dominates the small field. The Cessna is parked just outside the door on an asphalt spar leading to the runway.

"Hey Terry, how ya doing," the two pilots call out. They rehearsed the scene with Sparshott earlier that day.

4. Preston preparing to leave by plane. Preston, Sparshott and Carlos

"All set?" Sparshott asks.

"Ready to go."

Sparshott turns to Preston and hands him the attaché case

which they are certain Carlos believes is filled with money.

"Take this up to Ohio. When you get to the field, circle around. If the school bus is not parked where it's supposed to, get the fuck out of there and come on back. Don't land. If everything looks good, drop the money off. I'll see you in a couple of days."

"Okay, Terry." Preston climbs into the plane. "See you, Carlos."

The pilot revs up and taxies the few feet to the runway. Sparshott watches Carlos as the plane takes off and it looks like he's buying it, fucking impressed, man. They walk around the terminal to the Camaro. Carlos eyes Sparshott's car.

"Nice little Mercedes." He's been saving up. "I want a Porsche 944."

5. Sparshott and Carlos

"Wanna see it?"

Sparshott still has Macready's money laundering questions to pitch to Carlos, but first he wants to lure him inside the car close to the mikes behind the sun visor. He senses a fragile bond beginning to grow between Terry and Medina woven out of a common interest in dope, Panama, jewelry, and now cars.

Carlos climbs in the car, looks at the customized dash, feels the leather. "How much marijuana do you move?" he asks.

"One ton and above. My network is established. I can easily move coke through it."

"I made a quarter of a million since I, you know, started working with my man. I keep it in Panama."

"No shit! Can you give me the name of a bank down there to invest in?" Sparshott doesn't know if Carlos is bragging again or telling the truth, but he's sure of one thing, Macready will be so happy he'll shit C notes.

"Fuck man, you need more than a bank. You need an attorney, someone to set up the commissions. You gotta come down and talk to them. You gotta see how the system works. How much you wanna move?"

"Half a million . . . to begin with. Old Mike handles all my money. The guy's been a family friend for years."

Macready already lined up Old Mike as the IRS undercover, a pro from Florida, and asked Sparshott to prepare Carlos for him. Another base to cover.

"When you're down there," Sparshott says, "why don't you check it out for me? Find out who I gotta see, what's it gonna cost me."

"Okay man."

"And bring me back a case of beer for Christmas. Panama Beer . . . best fuckin' brew in the world. I can't get the shit up here."

"Fuck, man, that's it? A case of Panama?"

"Can you get me one of those nice molas?"

A mola is a hand-woven native tapestry. Tourists buy them faster than the Sandblast Indians can make them.

Carlos laughs. "Fuckin' hard to get, man. What's your phone number so I can call you when I get back?"

"I'll call *you*. I don't wanna give you my number until, you know, I see how things go, man."

"Okay, call me after the twelfth."

TWENTY

Burning to learn whether Carlos bought the scam, Preston flew with the pilots to Baltimore-Washington International Airport, twenty bumpy minutes from the airpark, then hitched a ride back to town. He hadn't been wild about the airpark idea when Sparshott first suggested it, but now he was enthusiastic. He and Sparshott had worked together so well there hadn't been a single miscue and, to him at least, it looked as if they had completely sucked Carlos in. Preston could almost see the guy counting the money he was going to make off Marty and Terry. Thank god for greed, what would a poor narc do without it!

But Preston was as confused as he was pleased. Was he supposed to be Terry's *full* partner in charge of marijuana distribution like an executive veep, or merely Terry's man in metro Washington? If he was just Terry's local boy, why did Terry send him to Ohio with a pile of money to buy a plane-load of marijuana? That implied that Terry not only trusted him but authorized him to negotiate drug purchases—the job of a full partner.

Naturally, Preston wanted the role of Terry's equal, but he had a feeling that Sparshott was pushing him further and further downstage without discussing the move with him or the team, and frankly it hurt. But what stung even more than playing Ed to Sparshott's Johnny was the growing realization that Tracy really didn't want him on the undercover team, that Tracy was tossing him bit parts like meeting Carlos in the airpark restaurant and carrying an attaché case on an airplane just to keep him happy. Scraps for the dog, demeaning and unfair. Sparshott, not Campbell or Tippett, seemed to be planning each undercover move, and Preston felt a faceless anxiety slowly strangling his undercover fun. Not confrontational by nature like Sparshott, he kept his feelings to himself.

As far as Sparshott was concerned, Preston's fear was justified to a point. In his mind, there could be only *one* lead undercover, someone on the same level as Roberto Tabares who could play one-on-one for the best and safest results. And there was never any doubt in Sparshott's mind who that lead had to be. Simply put, he had more chameleon in him than Preston, could scam and con better, and could withstand more undercover pressure. Both Campbell and Tippett chose him as lead undercover agent over the xenophobic objections of the Baltimore creds who didn't want a fucking local carrying their undercover ball.

But Sparshott really *did* want Preston involved in every possible scenario and for good reason—Marty Preston was good and he deserved it. No one had to tell Sparshott how he'd feel if, for example, Baltimore had managed to replace him with a Bureau undercover. Out of his mind fucking pissed. So Sparshott went out of his way to create what he thought was an important role for Marty in the airpark scam, and he had sketched what he thought were important parts for Marty in the four scenarios he was currently scripting and screening in his head. He hoped that Preston would get the message that he was the vital number two man and that he wouldn't fight it. Sparshott didn't want a major screwup over a power struggle. Or worse, he didn't want hurt feelings to make it impossible for him and Preston to work together, especially after Marty was already a key member of the Terry Petit marijuana-biker gang in Carlos' eyes. But if push came to shove, Sparshott was prepared to drive Preston right off the stage into the dressing room. He didn't think it would ever come to such a showdown, and he was counting on Preston's common sense and commitment to the investigation he, Preston, had begun, to keep the peace, no matter how fragile.

For his part, Bill Campbell barely sensed the dangerous friction developing between his two undercovers. Hell, he didn't have time. Carlos would be back in Washington in less than a month and there was so much to do without the freedom of a budget. Set up a beeper number and an answering service under the name Terry Petit in Frederick, Maryland, half an hour drive north from the airpark. Find, rent, and furnish an undercover house there. Keep the pressure on the creds for rented surveillance cars for the team and an undercover Mercedes for Preston. Work out the details of the next buy from Carlos—how much, when, where, backup. Finally, get Sparshott's and Preston's bosses to sit down with the Bureau SAC and ASAC in Baltimore to discuss FBI undercover rules for the Tabares investigation, then to sign a release which would say in part: Sparshott and Preston would work under the direct supervision of Campbell and Tippett; and the FBI would pay their overtime and protect them so they wouldn't ride home in a hearse.

Although he felt so good about the airpark scam he wished he had it in living color on video, Campbell wasn't absolutely certain Carlos had swallowed the bait. If the creds were as concerned about catching Tabares as they were about picking legal nits off the wiretap affidavit, he would have been able to read the actual transcripts of the phone call the DNR said Carlos made to Roberto right after the scam. That call had to be about Terry and Marty. But without those transcripts, he'd have to wait until Carlos returned from Panama on January 12 to find out for sure. As patient as Campbell was, a month is a hell of a long wait.

Naturally, Sparshott wanted to follow Carlos to Panama to see who his money laundering connection was, where Carlos lived, who he chummed around with, if he'd stop in Miami to meet Roberto. Naturally, Campbell had to tell him, "Sorry Tracy, no," even though the trip would be a smart undercover move. Logic is a stranger to bureaucracy, and Campbell knew the creds in Baltimore would never agree to the trip. He could hear them now:

There's no money in the budget you don't have, Special Agent Campbell. Even if there were, the trip would be dangerous. There is no time to arrange for backup and surveillance in Panama. And remember, we promised UCA Sparshott's MCPD superior officer that the Bureau would cover his back at all times.

Besides, he could get burned down there and if he did, he might never be able to talk his way out of Panama alive. Then what would they tell Montgomery County? And lastly, Special Agent Campbell, can you imagine the diplomatic fallout if a member of the Task Force investigation, sponsored by the Bureau, went undercover in a foreign country without going through proper channels which could take weeks if not months?

Naturally, Sparshott wasn't happy with Campbell's decision, not that he blamed Billy personally. What a wasted opportunity and what a fucking stupid excuse! It was only a simple surveillance job for chrissakes and he didn't need backup. When are we going to do something *right* for a change? I know what I'm doing. Doesn't anyone around here trust me?

Naturally, Campbell didn't blame Sparshott for wanting to go. But this was no undercover Camelot where the rain never falls till after sundown. This was the Bureau where the shit hits the fan before noon.

Fortunately for Campbell, the team had no trouble agreeing on the logistics of the second buy—a half pound for around $10,000 which they didn't have. Anything less than a half pound would be an insult, anything more a waste of money which, of course, would have to walk. They didn't have to impress Carlos or Roberto, merely show them they were serious buyers. Furthermore, a half-pound buy would keep Carlos on the defensive. Terry could say: "If the deal goes down smooth and the shit is good . . . the beginning of a beautiful relationship, man. If not, who the fuck needs it, you know what I mean?" Even Tippett supported the buy, a clear signal to the team that the creds would approve it. Christ, everybody knew Tippett kept his ear so close to their ass he heard every little fart.

Macready was especially interested in the next meeting between Sparshott and Carlos. He had convinced the IRS to loan Tracy the Mercedes for the duration of the case and Old Mike was ready to fly into Washington as soon as the footlights were trimmed. He could fit into any Sparshott scenario.

Ready for Carlos? Fuckin' ready, man.

But January 12 came and went and no Carlos. Sparshott beeped him, called his car phone, tried a third unlisted number which he assumed was Medina's home phone. Everything was quiet. Even the clone beeper lacked vital signs . . . Maybe—Raul Tabares warned his father about a big fuckin' badass biker pig with a beard. Maybe—Roberto then asked Carlos to describe this hotshot marijuana dealer with an airplane. Maybe—one of the half dozen lowlifes Preston had busted told Roberto about a narc with long hair and green eyes called Marty. Maybe—hey, bad guys don't have a monopoly on paranoia.

Sparshott finally reached Carlos on January 14 and everyone began to breathe easier:

"Carlos, this is Terry, man."

"Hey Terry, what's up?"

"You tell me."

"Hangin' around man. Just takin' care of some shit."

"I just got out of a party at the Sheraton up in Frederick." Sparshott is preparing Carlos for the eventual undercover house and answering service there. He wants Carlos to understand that he doesn't actually live in Frederick, just uses the town for business meetings. Where he actually lives—Hagerstown about an hour north of Frederick—is still a secret. And he dares Carlos to call the toll-free Sheraton number to see if the chain actually has a hotel in Frederick. "I slept there last night. I get a room there sometimes."

"That's cool."

"I'm gonna be in town next week. I got some business down where I met you last time."

"I found out everything you asked . . . you know, the favor." Carlos sounds proud of himself. "You're gonna love it. We gotta sit down and talk."

"Next week, man." Sparshott grins. Too bad no one is there to share the moment with him. Not only did the airpark show work, the sucker is actually *eager* to meet again. But Sparshott knows that bad guys lie as much as narcs, so he tests Carlos to make sure he actually went to Panama over the holidays. "Did you bring me my beer?"

Carlos laughs. "It's right here, man. I drank two already."

"Hey, that's *my* beer, motherfucker!"

"You know those molas?" Carlos is as excited as a kid at Disneyland. "Well, I got you a couple . . . I gotta show you the ring I bought, man. You're going to be jealous—the one with the diamonds."

"The full bezel or just the . . . "

"The full bezel, baby."

"How much?"

"Beautiful!"

"How much?"

"I'll get you one. Beautiful, man. So when we going to talk?"

"Next Tuesday . . . I'm gonna get a room down there for one day." Sparshott needs the weekend to prepare for the meeting and to set up the mechanics for the half-pound buy. He has an uneasy feeling that the FBI creds will somehow manage to create another crisis and he knows Montgomery County won't bail them out this time. He tells Carlos he'll be in town for one day only as an escape hatch in case the kid wants to socialize—Sparshott can feel a bond growing stronger with each contact—or insists on making the buy too risky. "I made some contacts over the holidays about, you know, and things look really good, man."

"Okay . . . if you don't catch me in my car, beep me."

"I tried you at . . . " Terry fishes to identify the third phone number Carlos gave him. "I guess it's your home number."

"Yeah."

"What's the best time to reach you?" More fishing. Sparshott wants to know Carlos' class schedule so he can manipulate the times for meets and buys. "You got school, right?"

"Yeah, I gotta be in class from ten o'clock till like four. So call between eight and nine-thirty."

"I'm interested in gettin' things rollin'."

"Me too, man . . . Hey Terry? I need a favor . . . I told you about the car I wanted to buy—"

"Yeah, the Porsche."

"I don't know what to do because, you know . . . That's why I wanna see you."

"Shit, I got a good connection, man." Sparshott understands Carlos' problem. He doesn't want to talk money on the phone because he's afraid it might be bugged, and he has the cash for the car but is afraid to spend it because car dealers are supposed to report any cash purchase over $10K. He's hoping Terry can sneak him around the law, and at the same time he's trying to impress Terry that he's a man of his word, if he says he's going to buy a motherfucking Porsche, then he's fucking going to do it. Sparshott sees the "favor" as an opportunity to sink his hooks deeper into Carlos' life and he grabs it with a devilish grin on his face. Hey Macready, you gotta get your guys to seize a Porsche so I can sell it back to Carlos. Recycle, brother, save the environment. "Same place I got my little Mercedes!"

"You serious man? Then we *gotta* talk!"

"Okay, but I'm gonna be in New Orleans over the weekend." Sparshott's wife is taking a business trip and Tracy gets to go along free. Always thinking scam, he uses the occasion to make Carlos think he's going south to line up a reefer deal. "I'm goin' down to meet, you know, a friend for dinner Saturday night. I might just call you to say howdy."

"You motherfucker . . . you gotta take *me* next time!"

"You sure you wanna go with me? People stare, man, they think I'm just a piece of biker shit."

Carlos laughs, how true, man. They agree to touch base the following Tuesday.

TWENTY-ONE

3:00 P.M.

Preston turns on the tape recorder attached to the telephone. "Carlos . . . This is Marty," he says.

"Hey, what's up Marty?"

"Same old stuff, man. Terry's here. Hold on."

They're calling from a pay phone in the lobby of the Greenbelt Hilton not far from Carlos' house. They figure the kid's sure to know the place and be impressed, you know, fucking Terry, man, looks like shit but travels first class.

Sparshott keeps Carlos waiting a few beats, then: "Hey man, this is Terry . . . I'm in town."

"Terry! My *man's* here, too." The kid can't wait to get the words out, he's so damn excited. "But you and me gotta talk first, motherfucker, then if you want—"

Sparshott pisses on his parade. "Shit, man, I don't want to meet anybody now."

"Hey, whatever you want, man." Carlos can't hide his disappointment. "Where are you?"

That Carlos wants Terry to meet Roberto means either Carlos is impressed—or Roberto has doubts. Whatever, Sparshott wants Carlos on trial not Terry Petit.

"At the Hilton in Greenbelt."

"How long you gonna be there?"

"Couple hours, I got to get back to Frederick." Sparshott needs an excuse to get rid of Carlos in a hurry if he has to.

"They're talkin' snow storms and I got stuff, you know, I gotta do before the fuckin' snow hits. We'll have a drink in the bar then go take a ride."

"Okay Terry."

Carlos knows the Hilton—he once met some chickies there—and walks into the cocktail lounge where Sparshott and Preston are waiting an hour later. His face lights up.

"How they hangin', man?" he says.

"Grab a seat, man!" Carlos sinks into a padded chair.

"Have a drink, you motherfucker."

Sparshott signals the waitress. As they chit-chat, he and Preston are careful to avoid business. Neither is wired and the attaché case recorder at Sparshott's feet is off. The bar noise would ruin the quality of a recording. And since the purpose of this meeting is to learn as much as possible about Carlos and Roberto and negotiate the terms of the half-pound buy, they want to hustle Carlos into the wired Mercedes where it's quiet and less distracting. And they want to get out of the hotel before their ice cubes melt because the place is a calculated security risk. Someone they know might spot them. If that happens Preston can cover himself because Marty lives in the area, but Terry's from western Maryland. How the fuck would he know someone in Greenbelt of all places?

Sparshott and Preston down their drinks like closet alcoholics, then Sparshott tells Marty to go take care of that little business matter and meet him back at the hotel in an hour. The errand-boy brush-off stings, but what can Preston say? With him present, the odds of a slipup increase—more pressure on Sparshott. And with him present, Carlos has to divide his attention between Terry and Marty—good for building relationships, bad for gathering intelligence. A true team player, Preston doesn't signal his hurt.

Sparshott leads Carlos out to the Mercedes, then eases his hulk into the car and slides the recorder switch at the side of the seat to the on position. It's time to play twenty-questions.

Carlos isn't ready for games. He's suspicious and he's no longer sure what to think of Terry. When no one stopped him at the airport on his way home to Panama for Christmas—he was carrying $18,000 in cash—he concluded that Terry wasn't a narc because Terry knew he'd be carrying money and in his stash would be the $800 Terry had paid for the quarter ounce. Fuck, there wasn't a narc this side of Bogotá who could pass up the chance to take him down when his pockets were full of money. But when he stopped in Miami on the way back and told Roberto about Terry and Marty, the airplane, and their marijuana operation, Roberto said he smelled a narc. Carlos respected the old man's judgment—if anyone could smell a narc from a thousand miles away, it would be sly old Roberto.

"Hey man, why the fucking ride in the car, man?" Carlos demands. He goes hinky without warning, almost as if he hears the recorder humming, and catches Sparshott by surprise. Fuck, you never know when a dealer's gonna turn on you like a pet tiger. "Why not talk in the bar?"

"Be cool, man, I saw some motherfucker in the hotel giving me the eye. Marty said the sonofabitch was hotel security. Who needs that shit?"

Carlos doesn't buy it. "You recording this? You getting this on tape, motherfucker? Let me see the wire and shit!"

Another critical moment. It could go either way. It could be over before it begins. Campbell, Scooter, and two other FBI agents are covering the parking lot entrances and exits, shit, a lot of good that's gonna do if the guy wants to walk.

Sparshott says: "Fuck you—you wanna search me, huh? Well, go ahead, motherfucker."

Carlos hesitates.

"He-e-ey—wait a minute pal, you got a fuckin' wire on *you* or somethin'? Is that what this is all—"

The tension eases. "Fuck Terry, you watch too much Miami Vice, man!"

"Yeah, I watch it . . . just so I learn!"

Carlos gives a nervous chuckle. "You know, I don't trust you fully."

"In time . . . I'll feel a lot better when I can take you to my house and you can take me to yours. I'll give you my phone later."

"The reason I say I don't trust you," Carlos confesses, "my man doesn't want to sell shit to you. He says to me, 'Why would this guy come to you, if he's got so much money?'"

"Hey man, my business is private." Sparshott now knows he's got a long way to go before he's in like Flint. "I ain't gonna tell you *everything* I do."

"I told my man . . . 'pure coincidence' . . . and he said . . . 'Well, I don't believe in that kind of shit.'"

"I wouldn't respect him if he did."

Sparshott inches onto the beltway and drives east toward Route 450, Annapolis Road, a two-lane highway with less traffic and fewer distractions than four-lane Route 50. Macready follows him. Sparshott needs to concentrate on talk not traffic. And he doesn't want Carlos' eye to wander too much.

As soon as they turn off the beltway and onto quiet Annapolis Road, Carlos blurts out like a man with a secret he can't hold any longer:

"Now listen, Terry! They said you gotta take your five hundred thousand, open ten different companies and put fifty in each, then you can deposit up to fifty a day in each one. Your name's not gonna appear anywhere."

"No problem."

"It's gonna cost you forty-eight to set it up . . . wash money . . . one initial fee. You can take up to ten million in cash out of Panama, man. It's all fucking legal and you don't even have to pay tax on the interest. You can't beat the price. All you gotta worry about is—getting the money *into* Panama. We'll go down and you'll see."

You bet your brown ass we'll go down, then *you'll* see, baby. Sparshott knows Macready will jump right out of his skin when he hears the tape in living stereo. Carlos just laid out the whole laundering scheme. Christ, he can't wait to go down there with Old Mike and a suitcase full of cash and set the fuckers up. Carlos continues:

"They work for this badass company. They do it for some

of the Cubans I work for. They told me they just opened an account for a guy from Atlantic City . . . a million bucks . . . and the guy wants to post another one to two mil a month."

"Let's say I start with fifty thou just to make sure everything works smooth, then have Old Mike put in three hundred, let's say, a month later."

Macready had told Sparshott that the IRS would never come up with half a million wash money. If the news disappointed him, he can imagine what it's doing to Carlos.

"Fuck man, I don't know if they'll . . . You should of told me that before because . . . "

Carlos is so upset he stammers. When Terry brought up money laundering at the airpark, he saw an opportunity to make some quick, easy cash as a go-between. So he told an attorney friend in Panama about this rich American who needs someplace to wash money, half a million to begin with, and now Terry's talking about a pissing fifty thousand.

"Shit, Terry, why don't you take this guy Old Mike with you and me and go down there? I'm not tryin' to rip you off, man. Don't worry about taking half a million down there. You take fifty, you take a hundred, it's gonna cost you the same, you still gotta pay forty-eight . . . I told them you're a bookie, man. He's—"

"Bookie?" The ride is turning into a fucking soap opera. Sparshott's played a lot of undercover roles in his life but a bookie? "Fuck, I don't know nothin' about bookies, man."

"Well, he's not gonna ask you any questions about it. He just needs to know you're no fuckin' dealer, you know, to cover his ass . . . I don't want the Cuban guy to know I'm doin' this for you. He's too touchy, you know what I mean? He doesn't believe in that kind of shit."

"Yeah, I know what you mean, man." A beautiful opening, thank you Carlos! "What's he do with *his* money?"

"Invests it, man. Liquor stores, man. He has a couple of corporations and shit."

Sparshott doesn't want to appear too nosy. Macready can always check with the Florida liquor license people for details. So he changes the subject and gives Carlos an opportunity to suggest that Terry show him his reefer business. He asks:

"Tell me Carlos, what's the Cuban gonna need to trust me?"

"You gotta *show* something, Terry. I've been tryin' to find out more about you but I haven't been able to." He asked one of his customers to check out a reefer dealer from Western Maryland by the name of Terry Petit. No one ever heard of him.

"Well I *wanna* show you something, man." Sparshott now knows he has to shift into the next scenario before it's too late. Roberto thinks he's a narc, and Carlos is no longer sure he is who he says he is. "You pretty strong? You in good shape?"

"Strong enough."

"Well, I might need some help in liftin' some stuff."

"Shit man, go pay some niggers."

"I don't want anyone to know what I'm liftin' unless I already got'em by the balls, you understand?"

"Yeah . . . where?"

"Up around Frederick! Shit man, you'd look good in camouflage pants and shirt. But I might have to blindfold you first."

"Fuck Terry, why do I have to trust *you* and you can't trust me?"

"Cuz it's a dangerous business and everybody tries to rip you off."

"I won't."

"What about the Cuban? You trust him?"

"Fuck man, if he's got the nerve to front me three keys, how can I *not* trust him?"

"Well, I'm comfortable in my business and I'm takin' a big chance with this new shit."

"You know what I would do? I'd buy *one* key from him!"

"Okay, I'll tell you what. I'll buy a half pound if you break it into four separate packages so I can get the shit right out to distributors, you know, the guys who didn't get to sample the first quarter ounce. If I—"

"Under a key, you deal with me."

"I trust you, man. If I like it and everything goes good, then I'll buy the one key. If the Cuban feels comfortable with that and—"

"Half pound . . . eight ounces. Okay, but you have to pay *my* price."

"What's that?" Carlos hesitates. It's clear that he hasn't dealt in pounds before. "Hey, you want a calculator?"

"Yeah . . . The Cuban's like you. He works hard to get what he has."

"Fuck man, don't we all!"

"Except me. That's why he always makes fun of me, that motherfucker . . . 'Rich little kid' . . . That's what he calls me all the time. Back in Panama I had a Mercedes ever since I was fucking seventeen, man. All my life I've been around rich people and I'm not gonna change my style now because of, you know, what I'm doing. Not the Cuban, he's as cheap as shit, he's afraid to spend his money . . . Eleven thousand."

While Sparshott weighs the half-pound price, Carlos turns the conversation to the Porsche he intends to buy. "I want an '84 or '85 . . . a 928 . . . but I don't want to pay no more than thirty-five or forty thousand. It's not that I don't have the money, I just want to be humble about the car."

"The 28's a nice car, man." Sparshott understands. A Hispanic kid going to school fulltime and driving a brand new Porsche? Who's kidding who? "So what color do you want?"

"Red . . . Can you get one for me? Can you get me a good deal?"

"Talk about *him* bein' cheap, man! I'll look around for you . . . You gonna front me a half pound?"

"You crazy? I don't front."

"You'll feel real silly if I turn out to be a hundred kilo dealer. And you know what? I'm gonna remind you . . . a year from now I'm gonna say, 'Carlos you didn't even trust me for a fuckin' half pound.'"

"I wish you luck, man." Carlos is clearly uncomfortable talking about fronting Terry so he quickly changes the conversation again. "You wanna buy an Uzi? A friend of mine wants to give me one."

"I might . . . show it to me as soon as you get it."

Christ, that's all Sparshott needs is to have some fucking local catch Carlos with a submachine gun before he gets his introduction to Roberto. He can hear Tippett sputtering now. "What? You want to buy an Uzi? But Officer Sparshott, they're illegal. I'll have to call a seance to see what J. Edgar thinks." Sparshott spots a liquor store and suggests they stop.

Carlos checks his watch.

"Man, you made me miss a fuckin' class, shit!"

"Then I'll write you a note . . . 'Dear teach, please excuse my friend Carlos because he was busy selling me a half pound—"

Carlos is having a great time with his new friend Terry, fuck school. They go into the liquor store where Sparshott buys some Jack Daniels and Coke, then they head back to the Hilton.

"Okay man, eleven thousand—four packages—two O's each," Sparshott says. "But I don't want to touch the shit and I don't want you to touch it, either. You got somebody to hold it?"

"Yeah."

"If I start picking up my stuff down in Miami later on, you're still gonna get your cut, right?"

"I hope so . . . so how much you gonna be movin'?"

"The potential's there."

"Well what you call 'potential' ain't shit for the Cuban. It's like there's nothing you can do to impress him, man."

"Fuck, I don't ever try to impress anybody . . . Marty was tellin' me that we should grind it, cut it maybe in half, then press it back again into rock and—"

"You don't wanna do that, Terry. If your people find out, you're gonna lose customers."

"That's smart."

Sparshott is still worried that Carlos might do something stupid before he gets to Roberto, like get arrested in D.C. or Miami or Panama. So he plays undercover nursemaid. Hey, sometimes it pays to coddle criminals.

"Listen man, if you and me are gonna work together you're gonna have to be careful. Once we get rollin', I'm goin' back on up to Frederick. What happens to you down here happens to me, right? I once had a guy that started sprayin' PCP shit on my reefer and you know what happened? We had a shootout in West Virginia. You know what happens when you have a shootout? Every-fucking-body starts askin' questions. Who needs that shit?"

"Tell me about it, man. Don't worry, I go over *every* detail before—"

"Okay then, I'll give you my beeper number. It's in western Maryland. I got an answering service—twenty-four hours—I don't want no motherfucker callin' in the middle of the night. That's why I don't give my phone number to nobody . . . just my beeper. Say to the girl, 'This is Carlos. Tell Terry I want him to call me right back.'" Sparshott gives Carlos the beeper number. "In a couple of weeks—when things get rollin'—we'll go down to Miami, get a bigass boat, and do some deep sea fishin'. I gotta talk to the Cuban about prices and I gotta find some airfields."

They pull back into the Hilton lot. "I gotta get back home tonight," Sparshott continues. "They're predicting ten fuckin' inches, man, can you fuckin' believe it? But I still got some time. You wanna come in for a drink? You wanna eat something?"

Eat your heart out, Tippett baby. A nice dinner with plenty of drinks, an Uzi, a trip to Miami, maybe another to Panama City, a charter fishing boat. You know what big spenders we F.L.'s are.

Carlos hesitates. "I gotta see the Cuban at seven and—ah, what the fuck, my girlfriend's not around, let's go eat."

TWENTY-TWO

Jerry Macready began to chuckle even before he turned the Mercedes tape on. Somewhere on the way to Annapolis, he had lost Sparshott and Medina and called Tracy on the car phone.

"Where the hell are you?" he had asked quietly. Not that he was worried about Carlos getting suspicious. Sparshott could bullshit himself into, out of, and around anything.

"Hey, Jerry, what's up, man?" Sparshott had answered. "Just cruising down 450 near Bowie . . . Okay, see ya later. Wait a sec . . . say hi to a friend of mine."

The next thing Macready knew, Carlos was on the line. Sparshott loved to pull those kinds of mind-fucking stunts—the surveillant actually talking to the surveillee. Macready had had a good laugh when Carlos finally hung up. Now he settled back with pad and pencil and turned on the tape. The longer he listened the more excited he became. A fishing boat . . . liquor stores . . . dummy corporations! Leave it to Terry—hell, now even he was calling Sparshott "Terry." Carlos Medina was actually telling Macready where to look for the assets of his boss Roberto Tabares. "You dumb sonofabitch," he whispered to himself. And if that wasn't enough, in the course of one hour, Sparshott got Carlos to answer the team's slate of questions, conned him into explaining how to launder money in Panama, negotiated the next buy, wheedled an invitation to Florida and Panama, invited Carlos to go deep-sea fishing, made an offer for an Uzi, and promised to get his old buddy Jerry Macready to help Carlos buy a Porsche 928—thanks a lot brother. No wonder Sparshott's boss held his breath every time Tracy went undercover.

But Macready didn't have time to worry about such trivia as finding Carlos an '85 or '86 red Porsche 928 in mint condition. A mountain of work was waiting for him in Miami. Besides finding and listing Tabares' assets, he had to form a rough idea of what Tabares was worth and how much he spent so he could quickly put together a net worth/expenditure case after Roberto's arrest. Your typical tax argument . . . Members of the jury, Roberto Tabares declared on his tax returns an average of $5,000 income for each of the last six years—or $30,000. During that same period of time, records show that he spent on an average of $200,000 a year—or $1.2 million. Where, pray tell, did that money come from if not from the drugs the court established he was selling?

The undercover investigation didn't make Macready's difficult task any easier. Until Tabares was actually arrested, he had to play invisible T-man without benefit of a single subpoena. Even with gags, subpoenas tend to leak. And a leak in the Tabares case would signal Roberto that he was under investigation and drive him and Medina underground. So Macready would have to rely exclusively on public records which entailed visits to the recorder of deeds to see what Roberto owned, the taxing authority to see if he was paying for property "belonging" to someone else, the licensing board to find his liquor stores, and the state corporation bureau to uncover the shells he used to hide and launder money. Somewhere in the hard copy, Macready knew he would stumble on the names of co-owners, cosigners, accountants, lawyers, mortgagers, bankers. All of them potential witnesses or co-conspirators whom he could interview after Roberto's arrest. All holding or hiding financial records just begging to be subpoenaed. Paper trails of monthly statements, canceled checks, deposit tickets, wire transfers, CD's, cashier and traveler's checks, money orders, currency transfer reports. A set of keys to unlock hidden real estate, buried brokerage accounts, secret safety deposit boxes, out-of-state banks, and big cash purchases. Each a fiscal nail in Tabares' coffin.

But whatever he ultimately learned about Roberto's

finances, Macready was smart enough not to expect much cooperation or gratitude from the FBI. When it came to drugs, the law enforcement system was so myopic it could only see the color green and make out the shapes of big objects like houses and cars. In its eyes, an IRS money laundering case was at best a prop to support more drug conspiracy charges, at worst, a feeble alternative to the charges themselves. The system believed that finding and dismantling a money laundering system jeopardized undercover operations, took too long, was too complex for a jury to understand, and earned light sentences. What a pity. For all educated lawyers, the system still didn't get the point—smashing a wash machine was critical to winning the law enforcement side of the war on drugs. Capture the ammunition, the enemy had nothing to fight with. Seize the drug organization's laundry and the money in it, the dealer had nothing to deal with. So elementary.

But to be perfectly honest, Macready wasn't surprised at the near blindness of the system. It took time for new ideas to filter through the crusty layers of bureaucracy and the IRS didn't give them much of a boost. It feared the public stage so much it ran every time the footlights went up. Hell, even cops didn't know that the IRS has an autonomous criminal investigation division with real T-men armed with guns, badges, subpoenas, and search and seizures. Like it or not, the IRS was the wallflower at the federal ball which didn't encourage the FBI to appreciate its unique talents.

If Jerry Macready had a lot to accomplish in Miami, Bill Campbell had a pressing need to make a "research" trip of his own there as well. He had to forge ties with the Miami Bureau, the Dade County police, and the *real* Miami Vice. Courtesy aside, he would need them for background information about the Tabares family and for backup on any future Miami meets, buys, searches, seizures, subpoenas, and arrests. He too had to conduct surveillance on Roberto and his son-in-law mule, Gustavo Rodriguez, to see where they lived, what kind of cars they drove, and who they dealt with so there would be no major surprises later. Like a scout, he had to survey the Miami terrain, gauge the strength of the enemy, and snap pictures of every known soldier and site.

Campbell had asked the Miami Bureau to conduct the preliminary surveillance for the team, but it had moved so slowly and sloppily he decided to do most of the legwork himself. If all went well in Washington, Sparshott would soon be undercover in Miami, and Campbell for one was not about to place Sparshott's life in the hands of an indifferent Bureau.

Unfortunately, there was no money in the budget which Campbell still didn't have to pay for the trip. The IRS agreed to cover Macready's expenses and the creds in Baltimore sprang for Campbell's, mostly because he said he had to talk to the Miami Bureau which made the trip sound "official." But the creds refused to allow Campbell to take along Special Agent Jeff Favitta who had already done surveillance on the Tabares case and who had once worked for the Division of Alcoholic Beverages and Tobacco in Miami. That Tabares owned a liquor store or two made no difference. And the creds hassled Campbell for two exhausting days over Sparshott's ticket even though he was lead undercover. They couldn't understand why it was necessary for Sparshott to actually eyeball the place before he went undercover there.

Although the creds couldn't see it, the squabbling over pennies made no fiscal sense. Forget professional pride and personal safety. The more money you spent hunting hidden assets, the more assets you found. The more you found, the more you seized. The more you seized, the deeper you wounded the enemy and the richer you became. If the team found just one extra buried account or one extra piece of hidden real estate in Miami, the team trip would pay for itself ten times over.

In the end, the creds reluctantly agreed to let Campbell take Sparshott but not Preston to Miami. Campbell felt bad about excluding Marty especially since the guy loved scuba diving. He knew the value of team building and to have Sparshott, Preston and Macready with him fulltime, shielded from the distractions of home and office, would go a long way to make them one. If anyone could benefit from the bonding, it was Marty Preston who was the least gregarious member of the team. But under the circumstances, Campbell felt fortunate just to have gotten a ticket for Sparshott, and he had no energy to wage a second battle over Preston. He had to hustle down to Florida and be back in three days in order to set up the half-pound buy before Medina backed out.

Marty Preston was hurt when he got the news he was staying behind and he didn't buy "the budget made me do it" argument for a minute. Heck, the FBI had more money than Ivory Liquid had suds. The Bureau was going out of its way to treat him like a second class team member—again—and the scrawl on the wall was clear. If he wasn't making *this* trip to Miami, he probably wouldn't be making other important trips either. In one way, he couldn't blame Bill Campbell for a bureaucracy that didn't respect locals. Hadn't Tippett removed the name "Martin Preston" from the wiretap affidavit that he, Preston, had originally drafted. Jeez, how subtle can you get. Tippett had argued that headquarters scratched his name because it permitted only *one* author on a wiretap affidavit for legal reasons. Sure, Stew, and God snorts cocaine.

But in another way Preston *did* blame Campbell. Billy should have fought for his ticket, he should have told his boss that the Tabares case was Preston's to begin with, that he was too critical to the undercover team to leave behind. But Preston only found out about the trip after Campbell already had one foot on the airplane. Although he complained, Preston didn't do what Sparshott would have done—bellow like a wounded bull, demand to talk to the creds himself, and threaten to withhold the chief's van from the team. Preston merely nursed the hurt in the privacy of his undercover car.

□ □ □

The team stayed at the Brickell Point Hyatt Regency close to Little Havana where both Roberto and Gustavo lived, and central to the places they had to visit. It also sat on the edge of Miami's financial district, an irony that didn't escape them since Miami's economy, like Bogotá's, floats on coke-dollars. It was important that Sparshott and Macready learn the hotel which would be their undercover home in future buys. Not that they complained to Campbell who usually stayed there when he was in town. Cops are used to cheap motels and Brickell Point was a treat.

Over the next three days, the team made surveillance forays into the unassuming world of Roberto Tabares. They snapped pictures, diagramed streets and houses, ran checks on car license numbers, studied dusty records and deeds, followed Roberto and Gustavo, and learned:

Roberto Tabares owned an impressive two-story, cream-stucco house with a red barrel-tile roof in a swanky area of Little Havana. He parked a new Cadillac Cimarron outside. From the pool in the backyard, you could see the Brickell Point skyline. Two large carved wooden doors graced the entrance and the windows were barred. There were so many drug dealers in the neighborhood that nothing was safe. Roberto had paid $178,000 for the house in September 1986 just after the FBI decided he wasn't big enough to catch. His neighborhood was a grid of quiet interlocking streets. Ideal for surveillance because there were plenty of places to hide. But there were few cars parked on those streets. Bad for surveillance because a strange car would be about as unobtrusive as a tour bus.

Roberto's son-in-law Gustavo lived a ten-minute drive away in a modest white-stucco house with a red tile roof in the working class section of Little Havana. The house, which Roberto had bought for $72,000, sat on a corner lot. Good for surveillance because it would be easy to watch from any direction. But Gustavo and his neighbors parked their cars in driveways and garages. Bad for surveillance because a car sitting on the street would stand out like a snow mobile.

Roberto moored his twenty-six-foot fishing boat, *The Excuse*, in the Miami Beach Marina just across the MacArthur Causeway near Brickell Point. It was a seaworthy, twin-engine Starcraft powerful enough to make drug runs to the Islands and was worth a modest $20,000. Roberto used a friend to front the boat for him. Bobbing in the sea with hundreds of other yachts, sailboats, and fishing craft, it looked quite ordinary—which was the whole point.

The "Tabares Liquor Store" and adjoining nightclub sat on the corner of Flagler Avenue and 48th in Little Havana, a good location. Flagler, which divides Miami north and south, is lined with small shops and businesses. Traffic was heavy. Roberto paid $40,000 for the liquor license which usually ran $100,000 to $150,000. He bought it from a woman who in turn had purchased it for $50,000. Who was kidding whom? Why would she sell it for less than she paid for it? The store, whose shelves and coolers were filled with an estimated $70,000 worth of liquor, was one of a string of businesses in a short city block. On paper, Roberto "leased" the block from private investors, then sublet the stores to other businessmen. Recently, he had begun to pour thousands into remodeling the nightclub which was temporarily closed.

The liquor store-nightclub was a beautiful launderette. Like Las Vegas casinos, it could wash and dry dollars with ease and left few soap stains. All you had to do was stuff your drug profits into the cash register, then tell your accountant to cook the books. The accountant could either overstate revenue or overstate expenses. If revenue—you paid taxes on the income. If expenses—you pocketed the drug money as a business loss.

A quick check with the banks that Roberto listed in public documents turned up three Currency Transaction Reports of cash deposits over $10,000. And Florida corporation records revealed that from the time he took over the cocaine operation from his son Raul, Roberto had owned four import-export companies, none of which ever declared income or paid a penny of tax. Two of the shells were still active.

Two houses, a new Cadillac, a fishing boat, a well-stocked liquor store, a nightclub undergoing a facelift, an entire city block, and a string of shell corporations. All purchased on an average annual income of $5,000. The guy was a fucking financial wizard.

For the Task Force team, the Miami visit did more than just uncover real and possible assets and identify records and witnesses to be subpoenaed later. It welded three egos of iron into a team as Campbell had hoped. Like epoxy, secrets bond. And Sparshott, Campbell, and Macready shared the secrets of Roberto Tabares. They became financial voyeurs who peeked into houses and cars and corporate books and records without getting caught. Each new fact they mined and each financial connection they made drew them closer. And they sensed it.

6. Billy Campbell in Miami

Sparshott, who could smell a fresh watering hole like a camel, found a quaint pub in a Brickell Point alley near the Hyatt. The team spent the nights there washing street and ledger dust from their throats. Then in the wee hours, they weaved their way back to the hotel. In the morning, they met for breakfast at the Hyatt coffee shop which overlooked the Miami River wharf where the U.S. Customs Service moored its Blue Thunder interdict boats. And each morning, Sparshott felt his heart thump when the boats revved up their twin-engines and putted up the waterway into Biscayne Bay and the open sea, hunters on a drug safari. A speed freak, Sparshott had lusted after a ride in one ever since he saw his first Blue Thunder on "Miami Vice." There were only thirteen of them. In rough sea, they could outrun the sleeker cigarette because they were heavier and waves had a harder time lifting them out of the water.

"Jerry, did you hear those Blue Thunders," Sparshott asked

Macready one morning. "I'd love to take a ride."

7. Jerry Macready on the boat

"No problem. I have a friend who pilots one in Lauderdale. I can arrange it."

8. The Blue Thunder arrives

"You get me a ride, brother, and I'll blow you, man."

The friend was Macready's former partner and he told Macready to meet him at the dock in Fort Lauderdale at noon. Campbell didn't like the idea. He'd have to change flight schedules and after all they were supposed to be working. What would he tell the creds? What would he tell his wife? What would . . . Sparshott told him to, hey, loosen up, brother. All work and no play helps the bad guys get away.

It was a fantastic half-hour ride. The little fucker had a rail around it like an amusement park ride and could really fly. It climbed a wave, pointed up like a rocket waiting for the countdown. Then it hit the water with a thud that sent painful shudders down their backs. Real fun, brothers.

9. Jerry didn't have to ask Sparshott twice to take over the helm

The team flew back to Washington on a high. They were closer than ever before. They knew they had Roberto swinging by his financial balls. They were familiar with his Little Havana world. And they looked forward to the half-pound buy from Carlos the following week. All they needed was the $11,000 buy-money Campbell had requested from the creds before he left for Miami.

TWENTY-THREE

Campbell should have known better. The creds began to screw up faster than even he thought possible. First, Baltimore told him that since he didn't have a budget, headquarters would have to give him the $11,000 buy money. Another telex, more fine print, another delay. As long as he was going through all that hassle, Campbell decided he might as well make it worthwhile. He asked for a $50K advance against the $700,000 he had requested over a month ago so that Sparshott could make a second half-pound (or larger) buy without begging. Then he told Sparshott to pick a date, not to worry, the money was as good as in his pocket . . . he hoped. After all it was only $11,000, hardly a dent in the Bureau drug-money budget. Sparshott chose February 6.

Four days before the buy, Campbell asked headquarters where he should pick up the money. It told him that the cash would be wired any day now directly from the Department of the Treasury to the First National Bank of Baltimore. Pick it up there, keep checking. Campbell waited two days, then called First National.

"What money? No one told us."

The same day, the DNRs suddenly turned schizophrenic. Instead of scribbling phone numbers, they printed neat rows of "1s" and "2s" and nothing more. Although the U.S. Attorney needed their records in case Roberto came to town before or during the buy—calls to Carlos would help establish a drug conspiracy case—Campbell couldn't convince FBI technicians in Baltimore to repair them.

"Drive all the way to Hyattsville? You got to be kidding!"

Finally, Campbell put in a request through Tippett who handled all the paperwork to headquarters for Sparshott and Preston to visit the Bureau vault and to sign out whatever jewelry they wanted. He had noted Carlos' keen interest in gold, how he had told Sparshott on the way to Annapolis that he could spot a fake Rolex a foot away, how Sparshott had asked him whether it would have made a difference if he had been wearing a fake the first time they met, and how Carlos had replied poetically, "Fuck, yes, man!" It was clear to Campbell that Carlos was impressed by the little things that go into building a scenario, a homily Sparshott had never stopped preaching.

Headquarters told Campbell that Sparshott and Preston were certainly welcome to help themselves, that's what the stuff was there for, no dollar limit, but that, sorry, all three agents authorized to open the vault were out of town. Gee guys, thanks for nothing.

If all that wasn't discouraging enough, Campbell learned the day before the buy that his request for $50K had *not* gone to Treasury but was still at FBI headquarters waiting for three fucking, pardon the foul language, signatures because $50,000 exceeded the one-signature threshold. But not to worry, headquarters promised that if he agreed to accept just $11,000, which was within the one-signature threshold, he could pick up the money at First National by three the next afternoon. Big choice! Both Campbell and Tippett agreed.

Campbell called the bank the next morning, then again at noon, then again before three. Still no money. Headquarters apologized saying the cash was frozen in the pipe, who knows exactly where, probably at Treasury. But not to worry, these things take time. Campbell then called a team meeting for the morning of the day the buy was supposed to go down.

If Campbell was embarrassed, Sparshott was pissing blood. He had told Carlos the deal would go down on the sixth, exact time and place to be determined. Now his credibility was at stake, not that the creds could ever understand what that means to an undercover. Big words like "credibility" weren't in their vocab. To change the date now would crack the foundation he had laid so carefully at the airpark—Terry Petit's reefer business ran like a Rolex. And during the ride to Annapolis, he had led Carlos by the nose into demanding proof that Terry Petit was for real—put up or shut up time, man, piss or zip up. Now big herb dealer Terry Petit, a guy who sold in five states and used airplanes to fly weed around the country, couldn't even piss eleven big ones. Fuckin' FBI snack food money for chrissakes. Well, however he talked his way out of the delay, and it would have to be a damn good yarn, he ran the risk of looking about as reliable as a snitch.

Tippett was the only team member who took the delay more or less calmly. It was no secret that he thought Sparshott was pushing the undercover investigation too hard and too fast. Eleven thousand dollars was a lot of money and Sparshott was a big pain in the ass. So Tippett suggested they put off the buy indefinitely.

Sparshott exploded like a flash-bang. There was no way he was gonna postpone the buy until some fatass cred finally decided to lift his finger and push the money button. His rep was on the line, he had to prove himself to Carlos, and if Tippett couldn't understand that, he should go back to catching bank robbers.

After the meeting broke up on a sour and cynical note, Sparshott followed Campbell into his office and closed the door. "Shit Billy, how am I going to tell Carlos I can't make the deal?" he complained. "Would it help if I called Roberts?'"

"That should do it," Campbell said.

"Give me the number. Don't worry, I'll take the heat."

U.S. Attorney Tom Roberts had replaced Bob Bonsib on the Tabares case several months earlier when Bonsib moved back to Prince George's County as Deputy State's Attorney. Sparshott knew that if he called Roberts, the prosecutor would waste no time. Word would get back to the Baltimore SAC that someone had gone over his head, SAC would kick Tippett in the ass, and there'd be hell to pay in Hyattsville. Bureaucratic dominos. But Sparshott didn't mind being the fall guy. Better him than Campbell who had to live with Tippett and the rest of the creds.

"What the fuck's going on, Tom? You're in charge of this case." Sparshott wasn't putting on a show as he sometimes did for effect. "We're getting jerked around."

"You're kidding me, Tracy!"

Roberts wasn't playacting either. He had begun his career with Bonsib in Upper Marlboro. A year later, he took a job as Assistant U.S. Attorney in D.C. Ten years and hundreds of drug cases later, he and Bonsib found themselves sharing an office again, this time as Assistant U.S. Attorneys in Baltimore specializing in narcotics. When Bonsib moved on, Roberts was a natural choice to inherit the Tabares case. He was an aggressive and ambitious team player, a big-picture man, and a legal risk taker who immediately saw the potential of the case. He also saw wrinkles on the fabric of the team but sensed they would iron themselves out as the case progressed:

Bill Campbell and Tracy Sparshott were a perfect match. Campbell could manage case details leaving Sparshott free to choreograph his undercover dance. Sparshott was bound to get snarled in red tape but like the cat he was, he'd land on his feet. Marty Preston was the team memory, critical to an ongoing narcotics investigation. He was bound to get hurt, but in the end he'd put the case before himself. If anyone could build a solid net worth/expenditures and money laundering case, rainmaker Jerry Macready could. But Macready was bound to be the first sacrifice on the altar of statistics. And as for Stew Tippett—well Tippett was right off the Bureau assembly line, a play-safe and unimaginative captain-may-I kind of special agent, he and Sparshott were bound to work together like flint and powder.

"They told me they *had* the money," Roberts said, "I thought it was all set."

"They're bullshitting you, Tom," Sparshott continued. "They don't have it and they want me to put the deal off. This whole fucking investigation is going right down the shitter."

"I'll check it out. Sit tight."

Roberts walked down two flights of courthouse stairs to Bill Tucker's office and asked where the money was. Tucker said he hadn't heard there was a problem getting it. As they discussed the eleven thousand—Roberts wasn't exactly whispering and the Task Force hub wasn't exactly designed for privacy—the DEA coordinator walked by. The DEA was an advisor on the Tabares case but so far no one had asked its advice, "I just got my monthly buy-money," he butted in. "There's plenty. I'll give you the eleven thousand, Tom."

"Sure you will," Tucker said before Roberts could shake on it. "Then you'll want the *stat.*"

"Damn right. My money, my stat."

Tucker turned to Roberts. "Let me see what I can do, Tom."

Roberts agreed to wait. He wasn't sure whether the DEA coordinator was bluffing or not, but who cares, whatever works.

He called Campbell back and told him the money was as good as in the bank. Campbell hoped so. He set Tuesday of the following week as the new buy date and asked Sparshott to stall Carlos until then.

Through Stew Tippett who still had police contacts in Richardson, Texas, where he used to be a fucking local, Sparshott arranged a call-forward scam: he'd call Carlos' beeper from the squad room in Rockville and leave a Texas callback number; Carlos would return the call which would be forwarded to the undercover phone in the squad room; Carlos thinks he's talking to Terry in Texas and his phone bill reflects a long distance call.

After he tested the call-forward connection, Sparshott asked Terry Petit's answering service in Frederick to find Carlos Medina and tell him that Terry was in Texas and would try to catch up with him later that day. Then he waited. Washington was digging out of two back-to-back snowstorms, fourteen and ten inches each, followed by a three-inch duster. D.C. Mayor Marion Barry got caught with his plows in the barn and Maryland Governor Donald Schaefer had a state of emergency on his hands. If Sparshott played Texas against the snow, Carlos might just buy the delay:

□ □ □

The undercover phone rings. Sparshott jumps into the booth, closes the glass door, and activates the tape recorder. "Hello?" he says without identifying himself. The call could be for any narc in the room.

"Who's this?" Carlos asks.

"Terry."

"What happened, man? Where you *been*, man?"

"In Texas . . . one of my warehouses up in Garrett County where I got some stuff stored—shit—I don't want to say too much on the phone. Well a roof caved in and it caused a lot of damage, man. I'm tryin' to make good down here on some *very wet* property . . . you know what I'm sayin'?"

"I read you, man."

"Hey, you wouldn't believe all the shit this fuckin' snow is causin' me. Is it melting there yet?"

"Fuck no . . . How long you been in Texas?"

"About two weeks. I'm gonna fly back next week . . . on Tuesday. Can we go ahead and do the thing, you know, what we talked about?"

"No problem." Carlos sounds as if he means it. "Man you are tempting me b-a-a-d with those beers. There's just three left."

"You better save me one, you motherfucker." Sparshott knows Carlos is buying it, he can hear it in his voice, not a hem or a haw of doubt, no skeptical questions, no putting the screws to him. The Panama beer dig tells him that. Why not go for an extra day? The way the FBI is blowing smoke out its ass, he'll probably need it. "I'll call you Tuesday when I get back. I might want to do it then . . . maybe Wednesday."

"Tuesday morning I'm gonna be in school."

"Then I'll call in the evening. I got a lot of wet stuff, you know, man, to check up on."

"The evening's fine, man."

"How you been?"

"Studying like a motherfucker but everything's cool."

"All right buddy, take care."

"Okay Terry."

From the moment Sparshott hung up on Carlos nothing went right. Roberto slipped into town—street sources said with thirteen keys of coke—and back out with a suitcase full of money and there had been no way to speed up the buy from Carlos. Of course, it would have been ideal to do the half-pound buy while Roberto was in town so they could monitor the DNR traffic. But what the fuck, the FBI hadn't gotten around to repairing the DNRs anyway.

Monday came and went without the promised buy-money. Headquarters told Campbell it was on the way, any hour now, everyone had signed off, don't be such a worrywart. Then Tuesday came and went and no money, guaranteed to be at First National first thing Wednesday morning, don't be such a worrywart.

Since Carlos had afternoon classes at George Washington University—it was his second month there—they had to do the deal either Wednesday morning or Wednesday night. They chose eleven o'clock in the morning since it was easier to get FBI backup during the day. It promised to be a close call. Campbell would have to sign out the money at the bank at nine, then pony express it to Washington by eleven.

Sparshott waited until ten o'clock Tuesday night, then called Carlos as he had promised.

"What's up man?" Carlos sounds pleased to hear from him.

"I just got back an hour ago."

"So how *was* everything, you know, down there?"

"I got what I needed."

"That's cool, man."

"How about tomorrow?"

"After I get out of school . . . around seven is fine."

"Can you do it in the morning? How about eleven?"

"Eleven's okay but I gotta be in school by twelve."

"We'll be done by then. Why don't you plan on being in your car at ten and I'll call you. Did you talk to your people? Everything the same?"

"Everything's cool."

"We're gonna do it with two people, right, so the shit's not around me?"

"Yeah."

"You gonna have the same guy as last time 'cause I think Marty remembers him."

"Yeah, I'll have him."

"What's his name so I can tell Marty?"

"Santiago . . . Shit, I'm studyin' like a crazy motherfucker. You wanna go get something to eat when I get out of class tomorrow night?"

"I gotta drive the shit, you know, back home and send it out to some people to test. Some other time."

"No problem." Carlos sounds disappointed which is great for Sparshott's next scenario. "So give me a call."

"See you later . . . "

Fuckin' alligator, thanks for the name of your man, man, thanks for agreeing to sell shit during FBI banking hours, thanks for buying the line that I gotta get out of town so I can have my people test the shit.

Sparshott sensed that Stew Tippett wasn't so happy. The Baltimore SAC had told him how Sparshott had seduced Tom Roberts into the money-game and he seemed as a mad as a cuckolded husband. Hey, *somebody* has to put discipline into this rogue undercover operation. Who better than him? The Tabares case is no longer a game. Real money is at stake for the first time, and a pro has to make damn sure no fucking local loses it.

TWENTY-FOUR

It was almost ten o'clock. Carlos Medina was waiting in his car for Terry Petit's call. Bill Campbell was somewhere between Baltimore and Washington. The rest of the team sagged around a table at the FBI office in Hyattsville. Everyone was edgy. The buy was supposed to go down in an hour, there still wasn't any money, and Tracy Sparshott was fighting the urge to kick the shit out of Stew Tippett.

Tippett had just finished telling the team—or so Sparshott thought—that since he couldn't block the buy which he considered ill-conceived, he was making damn sure hotshit Sparshott didn't lose the Bureau's $11,000. He and six other special agents would back Sparshott and Preston, and an undercover vehicle would be designated as the "crash" car. If Carlos Medina tried to rip and run with the money, the crash car would pin him to the steering wheel before he could reach the street. Remember men, Tippett said like Patton: "Bullets may fly . . . men may die . . . but the money never walks."

Spoken like a true cred.

But Sparshott kept his fists and his thoughts to himself. He had gotten what he wanted—a half-pound buy, on *his* terms, and a buy-plan he hoped would satisfy everyone. So let the asshole blow this time. He'd prove to the creds, especially Tippett, that he knew what he was doing and they had better start trusting his undercover instincts or the whole case would go right down the old shitter.

What was really bothering him was something he'd never tell Tippett. He was beginning to feel the pressure. Hell, the buy was the easy part. Reshaping his image as a reefer dealer who runs a tight operation was the hard part. Keeping the good guys on his side happy was the impossible part. There were just too many fucking creds who wanted to be near the TV cameras in case Roberto Tabares turned out to have sound-bite value. Then they could shout, "Hey, over here! We did this and we did that . . . "

For another thing, Tippett had touched the raw nerve of a deep insecurity that Sparshott managed to hide even from his partner. The Montgomery County Police Department had adopted a rule that only college graduates could be promoted. Sparshott, who frequently blamed himself for not finishing school, thought it was a good regulation but grossly unfair to make it retroactive. Unless he went back to school, he'd always be a corporal no matter how many awards he won or stats he collected. But he couldn't go back to college, even part-time, because he knew his police work would suffer if he did, and he had too much cop-pride for that. So he sat by and watched officers younger and less productive than him step up the ladder, and he nursed the need—he knew it was dumb—to prove himself over and over again as if to say, "Fuck, never judge a cop by his stripes." Tippett was feeding into that secret need by telling him—or so Sparshott thought—that he couldn't be trusted because not only was he an F.L. but only a fucking corporal as well.

The phone finally rang at almost ten on the dot. It was Campbell, he was still in Baltimore, he had the money but didn't think he could make it back to Washington by eleven. Wouldn't it be wiser to push the deal off until that evening?

□ □ □

"Hey Carlos . . . Terry."

Fucking creds, can't they do just one thing right?

"What's up, Terry?"

"I'm havin' problems with my car, man." There's not a hint of piss in Sparshott's voice. "It's been sittin' here for two weeks while I was in . . . you know. I can't get the fuckin' battery goin'."

Carlos thinks it's funny. "Is that supposed to be a *Mercedes* or what?"

"Shit, man, you'd think they'd put a decent battery in the motherfuckers . . . there's no way I can make it down the next hour or two."

"So how long is it gonna take you to get here?"

"I don't know. I'm waitin' for the tow truck now. You gotta be at school at twelve right?"

"Yeah man, I'm gonna have a test."

"So what time do you get out of class?"

"Fuck . . . late man. I get home at six, six-thirty."

"Okay, how about between six-thirty and seven?"

"I don't see a problem. I just wanna make sure it goes real smooth this first time. If you're *not* gonna be here at that time call me, man . . . I gotta, you know, see my friend and give him the letter for you."

The "friend" of course is Santiago and the "letter" is the cocaine. Sparshott plays along. "I called Marty and told him I'm havin' car problems. I said it would probably be around seven when you get out of school . . . hey, wait a minute, buddy, I think the tow truck's here." Sparshott covers the receiver for a long minute—still smoldering at the creds—then gets back on the line. "I thought you and I could meet at the Hilton again. We can sit and chit-chat, and I can call Marty, and you can call your guy, and your guy can show Marty the letter and I can show you the book I bought."

"Okay."

"If you like *my* book and *your* letter looks good, then they can go their separate ways. You and I are both covered."

"Cool . . . call me at six-thirty, I'll be waiting here."

"All right, buddy . . . hey, pass your test."

7:00 P.M.

Sparshott is sitting in the Greenbelt Hilton lot in the

Mercedes which is still wired and he's still pissed . . . at the Bureau, at Tippett, at himself for not punching the jerk out and for being pissed to begin with. What a way to begin a buy.

Sparshott wears a transmitter as well so that Campbell, who holds the receiver in his undercover car parked close to the exit, can hear him. He has a code word to use if he suddenly needs help. The money is in a paper bag on the floor behind the driver's seat. A second FBI car guards the other exit and the crash car is ready to block Carlos if he tries to escape with the loot.

Carlos pulls into the Hilton, which is in PG and makes Preston's bosses happy, in the white Camaro and parks next to Sparshott, driver's window to driver's window. He declines Sparshott's offer to join him in the Mercedes because he's waiting for Santiago, who has the four packages of shit, two ounces per, to call him and say everything looks good.

Sparshott and Carlos make small talk. When Santiago doesn't check in with Carlos after half an hour, both men get suspicious. Carlos thinks that, hey, maybe Terry set him up, maybe Marty and other members of the Terry Petit gang ambushed Santiago, grabbed the shit and ran. For his part, Sparshott figures that either Santiago screwed up and went to the wrong place, or that he didn't like what he saw and drove away without dealing. So Sparshott tells Carlos to go find his man and straighten things out, they can do the buy later that evening. Carlos drives off. The phone rings in the Mercedes.

□ □ □

Five miles up the beltway at Bob's Big Boy, which is in Montgomery County and makes Sparshott's bosses happy, Preston is on the phone in the chief's van parked in the same spot where he and Sparshott met Carlos the first time. Using two locations instead of one calls for more FBI backup and that makes the creds happy.

Preston is almost as miffed as Sparshott but for different reasons. When Tippett had said that morning, "Bullets may fly, men may die, but the money never walks," Preston took it as Bureau humor, which it was, and smiled. Now he doesn't think it's so darn funny. Tippett assigned more men to watch the money at the Hilton than he did to cover him at Bob's and *he's* the one in the most danger. Carlos won't be armed because he has nothing to be ripped off. Santiago will be packing because he's holding the dope. At least the van is wired.

For once, Preston thinks, he and Sparshott are in perfect agreement. The Bureau is treating them like—how would Tracy put it—fucking pieces of shit. But there is no time to argue the point now. He'll just have to be extra careful especially since Tippett is doing it again. He and Macready have the receiver in their red IRS Corvette which is parked too close to the van. Surrounded by Fords and Chevys, the Vette stands out like Lady Godiva in a convent. Preston can't believe Tippett could be so careless. The guy knows Santiago nearly burned him last time, he knows Santiago will make the delivery today, he knows Santiago is a cautious counter. Doesn't he realize that if the dirtball sees him a second time and makes the connection, the whole undercover operation will be over? Why didn't Tippett decide to back Sparshott at the Hilton where Carlos doesn't know him and where Tippett's precious eleven thou is?

"Where's Santiago?" Preston asks Sparshott.

"I don't know. Carlos just went to get him."

As the two undercovers try to figure out what the problem is—confusion, cold feet, setup—Santiago cruises into Bob's in a dark blue Sunbird.

"He's here. He's not in the Camaro."

Preston gives Sparshott a description of the car which he knows Tippett and Macready will hear and radio to the other back-ups, then hangs up. Although he's anxious to do the buy and get the hell out of there, Preston is relieved in a superstitious sort of way that Santiago is late. When a buy goes down too smoothly, he gets nervous waiting for the screwup that is bound to happen. And he worries that the screwup may be hot and wrapped in lead. Of course, Santiago is armed. Of course, Preston's not wearing a vest.

Yes, it's a comfort to have his gun tucked between the seat cushions behind him. But if draw comes to shoot, Santiago can reach his gun faster, and it's much easier to hit a target trapped in a parked van than a bobbing and weaving one outside. He knows he shouldn't worry, the money is well protected and everyone knows "the money never walks."

Santiago drives around the lot slowly just like he did the first time, then parks and gets out. He stands next to his Sunbird and inspects the lot just like he did the first time.

Preston gets a good look at him—mid-twenties, around six-one and 170 pounds, dark wavy hair and a mustache. He's wearing a black leather jacket and jeans with white tennis shoes.

Santiago sees Macready and Tippett, walks over to the Vette, and looks in just like he did the first time. They make like they are boyfriends caught in a lover's quarrel. Suspicious, he enters the restaurant and calls Carlos on the pay phone in the foyer just like he did before the first buy. Thank you, special agent Stevie Wonder.

□ □ □

Carlos drives back into the Hilton lot, pulls up next to Sparshott and says: "My guy's at Bob's but he doesn't like what the fuck he sees. Two guys sitting in a Vette. What the fuck's goin' on?"

All Sparshott can think of is Stew "Bullets Will Fly" Tippett. He quickly flashes the money—three packages of used bills, all denominations, new hundreds would look hokey—to take Carlos' mind off a rip-and-run and back to a sale. "If it's a ripoff, man," Sparshott says, "why the fuck would I bring the money? Let me call Marty and see what's goin' on."

Sparshott dials the van. "Hey Marty, buddy . . . Carlos said his man saw two guys sitting over there in a fuckin' Vette. His man doesn't like it, Here—talk to Carlos." Sparshott hands his car phone to Carlos with a silent "good luck, brother."

Preston gets the drift. "Hey Carlos . . . Marty . . . don't

worry about those guys. I saw 'em eating inside and they just came out."

Tippett and Macready hear Marty's end of the conversation over the wire loud and clear. They start the Vette and drive away like two guys who are in no special hurry. Santiago watches them turn left and head for New Hampshire Avenue. Then he walks over to the van wearing a stone face.

Preston is still giving Carlos a play-by-play on the phone when Santiago reaches the van. "Here's Santiago," he tells Carlos, "you can find out from him." He hands the receiver to Santiago who says a few words in Spanish which Preston can't understand. Preston tries to read the guy's face but can't figure out whether Santiago recognized Tippett or bought the "just finished eating" line.

Santiago returns the phone without a word, then walks back to his car, gets in, and points it toward the exit. Preston's heart sinks. Tippett blew it for good this time. But instead of driving out of the parking lot and into the street, Santiago pulls up next to the van and gets out. Carlos told him everything was cool, not because it was, but because he desperately *wanted* to believe Terry and in a strange way was too scared to back out of the deal. Santiago opens the door on the passenger side without a word and steps inside.

Santiago unzips his leather jacket slowly so as not to alarm Marty and pulls out a brown envelope. He isn't armed but Preston doesn't know that. Preston tears the envelope open. Inside are four plastic bags of rock cakes. He rubs a little White from one between his thumb and index finger. It's oily, about seventy percent pure he should think, good enough. Then he dips a key into the package, puts it to his nose, and fakes a snort. He picks up the receiver which he never hung up and says:

"It looks good. Go ahead and give him the money."

Back in the Hilton parking lot, Sparshott hands Carlos the three packets of cash which Carlos fingers quickly like a deck of cards without attempting a dollar-count.

"Gimme the phone," Carlos tells Sparshott. "I want to talk to my man."

"Marty, give the guy the phone," Sparshott orders.

Preston doesn't know what's going on at this point. Tippett is exactly where he's supposed to be—nowhere in sight, bye, bye backup. Preston knows the code word for a ripoff but Sparshott doesn't use it. His voice sounds relaxed, no urgency, no panic—like Carlos has a gun in my ribs. Assuming everything is good on Sparshott's end, he gives the receiver to Santiago who says a few more words in Spanish with a still expressionless face. Preston doesn't hear anger or fear in his voice and the guy doesn't reach for a gun.

"Everything okay?" Marty asks Sparshott when Santiago returns the phone.

"Everything's cool."

"Then I'm outta here, man!"

Santiago slips out of the van as fluidly as a gymnast, looks around the lot to make sure no one is about to attack or arrest him. Preston doesn't wait for him to drive off. He pulls out of the lot quite pleased with the way two fucking locals pulled it off once again. The wrinkles on the buy made it seem as real as life, not planned, staged, and rehearsed, and if Carlos is as smart as Preston knows he is, he will see it that way too.

Like Preston, Carlos doesn't waste any time. He tucks the three packets of money inside his coat and drives away. It's seven-thirty. All over in half an hour. Short, sweet, convincing. Bullets didn't fly and men didn't die.

This time.

TWENTY-FIVE

As far as Bill Campbell was concerned, the team was on a roll. True, he still didn't have any money, Preston didn't have his undercover Mercedes, and the u.c. wallet stuffers the creds finally produced, without the criminal record Sparshott and Preston had requested, were such dime store quality they were useless. But the half-pound buy was beautiful in spite of the goof which Tippett shrugged off—why all the excitement, I knew the guy would never make me, a different car and two people this time. And he was right. Although Santiago was suspicious at the time, he didn't recognize Tippett. After the buy went down as nicely as a good toot, Carlos was convinced the two guys in the Vette weren't narcs or they would have arrested him and Santiago on the spot. Fuck, no way the feds would let $11,000 walk, the cheap sonofabitches. So Carlos accused Santiago of snorting so much to settle his nerves that he became paranoid. Hey, fucking shit makes a narc out of a molehill. Even the creds seemed pleased with the buy. The coke turned out to be sixty-eight percent pure cocaine hydrochloride, good enough to be acceptable but adulterated enough to give Sparshott room to negotiate price. Scooter came up with a new confidential source. Headquarters let Sparshott and Preston into the vault. A judge signed the wiretap order. And Campbell finally found a nice undercover house in Frederick. Hey, who says no one loves good guys?

The confidential informant came to Scooter hell-bent on revenge. IT had been in the Presidential Towers apartment of Roberto's friend, Saulo Hernandez, and had seen fifty to a hundred keys of coke stacked on the floor like wax-wrapped blocks of cheddar cheese. IT had also seen Roberto in the apartment with the dope and confirmed what the team had long suspected—Roberto and Saulo ran separate but co-dependent operations and were supplied by the same Miami source. IT told Campbell that Hernandez had moved back to Miami and left Washington distribution in the hands of two Cuban associates and a guy called Frank—you guessed it—Jones.

The basement vault at FBI headquarters was a candy store of bad guy goodies. Racks of cocktail dresses, expensive leather jackets, and furs seized in raids. Drawers of jewelry lined up and labeled like safety deposit boxes—watches, rings, chokers and chains, earrings, necklaces, bracelets. Sparshott signed out $30,000 worth of jewelry—a heavy gold necklace, a diamond ring, and a gold ring with a ruby in a platinum setting shaped like the state of Texas which he would use to support the Texas part of his cover story. Preston selected a Rolex, a diamond ring for his middle finger, a gold nugget pinkie ring, and a necklace with a scuba diver on a gold medallion which he would use to support his interest in scuba diving. During conversations about the planned trip to Florida to meet the Cuban, Preston had told Carlos he was crazy about the sport.

When it finally landed on the bench, the wiretap affidavit was a smash hit. It took the judge only two days to read it and sign the court order. It had taken the legal creds more than two months to tear it apart and paste it back together. But hey, there was no time to look backwards. The bug was already in place and a team of FBI agents in the listening post was monitoring calls to and from Roberto's phones sixteen hours a day in two eight-hour shifts. They left the recorder running but unattended from midnight to eight. Campbell had managed to steal one of the Bureau's best translators, someone who knew the drug trade and could understand what the bad guys were *really* saying. Wiretap cases could stand or fall on delicate shades of meaning. Campbell didn't know whether the tap would produce any important evidence or any new leads, but he felt certain that Carlos would eventually talk to Roberto on the phone about Terry and Marty. Almost everything he said about them would help guide and protect them. Furthermore, the Title Three court order (legalese for wiretap) gave the Tabares case a bureaucratic legitimacy it didn't have before. Campbell could hear the creds thinking, "Golly, if the court gave us permission to eavesdrop on Tabares, then Tabares *must* be important. What the hell, any way you cut it, Title Three spelled men and money—the full $700,000 budget he had asked for two months ago, Campbell hoped.

The undercover townhouse Campbell found in Frederick, and none too soon, was no afterthought. From the first meeting at Bob's Big Boy, Carlos seemed intensely curious about where and how Terry lived. Sparshott had fanned that interest to lava red. First, he told Carlos that he lived in western Maryland, then he casually dropped the name "Hagerstown" which sat near the Pennsylvania and West Virginia borders over two hours from Washington. The city was far enough away to discourage Carlos from making a surveillance trip there on his own, and it gave Sparshott that all-important excuse, "Hey man, it's gonna take me a couple hours to drive down there."

But Sparshott didn't want an undercover house in Hagerstown itself because it was too far away to be useful. The only possible places along Highway 270 between Hagerstown and Washington for the next two scenarios he was planning were Gaithersburg and Frederick. Gaithersburg, the home of the Montgomery Airpark, was too close. Frederick was ideal. So Sparshott prepared Carlos for the undercover house by saying he sometimes stayed in Frederick when he had, you know, business in the area and that he had an answering service there.

To find a furnished house in the historic town wasn't as easy as it sounded. Just over an hour's drive from Washington, "for rent" signs are the exception not the rule. The city had bivouacked soldiers during the Revolutionary War, provisioned the covered wagons that headed west over the Blue Ridge after independence, and tended Union soldiers wounded during the bloody Civil War battles of Antietam and Monocacy. Francis Scott Key composed the national anthem there, and Barbara Fritchie, immortalized by John Greenleaf Whittier, waved the Union flag from her attic window at Stonewall Jackson as he pranced by: "'Shoot if you must, this old gray head, but spare your country's flag,' she said." The city had done a careful job restoring historic mansions, churches, parks and townhouses along Market Street, and Sparshott knew that Carlos, who liked class, would be impressed with the gaslights and bricked streets of Old Town. What better place for an undercover drug house than quiet, charming Frederick with its "Oh say can you see" and "Shoot if you must, this old gray head." Hey, just a little narc irony.

The FBI had a one-man resident agency in Frederick so Campbell asked the agent in charge to help him find a suitable place at a reasonable price. The agent eventually pointed out an old, shuttered brick townhouse covered with ivy just off historic Bentz Street and across from a city park—great cover for a drug dealer. There was plenty of parking out front—ideal for surveillance. An old carriage house in an alley behind the house served as a garage—nice for off-loading and storing marijuana. There was an alley entrance with a brick walkway—ideal for sneaking off-loaders in and out. And an added touch of reality to the cover—real dope dealers lived next door and no one knew it.

One look at the old townhouse and Sparshott knew exactly what he'd tell Carlos: "Hey man, my grandmother just died and left it to me. It's great. The neighbors know me and it looks like any old fuckin' place."

Fortunately, the budget came through before Campbell signed the lease on the house. Unfortunately, it was only for the $50,000 he and Tippett had requested before the half-pound buy, not the full $700,000. They weren't surprised. Competition for Task Force dollars was fierce, and Baltimore wasn't Miami or New York or Detroit.

Although the $50K wasn't much, it gave Campbell a taste of undercover independence. Not that renting a u.c. house was easy for an FBI agent. If he leased it in the name of the FBI, Campbell would need Bureau approval which would take up to three months. He didn't have three months. He didn't even have three weeks. Sparshott was hot and Carlos was ripe. If he leased it in the name of the undercover character "Terry Petit," he would have to tell the real estate agent the truth. For legal reasons—who would be liable for damages if there was a shootout in the townhouse? And for practical reasons—given his slim budget, Campbell would have to rent on a month-by-month basis which no real estate agent would agree to for an ordinary renter. And what would happen if the real estate company did a credit or employment check on Terry Petit and found out he didn't exist?

Campbell compromised. He flashed his creds and made the real estate agent swear on a stack of leases that he wouldn't tell anyone that the FBI was using the townhouse for an undercover operation. It was a prudent risk. Sparshott only needed the house for a month, maybe less, and he had promised on his shield that when he and Preston were finished driving Carlos around Frederick, Carlos would never be able to find the place again even with a map. In the end, the real estate agent was pleased to help out, anything to keep Frederick drug-free.

The "furnished" townhouse had a couple of beds, chairs, tables, and an old Victorian sofa. To make it look more lived in, Campbell cleaned out his closets and basement—blender, toaster oven, sugar and coffee jars, glasses and cutlery, TV snack tables, eggbeater, framed pictures. He raided the kitchen—cereal, mustard, catsup, cans of soup and vegetables, empty soda bottles, potholders and sponges. He visited the linen closet—sheets and towels, soap and toilet paper, extra shower curtain. Then he borrowed a few books and a couple of plants from the living room.

Campbell's wife Penny came home while he was loading the car. As a Bureau wife, she was used to secret plots, unpredictable hours, and cop and robber games, and she resented the stranglehold the Bureau had on her family. To steal her husband was one thing. But her housewares? No way was she going to turn into a Goodwill store because the Bureau was too cheap to give her husband a respectable operating budget! The nerve of those, those—creds!

But when Bill explained that he and Sparshott were setting up a beautiful sting, she jumped right into the spirit of the game.

She liked Tracy and had to admit there was a vicarious pleasure in watching him and Bill con the bad guys just like Newman and Redford. "Now make sure it looks like a *home*," she advised her husband. "And put the silverware drawer near the dishwasher or the sink. Take the lawn mower. And don't forget to . . . "

Meanwhile, Sparshott asked a neighbor for an assist. He was building his new home just outside Damascus—straight north on New Hampshire past Bob's Big Boy, past the last country store and gas station, through wooded estates and farms, down a logging road, past the mill, and into a five-acre patch of oaks. Every chance he could, he'd drive out to the building site to check progress and pound some nails, then stop by Wills General Store in Damascus for a cup of coffee or a sandwich. Over the months, he got to know the owner Bob Wills pretty well. He remembered that Wills said his father had opened a new restaurant in Old Town Frederick.

"Look, I'm working this undercover bit," he told Wills one day over a giant ham and cheese on rye. "I want to really impress a guy and I need someone to treat him like a king and treat me like a brother. So I'm going to take the guy to dinner. It has to be a cozy, friendly restaurant, a special table, and a great meal . . . appetizers . . . wine . . . the works. The guy's a drug dealer but it won't be dangerous. We'll have undercover agents inside and out. Can you and your father help me out?"

Bob Wills and his father loved the idea. Why not? A chance to help your country, become a footnote in local undercover history, create a story to tell the grandkids, and fill the till all at the same time.

There was still a lot to do at the townhouse to make it look like Terry's hangout. Of course, Sparshott had wanted Campbell to furnish the place with wall-to-wall flash—Carlos would be impressed—but he was happy just to have the fucking house and would make do. Hey, sometimes you gotta fight the war on drugs with mirrors and smoke.

Sparshott got a load of Harley shit from a friend—posters and pictures for the bedroom and extra leather for the closet—then arranged for mail to be sent to the house in the name of Terry Petit. He spread a few *Penthouses* around—the dope dealers girlie magazine of choice, more pussy for the dollar than *Playboy*—and the night before the dinner, he invited four Montgomery County narcs up to the house for pizza and beer on the Bureau. Enjoy brothers, the feds don't spring often. If he couldn't make grandma's place look like a drug dealer's house, then he'd make it look like a drug dealer's den, you know, like the mountain hideout of the Hole in the Wall Gang, B-movie stuff. They drank and ate, smoked and played poker, and listened to rock on the beautiful stereo Campbell rented—just for two days, of course. No need to be extravagant!

But in spite of all the dishes and towels, odds and ends that Campbell (Macready made a trip too) had carted to Frederick, the old house still had a bare Mother Hubbard look. If Terry's grandmother had lived there, she certainly would have accumulated more than a few sticks of furniture. On a hunch, Sparshott crept up the narrow stairs to the attic, picked the lock, peeked inside, then called Campbell. "Billy, get your ass on up here." He was as excited as a bargain hunter at a flea market. "You won't believe this. You *will not fuckin' believe this.* The attic is loaded with shit."

Sparshott, Campbell, and the narcs redecorated the house that night. Rugs, lamps with old fashioned fringed shades, stuffed chairs, end tables. They even found the pictures that matched the dust marks on the wallpaper. It was like putting together an old puzzle and, after a few cases of beer, it was fun. They left the place a casual mess that night. Cigarette stubs in ashtrays. Empty beer cans leaving rings on tabletops—grandma would moan in her grave—pizza slices and crusts still in their boxes, potato chips in bowls, and torn Dorito bags with salty crumbs on the kitchen counter. The Hole in the Wall Gang couldn't have done a better job. It was time to bait the hook:

□ □ □

"What's up man?" Sparshott asks Carlos on the phone.

"Nothing much, man. Just studying. Another fucking test tomorrow . . . So how'd everything work out with the—you know?"

"Everything was real good, man. Listen, I was thinkin' about getting together for dinner tonight."

"That's cool."

"Up at my place. It's a bit of a drive but I want you to see it and get to know where it is."

Sparshott gives Carlos directions: the beltway to Highway 270 north—just as if you were goin' to the airpark—but keep headin' north until you see the exit to Frederick—about an hour up 270—there's a brand new Sheraton there, you can see it from the highway. Get off.

"Me or Marty will meet you in the hotel parking lot."

"Okay, man."

"So how's business with you?"

"Better than *ever*, man . . . We gotta talk."

"Great . . . You sure you're not gonna be tied up?"

"No, no, no, no, man." Carlos gulps the bait.

"All right buddy."

"Okay Terry."

TWENTY-SIX

8:30 P.M.

"He's here. I see him!"

Carlos is a half hour late and everyone is relieved the curtain is finally up and the show ready to begin. Bill Campbell in an undercover car parked down the street from the restaurant. Bob Wills, Jerry Macready and Kathy Day, an IRS criminal investigator, inside the restaurant. Two more IRS investigators in the Red Horse nightclub. Tracy Sparshott in the undercover house. And Marty Preston on the radio in the chief's van sitting in the parking lot of the Frederick Sheraton Hotel.

"He's in the lot . . . he's parking . . . he's getting out!"

Carlos rushes over to the van like a man late for dinner and climbs in. "Sorry Marty . . . fucking transmission man. Shit, the thing's all fucked up. I'm lucky I got here."

"No problem . . . Terry had a little business to take care of first," Preston says as he drives out of the parking lot. "He's running late himself. We'll meet him up at the house."

Preston turns right and begins the zig-zag through town he rehearsed earlier in the day so Carlos couldn't possibly find the undercover house again. The drive takes twice as long but, hey, it pays to be cautious. When they reach the house, Preston drives by, then turns left into the alley. No lights or movement, no noise—Carlos seems a little scared which is perfect, a drug smuggler's paradise. Preston parks in front of the garage, then leads Carlos inside through the back door.

As planned, Sparshott is in the bedroom dressing for dinner so he'll have an excuse to invite Carlos inside and let him "discover" his Harley shit. Preston heads straight for the refrigerator as if he owns the place, grabs three beers, then leads Carlos into the living room where the rented stereo is playing. The place looks as if the Terry Petit gang just rode through.

Preston opens the beers, hands one to Carlos, and tells him to make himself at home while he checks on Terry. All planned to give Carlos an excuse to snoop. They hope he checks the mail addressed to Terry Petit sitting on the table by the telephone.

Sparshott sticks his head out of the bedroom. "Hey man, come on back while I finish dressing," he says. Preston takes a few big gulps of beer then excuses himself. "I'll meet you guys at the restaurant . . . business."

The IRS Mercedes is a two-seater and Preston wants to make sure that Carlos rides with Sparshott since the Mercedes is wired and the van isn't. Tom Roberts has a thing for transcripts.

Sparshott slips into a dinner jacket while Carlos admires the badass biker decor and the leather hanging behind the open closet door. He watches Carlos' face and listens to his voice for hints of skepticism or doubt. Carlos seems to be buying the cover. Sparshott swills his beer, then ushers Carlos out the back door and into the alley. No use overacting.

The whole visit takes less than five minutes as planned. But every minute is an hour during which Carlos can spot something the team missed, or catch Sparshott and Preston making a slip, or start asking himself the wrong questions. All they want is for Carlos to make grandma's house real in his mind, to believe that Terry lives there sometimes and Marty is at home there, and to conclude that they aren't trying to hide anything.

"My grandmother would toss in her grave if she knew what I'm usin' her place for," Sparshott says on the way to dinner. Carlos laughs. He seems relaxed now that the house holds no mystery and he's ready to have a good time. All Sparshott and Preston have to do is let Bob Wills, good food, alcohol, and friendship spin their magic.

Like Preston, Sparshott takes a devilishly devious route to the restaurant, the Bull on the Mark, one of a dozen restored townhouse cafes and bars on North Market Street. He's wearing a tiny transmitter sewn into his dinner jacket (Campbell has the receiver) and a battery-powered recorder in a harness under his arm. No one expects Carlos to demand a body search. After all, it's only a social evening with drug-dealing friends.

Sparshott parks in the spot Wills reserved for him in front of the restaurant which occupies the ground floor of the rowhouse. Above the restaurant is an apartment with a private entrance. He leads Carlos inside through double doors of wood and frosted glass etched with the words, "Bull on the Mark."

It's a small place. Besides the dining room which takes up most of the downstairs, there's a little bar to the left where Macready and Day are playing boyfriend-girlfriend so unobtrusively that even Wills doesn't know they're undercover agents. As soon as Wills seats Sparshott and Carlos, they'll move to a table in the dining room where they can hear without being seen.

"Hey, Terry!" Wills beams as if the guy were the mayor of Frederick. "Good to see you."

"Hi Bob, what's goin' on brother?" He turns to Medina. "Bob, this is a friend of mine . . . Carlos."

"Nice to meet you, Carlos."

Handshakes all around.

"I got your favorite table, Terry. So how you been?"

"Good, brother, good."

"Didn't you tell me you were headin' down to Texas?"

"I just got back. How's dad?"

"Doin' fine. He picked a nice wine for us."

"Super . . . thanks for the parking place. I mean I pulled my car right up front."

"Anything for a friend, Terry." Wills is having a great time.

"You heard about my grandmother?"

"Oh yeah, I'm sorry, man."

"It happens. She really liked you a lot, Bob."

Wills leads them to Terry's "favorite" table which sits in a raised alcove like a private dining room, cozy and intimate. Just the right touch, brother Wills.

"Fuck man," Sparshott says to Carlos, "I didn't think you'd ever make it tonight!"

"Shit, don't *tell* me, man!"

Then to Wills: "Now don't get me wrong, Bob. Carlos knows how to drive but his fuckin' car broke down on the way over."

Everyone laughs. Good friends having a good time. "If you need anything, Terry," Wills says, "you just let me know. Your waiter's name is Donnie. I'll check in on you later."

As Wills leaves for the kitchen, Donnie arrives with a tray of stuffed mushrooms. Wills told him earlier that evening that three special guests were coming for dinner and that he wanted Donnie to serve them. "Do it perfectly, treat them like kings, and there's a big tip in it for you." Of course, Wills didn't tell Donnie that Terry and Marty were really cops and Carlos was a drug dealer.

Donnie sets the hors d'oeuvres on the table. "Good evening, gentlemen, will these be okay for you?"

Sparshott tastes one. "Excellent, Donnie, thank you."

"Then I'll be with you shortly."

Carlos is so damned impressed he can hardly express himself. "I tell you, Terry, you make my day . . . fuck . . . you make my whole year, man!"

Sparshott spots Preston walking through the front door. He's dressed like he's on his way to off-load a ton of grass. "Here comes Marty," Sparshott says. "Look at the guy, will ya? What a bum! I can't take him anywhere."

Carlos' eyes light up he's so happy to see Marty. Then he looks at Terry with his long hair and beard and badass biker shit and laughs. Look who's calling who a bum!

As Preston sits down, sensing he was just the butt of a Sparshott joke, Wills returns with a bottle of Pouilly-Fuisse. He shows the label to Sparshott who nods his approval, then pours each guest a glass. "One of my father's favorites," he says. Carlos is beginning to feel special.

Before Preston can even bite into a stuffed mushroom or taste the wine, Sparshott says he can't remember if he turned the Mercedes headlights off. "Go check, will you, Marty?"

Preston simmers. Hell no, man. What am I now, your valet? First you poke fun of me behind my back, then you neglect to tell me that Bob is a prop you obviously rehearsed. There's no excuse for that, heck, I could have made a dumb mistake. Now you're treating me like a piece of crap in front of Carlos. I thought we were partners?

But Preston doesn't show how miffed he is. Instead, he calls Donnie over to the table and asks him to please check the car lights, then quickly changes the conversation. "Hey Carlos, did you see Terry's Texas ring?" Carlos fingers the platinum and gold piece with a red ruby, sucks in his breath and says:

"I can't believe this guy, Marty! Is Texas *that* good to you, Terry? Hey man, did I ever show you the ring the Cuban gave me ? I bought it for him in Panama but he was so mad when he saw it, he gave it right back and told me to sell it. No way, man."

Thanks for the Roberto opening, Carlos baby, even if the ring bit is a crock of shit. During one of his first wiretapped conversations, Roberto had told a caller looking to score some coke that *Carlos* was his partner now and that Carlos was handling day-to-day business. Sparshott probes the new Roberto-Carlos relationship:

"Hey man, you told me the Cuban's got two guys bigger than you—and yet he's dealin' with *you.* Why the fuck would he do that? You blowin' him or what, man?"

Carlos laughs. He's enjoying the friendly banter and Terry's way with words. "Listen to that guy, Marty . . . Fuck no, man . . . He trusts me more—and I'll tell you why!"

Donnie returns with a pewter platter piled high with grilled Maryland crab cakes, lobster and shrimp, oysters and scallops, and fresh sole. He tells Preston not to worry, the Mercedes lights were off, then asks what kind of salad dressing they want and how they prefer their tenderloins.

After Donnie leaves, Carlos goes on to tell Sparshott and

Preston how he bought two keys of coke from the Cuban and paid in cash. The Cuban took the money back to Miami and gave it to his own supplier without bothering to count it. The Cuban called a few days later to complain that Carlos had been $7,500 light. Carlos told Roberto he was positive he had paid the full amount but that because he wanted everything to be smooth between them he would make up the difference from his own pocket. The Cuban seemed satisfied but not terribly happy. Either Carlos was a crook or a lousy businessman. Then later that same day, the Cuban called back to apologize. It seems his supplier had miscounted Carlos' money. It was all there after all.

"From that day on," Carlos says with pride, "the Cuban trusted me completely."

If true, the story could be the key to Carlos' relationship to Roberto. A critical piece of the puzzle. But there's no time to sort out the truth now, Bob's father is heading for Terry's table. Of course, Sparshott rehearsed "Dad" ahead of time which Preston easily figures out to his continuing chagrin. Sparshott says:

"Hi Dad! How you doin? Carlos . . . this is Bob's father—he runs the show. This is Carlos. And this is Marty."

"Where you been Terry?"

"Just got back from Texas, Dad. You heard about my grandmother passin' away?"

"I'm sorry, Terry . . . But it's *good* to see you again. Enjoy your dinner and behave yourselves now!"

"Okay, Dad, see you later on in the week."

Sparshott is convinced that Act Two is playing as well as Act One in the undercover house. Carlos is so hungry for family, he's lapping up the shit faster than anyone can serve it—the royal treatment Terry is getting, how Bob and Dad know and like Terry so much, the feeling of genuine warmth and friendship.

It's now time to play hardball. Sparshott begins by needling Carlos about his tired Camaro knowing it will lead straight to Porsche-talk:

"It's a long walk home baby. If I didn't know your shit is good, I wouldn't believe a fuckin' thing you've told me. How come you're such a big shot and still so fuckin' poor?"

Carlos is embarrassed at the junk heap he drives. It makes him look like a petty dealer, a bruise to his ego, when he wants Terry to think of him as an important newcomer in the trade, someone worth knowing and dealing with. He grins slyly, like he knows something Terry doesn't. The wine is working. He glows and says: "Because I like to be that way, man . . . When I retire—*then* I'm gonna be rich."

"That's smart, man."

"Next week this guy sees me, Marty, I'll have a Porsche and then he won't have shit to tell me."

Carlos explains that he found an '84 Porsche 944 he likes and is going to pick it up on Thursday. Sparshott and Preston bait him—sure you are, buddy, we heard that one before. When Carlos insists he's serious, Preston bets him a bottle of Dom Perignon he's just blowing hot air. Carlos rubs his hands together. He's having the time of his life. That's what American friends do, don't they? Jab, challenge, bet. Carlos takes the wager and shakes on it . . . U.S. Marshals here we come.

"Hey, Carlos, you got enough money to pay for it?"

Sparshott wants to give the kid a chance to brag a little, drug dealers are so vain. Carlos bites. He seems hurt that Terry is not taking him seriously yet. He's got plenty of money, he says. His cousin hides some of it for him. The rest he launders in Panama where Terry should be washing his bundle. Sparshott makes a note to check this "cousin" out so they can do a search and seizure later, then pushes Carlos even farther:

"If you got so fuckin' much money, why don't ya buy a *new* Porsche?" Hey man, more to seize.

Carlos gets defensive once again—afraid Terry thinks he's a cheap sonofabitch. He explains that he's buying a used car because he doesn't want to draw attention to himself—you know how those fucking narcs are, man, they see a new car and right away think drug dealer. Besides:

"You think a car shows everything? Well you're wrong, man! You know what the Cuban guy drives up here? A fucking

Renault Alliance. Yeah . . . go ahead and laugh. That's what he drives, man."

"Maybe he likes it."

"That motherfucker's got money coming out of his fuckin' ears, man . . . You know what? The car isn't even *his*, man. A guy owes him money and he just took the motherfucker."

"So if I meet your man I gotta run in a Renault?"

"A cab will be fine, man!"

Now they know where Roberto got the little beige car. Have to remember to check it out, see who used to own it, might be a good lead. Sparshott drops the car shit and lets Carlos steer the conversation to business.

It's understood that Terry's next buy will be for one kilo as Carlos suggested during the ride back from Annapolis to the Greenbelt Hilton. But they haven't agreed on price yet. Sparshott gave Carlos what he wanted for the half-ounce and the half-pound without a whimper of complaint. This time, he intends to drive a hard bargain. If he doesn't, Carlos might conclude that he's inexperienced or too eager. After all, haggling and dealing are two sides of the same drug coin. And the transcripts will make good courtroom reading.

Carlos announces that his single-key price is $32 thou, down from the $38 thou he suggested during lunch at the airpark but still high for Washington. He quickly adds that the multi-key price is lower.

On his way back to Washington from Panama after Christmas, Carlos had complained to Roberto that $36 thou per key was way above the going rate in Washington. Hey man, thank you, Terry. After a lot of arguing and moaning about overhead and shit, Roberto agreed to lower his price to $26 thou, especially since his friend Saulo Hernandez who helped him get a toehold in the Washington market was now trying to steal Carlos' new customers by underselling him.

Sparshott insists on the multi-key discount for the single kilo and says that his best price is $20 thou—ridiculously low. Carlos holds firm. Sparshott won't budge either:

"I'll fight you tooth and nail, man . . . thirty-two is bullshit . . . it sucks and you know it. It hurts me when you try to pull that on me!"

"Terry, Terry, you *know* what you're payin' for, man!"

"Yeah, sure, I'm supposed to be payin' for trust! . . . Well, that's bullshit too. Tell me, aren't your shoulders tired from liftin' it?"

"Hey, man, be cool . . . we'll work it out."

"All right then—I'll tell you what, Carlos. I'll pay *your* price if you drive the shit right up here and then deliver it for me."

Carlos laughs. "Where and when, man?"

"Seriously—everything went fine last time. Now I got people in *Texas* who want the shit. But I'm not gonna ask you to deliver it there—or here. So what about Miami? We said we're gonna do something there. What's the price in *Miami* gonna be? And don't tell me thirty-two!"

"Why are you so worried about business in Texas? You can do better right here."

Carlos eels around the question which tells Sparshott and Preston that either Carlos doesn't know Roberto's price or he has no authority to negotiate for Roberto. All he can do is make an introduction and take a commission, vesting the Tabares meeting with an even greater importance. Carlos continues:

"People pay outrageous prices here, Terry, and—"

"Well, I ain't gonna be one of them."

"You don't know what you're—okay man—thirty."

Sparshott feigns anger and shouts to Wills, "Hey Bob, bring me a phone will ya?" Then to Carlos, "No way Jose. You call your man right *now*, baby. Thirty's bullshit too!"

"Then buy more!"

"I'm gonna, I'm gonna, but you're the big man now, so talk to me."

"You want me to play big man? Well, it doesn't mean that I'm big man *now*." Carlos covers his ass as fast as he can. He's made a deal with Roberto that he, Roberto, will handle any sale over one kilo for the time being.

Sparshott pushes: "Hey, hey, wait a minute, pal! You sayin' you didn't get this big promotion yet?"

"Yeah, I got the promotion but I gotta wait . . . What a country, man. You know I love this country, I'm tellin' you!"

Carlos' evasiveness only confirms what Sparshott already concluded: the kid's still on trial. What better way to prove himself to Roberto than to deliver Terry Petit like whitefish on a pewter platter. Sparshott says:

"Well I ain't hurryin' you man—cuz you drive that piece of shit around. You're just lucky you made it here, you know that, motherfucker?"

No use pressing Carlos any harder for the moment. Terry already made his point—he's a tough badass businessman—and he doesn't want to spoil the dinner atmosphere. The evening is still young.

"I'm having fun, having *fun*, man," Carlos says. "You know like . . . I *like* you guys."

"Well I guess *so* . . . I'm buyin'!"

The problem is, Sparshott likes Carlos too, and so does Preston. And there are times in the course of the evening as they joke and josh over wine and food that Sparshott forgets he's a cop and that Carlos is a dope dealer who's fucking up hundreds of heads with shit. If Carlos weren't a bad guy, Sparshott would enjoy treating the kid to a beer at the Fraternal Order of Police club after a hard day chasing crooks. He knows that locking up Carlos is going to hurt someday but that's what he's paid to do, put crooks in jail. Hey, it's like making love to your leading lady. Just because you're acting doesn't mean you can't get a hard-on or actually fall in love with her.

Sparshott is planning a surprise for Carlos as the final scenario before meeting Roberto. He and Marty set the guy up for the scam while Donnie serves them tenderloins and a special red Dad selected for his good friends. Sparshott says:

"I'm gonna let you take a ride with me next week, Carlos."

"Okay, man."

"Marty's gonna hold a gun to your head."

"Cocked!"

"Yeah, and if you're lucky, we won't hit any bumps on the way."

Carlos takes Terry and Marty seriously and doesn't seem eager to take the ride. He doesn't pack and he's afraid of guns. But he manages to peep an unenthusiastic, "Okay, man."

"Hey, we're only joking man," Terry says.

"Come on, only joking, Carlos."

"I'll call you and let you know when."

Carlos seems relieved. Although gun talk makes him nervous, he appreciates the joke on himself. Isn't that what friends do? Pull each other's legs? Two really nice guys, this Marty and Terry.

They season what remains of their dinner with friendly small talk. Carlos, it turns out, is a ring-jock and wants Terry and Marty to come to his house to see his pictures posing with famous boxers—Panamanians Roberto Duran and Eliodoro Camacho, Mike Tyson, and Sugar Ray Leonard. He brags about once meeting fight promoter Don King, being a guest at Sugar Ray's house, and knowing Juanita Leonard well enough to get free tickets to her husband's middleweight championship fight with Marvelous Marvin Haggler in Las Vegas in April. Sparshott follows boxing and makes a mental note to lean on Carlos for a Leonard-Haggler ticket. Who knows? Maybe Carlos supplies boxers. Maybe he has a connection in Vegas. Maybe he'll introduce Sparshott to a Vegas dealer or money launderer. Hey, Tippett, you gotta think big in the drug biz or you lose.

The dinner is winding down fast. Bob Wills stops by to chat with Terry for a few minutes about family and town gossip. You know—who got married, who split, who wrecked a car, who had a baby, who moved, who died, who got fired. Bob leads, Sparshott follows—Arthur Murray shit—and they make it sound as if Terry Petit knows just about everyone in Frederick when he doesn't know a single fuckin' person besides Bob and his father. Donnie wheels in the dessert cart and Sparshott says:

"Let's hear the spiel, my man."

"Up front and to the left we have pecan pie, next to that is deep-dish apple pie. This one is called a fallen chocolate marquis, blueberry cheesecake, chocolate mousse cake, amaretto cheesecake, and in the rear we have caramel apple cake, cherry cheesecake and chocolate peanut butter pie."

Over dessert, coffee, and after-dinner drinks, Sparshott and Preston discuss a nightcap at the Red Horse Inn where two female IRS criminal investigators posing as horny flight attendants are waiting. What better way to strengthen their covers and get rid of Carlos than to have two women—not three, mind you—hot for them. You don't have to be an American to get the hint.

"I don't know," Sparshott says to Preston. "It might be too late to do the Red Horse. You know, I gotta fly out in the morning . . . over to Dayton."

"What the heck, Terry. I already got these two girls lined up—Mary and Mary."

They push their dessert plates aside and Terry orders another round of drinks. He has to be careful. Carlos is so damn mellow, happy is more accurate, that he starts singing in Spanish. They better begin Act Three before the kid is too far gone to appreciate it. Or perish the fucking thought—he buys it in a car accident on the way home. Hey, cops are such worrywarts.

"Okay Marty—let's paint the Red Horse . . . buy me a beer?"

TWENTY-SEVEN

11:00 P.M.

Sparshott, Preston, and Carlos step out of the Bull on the Mark onto North Market Street just as a pickup with those bigass wheels and mirrors scoots by. In one fluid motion, the FBI driver toots the horn, slams on the breaks, and sticks his head out the window.

"Yo Terry! When you get back from Texas?"

Sparshott waves to the FBI secretary in the passenger seat. "Couple days ago, how you doin' man. How's the little woman?"

"She's fine . . . You gonna play basketball with us this weekend?"

"Yeah . . . I should be back by then."

The timing is perfect. Carlos thinks Terry is the fucking mayor of Frederick. Everybody knows him. In the restaurant, on the street, who next?

If Carlos is impressed, Preston is not. He gets into the chief's van and heads for the Red Horse Inn a few miles away. He senses the evening is a great success so far. He has followed Sparshott's leads, supported his every move, helped score points, brought up things Sparshott forgot, kicked him under the table once when Sparshott called himself "Tracy," and has done everything he could to make Carlos feel like a drug-brother. But he's still stewing at the demeaning way Sparshott treated him, and the driver of the pickup didn't help change his angry mood. Once again, Sparshott forgot to tell him beforehand that the truck was a prop just like he neglected to tell him about Bob Wills and his father. He could have made an embarrassing mistake on the street just then. That Carlos might be too chilled out to notice is beside the point. Heck, there's enough to worry about in a three-way undercover operation without inviting problems. And whatever happened to professional pride?

For another thing, Preston feels that Sparshott is pushing Carlos—driving is more accurate—too hard on price. Preston sensed during dinner that Carlos was digging his heels in at $30K, high but acceptable. Why doesn't Sparshott just agree to the thirty and get on with it? If he doesn't, Carlos might walk away. It's too late now but he and Sparshott should have agreed on a bottom line before dinner so he could play the negotiation game with Sparshott. Well, at least the evening's not over yet, and Sparshott still has time to swallow a couple thousand and send Carlos home a happy kid.

While Preston is on his way to the Red Horse, Sparshott and Carlos head back to the undercover house so Sparshott can change his jacket. He wants Carlos to see the place again, now that the kid is relaxed, and he has to change the tape and batteries in the recorder under his arm.

Like Preston, Sparshott senses the evening is going well because he's beginning to feel the bond of friendship between him and Carlos who, he knows, must feel it even more strongly. The guy's lonely. Sparshott also senses he's envious. Terry has roots and family and is somebody. Carlos is a tumbleweed in a strange desert. He's homesick and misses what Terry has—community and the friendship of men. Chickies are fine. But they are no substitute for tough men who understand the risks and pressures of dealing drugs.

Sparshott also knows that Carlos is not yet completely convinced that he is who he says he is. Not that Carlos doubts Terry is a dope dealer. He's just not sure Terry is a *big* dope dealer because he hasn't shown anything to prove it. A nice Mercedes, a Rolex, a Texas ring and some gold, an airplane, a $300 dinner are only signs of wealth not proof.

Sparshott has also confirmed what he suspected. Carlos

can't set the multi-key price of coke and can't arrange for him to buy shit in Miami. All he can do is convince Roberto that Terry Petit is a successful reefer dealer interested in moving into coke, win some snow-points from Roberto for introducing Terry, then sit back and collect his finder's fee. Which is better than Sparshott hoped for. Fuck, he doesn't want to play with Carlos. He wants to step on the kid to reach Roberto even if that means leaving him with his face in the mud.

Sparshott parks in the alley behind the townhouse. He and Carlos go inside. The place is empty. Sparshott excuses himself for a minute and leaves Carlos alone to wander around, maybe check the cupboards and refrigerator for dishes and food, or see if the silver is in a drawer next to the sink. He inserts a new tape and fresh batteries into the recorder and changes into a leather jacket.

On the way to the Red Horse Inn, Sparshott continues their discussion of price while the Mercedes eavesdrops. Carlos stands firm on $30K and says:

"So when you want to buy the first kilo?"

"When the price comes down."

"Shit man, come on. I want to see some money *first*—so I know you're good for it."

"Fuck man, I wanna see some *cocaine* so I know you can deliver."

Carlos laughs. He's enjoying the ritual of jabbing and feinting, you know, like Sugar Ray and Marvelous Marvin. He and Sparshott both know they'll agree on price eventually. But Carlos is not about to give up his profit which he will have to if he meets Terry's price. And Sparshott is not about to let Carlos make a little bundle on a trial buy. Hey, Tippett, who says I'm a big spender, man?

It's ladies night at the Red Horse Inn and you have to be blind to miss the place on Highway 15 just outside Frederick. A big red horse frozen in a prance stands on the motel roof like a stallion with nowhere to go. The restaurant, which is quiet and classy, is in a separate building. The nightclub, noisy and stylishly tacky, is underneath the restaurant with its own entrance.

Sparshott and Carlos walk into the nightclub. The music is so deafening, Sparshott turns his body recorder off. The curved bar is so crowded that drinkers are shouting for Buds like brokers on the exchange, little clouds of tinted smoke drift up to the suction fans in the ceiling, every table is filled. Preston is sitting at a reserved table in the rear where he and Sparshott can see everyone and everything, especially the entrance and exit. He's the only Red Horse stud sitting alone. Campbell, Scooter, and another FBI agent are perched at the bar. Macready and Day cover the back door from a safe distance in case Carlos remembers them from the Bull on the Mark. It's the curtain call for Act Three and everyone is anxious to have it play well and be over so they can celebrate or cry—whatever the occasion calls for. It's still not too late for someone to blow it.

Sparshott waves to Scooter who shouts, "Hey, Terry." He waves to the FBI agent who yells back, "Where you been?" Ignoring Campbell who turns his face away from Carlos, Sparshott leads Medina to the bar and introduces him to both undercovers as his friend Carlos. They shake Carlos' hand and welcome him, you know, any friend of Terry's is a friend of mine, don't be a stranger now. Carlos is so damn impressed Sparshott almost has to drag him to the table where Preston is waiting.

Preston orders a round and while they drink, Carlos continues to press Sparshott on price. Even though he seems anxious to move the stalled negotiation forward before the evening's over, Carlos still insists on $30,000 rock bottom. Sparshott still laughs at it and calls Carlos a fuckin' cheapskate. Preston still thinks Sparshott is being unreasonable. They order a second round of drinks and Carlos says he has a little present for Terry. He remembered that Terry was going to a hockey game at the Capital Center with "Julie" the first night they met, so he thought Terry might appreciate two tickets to the Caps game on March 3, a few weeks away. His cousin works there and can get tickets any time.

Sparshott is so touched he forgets Carlos is a bad guy and thanks him with an arm around his shoulder. Carlos flushes with pleasure. Then, Terry remembers he's Tracy Sparshott and begins to ask himself if the Cap Center cousin might be the banker who hides Carlos' money. Sparshott makes another mental note to check out the lead. If he is, the team will need a name and address so they can get a search and seizure for the loot.

At that point, the two Marys wiggle their way between the tables and join Marty who introduces them to Sparshott and Carlos, orders drinks, and starts to get friendly with one—as planned. She lets Carlos know without saying as much that she digs Marty and won't be disappointed when he decides it's time to leave.

Sparshott, who manages to keep an appreciative eye on his own Mary, spots the bulldozer driver who excavated his house walking through the door. The kid knows he's a cop and Sparshott is worried that he'll see him, wave, maybe call him Tracy, and blow his cover. That's how it goes sometimes, like, you come all the way to Frederick where you're not known only to bump into someone you know.

Sparshott goes on the offensive. The evening's almost over and he doesn't want to introduce a doubt in Carlos' mind at a time when there will be little opportunity to erase it. He excuses himself and heads for the men's room. On the way, he sneaks up behind the kid who is standing at the bar and says:

"I'm working. Don't look at me . . . don't talk to me . . . don't say anything."

"Got it!"

The kid doesn't move a muscle—hey, Tippett, there's something you can learn here—and Sparshott continues on to the restroom. While he's gone, Carlos begins to play Marty against Terry. He likes both but each in a different way. Marty, he finds more easygoing and less threatening. Terry more dynamic and fun. He cries in his beer: "Marty, Marty, you got to talk to Terry. He doesn't like my price. But he doesn't know what the fuck's going on."

Preston is now more miffed than ever at the way Sparshott is handling Carlos. Forget the insults. Forget the cover story inconsistencies. Sparshott is blowing the whole damn undercover operation by trying to force Carlos to lower his price and to give up his margin of profit. Doesn't Sparshott understand that dealers aren't Franciscans? Money is what makes their world go 'round.

Preston tells Carlos to relax, enjoy the evening, he's Terry's partner, and he has plenty of money of his own. If Terry won't meet Carlos' price, he will, thirty thou is high but okay for a single key. I understand, man, you gotta make a living too.

Preston feels his decision to meet Carlos halfway is the only cautious and responsible one under the circumstances. He has a lot invested in the Tabares case which he considers his, and if Sparshott slams the front door on Carlos, then he'll save the case by holding the back door open.

Sparshott returns. It's now after midnight. Terry and Marty are getting anxious to take Mary and Mary back to the house and, you know. Sparshott explains to Carlos that he has to get up early for his trip to Dayton and that he'll drive him back to his car. Then he tells Preston and the women he'll meet them back at the house.

Sparshott is pleased that everything went well at the Red Horse. Act Three was flawless and the two Marys so convincing that he is looking forward to ribbing them into a deep blush later. But Carlos destroys the glow during the drive to the Sheraton. He brings up price one last time—bottom line, $30K. When Sparshott won't accept it, Carlos says: "Wait a minute, man. Marty is your partner. If my price is okay with *him*, why isn't it okay with you?"

Sparshott begins to bubble like a sulfur spring. The last thing he expected was a divide-and-conquer ploy at the end of the evening when he couldn't convincingly talk his way out of a dangerous contradiction. So he merely says that Marty only handles distribution in southern Maryland, then quickly distracts Carlos. Fortunately, Medina has had a few too many and isn't sharp enough to exploit the obvious weakness in the Terry-Marty cover story. They chat about the good time they had until Sparshott pulls up behind the Camaro. Sparshott promises to call Carlos next week to tell him where and when they'll meet for the "something" he has to show.

Carlos' car won't start which is the best break of the evening. He'll be so preoccupied with getting home he won't have time to think about why Marty claims he's Terry's partner and why Terry says Marty is only a distributor. Sparshott calls AAA on the car phone and they wait for the tow truck. Hey, cops are such caring people.

□ □ □

The team was already celebrating when Sparshott burst into the undercover townhouse laughing like a guy who's been holding back all night. He joined the fun but beneath the teasing, back slapping, and the "we got the sonofabitch," he was doing a slow burn. Before the Red Horse Inn, he thought he knew exactly what Carlos was thinking, what he would do next, what he would tell Roberto. Now he wasn't so sure. Carlos had found a crack in the Terry-Marty facade, and although he had quickly diverted the kid's attention from it, he didn't know if or how Carlos would use it. But one thing he did know with absolute certainty—he would have to make Marty's distributor role in the Terry Petit gang perfectly clear the next time out.

But Sparshott didn't want to spoil anyone's fun by bringing up a problem now. Everyone sensed but didn't know for sure that Carlos had bought the con and would soon be snorting from their hand. Bill Campbell would return the stereo equipment later that morning—every penny counts when you're almost broke. If Sparshott needed it again, he could always re-rent. There was still a small mountain of details to arrange for the next show and everyone agreed the team would have to move quickly before Carlos had too much time to think and Roberto turned even more skeptical.

They had to keep the momentum going, the Snow-ball rolling as it were. Hey, just a little narc humor.

After the taste of shared success and a few beers for wash, what the hell, the price of a key of coke seemed more challenge than problem. But not all the beer in Frederick could quiet the nagging doubt. What if Carlos *didn't* buy it?

TWENTY-EIGHT

Stew Tippett wasn't concerned about the friction between Sparshott and Preston. In a u.c. operation, there's no time to work out everybody's role in advance. You have to make up a lot as you go. As for Marty offering to deal with Carlos behind Terry's back, well, drug dealers aren't exactly known for loyalty. In fact, Marty's apparent treachery might actually convince Carlos that Marty and Terry really *were* drug dealers. Narcs would try too hard to make everything look lovey-dovey.

Tippett wasn't far off the mark. Carlos had been surprised and pleased at Marty's offer to meet his price if Terry didn't. But the more he thought about it, the more he distrusted Marty. If the guy is ready to turn on Terry for a few thou, what will he do to me? Carlos believed in loyalty, fuck, he was still miffed at Roberto for overcharging him. Shit yes, he had tried to play Marty against Terry to get a better deal, fucking business, man, but deep down he was also warning Terry, his friend, to watch his back.

Bill Campbell didn't take the Terry-Marty problem as lightly as Tippett. A few days after the Frederick scam, he called Marty into his office for a painful chat. He had hoped that the competition between Sparshott and Preston over undercover roles would never reach a point of open conflict. Now that it had, he wasn't looking forward to settling it. He liked and respected both cops and could easily understand how Preston might feel that his role was just an undercover crumb. Be that as it may, Campbell couldn't allow one person or one scenario to jeopardize the undercover investigation which had suddenly turned more critical than anyone could have imagined. Quite frankly, the wiretap on Roberto's phones in Presidential Towers was not a treasure trove so far. When the team began its Title Three safari through the jungle of the system, no one had anticipated that Roberto would turn his Washington operation over to Carlos Medina and, as a result, drop into town infrequently and only for a day or two to pick up his money. To put it mildly, Roberto's phones weren't keeping the listening post on edge with constant ringing. At this point in the investigation, a buy from Roberto was the fastest and best way to shut Tabares down.

Campbell handled Preston with cotton gloves. The upcoming marijuana show was more complicated than the airpark and Bull on the Mark combined. Resentment could ruin it just as easily as role confusion, real or imagined. After some uncomfortable small talk, Campbell stepped into the ring.

"We have a problem."

"Tell me about it, Billy. I thought I was supposed to be in charge of operations. I thought Terry wasn't supposed to know about the price of cocaine. That was supposed to be my job."

"You *are* in charge of operations, Marty."

"Then you better tell Tracy that. One minute I am, the next minute I'm a delivery boy, like, 'Hey Marty, go see if I turned the lights off in the Mercedes.' If Sparshott needs flunkies, give him some. You have all kinds sitting around here."

Campbell smiled at the dig, then chose his words as carefully as a Secretary of State. In Bureau language, Sparshott was lead undercover. But working cops don't make those inflammatory distinctions, like, "Hey brother, I'm the lead, you're the support." To define Preston in those terms would be to make him feel second-rate which he wasn't. "I agree with you, Marty. You're not Terry's flunky and shouldn't be treated that way. I'll make sure everyone understands . . . Terry handles the business side of the gang, Marty the operations side."

Roles clarified, Preston brought up the Miami trip again which stuck in his craw like a hat pin. He still wouldn't buy Campbell's explanation that he had stayed home because there wasn't any money. He said he felt as if the Bureau was treating him like a fucking local, and that, as operations manager of the gang, he should have gone to Miami with Sparshott. There wasn't a thing Campbell could say to convince Preston otherwise.

Campbell watched Preston carefully over the next few days and noted that he seemed to have lost some of his enthusiasm for the case and began spending more time in the listening post working the wiretap, sometimes up to ten or twelve hours a day when Roberto was in town. He was a valuable asset because he knew more of the characters Roberto called than anyone else on the team. Hurt feelings aside, Campbell knew he could count on Preston and his confidence was not misplaced.

Preston invited Sparshott to dinner a few days after the chat with Campbell to clear the air. He didn't fence with words: I'm not your flunky, Tracy, and there's no excuse to treat me like I don't count or like I don't have anything to contribute. You don't ask my advice, you don't tell me who the players are in each scenario, you order me around in front of Carlos, and you badmouth me behind my back. Come on, Tracy.

Sparshott understood Preston's anger and hurt. Fuck, if he had to play Marty to someone else's Terry, he'd—hell, he didn't know what he'd do. So he dealt with Preston as directly and diplomatically as Campbell had: Terry and Marty evolved scenario by scenario and the roles are clear now—I handle the business and the money, you take care of the dope and the distribution. Fuck Marty, I worked hard to keep you in every single scenario because I know how much this case means to you. Your role is important and I need you, brother. Shit, I'm not trying to belittle you. You oughta know how it is, man—you sometimes forget to mention details when things are going fuck-crazy. I respect your skill as an investigator and you oughta respect my skill as an undercover. Don't worry about Carlos. I'll put him straight next time out.

Although he felt Tracy was talking down to him, Preston believed the explanation and was satisfied with the role clarification, not that he didn't lust after a bigger part in the operation. But this was no time to be petty. He told Sparshott that all of them—

Campbell, Tippett, Macready, Sparshott, and he—had to hang together. If the Baltimore creds found even a tiny crack in the solidarity of the team, the Bureau would use it to take the case from them. The two cops then drank to the next scam.

It was a reefer show, one of those "if I ever had the chance I would like to" productions Sparshott had dreamed about for a long time. It was Tippett's last straw and he took his anger out on Campbell who, like Sparshott, saw the show as a logical and necessary step to reach Roberto. For Tippett, it was overly ambitious and too risky. It would require so much backup and support that it would have to be approved high in the Bureau where the air was thin. It would require an assist from the DEA and who knew what they might want in exchange. And when all was said and done, the whole scam was built around *one* undercover, Tracy Sparshott, a fucking local whom he didn't like. Come to think of it, it was getting to the point where the lead undercover was trying to run the whole u.c. operation. Sparshott was working for the Bureau now, and the Bureau should be calling the shots, not just providing support for his cockamamie scenarios like the Bull on the Mark and the Red Horse Inn. A dinner to cement a relationship with a drug dealer was one thing, but $300? The Department of Justice did not give birth to and rear the Federal Bureau of Investigation so that locals could have a night out on the town all expenses paid. The champagne bet—Dom Perignon mind you—was the absolute limit.

It was clear to Campbell that the issue was more power and personality than the wisdom of a particular scenario. If he didn't do something soon, Tippett's inability to work with Sparshott would destroy the whole investigation. So Campbell sat down with Tippett and told him he understood how draining the paperwork on the Tabares case was, how he knew Tippett was getting it in spades every time Sparshott spent a buck—and he was—and how racing back and forth to headquarters and Baltimore was sapping

Tidwell's energy and patience. That's why he, Campbell, had decided to take over the undercover field operation himself. Stew Tippett would remain case officer (only the creds could remove him), but from now on Campbell would make each and every undercover decision, including routine budget allocations, subject to approval from the SAC. Tippett accepted the diminished role. How could he lose? If the case was a success, he would get the career credit because he was case officer. If it failed because of an undercover faux pas, Campbell would get the blame. Besides, with all the paperwork, he had little time for undercover games, no matter how creative.

Since the marijuana show involved real dope, Tom Roberts had to approve the scenario which he did—great idea, get it on tape. So did the creds which they did. But they were nervous about having a fucking local as the star and held serious discussions behind Campbell's back about replacing Sparshott with an FBI undercover. They wisely concluded it was too late for a pinch hitter—Medina liked Terry and Marty, a new player would make him suspicious, and the whole idea behind the show was to sell Terry Petit. To make sure Sparshott didn't blow it, the creds assigned seven special agents as backup and bit players.

Sparshott wasn't exactly thrilled about using FBI actors. He needed people who looked like, talked like, and acted like badass bikers. Most of the special agents he had met weren't the type. So he did some creative casting. It was his job to find the location for the show, Campbell had to come up with the marijuana. Since Terry Petit operated out of western Maryland, it would be logical to stage the show there. But if he did that, Sparshott would never be able to use his own narcs as bikers because his supervisor would not allow them to work outside the county. Not to worry.

It just so happened that officer Ron Gadies, a Montgomery County brother, made off-duty security checks on a private hunting club in the far western corner of the county in exchange for hunting privileges there. The place was filled with deer, pheasant, grouse, rabbit, and squirrel. It was also perfect for a marijuana show—isolated, secure, in Montgomery County, and less than a half hour drive from Frederick. Gadies agreed to make the fields available without telling club officers in exchange for a bit speaking-part. When Sparshott explained to his boss how important it was to have narcs whom he trusted as actors rather than FBI special hams whom he didn't know, his boss gave him six men. Hey, somebody's gotta show the feds how the pros do it.

Meanwhile, Campbell lucked into a load of fresh marijuana sitting in the DEA's Baltimore warehouse. The agency had seized the shit—more than a ton wrapped in fifty-pound bales—during a raid in Mobile, Alabama, and it was scheduled to be burned. "Just tell us when you need it," the DEA agent in charge told Campbell. No three-week wait, none of that "I gotta check this out with downtown," no ream of papers to sign in blood.

Campbell rented a large truck, drafted a couple of agents to help load the stuff, then drove to the warehouse. He signed the dope out—DEA was happy to give it to him as long as he didn't bring it back—then parked the truck in the Baltimore Bureau yard under a surveillance camera and behind a locked gate.

The next afternoon, Campbell and the agents assigned to the show drove out to the hunting club for a dress rehearsal. Tippett drove the van with the grass. Given all the doubt in the Bureau, Campbell really wanted the scam to work. As set designer and manager, he positioned every agent with utmost care and planned their every move down to the second. He had never been part of such a big sting and neither had anyone else in the Baltimore Bureau.

But Campbell saw an unavoidable bureaucratic problem ahead. What should Sparshott do if Carlos asked for some marijuana? He could hardly say, "Fuck no, man, the FBI will get mad at me if I give you some." Bureau rules allowed the undercover to let the bad guys sample the wares. But afterwards, the case agent had to file a telex explaining what happened and why—names, times, amounts, details. Campbell warned Sparshott to play both Carlos and the marijuana strictly by the Bureau book. He said:

"You can take the stuff out and show it to Carlos. You can

cut open a bale. But don't tell Carlos he can have some. If *he* asks for it, give it to him. Tippett will take care of the paperwork later so don't worry about it."

After the dress rehearsal in the hunting club fields, Tippett parked the marijuana truck in the yard of a Montgomery County police officer who lived nearby. Then the entire cast went to the undercover townhouse in Frederick to eat pizza and wait for the curtain call.

8:30 P.M.

Sparshott smiles when Carlos pulls into the lot of the Frederick Sheraton in a white Porsche 944. No one follows him. Campbell and Macready are parked close enough to see him but far enough away so as not to be seen. They've been sitting for over an hour watching for any counter-surveillance scouts he may have sent ahead.

Everyone is just a little nervous, like actors who know they have a great script and a creative cast but can't predict how the audience will respond. The team is taking no chances. The Mercedes is wired as usual and Sparshott, who isn't armed, is wearing both a transmitter and a body recorder. Tippett has the receiver. It's not that the Carlos-Sparshott meet is physically dangerous. But it's potentially destructive. A major goof would tear down every building block of credibility Sparshott and Preston have so carefully laid.

Carlos steps out of the Porsche and leans up against it as if to say, "I told you so, motherfucker!" He's dressed like a cat burglar in jeans, sneakers, and a black leather jacket. Like Terry told him on the phone the night before, "Hey man, put on some dark clothes and don't wear good shoes 'cuz it might be muddy." All Carlos knows is that Sparshott wants to show him something that has to do with his marijuana business. But what? Where? And how dangerous?

Sparshott eyes the Porsche like a centerfold. He wants to

find out as much as he can about it for Macready without appearing too nosy. If Carlos paid cash and the dealer who sold him the car didn't file a currency transaction report, then—hell, let Jerry figure it out. Terry caresses the curve of the hood. "Nice . . . I'm glad you got a decent car. How do ya like her?"

"I *love* her, man."

Sparshott sneaks a look at the dashboard. "Beautiful . . . How did ya pay for it?"

"Cash, man."

"What kind of price did ya get on it?"

"I got it cheap, man." Carlos acts as if he just won a blue ribbon. "You thought I was barking out my ass, right? Well, you *lost* buddy. I want my champagne."

"That's Marty not me." We'll see who lost, buddy. "How cheap?"

"Cheap, cheap, cheap!"

"Come on, man!"

"Don't worry about it . . . But now I gotta build a garage on my house, man. Estimates and all that shit."

No use pushing it. Sparshott leads Carlos to the Mercedes without telling him where they're going. If Carlos is curious, he doesn't show it. It's like a game of chicken—I won't ask you where we're going until you tell me why we're going there. Sparshott fans the suspense. As soon as he drives out of the hotel lot and turns onto Highway 340 west, Campbell and Macready radio the team at the staging area that Sparshott and Medina are on their way, heads up, places everybody. Actually, the car trip was the alternate plan. Sparshott wanted to meet Carlos up at the College Park Airport close to Medina's house, then fly him to Frederick. But there were mechanical problems with the plane he had lined up at the last minute.

"So how's school?" Sparshott asks. Carlos seems uptight, like he's carrying Panama on his shoulders, and Sparshott doesn't know if it's because the guy is scared or if something's eating him. "You do okay on your test?"

"I'm fucking up, man."

"Hey buddy, don't. You gotta keep your cover, you know what I mean?" Hey, don't flunk out on us yet. We need you. "You gotta keep the school lookin' *good,* man."

"Well, I feel like shit! My phone lines are all fucked up, man, so don't call me at home anymore. There's something going on and I don't like that shit."

Dealers always talk as if the narcs are hiding in their phones. But Carlos sounds really hinky and his fear is too specific to dismiss. He doesn't say he's worried that his phone might be tapped. He says the things aren't working right and that bothers Sparshott. He knows Tom Roberts intends to tap Carlos but hasn't petitioned the court yet. Does the DEA have the kid under surveillance? Is this another one of those cases, as the old saying goes, where the right hand doesn't know who the left hand is jerking off? Or maybe one of Carlos' customers got busted and rolled over on him.

"Did you check it out, man?" Sparshott asks. "Has anything happened to any of your people?"

"Everybody's cool, man. Everybody. So I say to myself, 'Terry's the only motherfucker left.' So what the fuck's going on, man? Are you setting me up, you motherfucker?"

"Well it ain't me, I'll tell you that right now." Sparshott chuckles as if to say "you gotta be kidding!" He's now almost certain no one has a tap on Carlos. Medina told him some weeks ago that he was experiencing mechanical problems with his new phones—Sparshott called him a "cheap sonofabitch" and encouraged him to junk the shit—and the cellular phone in the Porsche is newly installed, maybe incorrectly. To divert suspicion away from himself, he needles Carlos about snorting. "Are you starting to do your own product, man? Tell me, 'cuz you're beginning to act paranoid, you know, like the idiots who use the shit."

"Fuck no, man!" Carlos is hurt that Terry would even ask him if he toots which he does, too much, which he knows. Is it showing? Is the shit really turning him hinky like Roberto, Jr., whose old man didn't even trust him? "Tell me about it man. I can't stand people like that."

"Well, I don't wanna deal with anyone who's using the shit."

"No problem." Carlos lies easily, then quickly does what Sparshott is so good at—changes the topic. "Let me ask you something, Terry? Can they tap a cellular phone?"

"Shit no! I've had people look into that for me."

"Well, I'm changing *all* my phones anyway. I got this guy coming to check everything out. He's like a fucking genius."

"Good. Do ya trust him?"

"Yeah, he can tell me right away if they've been trying to, you know, tap my phones. A real genius, man. I live in an old house so it could be the lines are fucked up."

Carlos just talked himself into believing everything's fine. Hey, it's hard being a drug dealer in a technological age. Terry turns off onto Highway 85 and heads south down a two-lane country road that winds through fertile farmland. The show begins.

TWENTY-NINE

9:15 P.M.

Other than a few house lights winking like fireflies through the moving trees, it's a black, moonless night and the road is deserted. Sparshott is concerned—worried is too strong—about missing a critical turn. He had driven the route from the hunting club to the Sheraton twice that afternoon. The first trip took twenty-five minutes, the second twenty-two. What he manages to see in the dark looks different than it did in the daylight. If he gets confused or lost, however, he has a plausible excuse ready.

Fucked up phones aren't Carlos' only problem. He confides in Sparshott, brother to brother, that a check he was expecting from Panama was late, and he thought maybe the feds who were tapping his phones took it. You know how sneaky those motherfuckers are. He waited a few days and when the check still didn't arrive at the bank, he called home.

"So my sister tells me mom is sick, and I say 'what happened,' and she says 'mom got into a car accident,' and I say 'don't tell me that the Mercedes is a total loss'."

"Is your mom okay?"

"Yeah, she's okay but all cut up and shit. She broke the windshield with her head . . . Everything's cool now. I went to the bank and got my check today."

"Well I'm glad your mom's gonna be fine." Sparshott is so into his role as Carlos' buddy that he really is concerned about the guy's mother—a lot more than Carlos is. The woman almost killed herself and all her son can think about is the damage to the fucking Mercedes and his lost check. "Shit, Carlos, you can buy her a new car. You're the *big* man now."

"Fuck, I'm *gonna* buy her a new one."

Not that Carlos would care, but Sparshott is driving him through history now. Nearby, Union soldiers thwarted a Confederate drive on the city of Washington in July 1864 during the Battle of the Monocacy. Antebellum lime kilns line the road on their right. Just ahead of them is Buckeystown, founded by the Buckey brothers who opened a smithy and a roadside tavern there in the 1770s. They called the place "Good Luck" back then and Sparshott hopes it will live up to its reputation tonight.

They pass through Buckeystown and back into a blanket of darkness. Campbell and Macready follow so far behind the Mercedes on the twisting, hilly road that Sparshott can't see their headlights. Like a confessional, the intimacy of darkness encourages Carlos to open up even more and he tells his friend Terry that being the Cuban's numero uno in Washington is getting to him. He's under constant pressure, he's worried about his health, if anyone can understand what he's going through, it's Terry. What he doesn't tell Terry is that his new girlfriend found out he was using and threatened to, you know, cut him off if he didn't stop snorting, talk about pussy power.

"I got this motherfucker in my ass twenty-four hours a day. I got headaches all the time. Two fuckin' days without sleep. I'm telling you man, I can't take no more of this shit. And now I gotta be flying down to Miami with *you*. I'm retiring very soon, man, and—"

"Did you tell the Cuban what I want?"

"You still DO NOT GET IT, Terry, do you? I told you I'm the man up here. The Cuban does what I say. I tell him, 'I want the shit here by such and such . . . you'll have your money by such and such.' You are talking to *the* man. Right here!"

Sparshott chuckles. "Sure I am . . . but first you get paranoid on me and then you're gonna fuckin' retire."

"What do you expect, man? A friend of mine got busted

with a half pound. They made it look like he was the biggest fucking drug dealer around!"

"Tell me about it!"

There's more. Carlos goes on to say that it's not just a case of narcophobia. He's so damn scared about being ripped off by his own people that he uses Roberto's apartment as his stash pad and he's constantly worried about someone breaking into his Porsche or his house when he's in school.

"That's smart to keep the shit someplace else." Sparshott tries to be sympathetic, dealer to dealer. By the way, thanks for telling us where your stash is. "Cuz if they think it's in your house, man, one of these idiots could—"

"That's what I'm saying, man . . . Could be a fucking war."

Sparshott turns right onto Highway 28 which is even narrower and more isolated than 85. He can almost hear Carlos thinking, "What the fuck am I doing out here alone with this badass?" It's going down even better than Sparshott hoped and he begins to fuck with Carlos' head. The more frightened the guy is, the less critical he'll be and the more he'll buy the scam. Sparshott says:

"I was gonna take your Porsche tonight. But if just *one* little thing goes wrong, somebody's gonna get hurt. I don't need that—and your car to worry about too."

"What, what, what's going on tonight?" Carlos stammers like a kid in a haunted cave.

"Nothing . . . You're just taking a ride, man. Be cool."

"No . . . you tell me what's going on, motherfucker. If something happens, man, I'm gonna be right there too!"

"It's too late now, isn't it?" Sparshott lets him squirm. "We're almost there."

"Well I'm not gonna worry about it." Carlos lets out one of those brave little laughs that can't fool anyone. "But I'll tell you—I *was* worrying."

"You don't have a gun, do you?"

"Shit yeah, I got a gun," Carlos bluffs.

"Well you better not!"

"Then I'll have to leave it somewhere, won't I?"

"Listen buddy!" There's a mean edge to Sparshott's voice. "You got one—or not?"

Carlos answers with another brave laugh.

"This isn't bullshit," Sparshott warns.

"So what's the deal."

"You'll see."

They cross the Monocacy River, then take a right—the turn Sparshott was worried he might miss—onto Mouth of the Monocacy Road which dead ends at the Potomac River a mile away. The trees that line the rocky, dirt lane create a dark umbrella against the lighter sky. They're safe inside the borders of Montgomery County now. Earlier that evening, Sparshott radioed in a code 1070 which tells all police officers to stay out of the area. All he needs is to have a patrol car stop him and say, "Oh, it's you, Trace! What's happening, brother?" He tells Carlos:

"Make sure no one's following me. That's all you gotta do . . . Things better be goin' good out there or Marty's ass is in the grass."

"Marty's around?" Carlos snatches the word as if it were a life jacket.

"Shit, he *better be*. He's got all my business with him."

"What a wonderful adventure, Terry." The presence of Marty, if only by name, lightens Carlos' mood like music. "Way out here in the country. I just *love* it, man."

The Mercedes creeps up a hill, then coasts down. Carlos is as quiet as a Trappist. The car crosses a narrow bridge which spans the B&O Railroad below, then crawls toward a farm gate and tractor trail on the left side of the road. The gate stands open. To its left are dense woods, to its right an empty field which gently rises to a knoll about a quarter mile away.

"Everything looks good." Sparshott turns off the road toward the gate. "Everything's open."

A man with a machine gun suddenly jumps out from behind a clump of bushes and all but blocks their way. Carlos sucks in his breath as if he's been hit in the gut. Sparshott stops and lowers the automatic window on the passenger side so Carlos can get a good look at the guard who stoops and peers into the window.

"Terry, how ya doin'?"

"Hey Ron! Everything okay?"

"Movin' in and out . . . goin' good."

Sparshott rolls Carlos' window back up as officer Ron Gadies disappears into the bushes to wait for the next car. Sparshott douses his headlights but leaves the ambers on. Now Carlos is really scared. What if some bad guys try to rip him off and there's a real gunfight? What if the narcs are setting Terry up? "You're not going to drive your *Mercedes* in there, are you?" It's a rhetorical question.

"Just be quiet," Sparshott warns as he heads down the tractor trail.

9:30 P.M.

The Mercedes follows the trail along the woods to a gentle curve in the road. An FBI undercover car flashes its headlights in the distance. The Mercedes answers, then moves slowly to a second bend in the dirt trail. Another FBI flash from a different direction. The Mercedes answers again. Sparshott doesn't explain. Carlos doesn't ask. Just like the fuckin' movies, man.

The Mercedes leaves the tractor trail and heads out into the field which is covered with hubcap-high grass with car trails running through like ski marks in snow. A silhouette holding a machine gun in the air and a flashlight suddenly appears on the rise in the field straight ahead. The flashlight waves the car forward. Sparshott cuts the amber lights and glides up the slope in darkness.

The Mercedes stops at the top of the rise where Preston joins the sentry. A large truck sits in the bowl below. Six men in dark clothes—all Montgomery County narcs—mill around motorbikes trying to shut out the early March cold. They talk quietly and laugh and drink beer. Each has a gun tucked into a belt or holster. Even from a distance, they look like a rough bunch.

"How's it goin'?" Sparshott asks Preston. "What you got left?"

"One van and he's late. If he doesn't come soon, I'm leaving. We've been here too long as it is."

"Fuck it! Other than that, everything cool? No phone calls?"

"No problems. These guys always want a price break, then they show up late."

Preston directs Sparshott to drive down into the bowl and park next to the reefer truck. It's clear that he's in charge of the off-loading operation. It's also clear that Carlos is scared. He gets out of the Mercedes and follows Preston around like a puppy. He sees the guns and says, "A lot of guns, Marty."

"There's plenty more around," Preston says. Then to Sparshott: "My men are freezing down here, Terry."

"Yeah, Terry," a biker pipes up, "and we're never gonna get any pussy standing around like this."

The horizon lights up with the flash of a headlight in the distance. "Here they come," the silhouette on the rise calls down to Preston. He begins his flashlight dance. Two amber lights creep over the rise like animal eyes.

"What do ya want to do, Marty?" Sparshott asks as if Marty is in charge. He had promised Preston to make sure Medina understood Marty's role in the gang the next time out, and now he is making good on that promise. "Have him come down here?"

"Yeah, tell him to park close to the truck."

Preston walks over to his crew and starts issuing orders while Sparshott motions to the white van, driven by an FBI agent, to glide down the hill. The van still has its parking lights on which pisses him. "Tell the asshole to turn the lights off," he calls up to the sentry. "I said tell him to turn the lights off."

"Dumbfuck!"

Sparshott shows the van where to park then chews out the driver. "You been followed?" he demands, like, what can you expect from a guy who's late and drives with his lights on?

"No one followed," the driver says.

Preston's team moves with the speed of men with pussy on the brain. One jumps into the truck and slides bales of grass up to the sliding door in the middle of the truck. Carriers pick them up and tote them to the van where another narc stacks them inside like a farmer putting up hay. The men are so fast and organized they look as if they off-loaded herb every night of the week. Carlos watches in silence as if he doesn't want to be distracted with talk. Sparshott lets him drink it all in for a few minutes, then says:

"I *never* do this, man. I never come—only for you . . . Hey Bill, bring me a bale and a knife . . . Somebody gimme a light."

Preston turns on a flashlight and hands a hunting knife to Sparshott who slits the plastic tape and paper wrapping around the bale so Carlos can see that the grass is real but doesn't ask Carlos to sample the goods. The plan is to have Carlos witness the off-loading into just *one* van so he can't spend a lot of time in the field. And if he peeks into the big truck and notices it isn't filled to the roof with dope, Preston or Sparshott can tell him the rest of the reefer moved in and out an hour ago.

Carlos needs no invitation. He reaches into the bale with two fingers and pulls out enough grass for two or three joints. Then he sniffs it, stuffs it into a cigarette package wrapper, and tucks the package into his pocket.

"All the shit loaded?" Sparshott asks Marty.

"That's it . . . let's go guys . . . we're out of here."

The off-loaders head for their bikes while the van, loaded down with more than half a ton of grass, begins to climb the gentle hill. Its wheels spin under the weight.

"Slow," Terry orders the driver. "Slo-o-ow!"

The driver shifts down and the van creeps up over the hill and out of sight. The bikers rev up ready to fly. Terry calls to Marty over the engine noises:

"Hey listen . . . hey Marty, Marty, Marty, MARTIN! I'll talk to you in an hour. Get on the horn. We can't have this fuckin' driver around anymore. They all know the cutoff time."

"Yeah, I'll take care of him. He's over."

"All right . . . good job everybody. Give 'em an extra hundred, Marty. But listen—don't tear out of here all at once. Wait a few minutes . . . Hey, Greg, how are the kids?"

"Doin' okay, man."

"The wife?"

"She's fine, man."

Sparshott waves goodbye, then he and Carlos get into the Mercedes and drive up the hill. "Now those are good people," Sparshott says as they head for the gate faster than they drove in. Sparshott explains the operation: His pilots flew the reefer in from Texas earlier that night. Marty and his men were waiting with the big truck when it landed. They transferred the shit from the plane then drove out here. Marty never uses the same off-loading site twice and he keeps changing the schedule around. We use ten vans—two for each distributor. Then:

"In about two weeks I'll be able to go up to the bank and count my money. Old Mike, you know, my accountant, will call and tell me everything's set. Ever been to Harrisburg?"

"No."

"Want to fly there with me? Leave in the morning, have lunch."

"If I don't have a mid-term."

"I'll show you my money. Then we can really start talking business—Hey, I wanna see your house."

As they reach the gate, a car full of noisy kids drives by. Sparshott tells Carlos that they like to go down to the river and make out, but to be sure he'll have Marty check. He reaches for the car phone. What the hell, might as well make the kids fit into the scam.

"Listen, Marty—a white Cutlass, just headed for the dock. If there's a problem, let Ron at the gate take care of it. Good job, Marty. And tell your people thanks again . . . don't forget the extra hundred."

They turn right onto Mouth of the Monocacy Road and head back to the Sheraton. "Marty's the best," Sparshott continues. "There ain't nobody better with people and shit. He's family, man, you could cut his fuckin' tongue out and he wouldn't say nothing. I took a chance tonight 'cuz you wanted to see something. Normally, I don't take fuckin' chances. That's what I pay Marty for."

"Where the fuck did all that shit come from?" Carlos asks. It's the first real indication he's impressed and buying the scam.

"Jamaica . . . but listen, I'm serious, man. You swallow that shit if we get stopped. I don't like it around me . . . You got any idea what Jamaican Sense goes for up here?"

"No, how much?" Sensamilia is the best grass around.

"Fifteen to two thousand a pound. I've been doin' this for ten years, man. You don't put something together like you just saw overnight. Everything has to run like a clock. If it ain't tickin' just right, I'm history."

"I know that, man." Carlos begins to count all the money he's going to make off Terry. "I'm telling you. I'll cut my fucking balls off if you don't make a killing on coke . . . What are you doing now?"

"Taking you back. Then I gotta hook up with Marty and make sure that guy doesn't drive any more. Then, fuck, I gotta drive all the way over to Westminster."

"I thought we were, you know, going to party tonight, man."

"This is a business night. Give me a call later on in the week. We'll go to Hammerjacks."

Carlos discovered Hammerjacks, a popular Baltimore meat market filled with chickies, right after he returned from Christmas in Panama and has been after Terry to go there with him ever since. Sparshott always found an excuse to turn him down because he wasn't ready to get chummy with Carlos yet. He still isn't but doesn't want Carlos to know that. So he directs the conversation to his next move—the meeting with Roberto:

"Does your man have some place in Florida where my people can load up? An airport close by?"

"Fuck, you don't need all that bullshit. Ten keys makes only two packages. We don't do anything by plane. All our shit comes by boat."

"Okay—then you gotta be honest with me, Carlos. Can your man handle the volume 'cuz if the price is right—ten, twenty, thirty keys once we get moving."

"Don't worry about it, man. Anything you want."

"We'll meet at a hotel in Miami and we'll have dinner. On your man. You tell him I said I'm fuckin' tired of buying. We'll talk and he'll know everything's cool."

The Mercedes pulls into the Sheraton lot and parks next to Carlos' Porsche. Sparshott and Carlos get out. Sparshott sees a pair of sunglasses on the dash, snatches them, and tries them on.

"Nice fuckin' shades, man. I think I'll keep 'em."

"Fuck, no. I need them."

"You cheap bastard. I wancha to get me a black pair just like these. And don't get me no cheap ones, man."

Carlos won't say yes or no. Instead: "Hey, the shit is ready and waiting, man. Any time you want to go down, the Cuban will tell you himself."

"All right, buddy."

"Bye, Terry."

Bye-bye, sucker.

□ □ □

They celebrated in the Fraternal Order of Police club in Gaithersburg. Mostly they laughed at how Carlos' eyes got as big as frisbees when he saw the guns and badass bikers, and how Tippett must have shit creds when he heard Carlos over the wire helping himself to federal reefer. Both Sparshott and Preston, who had spent the most time with Carlos that night, were convinced they had completely snowed the kid. Marty saw the admiration and fear in his face as he tagged along like a lost fawn. And Tracy heard the excitement and greed in his voice after the show—pushing Terry to meet the Cuban, advising Terry once again to wash his money in Panama, inviting Terry to pick up chickies with him at Hammerjacks that same night. Why all the enthusiasm if he thought Terry and Marty were setting him up?

But hairline cracks of doubt soon appeared on the mirror of their confidence. The show had played so perfectly it was downright scary. Maybe the scam struck Carlos as enticing but as phony as airbrushed pussy. Or maybe Carlos conned Terry and Marty into believing he bought the show so he could get the fuck out of the field, past Ron at the gate, and back to the safety of his new Porsche. Or maybe he bought the scam but would have second thoughts the next day. The night before looks so different the morning after. The team finally went to bed in the early hours feeling no pain but suffering a case of nagging doubt.

PART FOUR

The Kill
Spring 1987

THIRTY

"You wouldn't believe this guy's operation to move stuff . . . it's *fantastic*" Carlos told Roberto Tabares over the bugged phone in Presidential Towers. He was impressed with Terry for letting him walk away with a shit-sample, something *he* would never do for Terry. "We got ourselves a big fish here, Roberto."

Unfortunately, Stew Tippett was not as enthusiastic as Carlos Medina. Before the marijuana show—The Tracy Sparshott Show as he thought of it—Tippett worried so much about a mistake out there, wherever "there" was, that he started having nosebleeds even though he was no longer responsible for the undercover scenarios. The Sparshott Show put his career on the line. What if the Tabares gang ripped off a half ton of high quality marijuana? The DEA would be rolling in the gutters of Baltimore and, as sure as Hoover was gay, the DEA would never let the Bureau forget it. What would happen if there was a shootout and a special agent got killed? What would happen if Sparshott was as cocky with the bad guys as he was with him and blew it? And, then there was the issue of allowing Carlos to sample the marijuana. He had warned Sparshott to do everything possible to discourage Carlos from taking any grass because he didn't have the time or the energy to do the required paperwork.

But once his superiors cleared the marijuana show—not that he didn't have to do a lot of gutter fighting to get the final okay—Tippett began having fun. And as he listened to Sparshott, Carlos and Marty over the receiver in his car parked well away from the scam site, he was proud of the whole team, Sparshott and

Preston, Billy and his tight planning, the FBI backups and extras, the Montgomery County off-loaders. Then Sparshott spoiled it all by calling for a bale of grass and a knife when Medina didn't even ask to see the dope. Tippett just knew that Sparshott was giving him the finger in the dark and there was no way he could get back at the sonofabitch. It was the final insult.

Tippett's resentment of Sparshott had been seething for months. He considered Tracy the best and most creative undercover he had ever seen, and the worst. The guy seemed to pride himself on scoffing at the paperwork he, Tippett, had to do as case agent. Hell, he didn't create the bureaucracy and he frankly thought a lot of it sucked, but telexes were as much a part of the real war on drugs as buys, and if Sparshott thought anyone could take the bad guys down without them, he was pipe-dreaming again. Didn't anyone on the team realize that it was his job as case agent to urge caution when no one else would, question the wisdom and feasibility of scenarios, convince superiors that this scam was necessary, that expense vital, and if he couldn't convince them, turn Sparshott around 180 degrees or simply say no. The problem was that no one—especially Sparshott—would recognize the thankless but important position he was in. Hell, the first step in catching bad guys is to talk the bureaucracy into wanting to nail them. That was his job. Granted it wasn't as flashy as playing bigshit marijuana dealer in the Bull on the Mark—Baltimore gave him a hard time on the $300 tab and the Dom Perignon bet which Sparshott thought was funny—but damn it, it was just as critical and stressful.

Even after he learned the show had played to a spellbound audience, Tippett was still nosebleed-worried and Texas angry. More damn paperwork at a time when he was writing a stack of arrest, search, and seizure warrants. Would headquarters accept his explanation for the MUF—marijuana unaccounted for—which Medina had tossed out his car window on his way home so a fucking State Trooper wouldn't catch him with his dick out like Gustavo? Would it blame him for being reckless with DEA dope?

Tippett was so wired when his Hyattsville supervisor reminded him to telex headquarters about the MUF, he went off like a string of ladyfingers. He yelled, he cursed and threatened Sparshott, he told Campbell, "Kill him, Billy. If you don't I will. He's jigging me." Part of his anger was theatrical, part real. And he scared the hell out of his boss who asked Campbell, "What's wrong with Stew?"

"He's losing it," Campbell said. "Under too much stress. He doesn't have a sense of balance and perspective anymore."

"Well, all I did was talk to him about getting the teletype out," the supervisor said. "I'm thinking of getting him removed from the case."

Campbell argued against the action, not that the Baltimore SAC would have removed Tippett anyway, he thought the guy was doing a great job. The Tabares investigation was at a critical turning point and a new case officer would only slow it down. And there was no way Campbell could take over Tippett's paperwork and at the same time handle undercover logistics which included even more paperwork: planning a team trip to Miami, a one-kilo buy, and a wiretap on Carlos; leading undercover meetings; lining up surveillance and backup; debriefing Sparshott and Preston after buys and meets; writing reports on their activities; managing the Tabares wiretap; and supervising the preparation of all transcripts. What little time and energy he had left, he needed to protect the lives and safety of his undercovers, not to play Bureau bingo. In a word, Stew Tippett was irreplaceable. Put that way, their supervisor had to agree.

Campbell pushed Tippett aside for the time being. He had over a ton of marijuana to dispose of before some wiseass bad guy stole it to sell on the streets of Baltimore. Forget a telex explaining how Carlos Medina got a couple grams of Jamaican. Try one explaining how Special Agent William Campbell lost a ton of DEA herb.

Campbell had reserved the Baltimore city incinerator for the day after the marijuana show. He and a couple of special agents drove the truck through the chain-link gate to the dump, then locked it behind them to keep out trash men with quick hands.

They backed the truck up to a huge chute which tunnels

into an underground furnace and tossed the grass, bale by bale, into the gaping hole. As the shit slid out of sight, incinerator maintenance men called out, "Hey, what a waste . . . The whole damn town's gonna get high." Campbell had to admit to himself—not that he would dare tell anyone else, well, maybe Penny—it was fun. No one in the Baltimore Bureau had ever destroyed reefer before. Another war story to tell the grandkids.

The next day wasn't quite so much fun. Sparshott's Montgomery County bosses were bellowing like bulls. Tippett had paid them a visit and, although Campbell had not been present at the meeting, he caught the drift of what Tippett had said, secondhand of course: Tracy Sparshott was a great undercover but totally unmanageable. He was as selfish as a kid. He wouldn't listen to anyone, thought the Bureau worked for *him*, made promises and plans without proper permission, spent money like Onassis, and thought he was James Bond. Allowing Carlos Medina to sample government marijuana was the last ridiculous straw. Somebody had to do something before he destroyed the whole undercover investigation.

Campbell had heard it all before—many times—and couldn't blame Sparshott's superiors for being pissed. They had loaned the Bureau their best undercover narc—creatively unpredictable to be sure, but honest, productive and tireless—and the Bureau was bitching because it couldn't handle him. If the FBI didn't want the guy, hell, Montgomery County had plenty of cases waiting.

To save Sparshott, Campbell had to cut Tippett's legs off just below the balls. "Well, Tracy's kept *me* apprised of everything," he told Sparshott's bosses. "And I approved every single thing." Campbell went on to argue that not only was Sparshott under control, he was essential to the success of the case and that he, Campbell, needed and wanted him. And he, not Tippett, was in charge of the undercover investigation.

It took fast, hard talking but Campbell won the argument. Then he called the team together. The meet with Roberto in Miami will be within seven days, he said. Carlos was eager to make the introduction and to delay it would make him suspicious. But the team can't plan and execute the meeting in such a poisonous atmosphere. Therefore, there will be an important change which, he hoped, would help them all work together more smoothly. In the future, Tippett and Sparshott will only talk to each other through him, and they will only be present in the same room if there's an emergency. It's no one's fault, but the case can no longer withstand the aftershocks of their conflicts. End of discussion, which was just fine with Sparshott.

With Tippett and Sparshott out of venom range, or so he hoped, Campbell cleared the Miami trip with the creds in Baltimore. He insisted on taking Jeff Favitta along with him, Sparshott, and Macready, arguing that since Favitta had worked both in Miami and on the Tabares case, he knew the city and the bad guys by sight. His presence was necessary for the safety of the lead undercover. Preston would stay home to work on the wiretap. It would be too confusing for Roberto to meet both Terry *and* Marty, and too dangerous since *both* undercovers ran the risk of being made.

It came as a great surprise, but the creds gave Campbell what he wanted for a change. Who knew why. Perhaps it finally dawned on them that they had a big case on their hands.

The team flew into Miami on March 17, the day before the meeting with Roberto, to conduct surveillance on Roberto, Gustavo, and Carlos when he got there. Although they traveled on the same plane, they didn't sit together. You never knew in the drug trade, Roberto could have planted someone on board to see if Terry was alone. A rented white Lincoln Town Car, easy to follow at night, waited for them at the Miami airport.

Three FBI agents joined them on surveillance that night and Campbell was as embarrassed as he was angry. He had given the Miami SAC plenty of advance notice about his surveillance needs and indeed the three agents he requested showed up on time. But two were dressed in suits and ties. They looked like feds on surveillance and weren't thrilled to be assigned shit detail after hours on another field office's case. The third special agent drove a surveillance car with a stack of two by fours he just bought for a home repair job sticking out the window. That made him even more conspicuous than his two desk-jock buddies.

Campbell had to make a choice. The Roberto meet was Sparshott's most dangerous undercover assignment so far. It would go down on Roberto's turf. Roberto would select the location and be protected by his own people. Roberto would decide when to come and when to go. If suspicious, he could have someone kill Sparshott, stow his body on *The Excuse*, and drop it into the Bermuda Triangle. The cuffs, as it were, were now on the other wrist.

Campbell wasn't surprised that the three agents assigned to him didn't know the first thing about narcotics surveillance. Most FBI agents spent their days behind computers and desks. What little they had learned about undercover surveillance at Quantico, they soon forgot through disuse unless they were assigned to the Bureau's Special Operations Group which specialized in surveillance and were a unit to be proud of.

It was too late for Campbell to trade in the three duds for three new ones who might be just as rusty. Either he had to keep them and risk Roberto burning them, or he had to fire them and risk leaving Sparshott out in the cold without enough backup. Given those options, Campbell chose to cover Sparshott without the Bureau. It was much safer to be short handed than left handed.

The team was waiting at the airport for Carlos at noon on Wednesday. They knew which Eastern Airlines flight he was on and that Roberto would pick him up because Carlos had discussed travel arrangements on the bugged telephone. They watched him get into Roberto's Cadillac Cimarron and tailed him to Roberto's house in Little Havana. They waited down the street to see if anything of interest might develop and when it didn't they drove back to the Brickell Point Hyatt to review the strategy for the dinner meeting later that night:

Terry would encourage Roberto to select the restaurant. It was his town, his meeting, his treat. But he would insist on driving Roberto to dinner in the Town Car which Bureau agents had wired with a transmitter. On the way, he would casually drop the name of the restaurant Roberto chose and ask directions street by street. Macready and Favitta would hear the conversation on their receiver and follow Terry at a safe distance. And because Terry didn't know Miami, it would not appear strange to Roberto if he drove slowly.

All in all, a practical plan. But like all plans, it was built on assumptions, and as everyone knows, assumptions, like bullets, can kill.

THIRTY-ONE

6:30 P.M.

Sparshott waits in his room for Carlos to return a beeper call. Campbell is watching for bad guys in the cavernous hotel lobby where he's been for several hours. So far he hasn't seen anyone suspicious, not even a house dick. Macready and Favitta are parked out front looking for signs of counter-surveillance. When Sparshott leaves the hotel, assuming he and Roberto don't eat inside, they'll follow the wired Lincoln, which is parked in the lot behind the hotel, all night. Like Campbell with whom they are in radio contact, they see nothing unusual.

The room phone finally rings. Sparshott picks it up. It's Carlos and he's as wary as a rabbit.

"Hey, what's up, Terry?"

"Where are you?"

"Listen, we're going to pick you up. Do you have reservations?"

"No, I was gonna see where you wanted to eat."

"Good . . . just wait for us."

"Where we gonna go?"

"To a restaurant. Are you ready?"

"I was just gonna jump in the shower."

The plan is to have Carlos come up to the room while Sparshott is still wet so Medina can snoop around and find the goodies he planted: a wallet with a "Terry Petit" driver's license and credit cards, a piece of paper with drug calculations, a biker's outfit on a hanger next to the door (Sparshott told Carlos he flew in from Houston), and a fake itinerary with real airline tickets to match—Washington to Houston, Houston to Miami, Miami to Washington. The itinerary supported his broad Texas cover story and allowed him to slip into Miami quickly and quietly.

So much for carefully laid plans. Now, whether Carlos comes up to the room or waits in the lobby is a moot undercover point. Carlos intends to take him to an unknown restaurant in an unknown car and he has to change Carlos' mind. A piece of u.c. cake, man.

"Just give me the address and I'll meet you there," Sparshott suggests. "I wanna shower and pick up something on the way."

"What?"

"Like a fuckin' blow job!"

Carlos starts to laugh even though he still sounds tense. That Terry has such a way with words. About to meet the *man* and he's thinking blow job.

Sparshott hears a doorbell ring on Carlos' end and assumes he's calling from Roberto's house. But the situation is suddenly too dangerous for another assumption. He wants facts. If the Miami feds weren't such undercover assholes, he would know *exactly* where Carlos and Roberto are. And he would learn what car they are driving three minutes after they started the engine.

"What's that noise?" Sparshott fishes.

"That's bells."

"Doorbell? Sounds like church."

"I know." Carlos doesn't bite. "It's funny."

"Why don't you just give me an address for the restaurant so I can—"

"Tell me what time you're gonna be ready and we'll pick you up," Carlos says. Roberto warned him to be firm and not allow Terry to dictate terms like he did in Washington. Miami was *his* town and he intended to call the shots.

"I'm fuckin' starved, man," Sparshott says. "What kind of food we gonna have?"

"Eight?"

Sparshott tries another tack. "Make it seven-thirty. I got a car. I'll just wait for you out front and follow."

"Seven-thirty's okay . . . but I'll wait for you downstairs. Our car. What room you in?"

"2237"

The situation is getting worse by the minute. Carlos won't tell Sparshott where he is or where they are going. He won't let him drive them to the restaurant or follow in his own car. Since he's convinced he can still talk his way into the Town Car, Sparshott doesn't warn Campbell about a possible change in the game plan. Understaffed, Campbell has enough to worry about.

7:10 P.M.

Sparshott's room phone rings. He's a little surprised. As planned, he's not dressed, but if Carlos is early it's something new. He picks up.

"I'm downstairs," Carlos says.

"Hey man, you're fifteen minutes early. I'm still dressing. Come on up."

"No . . . I'll wait for you down here. Don't take too long."

"Okay, I'll meet you by the bar."

Sparshott finishes dressing in a hurry so he doesn't keep Roberto waiting. He's disappointed that Carlos won't come up to sniff out his room. Fuck, the visit would buy an extra three minutes to find out why Carlos is so secretive—the guy's never been like this before—and where they're going for dinner. The night is definitely off to a bad-guy-start. Carlos is in control and Sparshott doesn't like it one damn bit.

Sparshott steps off the elevator dressed in a three-piece suit and looking about as comfortable as a bear in a tux. He spots Carlos standing outside the cocktail lounge and Campbell sitting in a chair halfway between Carlos and the front door. As he walks across the lobby, he's comforted by the thought that Campbell has already radioed Macready that Carlos is in the hotel.

Carlos watches Terry lumber across the lobby and is in stitches by the time Sparshott reaches him. He holds his gut and points at the new threads. That badass Terry, he's such a scream.

Sparshott enjoys the joke on himself, then suggests that he drive everyone to the restaurant in the big Lincoln he especially rented for the evening, but Carlos says that Roberto is waiting outside in *his* car. Sparshott offers to follow Roberto so he won't have to return to the hotel after dinner, but Carlos says Roberto wants Terry to ride with *him*. Sparshott tries to pry out of Carlos where they're going to eat so he can drop the name of the restaurant as they walk by Campbell, but Carlos just smiles like a kid with a secret.

Sparshott follows Carlos to the front door. He has one last chance to cover his ass. Roberto couldn't possibly take his refusal to ride with him as insult. There isn't a fucking drug dealer this side of Antarctica who'd willingly agree to a ride in a strange drug dealer's car.

Sparshott steps outside. A white stretch limo with tinted blue windows hogs the curb, motor humming to cool its leather seats for some out of town celebrity or corporate VIP. He glances up and down the crescent driveway but doesn't see Roberto or his Cimarron.

"Surprise!" Carlos says as he opens the back door of the limo with a flourish.

"Wow, this is really nice," Sparshott says. His mind is racing. Fuck, that's what the sonofabitch had up his sleeve. Well, there's no way I can refuse a limo ride . . . what if Macready doesn't see me step into the stretch, shit, I'll lose his backup for the night . . . pass the fucking Maalox.

Sparshott paces the length of the limo to give Macready a chance to see him and shamelessly gushes: "A great car . . . and what a surprise!" As he stalls for precious seconds, he reassesses. Roberto and the limo are sending him one of two messages. Either, "You showed my man a good time, now I want to show you a good time." Or, "Adios, amigo narco."

Carlos is getting impatient. "Come on," he says. "Let's go."

As he stuffs his hulk through the door, head low so he doesn't bang it on the roof, Sparshott sees two pairs of shoes. He slides into the cool leather seat facing the rear next to the curbside door. If he has to jump out, he'd just as soon not roll under Macready's wheels. He looks up. Gustavo is sitting across from him, Roberto is next to Gustavo facing the driver, and a bouquet of red and white carnations rests on the ledge behind them. Roberto watches him with cold curiosity as if he were a specimen in a petri dish.

Carlos crawls past Sparshott, takes a seat across from Roberto, then raps on the window that separates the back seat from the driver. The limo pulls away, glides down the driveway as smoothly as a skater on ice, then turns right on Brickell Avenue toward Roberto's house. Roberto hands the bouquet of carnations to Sparshott who says thanks—the only words spoken so far—then plucks a white flower and slips it through the buttonhole of his lapel. His mouth is dry and his nerves as taut as fiddle strings.

"You want a drink?" Carlos finally asks.

"Yeah, I'll take a rum and coke."

Carlos reaches into the bar which is lodged between him and Sparshott and takes out a decanter. The only sound in the limo is the tinkle of ice against crystal and the fizz of Coke. Carlos hands the glass to Sparshott. It's not that he's thirsty. He just wants to have something in his hand for Gustavo, you know, just in case. What a fucking way to make a living!

"Terry, this is Roberto," Carlos says. He points to Tabares in his gray suit, open collar, and elevated shoes. Roberto doesn't blink.

"How ya doin'," Sparshott says as cheerfully as he can. "Where we goin'?"

"We got a *nice* place picked out," Carlos says.

Sparshott tries to read the mood. Roberto seems hostile as if waiting for him to prove himself. He's probably worried about Terry being armed or wired or both. Gustavo is as cautious as a panther. He's probably armed or has a gun hidden in the limo cushion behind him. Carlos is as cool as the leather seats. He obviously doesn't want to let on to Roberto that Terry is more than a business contact. Fucking Terry is his friend, man.

The limo turns down Coral Way. It's a wide street with a median strip and not terribly busy on a weeknight after the rush hour. Sparshott glances out the window a few times as if to take in the sights. He doesn't see the surveillance car which pleases him as much as it makes him feel lonely.

Carlos breaks the awkward silence by saying he hopes Terry will take over his string of Washington customers so he can retire. It's an opening Sparshott didn't expect so early in the evening and he seizes it to make a point Roberto can't possibly miss.

"I have my own people, buddy," he tells Carlos. The words sting the kid like a nettle. "I don't wanna work for you. I got my own sweet operation goin'."

Sparshott relaxes when the limo pulls up to the front door of the Studio Restaurant less than ten minutes after it left Brickell Point. Southwest 32nd Avenue, which runs in front of the place, is busy and the parking lot nearly full—ideal for Macready. Roberto rattles something in Spanish to Gustavo who opens the door next to Sparshott and gets out. When Sparshott makes a move to follow, Carlos tells him to wait.

Gustavo does the usual scan-dance to see if they were followed or if there are any suspicious looking people sitting in parked cars. Hey, thank God Tippett stayed home. Then he strolls to 32nd Avenue and looks up and down the street. Sparshott gets a good look at him through the one-way tinted glass window. Mid-thirties, black hair and green eyes, two hundred pounds piled on a six-foot frame. Kilo for kilo, an even match. He hopes Macready isn't too fucking obvious.

As Gustavo returns to the limo, Sparshott prepares himself mentally to leap through the door, knock Gustavo on his ass, and disappear between the parked cars. But Gustavo doesn't seem shifty or on edge. Sparshott allows himself to relax again so he can conserve his energy. He senses he's going to need it. Gustavo and Roberto are too cautious, Carlos too cool.

Roberto lowers his window and tells Gustavo something in

Spanish. The guy walks to the front door of the restaurant and enters. Sparshott figures that Roberto just sent him on ahead to make sure his table was ready. When Gustavo comes back out and nods to the limo, Carlos says, "Okay, Terry, let's go now."

The Studio looks like something straight out of Havana. Palm trees, fishnets, very expensive cigar smoke, little guys in white evening jackets, senorita waitresses, and Latino music to shake their cute asses to. The Cuban owner is waiting for Roberto at the maitre d' stand like Bob Wills waited for Sparshott in the Bull on the Mark. He says something warmly to Roberto in Spanish, then hugs him like a brother. Sparshott smiles and really relaxes, well, as much as a white unarmed undercover cop without a wire and surrounded by dope dealers in Little Havana can.

Gustavo leads them to a reserved table in a quiet corner, but before they sit down and order a round of drinks, Roberto spits out another stream of Spanish. Carlos looks like he just swallowed a bad oyster. "Sorry, Terry," he says. "They want to see you in the men's room."

Sparshott walks to the back of the restaurant between Gustavo and Roberto. It's possible but unlikely, he thinks, that they have dope hidden in a john commode, you know, like in the movies, and want to show it to him before dinner so they can all relax and have a good Latino time. It's more likely they don't trust him and want to find out who he is. Or maybe Gustavo made Macready in the parking lot and didn't want to create a scene outside. Maybe they *know* who he is and are taking him to a back room or the back alley. Sparshott thinks of his daughter Morgan. He knows he can handle Gustavo. What the fuck am I doing in Little Havana so far from her? He knows he can take Roberto. She needs me. But both guys at once?

THIRTY-TWO

As Medina and Sparshott reached the front door of the Hyatt, Bill Campbell got up from his seat in the lobby and started walking. Keeping his back to the entrance, he pressed the transmission button on his radio and said to Macready: "They're leaving through the front door right now." He waited for two minutes then got on the radio again, "Did you see him?" Macready didn't answer. "Jerry, did you see him?"

When Macready still didn't answer, Campbell wasn't sure what to think. Maybe Jerry was so busy tailing Sparshott he didn't want to take his eyes off the road. Or maybe Tabares entered the hotel when Campbell's back was turned and decided to eat in the Esplanades Restaurant next to the entrance on the right. Wouldn't that be great for surveillance!

In spite of his curiosity, Campbell didn't peek into the Esplanades for fear of being made. Instead he strolled out the front door like a hotel guest in no great hurry. Momentarily relieved that he didn't bump into Sparshott, Medina, or Tabares standing outside, he tensed when he spotted Macready still sitting in his surveillance car not far from the cab stand. Campbell hurried over to him, figuring Sparshott must somehow still be in the hotel.

"Where is he?" Campbell asked.

"Shit, I don't know. I never *saw* him."

"What about Medina? Tabares?"

"Shit, I never saw them either."

"Where the hell *is* he then?"

Macready felt panic rumbling in his stomach like gas. He

knew Tabares was coming to get Sparshott and he knew Sparshott would be leaving through the front entrance or be carried out on his shield. There was no way, Tracy had promised, that he would allow Carlos or Roberto to lead him out the back door or a side exit. Macready reconstructed the scene out loud:

A white stretch limo pulled up to the entrance and parked. He didn't notice anyone waiting for it or getting out . . . Then Campbell radioed saying Medina and Sparshott were leaving the hotel, but he didn't see them exit because the limo partially obstructed his view. And he didn't notice anyone enter the limo because he couldn't see the curbside door from his vantage point. When the stretch finally drove off, the sidewalk was empty . . . The limo turned right onto Brickell Avenue then disappeared around a sharp curve. He remembered asking himself at the time, "I wonder if the sonofabitch picked Tracy up in a limo." But since he hadn't seen Sparshott, Medina, or Tabares, he dismissed the thought.

Nobody was kidding anybody. As soon as Macready said "limo" all three investigators knew exactly what had happened but couldn't face the consequences. They talked themselves into believing Sparshott was still around the hotel somewhere. He would never vanish into a muggy Miami night, unarmed, without a wire, and without backup! That's not the way undercover work is done.

While Macready waited outside the hotel in case Sparshott magically reappeared—Tracy always had a fucking rabbit up his sleeve—Campbell and Favitta raced to the hotel parking lot. The Lincoln Town Car hadn't moved an inch and its hood was still night-air cool. Next, they slowly drove around the hotel looking for—who the hell knew what—Sparshott taking a piss under a palm tree, Tabares' Cadillac Cimarron parked in the bottom of the swimming pool, a white stretch limo with a flat tire. When they found no trace of Sparshott or the limo, they drove back to Macready.

"I'll check inside," Campbell said. "You and Jeff wait out here."

Campbell walked back into the lobby as calmly as he could

under the circumstances. He took a slow look around, he checked the Esplanades—screw getting made—he peeked into the bar, he called room 2237. No sign of Sparshott, not the smallest undercover spoor.

The three investigators stood outside the Hyatt and debated what to do next. "It *had* to be the limo," Campbell finally admitted. No one argued with him. He told Macready to stay at the hotel in case Sparshott returned while he and Favitta went limo hunting. Miami might be a big town, they told themselves, but Little Havana is small and how many white stretches could there be out there on a weeknight?

Macready felt so sick as he watched Campbell and Favitta disappear around the curve on Brickell Avenue, he wanted to vomit his anger, fear, and shame into the bushes. He had the eyeball on the front door. It was a simple enough job. How the fuck could anyone miss seeing Tracy, the big lug! What if something happened to him? What would he tell Tracy's wife? All bullshit aside, he fucked up and there was no one to call for help and nothing to do but cruise the streets of Miami and wait outside the Hyatt like a fucking rookie.

□ □ □

Campbell and Favitta followed the tracks of the limo down Brickell Avenue to Coral Way, then headed north just as the limo had done. They reasoned that if Roberto lived in Little Havana, he probably took Terry to a Cuban restaurant there. So they headed for the restaurant strip. Hell, no one had to tell them they were clutching at straws, but looking for a limo beat waiting back at the Hyatt for one to turn up.

Traffic was heavy, the streets of Little Havana noisy, the restaurants busy. They drove by Roberto's house. They dropped by Gustavo's. They checked the Tabares Liquor store and looked in the parking lot in the back. No sign of the white limo which was parked outside the Studio Restaurant in Coral Gables, a mile north from where they searched.

"We might as well go back to the hotel and wait," Campbell finally said. "Maybe Tracy will notice we lost him and find a way to call."

Campbell felt like shit. He couldn't blame Macready for not spotting Sparshott. The poor guy couldn't be expected to see everything. He couldn't blame Sparshott for not warning him he'd be going to dinner in Roberto's car. It would have been a risky move. He blamed himself. Given all the unknowns and the danger, he should have had at least five cars protecting Sparshott's back. He had simply made the wrong choice when he fired the Miami Bureau.

Never in his life had Campbell felt so utterly helpless. He didn't know where Tracy was, who he was with, what he was doing, if he was in danger, if he was dead. Over the last six months, Tracy had become a real brother and now that the guy needed him there wasn't a goddamn thing he could do but pray to the god of all narcs.

Macready and Favitta waited in the surveillance car outside the hotel, Campbell waited inside. He couldn't sit still. He went to his room and sat by the phone in case Sparshott called, he paced the lobby, he talked to Macready on the radio, he checked the front desk for messages, he went outside to chat with Macready and Favitta because sharing his fear with them made him less afraid. More clutching at more straws.

THIRTY-THREE

7:45 P.M.

There's a guy standing at the urinal with his dick in his hand when Sparshott steps into the Studio men's room followed by Gustavo and Roberto. Sparshott thinks about how to use the guy to get the fuck out of there, but Gustavo tells him to scram, "vamoose," like in the movies, and Sparshott knows Gustavo means business by the sound of his voice.

After the guy rushes out of the john still trying to zip his fly, Roberto blocks the door. "Check, check," he orders Gustavo in English so Terry can understand and won't panic. As Gustavo shoves Terry into an empty stall and begins to pat him down, Roberto moves away from the door to watch.

Sparshott feels relieved in one sense—shit, he's not stupid enough to wear a wire—but still scared. What if the search is only a preview? Raul Tabares is convalescing in a Miami hospital. What if Roberto told his son he's meeting a big badass marijuana distributor from Maryland called Terry who wants to move into coke? Does Raul know him? Know him, Papa, know him! Put a hole in the motherfucker for me will you?

Gustavo finds a small can of spray cologne in Terry's coat pocket and examines it carefully, as if it's one of those trick microphones. "What's this?" he asks.

"Cologne . . . it's spray . . . give it to him."

Gustavo hands the canister to Roberto who pockets it. "Look under shirt," he says.

Sparshott doesn't resist as Gustavo unbuttons his shirt and checks his bare skin for a wire, then unzips his pants and feels his legs and crotch.

"Okay," Gustavo tells Roberto who smiles for the first time.

"Okay," Roberto tells Terry.

"Fuck okay!" Sparshott says.

He slams Gustavo against the wall of the stall keeping his body between him and the opening, then pats him down, balls and all, without making him unzip. Gustavo's first reaction is to struggle but on second thought he submits as Terry did. Roberto watches in silence, like, hey hombre, I no blame. Sparshott finds a switchblade which he returns to Gustavo when he's finished.

While Gustavo straightens his clothes, Sparshott reaches through the opening of the stall and pulls Roberto inside by his shirt. Like Gustavo, Roberto is shocked but doesn't resist. Sparshott pats him down thoroughly, his eyes badass biker hard, then steps back.

"Now . . . okay."

Roberto laughs as if he half expected Sparshott to pull a stunt like that. Didn't Carlos warn him that Terry is such a scream? "I sorry," Roberto says. "I sorry . . . necessary."

"Hey, don't mention it, pal."

Back in the dining room, Carlos looks like a defendant waiting for the jury. One look at Roberto and he knows the verdict. The guy is smiling as if trying to remember one of Terry's dirty jokes.

They sit and Roberto sends Gustavo to the bar for a round of drinks. Sparshott appreciates the move—Roberto wants him to know that Gustavo is just muscle, nothing more. As they settle into their drinks, a waitress brings menus. Carlos waits for Sparshott to open it, and when he doesn't, he asks, "What do you want to have?"

Sparshott couldn't care less about food after his visit to the men's room. He's pleased with the way he managed to turn the table and take command, but he's still anxious, and a long list of unknowns nibble at his appetite. He thinks of Macready and Favitta waiting outside and cussing. Fucking Tracy has all the fun, we gotta sit out here without air, he's inside checking out the cute little asses and eating like a pig. Hey, just a little narc humor.

"I'm *his* guest," Sparshott says. "Let him order for me."

Roberto beams with an almost childlike pleasure, so different from the hard-assed drug dealer in the john. He orders one of each appetizer on the menu and a bottle of Cuban wine, then selects the main entrees with great authority and in Spanish as if he planned the dinner in advance. Pleasure out of the way, he gets down to business, none of that did you have a nice flight, how do you like our Miami weather, do you have a room with a view?

"My English no good . . . I sorry," he says.

Carlos explains that if either man doesn't understand the other, he'll translate. The kid's tense and knows he playing to two juries at the same time. He wants Terry to impress Roberto so Roberto will sell to Terry. And he wants Terry to conclude that Roberto can deliver so Terry will buy from Roberto. Fuck, man, what a way to pay for college.

Roberto pauses, then begins by stressing that Carlos is his man in Washington now and Carlos handles all sales and money transactions. He himself is gradually retiring from retail distribution and moving exclusively into wholesale supply.

Christ, not *another* retiree, Sparshott thinks. Tom Roberts better hurry or the whole fucking Tabares organization will be on social security. Then Sparshott waits for the other shoe to drop. His biggest fear in coming down to Miami is not that he might blow the meet or fail to win Roberto's trust. It's that Roberto might simply tell him, "You deal with Carlos . . . not me." If he does, Roberts might just as well arrest everyone as soon as the team returns because he'll never get any closer to Roberto than searching his balls in a shitter. But Roberto doesn't tell Sparshott to deal exclusively through Carlos, so buying directly from Roberto, powder on his fingers and all, is still a real possibility.

His own role clarified, Carlos leaps into the conversation like a guy with hot poker up his ass. "I have *one more* thing to check out on you, man," he tells Sparshott trying to assert a little authority. After all, he's Roberto's man in Washington. "Money . . . money, man . . . we're going to Harrisburg, right?"

"Right!"

"When?"

"How about next week—Thursday. Old Mike's gonna be there."

"No problem."

Sparshott knows Carlos posed the question for the benefit of Roberto, like, Terry, tell the old man what you told me about seeing your bankroll, he doesn't believe me. Sparshott thinks he saw a furtive gleam of greed in Roberto's eye at the mention of money. He senses the money show is the last critical test in their eyes so he set a firm date without permission. Hey, Tippett, fuck you and your cred bullshit, pal. That's the thing about creds. They don't understand that when you're under pressure and your fuckin' credibility is on the line, you gotta make commitments and worry about the details later.

Roberto is so delighted with the promised money show that he asks like a kid who needs to take a pee, "I go too?"

"Great," Sparshott says and means it. "Glad to have you along, buddy."

Roberto's wanting to see and feel Terry's money in Harrisburg is a wonderful surprise. After a few false steps, it's turning out to be a good-guy night after all as Sparshott wrests more control by the minute. Thursday is enough time for the IRS and the FBI to get the flash money, Old Mike to fly up to Washington for a briefing, and Campbell and Tippett to find a bank, airplane, and pilots.

"So when we actually going to *do* something?" Carlos asks.

"When Old Mike tells me my money is right, you know, from the last shipment."

"How much you want to do?"

"One kilo up there . . . then one down here to make sure everything goes smooth."

The second kilo buy in Miami is more than insurance. It

gives the team a second option for future buys and a chance to see Roberto's operation up close which means more arrests and seizures. It will establish Terry as a cautious buyer who isn't afraid to spend money to test the supplier and the shit, so unlike those cheap feds who spend as little as they can get away with. Maybe Sparshott can even con an introduction to Roberto's supplier. Ever since Carlos confided on the ride to Annapolis that there were three big Cuban coke dealers in Miami and Roberto was the right hand of one, Sparshott has been drooling down his Harley shirt.

Roberto likes the two-buy proposal and Sparshott begins negotiations. He tells Roberto he wants to pay the lower Miami price for the buy in Washington even though Roberto has delivery costs. Roberto suggests $26K per key as a fair price which is halfway between the thirty thou Carlos asked and the twenty-two Sparshott offered. Roberto explains that the price is a little steep because he guarantees high quality coke delivered on time.

Sparshott knows that coke goes for around $20K in Miami. Although Roberto's price is in deep center field, it's still in the ballpark and Sparshott doesn't mind giving in. He stood his ground, forced Carlos' price down, and won. Roberto will be more convinced than ever that he's not a narc—feds take dope at any price just to get the deal behind them—and will owe him one for agreeing to the compromise.

"How much buy later?" Roberto asks. He obviously knows the answer from talking to Carlos but wants to hear it from Terry himself.

"Fifty kilos."

"No problem . . . need time. You call, I ready fifteen days."

"I'll pay for forty on delivery and the rest in a week. When we're really rollin' my people can pick up the shit in airplanes and make deliveries to Maryland and Texas."

Roberto objects and confides to Terry that he has a better way to move cocaine. His people own an auto repair shop where they can remove the back seat of a car, create a womb, then pack in the tightly-wrapped kilo packages. "Safer than air," he says. "You visit after buy in Miami . . . you see."

Christ, a chop-shop. That juicy piece is worth the cost of the trip to Miami and the $26K for the toot. Seize the whole fucking place, equipment and cars, make another string of arrests, who knows, maybe the shop deals in hot autos or customizes them for other shit peddlers, watch 'em for a week, then clean out half of Little Havana. Ain't it enough to make a narc weep?

For the most part, it's a pleasant dinner. The icy Roberto Tabares of the limo slowly melts into an open, warm, and funny guy. Never in a narc lifetime would you pick him out of a crowd as a dope dealer. He seems too gentle to even own a gun much less shoot it, and he treats Terry like a new friend he's eager to please. But under the surface of the dinner runs a current of anxiety. It's as if Roberto has something on his mind and can't relax until he settles it. He eats quickly and without relish, doesn't order dessert, and won't suggest an after-dinner drink at the bar. Instead, he calls for the check, hands it to Gustavo without looking at it, and says something in Spanish which Carlos translates:

"He says you did me a favor by showing me your business. Now he wants to return the favor. He says you're going to make more money than you ever dreamed of."

Tell me about it, motherfucker. A fishing boat, liquor store, nightclub, two houses, bank accounts, a string of cars, and now a fuckin' chop-shop.

9:00 P.M.

Motor purring and dripping air conditioner water, the limo is waiting outside the Studio. Roberto and Carlos get in. Sparshott stretches and takes a deep breath like a guy who just ate too much lobster and shrimp and shit, and looks around for the undercover car. When he doesn't see it, he's pleased. Nothing worse at this point, now that he's almost home free, than to have Gustavo burn Macready.

For his part, Gustavo takes one last look around the lot and the street, then ducks inside the limo and shuts the door. The stretch pulls away. With no idea where it's taking him, Sparshott feels more pressure than tension. He knows Roberto is going to show him some coke and he's no longer afraid Gustavo might try to kill him. He could tell from the dinner conversation that Roberto accepts his cover story but isn't convinced yet that he's good for $1.3 million which is what fifty kilos of coke will cost. That's why Roberto's so anxious to see Harrisburg. But Sparshott knows he can still make a stupid mistake that could blow his cover, and that Macready can still get burned.

The limo turns south onto 26th Avenue and glides by Hondas and Toyotas parked in driveways, a long white ghost on wheels looking for a place to rest. After a few blocks, it slows, then turns into the curved driveway of a corner house, but the stretch is so big it doesn't fit. Since Roberto's paying for door-to-door service, the driver isn't sure what to do. He parks half in the driveway and half on the street and hopes he doesn't lose his tip.

Even before the limo turned into the driveway, Sparshott knew it was heading for Gustavo's place. He climbs out of the car and glances down the street. Thank fucking goodness, he doesn't see any headlights and reminds himself to tell Macready what a great surveillance job he and Favitta did.

Gustavo disappears around the corner of the house and raps loudly on a window. A minute later, his wife Nicky opens the door with a radiant smile, happy to have her father visit her humble home which, of course, he owns. She ushers her guests into the dining room on the left where Roberto offers Terry a chair at the table and orders Gustavo to fetch drinks.

Gustavo hurries into the kitchen, returns with a tray, then disappears into the rear of the house. When he comes back a few minutes later, he's carrying a yellow nylon bag which he presents to Roberto who barks another order in Spanish. If it wasn't clear who's in charge, it is now.

Roberto unzips the bag and takes out a brick wrapped in green duct tape with "kilo" printed on it in black magic marker. Gustavo returns with a cutting kit—knife, razor, spoon, and mirror. Roberto takes the knife, slits the package, just like Terry did for

Carlos, drug-tit for drug-tat, then spoons out a G of powder which he piles on the mirror.

"Here!"

Roberto slides the mirror to Terry. It's the final test. Terry's a reefer dealer who's never dealt coke so he can't appear to know too much about it. But he's also a careful buyer so he has to know what he's doing.

Sparshott takes a pinch of the coke and rubs it slowly between his fingers. Roberto watches him like a diamond merchant. The coke is quite oily, at least 85 percent pure. Terry looks at his fingers and nods almost imperceptibly to Roberto. Then he rubs a little cocaine residue on the inside of his lips, careful not to swallow any, fucking Tippett would arrest him for use of a controlled substance if he did. Aware of his rapt audience of three, he takes his time and waits. His lips immediately turn numb and remain so for a minute. Then, he silently nods his final okay.

Sparshott isn't certain whether Roberto expects him to snort or swallow the shit and is prepared to argue the point when Carlos grabs the spoon before Gustavo can whisk away the candy, dips it into the package, and builds a mound of coke on the mirror. Then he takes the razorblade, draws a line, and fishes a twenty dollar bill from his pocket as if he knew in advance he was going to get a free hit and wanted to be ready. He rolls Jefferson into a straw, then snorts the shit like a junkie. Thank you Carlos, you dumb shithead.

Sparshott wants out of Gustavo's house. He wants to drink and party and put the stress and tension behind him. He's passed every single test Roberto put to him. He turned in a flawless performance and is excited. He's fluid, loose, like he can fit any form, squeeze into any tiny corner. He doesn't even feel the strain he knows is there. He wants to shout, "Hey Tippett, you sonofabitch, I did it. I'm in!" But he still has a few more lines to recite before the final curtain and he wants them to be memorable.

"Fuck man, I don't allow my people to do shit," Sparshott slowly and calmly tells Roberto so he doesn't miss a word. His eyes aren't angry just flinty. "I don't like dealing with people who do shit. And I don't like being in the same room with so much fuckin' shit."

Roberto stumbles all over himself with embarrassment. He lectures Carlos in a stream of angry Spanish and you don't have to be a linguist to catch the gist. Carlos' coffee brown face flushes a delicate purple. Then, Roberto turns to Sparshott and apologizes for Carlos' behavior and for placing him at risk. "I sorry . . . I sorry . . . no more." He's defensive and disappointed that his cocaine show is not as impressive as Terry's marijuana show. Fuck man, a perfect ending to Act Two.

10:05 P.M.

Macready still waits in the surveillance car outside the Hyatt. It's been the longest three hours of his life. Not knowing when or if Tracy will return. Of all the IRS criminal and undercover shit he's done in his life, there's nothing to compare to the wrenching fear of those three hours. To say it's been the worst night he's ever spent doesn't even begin to describe his pain. There's anger at the Bureau for not sending their best surveillance teams, terror that maybe Tracy is dying at that very moment or already dead, anxiety that's he's alive but the case is dead, embarrassment that he lost the guy to begin with.

Then he spots the white limo round the bend on Brickell Avenue and feels like shouting, "Tracy, you wonderful, crazy sonofabitch." Instead he grabs his radio and says calmly, the total professional, "Here comes the white limo."

The stretch door opens and Sparshott is the first one to step out looking like he's ready to drink his buddies under the table. He waits for Roberto and Carlos with a confident stance that says, "I got you, motherfuckers." Macready is so happy he feels like running over and kissing the sonofabitch right in front of the Brickell Point Hyatt for all Miami to see. Instead he says: "It's Tracy. Let's get *on* him."

Sparshott leads Roberto, Carlos, and Gustavo up to his

room with the excuse that he has something special for them there. In reality, the room is wired for sound and he wants to get Roberto on tape for Tom Roberts and to finally give Carlos that chance to snoop.

After a visit to the john, door closed, Sparshott steers Roberto into a recap of their dinner negotiation: $26,000 per key . . . one buy in Washington . . . one in Miami . . . a large buy of fifty keys later. Then he gives Roberto a Harley hat and Gustavo a Harley t-shirt. They're as happy as bikers at a rock concert. Carlos, who is still angry at Terry for bitching about him in front of Roberto, doesn't get a present and that miffs him even more.

Sparshott invites everyone down to Currents, a cafe-bar in the lobby, for dessert and a nightcap. It's a perfect ending to a perfect night. Roberto is as relaxed as a kitten by the fire. He tells Terry that he wants to expand his business into New Orleans and wonders if Terry can help him. Carlos obviously bought the New Orleans scam and Sparshott promises to do what he can. Then, just before Sparshott can call it an early night—it's only eleven—Carlos says, "my man is *very* happy with the way things went tonight."

"Yes," Roberto adds. "I show you me . . . I show my business."

Then he rapid-fires something in Spanish and he and Carlos laugh until tears come to their eyes. When he finally gets his voice back, Carlos translates.

"My man says you don't look like a DEA agent."

This time Sparshott laughs until tears come to his eyes. Hell no, pal . . . I'm no fed, I'm a fucking local. The compliment of his career, his bouquet of roses and his curtain call. He nearly floats back into the lobby and feels an uncontrollable urge to ham it up for the gallery. Roberto is carrying his new Harley hat in his hand. Sparshott takes it and puts it on Tabares' head. He knows Campbell is watching from somewhere and will get a kick out of it. The hat is so big it comes over the guy's ears. Christ, what a picture. Roberto Tabares in his $500 gray silk suit, standing in the lobby of a hotel filled with women wearing diamonds and silk in a

Harley hat that makes him look like an FBI agent undercover. Even Gustavo smiles.

Sparshott leads his friends out to the limo where he says good night, reminding Roberto about the trip to Harrisburg the following Thursday.

□ □ □

When the stretch pulled away, Sparshott walked back into the lobby and took the elevator up to his room. He suddenly felt drained. His armpits were damp from sweat, he craved a shower, he wanted to compare notes with the other guys, and he lusted after a Captain Morgan's rum and Coke. Like Circe, the back alley pub was calling to him, and a barstool there had his name on it.

Sparshott took off his jacket and tossed it on the bed. He was still smiling over how stupid Roberto looked in the Harley hat when the phone rang. He grabbed it as he kicked off his shoes.

"Is it clear?" Campbell asked.

"Yeah, all clear."

A minute later, Sparshott heard a rap on the door and yanked it open. Campbell and Macready stood there as white as albino shit and as wired as Roberto, Jr. Sparshott's first thought was that Tabares got shot on the way home.

"What the fuck's wrong?" he asked.

"We lost you!"

Campbell and Macready slapped him on the back and hugged him like he was an MIA fresh from the jungles of Laos.

"So what?"

Sparshott figured they must have hung back when the limo left the Studio after dinner, or maybe turned down the wrong street on the way to Gustavo's, or got there late or not at all. It can happen to anybody, shit, one-car surveillance is Russian roulette.

"When did you lose me?"

"As soon as you left the hotel."

"You mean I was—for chrisssakes, how the fuck could you lose a limo?"

A good question and so funny they had to laugh, goddamn funny when you get right down to it. Losing a white stretch limousine parked fifty feet away, fuck, like one of those illusions that David Copperfield pulls on TV.

They partied until four and agreed not to tell anyone what happened, especially Tippett who'd have a cred fourth of July with the news. Every now and then someone would say after another round, "Hey, should I tell him to bring a limo?" and they'd crack up all over again.

THIRTY-FOUR

Jerry Macready did a slow burn as he waited for Bill Campbell and Stew Tippett in the cluttered, shared cubicle he called an office. He knew why they were coming. Sparshott had called to warn him.

"Have you heard from the Bureau yet?" Tracy asked.

"No, am I supposed to?"

"Let me put it this way . . . your friendship is more important to me than this case—you're going to get *fucked,* brother."

Macready chuckled. With Tracy every fucking thing was a big fuck. "Now what?"

Sparshott had become brother-close to Macready during the six months they had worked the Tabares case together. Losing Tracy in Miami was the glowing iron that cauterized their friendship. Sparshott knew that the pill would go down easier coming from a friend than from a cred. If the creds ever got wind that Sparshott had tipped Macready off, they'd have the excuse they were looking for to get Sparshott booted off the case. Fuck the limp-prick creds, Jerry Macready was worth the risk. As much as he wanted to do the big hand-to-hand buy and take down Carlos, Roberto, and their Miami connection, he'd stop the case dead in its tracks if Macready asked him to.

"They're going to cut you out of the undercover," Sparshott said. "They're flushing Old Mike right down the shitter."

The news hit Macready blindside like a boomerang. He couldn't see it coming but he should have heard it. When he volunteered to line up the bank for the money show, Tippett had said no thanks the Bureau will do it. When he volunteered to get the flash money, Tippett had said no thanks the Bureau will do it. Looking back, Tippett had been pissing on every fire hydrant in Harrisburg to stake a Bureau claim.

What hurt Macready even more than the FBI trying to steal the show was not telling him so he wouldn't have time to challenge the Bureau to a brawl. The Baltimore SAC had debriefed him the night he returned from Florida without even hinting that Old Mike was already dead. The next day, he and Sparshott met with the creds again to plan the money show. Not a word about cutting the IRS out, a flawless bureaucratic undercover move. And Tippett knew Old Mike was flying up from Miami—at IRS expense of course. Not even a suggestion that the trip might be premature. It was fucking embarrassing. Sparshott and Preston had already briefed Old Mike about the money show. He impressed them both. They were asking him to play a difficult role—fit into *their* show—and he not only agreed to cooperate but spun out a dozen scams to sort through Tabares' laundry and steal his money. Damn impressive, and now he had to tell the guy to pack up and go home because the Bureau wanted the whole enchilada. Macready had thanked Sparshott for the tip and told him to stay cool, the IRS would work it out with the Bureau.

□ □ □

In the parking lot of the National Bank of Maryland on Georgia Avenue in Wheaton, two stories below Macready's office, Bill Campbell took a deep breath. He had no idea how to break the news to Macready, especially after the guy sweated blood in Miami. He resented the fact that the Baltimore SAC had appointed *him* the messenger of death and had ordered him not to say a word until the last minute when it would be too late for Macready to bellow. To soften the blow, Campbell had leaked the decision to Sparshott, hoping he'd warn Macready in advance.

Simply put, SAC had called Campbell into his office and

informed him that the Bureau had killed the money laundering investigation. The decision was final and Campbell was not to breathe a word. SAC said he didn't want to jeopardize the whole narcotics investigation, now that it looked promising, by planting an IRS undercover in the middle of it.

SAC, it turned out, had once worked a big money laundering case with the IRS in Miami where he was also agent in charge. By the time the last bad guy was arrested, a lot of money had walked, he himself had spent two weeks on the stand, and the list of white collar crooks who had gotten respectable time was unimpressive. Rumor had it that headquarters punished him with a job in Baltimore.

Campbell was stunned, humiliated, and angry. What could he say? Of course, asshole, it's risky to wed money laundering to narcotics. Of course, two investigations and two undercovers are at least twice as dangerous. But he merely pointed out that the Bureau had agreed to the parallel undercover investigation right from the start and that the bad guys were already expecting to meet Old Mike at the money show in Harrisburg.

SAC gave Campbell a deep cred frown and told him not to worry, he'd work out a smooth transition with the IRS. The words were no comfort. Campbell knew that when a cred said "not to worry," you better watch your butt. He wanted to ask whatever happened to honesty, fairness, and loyalty, but he knew it wouldn't do any good.

"If we tell the IRS they're out," he argued instead, "they're going to take their car back. And that car is *making* this case . . . I'm serious. It's been three months since I asked for one. It's nowhere in sight."

Campbell knew it was a lame, petulant speech, and he was angry at himself for not coming up with a real harpooner. SAC didn't even grace the outburst with a comment. He simply dismissed Campbell like a Quantico trainee.

Campbell got out of the car—Tippett was with him—and walked across the lot to the side entrance. Ironically, he felt a deep sense of relief which had nothing to do with Macready waiting in his office above the bank or the shitty task at hand. For months now, he had been wrestling with doubts about the Bureau to which he felt genetically bound. Early on in the Tabares case, he had begun daydreaming about leaving the FBI but he batted the heresy away like a schoolboy fighting an impure thought. But the daydream grew into a deep-felt need, and the need into a firm decision. He would turn in his gold-edged credentials as soon as the Tabares case was over. He wasn't sure he could handle his father's disappointment, maybe even rejection, but he was absolutely certain he could not survive much longer as Special Agent William Campbell. The meaningless bureaucracy and lack of Bureau support for narcotics work, his special love, was making him as bitter and angry as his father was proud and satisfied.

Macready met Campbell and Tippett in the outer office, then led them into his cubicle and closed the door. As calmly as he could, he let Campbell tell him what he already knew. As he listened in silence, the words stung like iodine. What hurt the most was Tippett's pharisaical cred brush-off: "We both feel bad, Jerry, but there's nothing we can do." Sure, brother, sure!

Macready's red face got redder. He controlled his anger but couldn't disguise his bitterness. "I'm not sure what this decision will do to the rest of the case," he finally said. "Management will have to decide. It might take the car back. It might take me off the case. We'll just have to wait and see."

After Campbell and Tippett left his office, Macready began to fantasize. He saw management repossessing the little white Mercedes as a symbol of its disgust. He heard management tell the Bureau that the IRS was pulling Macready off the case. He watched IRS agents sneak up to Tabares' door and, without informing the Bureau, announce he was under investigation for tax fraud. And he heard the FBI sputter, "foul, foul." It would serve the Bureau right and it wouldn't be the first time one federal agency stole a case right out from under the ass of another. But Macready knew management was too much of a team player to screw up an investigation just to punish the Bureau. And deep down, he didn't want it to either.

In the end, the IRS and the Bureau hammered out a wimpy compromise: The IRS would drop its money laundering investigation, allow Macready to do surveillance and backup as needed, and give the team the use of the Mercedes for the duration of the case; the Bureau would allow Old Mike to play his part in the money show as long as he and Sparshott promised not to introduce the topic of money laundering in their conversations with Tabares.

Politics settled, strategy agreed on, parts assigned, and money in place, Sparshott called Carlos on the undercover phone to set time and place and to kiss and make up. He was miffed at the way the Bureau had shafted Macready, angry at the IRS for caving in like a fucking taxpayer, and pissed at the utter stupidity of cutting off the money-laundering arm of the investigation. But hey, what's a narc to do except keep on goin'.

Sparshott knew Carlos was still upset at how Terry had embarrassed him at Gustavo's house in front of his man, and he couldn't risk allowing that anger to color the money show. Not that he blamed the kid for being sore. But fuck, if he were Roberto, he would have kicked Carlos' ass from Little Havana to Panama City and back.

□ □ □

"What's goin' on buddy?" Sparshott says.

"Nothing much, man."

"That was real nice the other night . . . Everything set for this week?"

"Yeah."

"Like I told Roberto . . . we're leaving Thursday morning—at eleven."

"Well, I guess I have to call my man and tell him to be here Wednesday then, won't I?" Carlos is so cold you can hear icicles tinkling on his tongue.

"Why don't you have him call my beeper so I can call back and thank him personally."

"Just say your thanks when he's here."

"What the fuck you tryin' to do now, you sonofabitch, control me?"

"Yeah . . . I'm the main man now. *You* have to do the fucking work not me . . . so the next time you see him, you don't complain about me, you motherfucker. Lucky I didn't make *you* do a line, okay? So don't you complain about shit."

Sparshott laughs. Now that it's out in the open he can deal with it. Soothe him, stroke him, like, no hard feelings, man.

"You mad at me?"

"Complaining about me and then telling me, 'Let me talk to Roberto' and shit. Shame on you, man . . . What time are we coming back on Thursday? I'm already going to miss a class."

It's almost over now. Carlos is getting back to his old greedy self. Sparshott lances the boil one more time.

"Now there you go again—bitch, bitch. First you give me a hard time 'cuz I want to talk to your man, then you give me a hard time 'cuz you're gonna miss a fuckin' class."

"I wouldn't have done that to *you* Terry. I didn't put you with Roberto so you could complain about me because you don't have no reason to complain, man."

"Be cool. I took him aside and I told him I liked you . . . a lot."

"You don't have to lie, you motherfucker. And you don't have to complain either."

"Did he give you a hard time?"

"NO HE DID NOT give me a hard time. Business is great. He has nothing to complain about . . . So when will we get back?"

"Say about forty-five minutes to get there . . . couple of hours there. Be back by four. Is that okay?"

"Ah, what the fuck! I can miss another class. I'm fucking up so bad at school, my mother called. I guess I'll have to buy her a new Mercedes then she won't give me any more shit."

"Hey listen, I got a Harley hat and a nice shirt for you. I didn't want to give you that old t-shirt down there, but I figured it was good enough for Gustavo . . . You know what Roberto told me? You're such a cheap motherfucker you take him out to dinner at McDonald's."

Carlos giggles. That Terry is such a scream.

"Hey, I really didn't mean to give you a hard time. I apologize." Sparshott waits for Carlos to respond. When he doesn't, Sparshott continues. "Look, I don't apologize often and this is probably the last time you're gonna hear me do it. So don't be mad at me, you sonofabitch!"

"I'm not mad at you."

"Okay, buddy. Was he happy with everything?"

"Everything's cool. He's happy and I'm happy. What airport?"

"Same place as last time. Remember when we walked out to the plane?"

"Yeah."

"When you get there, just come out back. I should be landing at eleven. That way I don't have to run inside and try to find you."

"That's cool."

"Hey, bring yourself a little rubber bag so you can puke in it."

Carlos had told Sparshott he didn't like flying and that Roberto was so afraid of planes he wouldn't go up with Terry if he didn't like the look of his aircraft. He'd rather go commercial and meet him in Harrisburg.

"Don't fuck with me, man," Carlos says. "You know I do not like those fucking planes."

"Okay, man. See ya at the airport."

"Bye."

THIRTY-FIVE

11:00 A.M.

Campbell radioes Sparshott in the twin-engine plane circling above the Montgomery Airpark that Medina just pulled up in his white Porsche. The eight-seater banks and, as it makes its final approach, Sparshott can see Carlos and Roberto standing outside the back door of the terminal. He specifically requested a twin because two engines would make Roberto feel more secure, and an eight-seater because the craft was supposed to haul reefer. He even removed a row of seats and piled cargo nets in the back to make sure Roberto couldn't possibly miss the point. Hey, undercover success, like the devil, is in the details.

The plane lands and taxis to the back door where Roberto waits nervously. When Sparshott hops out to get him and Carlos, he refuses to climb aboard. Instead, he walks around the aircraft, you know, to make sure it has wheels and the tires aren't flat and the props are really spinning, then announces, "I go commercial."

Sure, buddy, like there are three flights a day from Montgomery Airpark to Harrisburg, Pennsylvania. Sparshott grabs him by the elbow. "Come on, Roberto, the money's waitin', let's go, buddy." He half pushes the old man through the open door. Once inside, Roberto can't fasten his seatbelt quick enough. As the plane races down the runway and lifts off, he stares at the floor and clenches the armrest until his brown knuckles turn white.

The attaché recorder sits at Sparshott's feet—Tom Roberts is getting an insatiable appetite for transcripts—but Sparshott doesn't bother to switch it on. The plane is too noisy and Roberto and Carlos are too scared to talk. Sparshott can't blame them. How do they know the airplane is sky worthy and the pilot good? Kidding aside, he's pleased they're frightened. They'll be so busy worrying about crashing into the Catoctins below, they won't have the energy to get suspicious.

Sparshott does all the chatter during the one-hundred-mile flight north over Frederick, past Camp David, across the Penn state line, past Gettysburg. To flash money in a bank so far from Washington is an important complement to his cover story. If Terry Petit deals reefer in five states, wouldn't it be logical for him to deposit his cash in regional banks? And if Terry were really a narc, wouldn't he show money in a bank closer to home? Christ, every dealer worth a snort knows how fucking cheap the feds are!

As they near the Harrisburg airport at the foot of the Alleghenies, they fly over Three Mile Island on the Susquehanna River which tumbles through the state capital on its way to the Chesapeake Bay. Sparshott encourages Roberto to look down at the reactor cones, after all the place is history, but the guy still won't lift his eyes from the floor.

Roberto is so happy to see the tarmac after the bumpy half hour ride that he bounces off the airplane into the waiting car. For Sparshott, the car is the Ferguson test of the whole money show. The chauffeur is an FBI agent, not Old Mike whom Roberto expects.

The day before the show, the team had a tiff with Tippett over using a special agent as a driver. They argued: Why introduce a *new* player at this point? He's not necessary and it's too risky. Why not let Old Mike drive. But Tippett told them they were exaggerating the risk, drug dealers see new faces all the time, and he wouldn't budge. It was clear to the rest of the team that he viewed the money show as a Bureau production which, unfortunately, had to feature a fucking local and an IRS accountant. Production values won the day.

Once he settles in the backseat of the car, eager to put distance between him and the airplane, Roberto studies the FBI driver with the same cold detachment he treated Sparshott to during the limo ride to the Studio Restaurant. He says something to Carlos in Spanish and Carlos answers back in Spanish. Sparshott figures Roberto asked Carlos if he knew the driver. He watches Roberto carefully and, for a brief moment, thinks the guy is going call the show off, get out, and hop the next commercial flight out of town. But the urge to flee in the face of doubt finally succumbs to greed.

The FBI couldn't have selected a better bank than the little red brick branch of the Dauphin Deposit Bank on the outskirts of Harrisburg, a ten-minute ride from the airport. Guarded by two tall spruces and a waving flag on a pole, it's just the kind of bank Terry Petit would choose—small, unobtrusive, very clean, and quite friendly. A perfect cover for a badass marijuana dealer.

They park in front of the bank. Macready, who had only three hours of sleep and is running on coffee nerves, has the eyeball up the street. He knows enough to keep his distance in case Roberto or Carlos saw him hanging around the Brickell Point Hyatt. Tippett has a second eyeball across the street.

Old Mike DuMond waits inside. He's Roberto's age, speaks with the gravelly voice of authority, and looks like he just stepped out of a board meeting. Under the circumstances, he's calm. When he learned that the Bureau had cut him loose and why, he called every special agent in shouting distance an "empty suit." He didn't so much mind the personal rejection, but he felt goddamn sorry for Macready who was completely crushed. Typical Bureau, Old Mike thought, it wants all the credit, which only served to remind him of his favorite FBI story:

The Bureau got a tip that some bad guys were planning to rob a bank so it sent out a team of special agents to watch it. They sat and sat and nothing stirred. When noon rolled around, they all went to lunch together. The bad guys robbed the bank while they squirted catsup on their fries . . . Maybe the story was true, maybe not. Given how he felt, Old Mike was not about to give the fucking Bureau any benefit of any doubt.

Sparshott leads Roberto and Carlos up the red stone steps

into the bank where he introduces Old Mike to Roberto. Although he hasn't been to the bank before, he feels secure playing second to the IRS man. The "bank manager" (an FBI agent) greets Terry by name as if he's a special customer. After Old Mike gives him the renter's key to a safety deposit box—he already has the bank's key—the manager leads everyone through the bank, past a row of tellers, and into a small viewing room with a table. He excuses himself, walks into the vault to the left of the room, and returns with a safety deposit box which he offers Sparshott. When Sparshott points to the table, the manager sets the box down and leaves, closing the vinyl accordion door behind him to insure privacy.

Sparshott lifts the lid. Inside are twenty stacks of hundred dollar bills, five thousand dollars per stack, a hundred thou total, which FBI agents counted and packaged the night before. Roberto is not expecting to see more money than that since he knows from Carlos that the Dauphin Deposit Bank only holds Terry's take from his southern Pennsylvania operation.

Carlos steps forward. Roberto hangs back a few feet. Carlos eyes the pile of money like a boy looking at his first naked woman. He caresses the top bill with his fingertips as if to prolong his pleasure. Then he picks up a stack and slowly strips back each bill to make sure the pack isn't padded. His curiosity satisfied, he replaces the stack and reaches into the bottom of the box for another. Sparshott can feel his total concentration and smell his greed as he examines the second stack bill by bill but more quickly. He replaces it, takes a third stack and thumbs through it like a deck of cards, then closes the lid as reverently as if it contained his mother's ashes.

"That's a hell of a lot of money to keep in one place at one time," Carlos says. He's pleased but disappointed. He had hoped Roberto would get to see even more cash.

"We own a piece of the fuckin' bank," Sparshott says. "It won't get ripped off."

Roberto, who watched the show with the same expressionless face he had in the stretch limo, steps up to the box, opens the lid, and rifles through the stacks to, you know, prove it's real. Then he breaks into a smile just as he did in the Studio shitter after the body search.

"Now we see," he says. "All good."

"A hundred thousand," Sparshott explains. "This is only *one* of my banks . . . but that's really none of your business, is it? Let's go eat."

1:00 P.M.

The creds had laid out the rules for lunch at a Sheraton near the airport with split-hair precision. If Roberto brings up the topic of money laundering—without any prompting on Sparshott's part, of course—Sparshott is to say no more than he absolutely has to. Under no circumstances is he to make any wild Tracy-promises. To make certain that Roberto is not tempted to talk money laundering, Old Mike is to sit at a table by himself. Christ, it's like the Bureau telling Roberto, hey, we'll give you a bonus, buddy, if you don't tell us where you wash your dirty money or ask Old Mike to clean it for you. An interesting case of obstruction of justice.

There's a slight problem. The maitre d' eyes Sparshott who looks his usual badass biker self and doesn't want to seat him, like, come on, gentlemen, this is the Sheraton not Roy Fucking Rogers. Old Mike reaches into his Brooks Brothers pocket, pulls out a fatass flashroll, and peels off a sawbuck. "He's my friend," he tells the maitre d' in his banker's voice. "Treat him well." Carlos can't stop giggling. That fucking Terry, he's such a scream. Hey, don't rap it, sometimes the best material comes off the cuff.

Sparshott makes sure the attaché recorder is at his feet and running. He thinks the FBI lunch rules are a crock of cred shit and he told Old Mike before the show that he'll toss *all* money questions to him. If Roberto brings up laundering, what the fuck is he gonna say, hey, man, the FBI said we ain't supposed to talk about that shit. Eat your sandwich.

Once they have a drink and Roberto begins to relax, it

becomes clear how impressed he was with the show in the bank and how eager he is to set a date for the first one-kilo buy. When Sparshott suggests the following Friday, Roberto nods his approval.

Sparshott spells out how he wants the deal to go down. The one-key buy is a dress rehearsal for the fifty-key buy, he emphasizes, and it's important that it fly *exactly* as planned. He suggests that the kilo be divided into five packages, each package kept at a different location. He will hold the money and wait with Carlos until Marty tells him the shit is good.

Roberto is so impressed with the plan he tells Sparshott he wants to be present Friday when the deal goes down. Hey, what a fan-fucking-tastic idea. You just made your buddy, Tom Roberts, real happy, pal.

The date and details of the buy agreed on, Roberto turns curious about Terry's use of hundred dollar bills. Sparshott waves Old Mike over to the table.

"Why all hundred?" Roberto asks.

"Easier to move."

"You can sell hundred?" Christ, the guy has a thing about C notes.

"You bet. They're easy to move and don't attract attention."

"You buy kilo Friday in hundred?"

"Why not?" He asks Roberto how he wants the money bundled—with rubberbands, in wrappers, sealed in plastic. He then gives the guy the weight of each in case he wants to weigh the bills instead of counting them. Then Old Mike explains how he washes Terry's cash: he collects all the small bills from Terry's people, converts them to hundreds, then moves the big bills off-shore, invests them in dummy corporations, and deposits the washed money in a string of banks. Terry remains invisible, the only money he *ever* touches is squeaky clean, and the money and the dope are never in the same place together. Fucking sweet, man.

It's a perfect opening for Old Mike to lead Roberto into a discussion of a joint Tabares-Petit money laundering operation, but Old Mike honors the FBI gag order and Roberto doesn't take the bait. He has his own liquor store and nightclub laundry, and what isn't tied up there is hidden in an air conditioning duct in his home. The guy doesn't trust accountants and off-shore banks.

Old Mike returns to his lonely sandwich. In his twenty years as an IRS criminal investigator, he's never seen such utter stupidity. And he hopes that if he hangs around for another twenty years he'll never see the likes of it again.

After a few minutes, Sparshott motions Old Mike back over to his table for some undercover fun. He pulls out a Harley brochure and starts pointing at some fancy bikes. "Stew likes this one," he says. "Greg likes that one. Fuck—get one of these and six of those!"

"This is going to cost you, Terry," Old Mike says. They had rehearsed the scene the previous night. Carlos and Roberto are all ears.

"Who gives a fuck," Sparshott says. "After all they do for us, they deserve it."

"Okay, let me see . . . looks like the total package is going to run around two-hundred thou."

"No problem." They talk about how to draw the cash from Terry's stashes in his other banks.

At the end of the lunch, Roberto says he'll be driving his family up to Washington soon and would like Terry to meet them at Carlos' house. Sparshott tells him it would be a great pleasure. The undercover scam is turning into a fucking minuet, man:

Terry treats Carlos to a special dinner and shows him his reefer. Roberto rolls out the red carpet for Terry and displays his cocaine. Terry shows Roberto his money. Roberto offers Terry a tour of the chop shop. Roberto invites Terry to meet his family. Terry is expected to show Roberto where and how he lives in Hagerstown. Roberto goes to jail. Terry goes back to Montgomery County.

□ □ □

The return flight to Gaithersburg is more relaxed than the ride down and Roberto seems less afraid. He even ventures a quick look out the window during takeoff, watches the pilot play with the stick through the open cockpit door, and through Carlos asks a series of questions about the airplane. How much did it cost? How much does he pay the pilot and copilot? Will Terry help him buy one so he can cut his overhead? Not that he's serious, mind you. Roberto avoids flash like herpes.

Sparshott feels another one of those uncontrollable urges to have fun. The money show was a standing-room-only hit. Roberto didn't burn the FBI driver—Tippett was right—Old Mike was low-key perfect, the bank manager as good a bit player as Bob Wills, Roberto asked to be present during the one-kilo buy the following week, fuck, he even invited Terry to meet his family. It's time to shake things up a little.

Over the noise of the engines, Sparshott shouts to the pilot, "Hey, why don't ya show them what this baby can *really* do!" Then he grins to himself and sits back to watch the final scene of Act Three.

The plane goes into a nosedive. Carlos and Roberto let out a long, angry stream of Spanish and clutch their armrests. The plane pulls out of the dive and climbs—almost vertically it seems—then levels and does a roll. By the time it lands at the airpark, Roberto and Carlos have no further questions.

THIRTY-SIX

Campbell had to be out of town. That left "Bullets Will Fly" Tippett in charge of the one-kilo buy, and Sparshott sensed the guy was so scared his lead undercover would lose $26,000 of Bureau money that his nose refused to bleed. When Sparshott tried to reassure him—everything the team had done so far worked perfectly and this buy would too—his self confidence, which Tippett interpreted as cockiness, made Tippett seem even more edgy.

The buy was important because it would be the first time the team had Roberto present during a dope deal. If the investigation fell apart afterwards, Tom Roberts would still have a solid case against Tabares. The problem was—Sparshott had suggested holding the dope in *five* places as a practice run for a later fifty-key buy and Roberto went for the idea. Under the best of circumstances, the Bureau would shit ram-cars over any buy that called for surveillance and backup in six locations—five for the dope and one for the money. With Tippett in charge, which Sparshott considered the worst of circumstances, it was clear the Bureau would reject even four locations. Hey Billy, thanks brother, hope you have a fucking good trip.

Sparshott's choice was starkly clear: either devise a plan simple enough to satisfy the FBI, plausible enough to maintain Terry's credibility, and safe enough to keep Tabares cool, or the crucial buy would go, you got it, man, right down the old shitter.

Sparshott and Preston had invited themselves over to Carlos' house a few days after the money show to manipulate him into changing the five-package plan. It was a typical bachelor's pad. Unwashed dishes stacked in the sink, unpressed clothes on the floor. Newspapers, Coke cans, and unopened boxes on every surface. The furniture was respectably modest but the stereo was top-of-the-line. Other than a few Panama beers and soda cans in the refrigerator, the larder was bare.

Carlos shared the two-bedroom bungalow with a pair of alligators in a tank and a parrot named Zeus who ate pistachios, lived in a room of his own, and had an ornery personality. With bird shit all over the floor and holes in the sheetrock walls—the fucking bird went crazy whenever Carlos overslept—the place looked like the home of a giant woodpecker. Carlos loved Zeus, bird shit and all. He had always wanted a parrot and when he saw one advertised in the paper, fuck, he went out and bought it.

Preston brought along the bottle of Dom Perignon he owed Carlos from the Porsche bet in the Bull on the Mark. Carlos was as pleased with it as Duran with a knockdown. He placed the champagne in the refrigerator, told Sparshott and Preston to help themselves to a beer, then excused himself to get dressed. He had just returned from a weekend with some chickies in Daytona Beach and had overslept. He badly needed a couple of hits. Zeus was drilling a new hole in the wall and without some shit and coffee Carlos was as useless as his old Camaro.

Sparshott and Preston snooped around. They noted correspondence from George Washington University, the middle name (Eugenio) and date of birth (February 5, 1964) on Carlos' driver's license, his mother's phone number on a telephone bill, and the name of his bank on a monthly statement. They found a small stack of index cards with drug calculations and a rolodex which Sparshott quickly spun to "S" where he found Santiago's number. A subpoena to the phone company would give the team a last name and address.

When Carlos returned dressed, freshly tooted, and ready to face the day, Sparshott challenged him to a second bet. Marty would have a Mercedes within a week—a gift from Terry for a job well done—or he'd give Carlos another bottle of Dom Perignon.

Carlos was sincerely happy for Marty and took the bet.

The FBI had seized a cream Mercedes 190E in a drug raid and sent it to Baltimore at the request of the ASAC for use in the Tabares case. But one of the creds liked it so much, he appropriated it for his own use without telling Campbell who bellowed like a branded steer when he found out. He had been waiting five months for the undercover car.

After they shook on the bet, Sparshott began to manipulate Carlos into simplifying the buy plan. First, he made the five location scheme so complicated he knew Carlos would reject it: Rent five storage bins with five different coded entry passes and five different storage bin keys. Santiago places one package of dope in each bin, then shows them to Marty. If the shit is good, Santiago keeps the keys, Marty holds the passes and calls Terry to say everything is cool. Terry then shows the money to Carlos who tells Santiago to give Marty the five keys. Everyone is happy.

Carlos laughed and said the plan was too crazy, you know, passes and keys and shit, and too fucking risky with dope in five public places, man. Why not use three rented cars, two for the dope and one for the money? If everything looks good, exchange keys and everyone is happy.

Although he ultimately wanted *one* car for the dope to keep Tippett's nose dry, Sparshott was satisfied for the moment. From five bins down to three cars—not bad. Next, he told Carlos he'd accept the counter plan but Carlos would have to pay for the car rentals since it was his idea. Carlos didn't like it one damn bit and said he'd have to check with Roberto. Hey, who said greed ain't a narc's best friend?

Carlos was supposed to leave for Las Vegas that night to watch the Sugar Ray-Marvelous Marvin fight. He had two free tickets to the match at Caesar's Palace and begged Sparshott to go with him. But Sparshott had to turn him down, Tippett's orders. For chrissakes, they had a $700,000 budget, or so he thought. What the fuck were they saving it for, defense bonds?

When Carlos mentioned he didn't have flight reservations yet, Sparshott immediately called his wife, a travel agent, and asked her to make the arrangements. That way he could keep tabs on Carlos even if he wasn't going along. Hey, don't rap it, every little edge adds up.

The buy was set for the afternoon or evening of April 8, the day after the fight. But the eighth dawned without word from Carlos or Roberto. Great news. It meant they probably hadn't rented three cars yet. Sparshott called Carlos at home but no one answered. Wonderful news. It meant the guy was sleeping off his trip. Sparshott had both Roberto and Carlos in a thumbscrew and he began to apply pressure.

11:30 A.M.

"Hello, Tabares Liquor Store."

"Is Roberto there?" Sparshott asks.

"He's speak."

"Hey, buddy, it's Terry."

"Hey man, what happen to you? I wait for you in my boat on beach."

"You're supposed to be *here* today."

"Today? I call Carlos . . . Carlos no home. No call me back on beeper. At Las Vegas . . . at box, remember?"

"I know . . . I helped him get the airplane tickets but he's supposed to be back. He told me it was definitely today. You know how I am. I like things to go *exactly* as planned. I already picked up the envelope you wanted. Can you come up?"

"Tonight? Terry, is it possible we delay for tomorrow? I call to Carlos, okay?"

"Okay, but it's kind of upsettin'."

"I understand."

"I'm gonna go over to Carlos' now and knock on his door."

Sparshott couldn't ask for more. Roberto is almost begging him to change the plan, wondering what the hell is wrong with Carlos, and worried he might lose the $26K sale. He hops into the Mercedes, races over to Carlos' house, and bangs on the door until the kid opens it. He's still half asleep even though it's almost noon, and he looks like he flew home in the luggage compartment.

"You're in *big* trouble," Sparshott says. "You better call the old man."

"You talked to him?"

"Yep."

"Is he here?"

"Nope . . . he said he don't know nothing about what's goin' on. He told me he can't come today and I'm pissed 'cuz I don't operate this way and you *know* that."

"Shit, I can work it out."

"I wanted to make sure everybody was going to be happy so next time there's no problems. You better find out what the fuck's goin' on!"

Carlos calls Roberto and speaks in English so Terry can understand his end of the conversation. In a commanding voice he lays the full blame for the screw up on Roberto: "Terry is *real* mad. We agreed on the date and now he thinks we're irresponsible. He's here now wondering what's going on with you. You failed him."

Roberto apologizes and promises to do the buy the following night. Perfect so far and it's only noon. Now all Sparshott has to do is talk Carlos into doing the buy that night as scheduled. Then there won't be enough time to set up a complicated three-car deal.

Sparshott and Carlos grab two beers and sit on the front porch. "I can't have this kind of shit going on." Sparshott tightens the thumbscrew. "I mean, it's gotta go—boom, boom, boom—just like that. You don't even have the cars, do ya? You're treating me like shit, you know that."

"Hey man, you think we *want* to fuck around, you're crazy, man!"

"Okay then, buddy, no fuckin' around . . . Can he get up here tonight so we can do it tonight?"

"Why not? Let me find him. Shit, he's the one who fucked up, not me!"

"After that, call your buddy Sandi—Sandi"

"Santiago."

"Yeah, Santiago and get everything set."

Carlos calls Roberto at the liquor store and tells him in no uncertain terms that he has to drop everything and hop a plane. The buy *has* to be that night or Terry will never trust them again. Carlos hangs up.

"He comes tonight."

"Shit, you know, it just the *principle* of the thing," Sparshott says.

"That's what I told him."

"And that's the way it's gotta be. So we'll have to do it with the shit in just *one* car. Have your man park at Bob's. Marty will be across the street in the little shopping center at the 7-Eleven. He'll drive his car across the street, look at the shit, then call me from a pay phone. If it's good, I'll give you the money. Santiago gives Marty the shit, like last time, and everybody's out of there."

"We gotta hide it, you know, behind the seat."

"Fuck, just put it in the trunk this time. We're not talking about a lot."

"Where you and me going to meet?"

"Same place as last time."

10:00 P.M.

Roberto exits Eastern Airlines flight 198 wearing his usual gray suit and carrying a large, heavy white box tied with string. He enters the terminal at Washington National Airport where an FBI agent spots him and radioes a surveillance car waiting outside the terminal to pick up his trail. They figure he has the dope in the white box.

Roberto stops at National Car Rental, then boards a shuttle bus to a parking lot where he picks up a silver Pontiac Sunbird, drives over the Potomac River across the 14th Street bridge, and heads for Maryland.

Carlos and Santiago wait for him in a Mercury Cougar

parked in the lot of Presidential Towers. When he pulls into the lot, Roberto doesn't even bother to go up to his apartment. Three keys arrived by mule earlier—one for Terry, one for Carlos, and one extra, some Lipton Tea shit Roberto had bought from a new supplier at a flea market price. Carlos took one look at how the stuff crumbled to the touch and said to himself, "No way, man."

Roberto places his white box in the trunk of the Cougar, gives the rental keys to Santiago, and joins Carlos. Both cars turn north on New Hampshire. The Sunbird drives under the beltway, takes the first right on Elton Road, then another immediate right into Bob's Big Boy. The Cougar heads east on the beltway toward the Greenbelt Hilton where Sparshott waits at the bar dressed to kill—jeans and leather vest over a Harley t-shirt.

10. Sparshott meets with Carlos (white hat) and Tabares at the Sheraton Hotel in Greenbelt, MD to pay for a kilo of cocaine

Sparshott is confident the buy will go down smooth unless Stew pulls another "Tippett" and blows it. The guy insisted on a contingency plan with the usual ram car and "the money never walks" shit. Fuck, with eight FBI agents as backup, Sparshott feels well protected even though Campbell isn't there to keep everyone cool. The $26,000 is stuffed in the tape-recorder attaché case at his feet. Ripoff is the furthest thing from his mind. Some bad guy or good guy getting hinky or running scared is his main concern. He's seen dozens of deals turn sour in seconds over the smallest thing, like the squeal of tires, the toot of a horn, a bunch of loudmouths in a station wagon, a patrol car cruising by. If Tippett or any of the

FBI surveillance cars make a false move of any kind, it's over. Bye, bye Tabares.

Roberto and Carlos join Sparshott for a fast drink in the Hilton lounge while Santiago and Marty make contact and set up their end of the buy. Sparshott can sense that Roberto and Carlos are nervous, as they ought to be. Marty could be ripping off Santiago or arresting him at that very moment. And they won't know whether Terry is a narc until the deal is over. They finish their drinks in fourteen minutes flat.

Sparshott and Roberto sit in the Mercedes so Sparshott can be near the car phone. Carlos parks the Cougar next to them in the usual driver window to driver window position. As they wait for Marty's call, Roberto and Carlos seem calm—the typical eerie quiet before the buy. Sparshott can almost hear them thinking, "It's too late to back out so let's get our money and see if we get busted."

11. Carlos (left) and Tabares (right) hardly look like the Washington cocaine source that they are

Meanwhile, Preston is suffering from a mild case of prebuy jitters in front of a 7-Eleven across Elton Road from Bob's Big Boy. This is no quarter-ounce or half-pound buy. Santiago will be delivering a whole kilo this time, and he knows the man from Miami is here to make sure he does it perfectly or Terry and Marty will be out of there, like history. Santiago is bound to be dangerously tense. Not exactly a comforting thought. Preston's new Mercedes 190 isn't wired and he's not armed. So if he gets into trouble, surveillance, which is hanging back, will have to *see* the problem before it can bail him out. Unfortunately, most of the FBI agents he's met don't have 20/20 vision.

While Marty talks to Tippett on the pay phone to make sure the backup covering his ass is in place, Santiago pulls into Bob's, cruises the lot, then drives back out across the street to check the tiny shopping center for suspicious cars. All part of his job. He spots Preston on the phone, but instead of going back to Bob's to wait for him as the buy-plan calls for, Santiago walks over to the pay phone.

"You take now?" he asks Marty.

Preston's not sure what's happening. Is there a change he doesn't know about? Is this a setup or a screwup? His people are positioned for a buy in front of Bob's not in front of a busy 7-Eleven fifty yards away.

"No," Preston tells Santiago. "It's supposed to go down across the street . . . same as last time." He drops another quarter into the pay phone and calls Sparshott who passes the receiver through the window to Carlos.

"This is all messed up, man," Preston complains. Since Santiago doesn't argue or make a move for his gun or drive off, Preston concludes the guy made an honest mistake, then uses it to hammer home Sparshott's dress rehearsal theme. "The deal is supposed to go down like the *big* buy. No way am I gonna take the shit in the middle of the street. And I'm not gonna deal with your guy again either."

Once again, Carlos is utterly humiliated in front of Roberto. First, he embarrassed his boss by snorting a line of coke in front of Terry, then he disappeared in Las Vegas and almost blew the whole deal, now his runner fucks up. "Don't worry, Marty, I'll fire him . . . I'll fire him!"

Hoping it was just a stupid mistake and that Carlos is not trying a rip and run, Preston tells Sparshott he and Santiago are going to start the buy all over again . . . strictly according to plan. Then he waits a beat for Sparshott to alert him that he's got a gun up his ass. The emergency code for this buy is "tenfifty" which is cop talk for officer in trouble. When Sparshott doesn't say something like, "it must be around ten-fifty or eleven now, I'll see you back here at twelve," Preston hangs up, then drives across the street and takes his usual spot—where backup expects him to be.

When Santiago parks nearby, Preston gets out of his car and walks over to the silver Pontiac. He moves slowly but deliberately, no use making Santiago more nervous than he already is.

Santiago stands by the trunk. When Preston arrives, he opens it and points to a shoebox. Preston lifts off the cover. Inside is a brick wrapped in red tape with the word "mono" written across it in black magic marker. Some kind of code word, Preston figures. He pierces the tape with a key, rubs a little powder between his fingers—definitely not as oily as last time but acceptable. Then he sticks his head inside the trunk so Santiago can't watch him and simulates a snort.

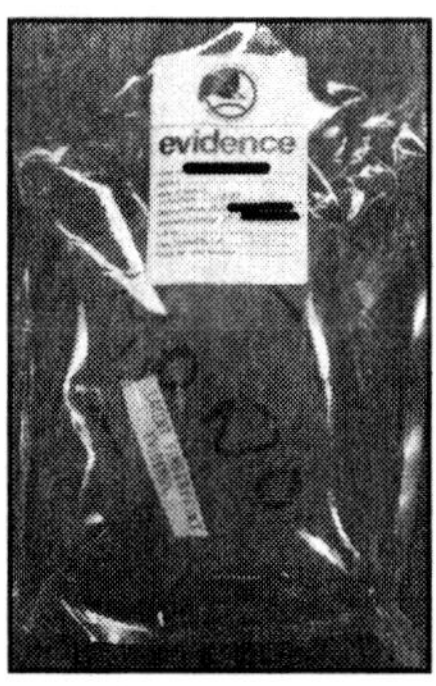

12. First kilo of cocaine Sparshott purchased from Carlos at the Sheraton

Preston shuts the trunk and takes the Pontiac keys from Santiago. They walk back across Elton Road to the pay phone in front of the 7-Eleven—the phone in the lobby of Bob's isn't private enough. Preston calls Sparshott.

"The shit's here. It looks good."

Sparshott reaches behind the driver's seat for a paper bag with five thick packs of fifty hundred dollar bills each and a thinner pack with ten hundreds. He already showed the money to Roberto when he saw how upset the guy was over Santiago's goof. Feeling and counting the cash seemed to soothe his nerves.

"Okay, I'm gonna give 'em the money," Sparshott tells Preston as he hands the package to Carlos through the window. "Take the delivery . . . give the phone to Santiago."

Santiago grabs the receiver, listens for a moment, then nods yes to Marty and hangs up. They walk back across the street like old buddies. Preston opens the trunk of Santiago's car, takes the shoebox, then tosses Santiago the keys. Hey, man, like history, I'm gone.

Roberto couldn't be happier. He tells Terry he has a gift for him, gets out of the car, and opens the trunk of the Cougar. Sparshott knows exactly what FBI surveillance is thinking at this moment, and he's more scared of them than he has ever been of Roberto.

"What's Tabares doing?" they're wondering. "Is he getting an Uzi? Did he burn Sparshott?" Hey, hurry, man, before Tippett comes racing to the rescue like the fucking cavalry or the crash car decides to play stock car.

Roberto reaches inside the trunk and, with a magician's flourish, pulls out a single bottle of Corona beer. Then he smiles in that sheepish way of his. Sparshott opens his trunk to load up the case of beer in the large white box Roberto had carried on the plane. Christ, the old man's such a thoughtful guy, too bad he's . . . fuck, no use even thinking about it.

13. After the deal, Sparshott lays it on to Tabares and Tabares takes the bait

Sparshott puts his arm around Roberto's shoulder and leads him back to the bar for a drink they can both use. Roberto is one gay caballero, Sparshott one happy narc. The buy couldn't have gone down better. Other than a little confusion on Santiago's part—it can happen to anybody under pressure—it was as smooth as a white lie.

Once inside the lounge, Roberto informs Terry with regrets that his family canceled its trip to Washington. But he would be honored to have Terry come to Miami the following week to meet his wife there, visit his home, see his boat, and maybe fish. No business, just friendship.

Sparshott turns lake-bottom cold. Raul Tabares is still in Miami. Does meeting Roberto's family include his son, Raul? If not, did Raul tell anyone about the big, bearded pig who busted him? And what about Raul's wife Lolita, would she be there?

THIRTY-SEVEN

The team was ready to fly down to Miami for Sparshott's visit with the Tabares family when they got the devastating news. Roberto Tabares had stepped onto his boat at the Miami Marina, headed out for the Islands on a cocaine mission, and never returned. The team learned about his disappearance from the tap on Carlos' phone which the court had approved the previous week, then confirmed it with the Coast Guard. Roberto's wife, who had called in the missing-at-sea report, was frantic and Carlos was as dejected as the team. The case was over. Tom Roberts would get Carlos, the sharks Roberto. As Campbell put it so succinctly, "Oh shit!"

Under the circumstances, the team had no choice but to make the trip anyway. How could Sparshott explain why he canceled the visit when he knew Roberto was calling his family together—Roy was coming all the way from Washington—just so Terry could meet them?

Sparshott, Preston and Scooter—Campbell was still traveling—booked rooms at the Brickell Point Hyatt until they could figure out what to do next. They watched Tabares Liquor Store, Pier J at the Miami Marina, and the Tabares house. They called the U.S. Coast Guard every hour. But there was no sign of Roberto.

Sparshott then called Carlos to see if he knew anything he hadn't already said on a bugged telephone. He was careful not to let Carlos know where he was staying in Miami just in case the kid was smart enough to send counter-surveillance to the hotel. If one of his people saw Sparshott talking to Scooter, Sparshott could be in deep shit and not the kind you snort.

□ □ □

"Hey, man . . . Terry."

"You down there?"

"Yeah."

"Have you called Roberto?"

"I called the liquor store and talked to somebody that said he wasn't there."

"It's fucked, man."

"What's wrong?"

"I *cannot* get a hold of him. I hate it when he does shit like that, man."

"You can't get a hold of him at *all*?"

"I got his wife."

"What did she say?"

"She didn't want to talk. When she doesn't want to talk, it means he's away . . . working on the shit, you know what I mean? With the boat. She told me he'll call me when he gets in. That's all she'll say."

"Okay, I'll check with you first thing in the morning and you let me know what's up."

"Where are you right now?"

"At a friend's . . . a business associate. We're getting ready to go out drinking."

"In Miami?"

"No, up in Lauderdale. He's into, you know, heavy farm equipment. I gotta leave the day after tomorrow and stop in Dayton to pick up a plane."

"I feel bad because—shit, call me collect tomorrow if you're using a pay phone."

"All right, but only if I'm not gettin' laid."

Carlos roars. That Terry, he has such a way with words. "Bye, Terry."

□ □ □

Sparshott, Preston, and Scooter sat in the alley pub behind the hotel and cried in their drinks. With each new round, the Tabares case became more hopeless. They were shocked. Roberto couldn't just go out and get himself drowned. That doesn't happen even in the fuckin' movies, man. Ripped off and shot behind the ear, okay, but shark-food? They were angry. What a fuckin' way to end a big case, just two steps away from the big buy. But they saw a glint of hope. Maybe he's just lost or has engine trouble and is bobbing around somewhere like a fucking cork. Speaking of corks . . . It was early morning when they finally got to bed and, although they all drank their share of pub grog, no one was in a happy mood.

The morning sun broke through the clouds unexpectedly bright and beautiful. Sparshott learned from the tap on Carlos' phone that Roberto was alive after all, heading for shore, rescued at sea by, you guessed it, the feds. Roberto's pilot had steered off course on the way to the Bahamas where Roberto had arranged a fifty-key buy, and *The Excuse* ran out of gas. The Coast Guard confirmed it had found the boat drifting north in the Gulf Stream, and that Roberto Tabares and two passengers suffered nasty sunburns but otherwise were fine. The creds sighed in relief when the Guardsmen didn't find any dope on board. After all the time they put into the Tabares case, they didn't want to give the stat to somebody else for doing practically nothing.

The team quickly moved from the Brickell Point Hyatt which was close to Roberto's house to an Embassy Suites motel in Fort Lauderdale—two fucking locals to a room to save Bureau money. They wanted to keep a reasonably safe distance between them and the Tabares family. Hey, no one's gonna drive up the coast to look for them. You know how lazy bad guys are.

When they were settled in, Sparshott called Tabares Liquor Store to see if the gig was still on and found a message waiting for him: "Roberto say you call Carlos," which he immediately did.

□ □ □

"Whatcha doin', man?"

"Nothing Terry . . . waiting for your call."

"Some guy at the store said I should get a hold of you. What's goin' on?"

"Roberto is out doing what I told you."

"*Now*? Hey, you're kidding me? I told him I was coming."

"He's probably landing right now. His wife told me, you know, he was out fishing." They both laugh.

Sparshott is still afraid of visiting the Tabares home and tries to use Carlos' and Roberto's feelings of guilt—they almost blew the last buy, now this fiasco—to change the visit to a public place, the sooner the better. He tells Carlos his schedule is so full, he has to leave for Ohio the next day, that he can only fit in dinner that night or breakfast the next morning. Carlos says he'll arrange something.

"How do I get a hold of you, Terry?"

"I'll call *you* at two."

"What are you going to be doing?"

"Fuck, I don't know . . . maybe I'll go fishing."

Carlos cracks up. That Terry. "You get laid?"

"I had a rough night, man. I was drunk and I got into an argument with this girl with big tits, and I said they were small, you know, just to get her a little mad. It went downhill from there."

"You fucked up, man . . . Call me later . . . bye."

Sparshott was nervous but wouldn't admit it even to himself. Of course, he was relieved that Roberto was still alive, but he found the confusion and the unknowns unsettling. He had checked on Raul Tabares and the quadriplegic was still in his hospital bed—good news. Tippett had arranged for the Miami Bureau's crack Special Operations Group to cover him—comforting. But he wouldn't be wired just in case Gustavo decided to tickle his balls again—uncomfortable any way you looked at it. And he still didn't know if he was expected to make an appearance at the Tabares house and if he was, who would be there—scary.

He called the liquor store once again. This time he reached Roberto who acted as if nothing had happened and suggested they meet at two o'clock that afternoon. Nothing about a private dinner with him and his wife or a quick breakfast in the morning.

2:00 P.M.

Sparshott pulls up to Tabares Liquor Store on Flagler Avenue and toots his horn, you know, like the Hispanics do just to drive everyone else crazy. He had suggested they meet at the store—one of his missions impossible, should he accept it—as a way to case the place for Macready. He's still not sure what Roberto has in mind, but now that he's on stage, he's more relaxed. Sitting on the floor next to him is a large houseplant for Roberto's wife, Nicole. He had called Campbell, just like a fucking school kid, for permission to buy it because Tippett ordered him not to spend a Bureau dime without prior approval. Christ, what a way to run an investigation, penny-wise and undercover foolish.

Roberto waves to Sparshott and motions him to drive around to the lot behind the store. Then he rushes out the back door to greet him like, well, like a buddy long lost at sea. When Sparshott gives him the plant, he's overwhelmed with the thoughtfulness toward his wife. It's the greatest show of warmth and friendship Roberto has demonstrated so far. He tells Sparshott he has a wonderful surprise for him—a little family party in Terry's honor at his home.

"Hey, great!" Sparshott tells Roberto.

"Oh fuck!" he tells himself. "Maybe it would have been better if the sharks got the guy."

Roberto is proud of his money laundry. He guides Sparshott through the store and even opens up the walk-in cooler to show him the stacked cases of cold beer. It's the best stocked liquor store Sparshott has ever seen and he's visited a few in his lifetime.

Next, Roberto leads Sparshott through an adjoining door into the nightclub which is still under construction. The bar, shaped like a large wooden lifesaver, is nearly completed. The lights are in place and the disco equipment is just waiting to mambo and samba. Roberto says the place will be open for business in one month.

After the tour, Roberto gives Sparshott two Tabares Liquor Store hats and t-shirts, then climbs into his Cadillac and heads for his house, a ten minute drive away. Sparshott follows in his own car, sorry, but I gotta meet someone later on. In reality, he needs a getaway car in case he has to bust out of Tabares' house and make a run for it. His mind is racing. He faces three serious problems and they all have the same last name—Raul, Roy and Nicole.

It's now three o'clock—five hours since he last checked to make sure Raul was still in the hospital, plenty of time for Roy to bring his half-brother to the house. If Raul isn't there now, he could always come later. Even if Raul doesn't leave the hospital, he could have told Roy about the big pig that busted him. Okay, forget Raul . . . Roy might recognize him from all the surveillance he did on the guy's house in Columbia, Maryland. Okay, forget Roy . . . what about Nicole? It's not uncommon for the wife of a drug dealer to kill a deal—and the buyer because she doesn't like the way he dresses. That means Sparshott will have to be charming for hours without allowing liquor to loosen his tongue or lower his guard. Hey, man, nothin' like a little family get together! Meet the little woman and shit.

Sparshott parks as close to the front door as he can without boxing himself in. He looks up and down the street like a house guest who wants to see how his host lives, doesn't spot Preston or Scooter or Tippett who is in Miami to coordinate the complex surveillance operation. Tippett's almost as scared as Sparshott and his resentment toward the cop is deeply buried under layers of worry. To walk into a bad guy's house for dinner without a wire or a gun is as dangerous as it comes in the undercover game. Tippett had offered Sparshott a chance to back out, your call buddy. Typical Sparshott, he said let's fuckin' do it. Tippett knows the guy will push the scenario right to the edge wherever the hell that is, and that makes him doubly nervous.

Sparshott follows Roberto up to the carved-wood front door. He stands there while Roberto rings the doorbell to give his wife the pleasure of formally greeting her guest of honor, and notes again that the windows are barred—can't toss a chair through one of those and dive out—and remembers that the backyard is fenced. That means his only way out is the front door he's staring at.

Nicole Tabares, dressed in a full length hostess outfit, smiles warmly and invites Sparshott into her home. When Roberto presents her with the houseplant, she seems as touched by the gesture as her husband was. As she steps away from the door so he can enter the tiled foyer, Sparshott freezes. His feet feel as if they're stuck in cement shoes and, for the first time in his life, his tongue is actually tied. His panic borders on cold fear.

Sparshott stares down a long hallway which runs the length of the house and opens onto a back porch. The sheer curtains which cover the porch windows flutter gently. It's funny how you notice little things like that when you're scared. Raul Tabares is reclining in a hospital chair on the porch enjoying the afternoon breeze, a blanket bunched up on his chest. All Sparshott can see of him are his feet, backlit by the late afternoon sun like two black jackrabbit ears.

Sparshott's thinking, oh fuck, I gotta get out of here, I gotta make it look good, I gotta come up with a fucking excuse they'll buy. But he can't think of any fucking excuse so he stalls for time. He tells Mrs. Tabares how much he likes her carved wood doors. She beams in pleasure. He tells her how attractive the tiled foyer is. She smiles graciously.

Then he suddenly has it. He'll tell Roberto that he forgot he had an early meeting up in Lauderdale with one of his pilots, sorry buddy, gotta go. But he can't get the cotton out of his mouth. His heart is pounding so wildly that a body mike would pick up the thunder.

Then the feet on the chair at the end of the hallway move. The footrest on the recliner folds back into the chair and a woman holding a baby in a blanket gets up and walks toward him. Sparshott recognizes her—it's Gustavo's wife, Nicky—but is still too stunned to think straight. He reaches for the kid. "Oh what a beautiful baby!" he says. Mrs. Tabares is delighted. A nice man who loves children.

The baby is Sparshott's insurance until he calms down enough to feel safe again. He takes a step deeper into the house, clutching the little hostage. He looks for Raul, he waits for another surprise, he quickly exhausts his vocabulary of baby talk. He notes stairs to the right of the foyer. No help there.

A living room with barred windows to the left. He feels as helpless as a yacht in dry dock.

Then Roy comes to meet him, drink in hand and already a little tipsy. Sparshott holds baby Gustavo a little tighter. He's ready to back out the door, the child as his shield, cowardly, but his choice is starkly simple. Danger has a way of doing that, making things simple—either Morgan becomes fatherless or Gustavo childless. Easy choice, man.

Roy doesn't recognize Sparshott. He just stands by the door and waits respectfully for his father to introduce him to the family's honored guest.

Sparshott breathes easier now. He takes a quick look around the place—kitchen to the left, living room across from the kitchen, small office on the right just before the porch, pool out back with kids splashing. When he doesn't see Raul, he hands the baby back to Nicky with one last goo-goo.

The spread on the porch is Cuban, catered, and expensive. Giant shrimp and lobster in heated metal pans, whole fish, barbecued chicken, roast beef au jus, fresh baked bread, a mountain of red beans, and a dessert tray with small pastries. There are several cases of Corona on ice and six bottles of Dom Perignon—how thoughtful. Hey, who says it's tough to be a narc?

When an hour crawls by and Raul doesn't appear and no one even mentions his name, Sparshott concludes he isn't coming and goes to work. His first job is to make everyone like him, especially Nicole. He compliments the women, drinks and backslaps with the men, and jokes with the kids. He watches faces and body language and constantly asks himself: Are they buying me? Are they comfortable with me? Am I impressing them? He can feel Nicole's eyes on him and it doesn't take him long to figure out that she dotes on Roy. So he spends a lot of time with the guy, like the way to a mother's heart is through her favorite son.

As afternoon grinds into early evening, Sparshott begins to relax a little. He knows he's out of immediate danger but he still worries about making a mistake. And he feels as slimy as a snitch when he begins his second mission—to snoop for the Bureau. It's one of those times when Sparshott and Terry argue.

Terry likes the Tabares family, most of whom are not involved in drugs and probably don't know Roberto is. They are warm and friendly people and treat him like a new cousin. But Sparshott keeps butting in. Like a prickly conscience, he reminds Terry not to enjoy himself too much, not to get too close, not to drink too much, hey Terry, keep your fucking eyes open and watch your ass.

Sparshott becomes a camera. He snaps pictures of everything in the Tabares house from the black lacquer table to the waterbed in the first-floor guest room. He photographs every lock and when he goes upstairs to the bathroom, he gets all three bedrooms on his memory film.

As afternoon flirts with evening, it becomes obvious to Sparshott that his host is dying to talk business. So when Roberto suggests a ride to the marina to see his boat—Sparshott doesn't like the sound of "let's take a ride"—he figures Roberto needs a private minute with him. To protect himself, he suggests they go in *his* car. You never know in the drug biz. Maybe Roy, who tags along, made him after all—Sparshott doubts it, the guy's half sloshed—or maybe someone's waiting on the boat. They pass the Brickell Point Hyatt and turn right onto the MacArthur Causeway. Roberto directs Sparshott to Pier J where *The Excuse*, which appears empty, rocks in its berth.

Sparshott follows Roberto on board and watches his every move. If there's any trouble, he can always dive overboard, you know, like in the movies. Roberto is as eager to show Sparshott his boat as he was the liquor store and, once again, Sparshott memorizes every detail from the size of the engines to the color of the cabin.

They sip Coronas on the deck as the late afternoon sun begins its journey to the sea and firm up the second one-key buy in Miami the following week. Roberto then turns his attention to the stone in his shoe that has troubled him all afternoon—the big buy set for May 5, three weeks away. And he has only two questions. Does Terry still want fifty keys, and is the date firm? He doesn't like the idea of sitting on so much dope even a day longer than he has to.

Sparshott tells Roberto he understands. He still wants the fifty and doesn't want to sit on $1.2 million longer than he has to. They freeze the date, no changes, no turning back. Roberto nods his approval. They set a tentative date for the second one kilo buy in Miami for the following week, then return to the Tabares house.

Never before has Sparshott taken so many chances at one time. The tension is beginning to tie strings of little knots in his head, but he tries to appear at ease, relaxed among new friends, even having fun. He feels like an actor with a migraine who still manages to move his audience to laugh and cry. No matter what the strain, he knows the litmus test of family is almost over.

Terry is so exhausted after eight hours with the Tabares family that he doesn't have the energy to fight Sparshott any longer. Fuck you, Tracy, give me a break will you, man? Terry *is* a dope dealer now, friend of Roberto and Nicole, Roy and Nicky, and Terry is beginning to have a good time.

It's late. Good time or not, Terry is mentally drained, like a politician who can't bring himself to kiss another baby or shake one more hand. He also knows he doesn't have to any more. He has won. Nicole is perfectly at ease around him.

"You come back again, Terry," she says at the door.

"More time in Miami, Terry," Roberto says.

"I'd like to. If everything goes well on the fifth, maybe the week after."

"Go fishing?" Roberto breaks into that almost childlike smile of his.

Terry laughs and puts his arm around Roberto's shoulder, but Sparshott pulls him back before he can get too close to the old man.

"Okay, buddy," Sparshott tells Roberto. Both he and Terry feel a twinge of honest sadness. "We'll go fishin'."

THIRTY-EIGHT

Bill Campbell came home to a cockfight over the planned second one-kilo buy in Miami. Tracy Sparshott wanted to make it. Stew Tippett wanted to kill it.

Sparshott argued that since he, not Roberto, had suggested the buy, he would be stepping out of character if he backed down. Now that he had earned Roberto's confidence, it was no time to raise doubts. Besides, if he jumped right into the fifty-kilo buy-bust, Roberto might suspect he was a narc. Fuck, every bad guy knows that feds buy as little as they can and set them up for as much as they can. And don't forget Roberto's invitation to see how his chop shop reupholsters cars, like in *The French Connection.* And don't forget that the original undercover proposal, approved by the creds, called for two separate one-kilo buys, one in Washington and one in Miami. And don't forget . . .

Tippett was as hardass stubborn as Sparshott. He argued that the Miami buy, which Sparshott had indeed suggested and without proper approval, wasn't necessary since Tabares had already agreed to sell them fifty kilos. Why risk something going wrong—you know how easily locals can fuck up—just to tour a chop shop? Besides, there wasn't enough money in the budget to buy a kilo at any price. If his supervisors in Baltimore had burned his ass for spending money on a plant for the bad guy's wife, what would they say to another expensive trip to Miami that wasn't necessary? Besides there wasn't enough time to go through channels all the way to headquarters to get it. And there wasn't . . .

Campbell sided with Tippett for a change. Theoretically, he

agreed with Sparshott that the buy in Miami was a logical undercover step and that a week was plenty of time to set it up. But practically, there really *wasn't* any money in the budget. So he reluctantly agreed with Tippett without explaining to Sparshott that when he couldn't get the $700,000 he had originally asked for, he had settled for a quick fix of $50,000 to keep the team in business. (Tippett immediately asked for another $50K but it hadn't come through yet.) They had spent nearly $38,000 of that slim budget on the three previous buys alone. Add travel and rent, and they were broke. Campbell felt that if the team knew their real financial condition, they would be demoralized. He asked Sparshott to phone Roberto and call the buy off.

What neither Campbell nor Tippett told Sparshott was that, if Roberto showed Sparshott the chop shop, the Miami Bureau not the Task Force team would be assigned the subsequent investigation, make all seizures and arrests, and bag all stats. The Baltimore Bureau wouldn't take kindly to spending its own cash to buy feathers for Miami's nest. Hey, who says the feds don't have teeth.

Sparshott didn't fight back. Neither did he buy the no money-in-the-budget argument which, he believed, was nothing more than a thin disguise masking the Bureau's contempt for him as an F.L. Shit, the sooner the team takes Roberto down the better. His five-year tour of duty as a narc was nearly up and he wanted to nail the Tabares organization before he had to move on.

While the team planned the big May 5 buy, the FBI agent monitoring the wiretaps intercepted a Tabares-Medina conversation with staggering undercover implications:

"It can't go the way they want," Roberto said.

"But I gave the guy my *word*," Carlos complained.

There was a long pause. Then a Hispanic called Tomas got on the line and reamed Carlos out for three minutes. Every time Carlos tried to break in, Tomas cut him off like a cleaver.

"I've been in business for fifteen years," Tomas said. "I run a national organization. Fifty is a small deal for us . . . we do that every day. But this smells like a setup and I don't like it. I think they're the feds. Only the feds would make such a big single buy. I wash my hands. If it goes bad, it's you—not me."

"I trust these people," Carlos said when Tomas finished. "I know these people. I gave my word."

Roberto then got back on the line and said, "Okay, Carlos, we'll do it. But we'll do it in parts . . . not all at once."

□ □ □

The team was so excited with the call that it was ready to snort a line. They had their first solid lead on Roberto's supplier. A last name to go with Tomas would only be a matter of time and patience, like finding out "the old Cuban guy" was Tabares. When Carlos had told Sparshott on the ride to Annapolis that Roberto was "the right hand" of the biggest cocaine dealer in Miami, the team suspected the kid was exaggerating. Now they knew. Fifty keys a *day*, less a few Gs of hype, was big even for Miami.

The team, especially Tom Roberts who carried the biggest stick—after all, the Bureau was supposed to be working for him not him for the Bureau—wanted to go for the whole pineapple and quickly agreed on a plausible plan: Sparshott will tell Roberto he's nervous about the way the one-key buy at Bob's went down and wants to do a smaller practice run of five kilos; given what they learned from the Tomas phone call, Roberto will jump at the offer; after the buy, Sparshott will tell Roberto he wants to meet his supplier.

Campbell called a round-table team meeting, which they dubbed "The Stew Tippett Show," in the conference room of the Hyattsville office. They were armed with reason and prepared to treat Tippett to a hell of a lot more than a bloody nose. Over the months and almost imperceptibly, he had become the eyes and ears of the Bureau. Simply put, if they couldn't convince Tippett to go for Tomas, it would never be done. Five kilos of coke at 26 thou per key came to $130,000. Either the creds in Baltimore had to approve that expenditure from the case budget, or, if there was no money in the budget, beg headquarters for it. As far as the creds were concerned, Stew Tippett was the Tabares case officer and what he did not recommend, did not get done. Not exactly what Campbell had in mind when he asked Tippett to join him on the case.

Both Campbell and Roberts were reasonably certain Tippett wouldn't go for a longer, broader, and more expensive investigation. Targeting Tomas was risky. The Bureau could not only lose a pile of buy-money—$130,000 for openers—but could blow part of the total case and maybe get Sparshott killed in the process. Unlike everyone else around the table, Tippett was no risk taker. He believed his career would rise or fall with the Tabares case, and it was no secret that all his case recommendations so far were influenced more by fear of failure than hope of success, or so the team thought. But even if Tippett suddenly caught a bad case of courage and recommended allowing $130,000 to walk, Roberts and Campbell were doubtful headquarters would approve. All the team had to go on was a single phone call from an alleged dealer without a last name. But in spite of their skepticism, they felt they owed it to themselves and the team to try and win Tippett over. They argued:

The team now knows that Roberto and Carlos are suspicious but still willing to sell them fifty keys—in parts—because they are greedy. They also now know that Roberto and Carlos will have to buy the dope with their own money. Tomas made it clear he wasn't going to front them because the deal reeked of feds. At a wholesale price of $13,000 per key, fifty will cost Roberto and Carlos $650,000. Even if they offered to sell Sparshott half now and half later, $325 thou was a big chunk of change to risk. So—if Sparshott tells Roberto he feels more comfortable progressing from one key to five, and if the five-key buy goes down smooth, Roberto will be convinced more than ever that Terry is an honest crook. Tomas will waver. Sparshott can then work on Roberto for an introduction to Tomas just as he manipulated Carlos for an introduction to Roberto. Once Sparshott has his hooks in Tomas, Christ . . . make a two hundred-key buy, sell the dirtballs airplanes, get leads on their massive money laundering. Just imagine—if the Tomas organization sells fifty keys a day at $13,000 per, that would come to $650,000 a day, $4.5 million a week, $18.2 million a month, $218.4 million a year. Hey, why can't the good guys get greedy sometimes.

Of course, Roberts and Campbell were right. When the team crossed the last "t" on the last argument—Sparshott was so nice he didn't even say, "I told you so, asshole"—Tippett simply said no, Baltimore had already told him it wouldn't go for it and Tomas would never buy Sparshott whom he's sure is a narc. After a five-kilo buy, Tippett argued, the team would end up with the same thing—Roberto and Carlos—minus $130,000. Let's take the two sitting ducks down first, then go for Tomas afterwards. Sure bro, send the locals back on the street to sniff out another big case while the Bureau keeps Tomas all to its fucking self.

Although he was badass disappointed, Sparshott was not surprised. He had run into the same fed Magoo-shit on his last big case with the DEA. The bad guy from New York had a supplier in Miami, maybe it was even this guy Tomas. Sparshott wanted to weasel an introduction to the Miami connection. The feds said no. The bad guy offered to introduce Sparshott to a heroin dealer in New York. The feds said no. The bad guy introduced Sparshott to two Washington PCP dealers who got their juice from L.A. Sparshott wanted to go under and penetrate the whole fucking gang. The feds said no. Christ, just like Carlos' friend Zeus. Hey, welcome to the war on drugs . . . fuckin' cockatoos for generals.

□ □ □

If the good guys were divided, the bad guys were confused. At first, Tomas was so convinced Terry was a narc—no one jumps from one to fifty keys but feds—that he even refused to sell the dope to Roberto for cold cash, forget about fronting any. When

Roberto couldn't find a new supplier, he went back to Tomas and practically begged for a deal. Weren't they good friends? Had he ever let Tomas down? Didn't he trust Roberto's judgment? After all *he* was the one who met Terry and saw his operation, not Tomas. He'd swear on the Cuban blood they had in common that Terry Petit wasn't a narc.

Tomas caved in—part greed, part friendship—and worked out a compromise deal: He would sell Roberto the first twenty-five kilos for $10K per instead of the usual $13K per. Roberto would then sell Terry the shit for $26K per key. In exchange for the buy money, Tomas would give Roberto another twenty-five keys which Roberto would then sell to Terry. In the end, each dealer would walk away with $650,000. Not bad for a couple days work and a little worry.

Tomas in place, Roberto offered Carlos a deal—either accept a kilo of coke as a finder's fee and back out, no hard feelings . . . or front $100,000, help with the buy, and make $100,000 profit. Carlos went for the money which he planned to use to open a legitimate business in Panama after graduation. Fuck, man, no way he was gonna beg his stepfather for money especially after the silkscreen business he had started after high school went belly up.

But the closer Carlos came to the bigass buy, his last deal he told himself, the more frightened he became. From a one-key per month dealer to a 50-key middleman in less than a year was one fucking big step. Christ, he had never seen more than three kilos parked in one place at one time in his whole life. He couldn't sleep, he lost so much weight he looked like a scarecrow in his six foot two frame, he was smoking two packs of cigarettes a day and drinking so much he couldn't concentrate on his books, his grades at GW were slipping, he'd lose his girlfriend if he didn't stop snorting. Fuck, he was addicted to the shit and he knew it. He was getting regular nosebleeds like some stupid junkie, he now needed several lines, not just one, as an eye opener, a couple of pick-me-ups during the day, you know, just to keep going, and an eightball at night to convince himself that his life wasn't falling apart. He made up his mind to stop snorting but couldn't. When he went to Daytona Beach on vacation, he purposely didn't take any dope with him to, you know, dry out a little. He ended up buying Gs down there to relax with. Now he needed the shit to get him through the big buy even though it was making him as paranoid as Zeus without his pistachio fix. Big doubts ate at him. What if narcs grabbed the dope before it got to Washington, like the fucking state troopers and Gustavo? What if Tomas was right and Terry was a fed? What if Tomas was wrong and Terry was a real marijuana dealer but the feds were already on his ass? What if Terry was on the level but Marty wasn't?

Fuck, Tomas and Roberto, who had fifteen years of experience in the drug trade to his one, didn't help any. First, Tomas was so convinced that Terry was a narc he refused to deal. Then he was willing to sell Roberto twenty-five keys below the market price. Well, fuckado! What if Tomas' first impression of Terry was the right one?

The big doubts got to Carlos. He phoned a friend who knew a cop and asked him to discreetly find out what kind of listening devices and shit pigs use. What his friend reported back—of course the phone was bugged—was so vague he could have learned more from a "Miami Vice" rerun. Next, he drove to a counterspy shop on 14th and K Streets in northwest Washington, about ten blocks from FBI headquarters—of course an FBI surveillance team followed him. The store was a spook's gadget-dream come true: telephone scramblers to fit any budget; tape recorders to fit any cranny; sweeps to find hidden bugs; bird dog pens that emit tracking signals; telephone analyzers to ferret out phone bugs; electronic bomb detectors; voice stress analyzers; night-vision cameras, binoculars, and gun scopes; counter-surveillance receivers to pick up covert radio transmissions; cameras in briefcases and car antennas, in fire-protection sprinkler heads and digital clocks which send continuous videos up to a quarter mile.

Carlos bought a pocket-size surveillance receiver which vibrates like a silent telephone beeper. You wear the $1,700 gadget in a pocket. It tickles you if it picks up a covert radio transmission. He also priced a top-of-the-line phone analyzer which he later asked Roberto to buy. Roberto said he trusted Terry so why waste $18,000 for a bug detector that probably didn't work. Carlos said he'd go fifty-fifty. When Roberto said no deal, Carlos invited Terry to dine with him and the vibrator. The thing never went off—Sparshott wasn't wired and surveillance was hanging way back—and that seemed to soothe Carlos' drug nerves for a while.

But too little sleep and too much shit made him replay all the nigglings he had had about Terry since they first met at Bob's Big Boy. Fucking Terry, every time Carlos felt the smallest doubt, the guy would do something to settle it. Was he a mind reader or what? After the first quarter-ounce buy, Carlos wasn't sure Terry was really a marijuana dealer. Then Terry takes him to the little Airpark and gives him a peek at his operation. Roberto said right afterwards that Terry smelled of narco-shit. Then Terry buys a half pound for $11 thou to prove he's got money and isn't a narc. None of his friends ever heard of a biker-dealer called Terry Petit. But then Terry wines and dines him in Frederick where every-fucking-body knows him. He was disappointed that Terry's house looked so cheap and wondered if the guy was exaggerating his operation, you know, like a typical dealer. Then Terry shows him his marijuana business. He worried about how Terry disappeared like a groundhog, kept putting off the one-pound buy, and tried to make everything so fucking complicated and, you know, clockworky. Then Terry meets Roberto and impresses him with all that caution-shit. He wasn't sure that Terry would be good for $1.3 million for a fifty-key buy. Then Terry shows him and Roberto a stash in a rinky-dinky bank which sells Roberto completely. And there were all the little things that didn't spell setup, like the bottle of Dom Perignon, the Rolex, the Mercedes, the Texas phone call, the roundtrip airline ticket to Dallas, the platinum Texas ring, the sample of grass, the bikers and machine guns in the fucking field, Marty's new Mercedes, the airplanes, the bikes Old Mike was buying for Terry's people. If this guy was a narc, he was fucking good, man.

Big and little doubts aside, Carlos still considered Terry his friend. So he brought him a present from Miami, Roberto Duran's autograph on a napkin. He had met the boxer in a Cuban restaurant where he and Roberto were settling the financial details of the big buy. And he invited Terry to go to Miami with him and his cousin Pinky the week after the big buy to see the Duran fight.

"Pinky?" Sparshott asked. He wanted the cousin's real name so Tom Roberts could add him to the target list. "Shit, man, nobody's named *Pinky*."

"Well, we just call him Pinky. Pincus is his name . . . Louis Pincus."

Carlos even introduced his good friend Terry to his sister who was visiting from Panama. She attacked Carlos' house with Mr. Clean but didn't know what to do with Mr. Pistachio Shit.

"I'm going to kill that parrot," she complained to Sparshott. "You want it?"

"Let's have it for dinner," Sparshott had said. "Better yet—give him to the fuckin' alligators."

Carlos liked Terry so much that he didn't want to disappoint him. When Tomas said no fucking way, man, he warned Terry that the deal might turn sour. "It's not me or Roberto," he apologized. "It's Roberto's partner. He says that's the way the feds do it—all at one time. He would normally front us, but to do the deal I might have to put up everything I have. This shit is really worrying me."

If all that wasn't bad enough, one of Carlos' people—he suspected Santiago whom he had met at PG Community College—had broken into his house and ripped off $15,000 cash he had just collected. He complained to Terry and asked for his advice, you know, drug brother to drug brother. Sparshott warned him not to do anything foolish until *after* the big buy and offered to have his people take care of Santiago later which, of course, they would.

For his part, Sparshott found Carlos' confidence in him both flattering and touching, and his concern for Carlos was real. The line between cop and friend had blurred. Carlos wasn't a bad kid. He had no criminal record in the U.S. or in Panama. He didn't come from a family of crooks. He didn't seem to have a violent bone in his skinny body. He was as warm and friendly as a puppy and just as needy. But he was spoiled, selfish, greedy, and hooked on shit. Sparshott was going to send him to jail as a cocaine conspirator and kingpin, you could bet a toot on that. But he would do anything he could to save the kid from a murder one rap.

With the team divided, Carlos hinky, and Tomas still wavering, Roberto came to town full of confidence to negotiate the final details of the big buy.

THIRTY-NINE

Sparshott invited Roberto and Carlos to lunch at the Gaithersburg Marriott not far from the Airpark and tooled up in a bigass Harley. Roberto loved it. Never great on small talk in broken English, he began negotiations as soon as they sat down. Carlos was his point man. Sparshott's job was to talk Roberto out of using three cars for the buy—a spinoff of his original five-location suggestion—without appearing to change the buy rules at the last minute. For once, Sparshott completely agreed with Tippett and the creds, surveillance and backup at three separate locations would be a logistical mess.

Carlos began the negotiation by rejecting both the Greenbelt Hilton and Bob's Big Boy as buy locations. Sparshott agreed.

Sparshott suggested a daylight buy so everybody could see what he was getting . . . in an open parking lot so they could both watch their backs. Carlos agreed in principle.

Sparshott then suggested the deal go down at the White Oak Shopping Mall which was on New Hampshire Avenue two miles north of Bob's Big Boy. He had given the location a lot of thought. Not only was it ideal for surveillance, backup, and takedown, but there were two highrise apartment buildings across the street with balconies. Perfect for the FBI sniper team Tippett ordered. Naturally, White Oak was in Montgomery County where Sparshott's brothers could take part in the biggest hand-to-hand buy and drug seizure in the history of the Baltimore-Washington metropolitan area. Carlos agreed.

Roberto then insisted on breaking the 50-kilo sale into three parts, not two: a 15-key buy for $390,000, followed by another 15-key buy a few hours later, and a final 20-key buy the next day. Sparshott agreed. There would never be a second or third buy. The first would be the bye-bye bust.

Sparshott suggested that the first buy be between Terry and Carlos, the second between Marty and Carlos, and the third on the following day between Terry and Roberto. Tabares rattled off something in Spanish, then agreed.

Finally, Sparshott suggested that since Roberto wanted to divide the buy into three parts, they ought to keep each as simple as possible: the money in one rented car and the dope in another rented car; after the buyer inspects the shit and the seller sees the money, they exchange car keys and drive away. He was hoping Roberto would agree to the buy-plan without his insisting on it which he was entitled to do because Roberto had changed the sell-plan.

Sparshott didn't have to worry. Roberto kept nodding yes, yes as he spelled it out. In fact, Roberto was so pleased with the final arrangements that he invited Terry to move to Miami after the buy and promised that if he did, he'd buy him a new bike and a new boat. Hey man, is this guy beautiful or what?

While FBI agents kept Roberto and Carlos under constant surveillance and monitored the wiretaps around the clock—they were looking for counter-surveillance clues, dope transportation plans, tips about possible shooters, hints about a rip and run—Tippett and Campbell drew up a complex "operational plan" which called for more than 130 FBI agents, IRS agents, and local cops from Montgomery County, PG, D.C., and Miami. Hey man, the greatest fucking show on earth.

Campbell personally knew every FBI agent in Hyattsville, Silver Spring, and Baltimore, and desperately wanted to help put the teams together because he didn't want "slugs" playing key roles. Bureau snipers were among the best in the country and Bureau Special Operation Groups were highly trained surveillance experts. But a lot of the desk jocks were so rusty and inexperienced

Campbell didn't trust them. He owed it to Sparshott and the rest of the team to make sure they had as few pre-raid gas pains as possible. But the creds told Campbell to mind his own business. When he finally got to see the list, hey, he *was* the operation coordinator, he demanded a meeting with the supervisor who had assembled it, a blue flamer with the street smarts of a debutante. The guy had placed in important slots special agents with as little savvy as *he* had, and Campbell had no confidence in their ability to make safe decisions under pressure. The most he could possibly expect from them was to be in the right place at the right time on the day of the raid. Campbell reasoned with the supervisor, he argued, he demanded, he did everything but crawl and weep. The cred refused to alter the list.

Having failed in Baltimore, Campbell asked the Miami Bureau to conduct tight surveillance on Roberto Tabares to see where and when he got the dope and how he was packaging it for the trip to Washington. But the Miami SAC declined to assist saying the assignment was too vague and the Bureau was too busy with its own drug cases. Gee thanks, guys.

Luckily, the team intercepted a phone call from Carlos to Roberto during which Carlos offered to send some white mules down to Miami to bring the shit back because, you know, the fucking state troopers would never hassle white guys. But Roberto declined the offer saying he would bring the dope up to Washington himself in a Winnebago with a couple members of his family as cover.

Everyone was ready. The teams visited their assigned locations and rehearsed. Campbell and Tippett asked all supervisors to do a dry run with FBI-supplied radios to make sure everyone was comfortable with the five-channel system they had devised for the complex buy-bust, arrests, and raids. The snipers selected the spot in the parking lot across the street where they wanted Sparshott to stand. Campbell chose the Hines-Rinaldi Funeral Home a mile north of the mall on New Hampshire as the raid staging area. The arrest and search/seizure warrants were signed and sealed in Washington and in Miami. Jeff Favitta and

Jerry Macready were in place in Miami to coordinate the fireworks there.

It was after ten. The buy was set for ten the following morning just twelve hours away. An FBI team in the listening post was monitoring Roberto's and Carlos' phones and watching the parking lot of Presidential Towers through binoculars on a tripod, cameras loaded and ready to go. All they needed was Roberto Tabares.

A white Winnebago with a green and gray stripe finally pulled into Presidential Towers shortly after ten. Roberto, his wife, and a young white woman got out of the RV with suitcases which they carried into the building. Roberto and the white woman came back out shortly and drove to the New Hampshire Motor Lodge not far from Bob's Big Boy where Tabares booked a room for her in his name. The team figured she was a courier assigned to bring the money to Tomas who was supposed to come but didn't. An acute case of last minute jitters.

The team huddled for the last time around midnight. Everyone was tense and exhausted, but relieved that the final play of the scrappy game was about to begin. Each had worked eighteen straight hours and needed a chance to rest before psyching up for the buy-bust the next morning.

But Tippett told the team that Baltimore wanted him to scrap the buy-bust and just raid the Winnebago and Tabares' apartment. Why risk almost $400,000 in buy money when the dope was sitting right under their noses? Tippett was inclined to agree with his superiors. The wiretap team had intercepted some messages which led him to believe that Tomas was sending up a team of shooters to protect his interests. A buy-bust could be deadly.

Sparshott, Campbell, and Preston exploded, and the last team meeting turned into a verbal brawl with everyone ganging up on Tippett and, through him, the creds in Baltimore:

How the fuck do you know Roberto muled the dope to Washington in the RV? No one saw him load the shit and no one saw him unload it . . .

Christ, Stew, if he did carry it in the RV, who's to say it's still sitting there or in his apartment . . .

Yeah, maybe Roberto stashed it in another apartment, there's no surveillance following his movements . . .

Or maybe the white woman has it in her motel room . . .

Our guys saw Roberto getting in and out of three different cars, Stew—Carlos' white Porsche, a silver Toyota, his own beige Renault . . .

The shit could be anywhere and nowhere . . .

You can't be sure they're going to have shooters . . .

Can't you see that to raid Roberto without a buy-bust first would be to risk the whole fucking investigation . . .

Caught painfully between the team and Baltimore, Tippett was in no mood for undercover logic. He wasn't sleeping well. Family tensions over long hours and late nights were growing.

The buy-bust was just too personally risky for Sparshott. He was calling it off. End of discussion.

Sparshott took the news as another cred kick in the balls. As far as he was concerned, substituting the raid for the buy-bust was just the creds' sweet way of saying they didn't trust a fucking local with a job an FBI agent should have had right from the start . . . It was Tippett's way of covering his puny little dick. If he raided the RV and the apartment and actually found the thirty or fifty keys of dope, he'd get a promotion. Hey, great job Stew! If he came up empty, he could blame the rest of the team for faulty information, hey, what can you expect from those fucking locals . . . It was the Bureau's way of cutting the locals out at the last minute and seizing all the credit along with the shit and the assets. Naturally, *Bureau* teams would smash doors and seize drugs, and crow before the TV cameras.

Sparshott was ready for action, not words. "No fucking way you're going to take this hand-to-hand buy away from me," he yelled at Tippett. "I deserve it." His fists were clenched and he was ready to do something he had wanted to for a long time—break Tippett's fucking jaw like a wood door on a wood frame. But Campbell pulled him aside and cooled him off.

Tippett wavered. The lines of tension showed in his face and the team thought for a moment that he might actually go for the buy-bust after all. Then again, maybe he had to clear the final decision with Baltimore. But, the pre-takedown briefing was scheduled for seven the next morning. How could he possibly tell a hundred well-rehearsed agents and officers that the Bureau had changed its mind? But then, how can you predict what a guy who gets nosebleeds over a marijuana show will do when he's faced with losing $390,000 of FBI money and has creds chewing on his ass?

In the end, Tippett stood his ground. As of that moment, FBI teams would raid Tabares' Winnebago and apartment and seize the cocaine after the morning briefing. Fuck it, a cred's jaw isn't worth an F.L.'s career.

FORTY

The final raid briefing was about to begin in the Prince George's County police station in Hyattsville just down the road from the FBI office which was too small to hold a hundred agents and officers. Both Campbell and Tippett arrived early. "I know we've had our differences, Stew," Campbell said. He looked as frazzled as a POW. It was his eleventh hour, now or never, pitch. "But we're almost there. Let's bury them . . . let's do this right."

Campbell hadn't gotten to bed until after midnight, then he had tossed and turned until three when he popped up worrying about coffee and donuts. Cops bitch if they don't have their early morning caffeine and sugar fix. Funny how the mind works in a time of crisis. Your house is on fire and all you can think of is saving your ten-dollar football trophy. After a shower and a shave, Campbell stopped at a Dunkin' Donuts for twelve dozen fresh ones and paid for them out of his own pocket. FBI rules did not allow special agents to use office funds for coffee served in a county police station.

Tippett didn't look like he just got back from Maui either, and the corner he had painted himself into looked a lot tighter up close. All the raid teams had worked and rehearsed hard. Every arrest and search/seizure warrant was signed. More than a hundred agents and officers were ready, eager, and waiting for FBI leadership.

"Okay," Tippett said, "we'll go the whole way."

"Thanks, Stew," Campbell said. He could have hugged the guy. Instead he went to find Tracy.

For a man who had only five hours of fitful sleep, Tracy Sparshott looked as cool as a rum and Coke. He had stayed up late with Captain Morgan replaying every fed fuck-up on the Tabares case, something he rarely did, hey, you gotta look forward, fuck yesterday. It had come as a shock to him to realize that he was no longer the same Tracy Sparshott who raided Raul's house with June Boyle almost a year ago to the day, and he didn't know if that was good or bad. When he first began the Tabares case, he had wanted to make narc history so badly he couldn't see much else. Fuck, he still wanted to set a new record, especially since the Medina buy-bust was supposed to be his swan song. He'd have to rotate out of narcotics soon and fat fucking chance he'd find another Roberto Tabares before then. But he no longer itched to make history for the same reason.

When he first began the Tabares case, he had wanted to catch a string of bad guys. Hey, that's what they trained him to do and rewarded him for with citations, plaques, medals, pay raises, and bonuses. He couldn't complain. More than twenty bad guys would be arrested here and in Miami for starters as soon as he gave the takedown signal, assuming Tippett changed what little mind he had. That ain't shabby. But he no longer wanted to see the bad guys go down for the same reason.

For seven months now, he had watched the feds shit on local cops. Treat them like Little Leaguers, laugh at them behind their exposed backs, prance around them with airs of superiority, use them like valets, and risk their lives with Bureau fuck-ups. He had hoped to prove one last magnificent time that local cops not only can do it, they can do it with style. The stakes were suddenly much bigger than Carlos Medina and Roberto Tabares. It had turned into a badass new game. The fucking locals against the feds. The F.L.'s versus the creds. Tracy Sparshott against Stew Tippett. It was Sparshott's war. It always was but he just never saw it until now. And like an aging athlete, he craved that one last chance to show his stuff.

Sparshott had set the alarm for five-thirty but got up before it sounded, not knowing whether he'd be making a buy or busting

Stew Tippett in the mouth. He trimmed his beard, showered, and picked up the suitcase with $390,000 in it from the feds, then drove to the Hyattsville station to see what asshole Tippett would finally do. He had long ago concluded that Tippett was one of those gutless wonders who push decisions off in the hope that circumstances would decide for him.

Sparshott was sitting quietly eating a donut like, hey, what a beautiful morning, when Campbell found him and told him it was a go. He was too numb to feel anything but relief that he was getting his big chance after all. He wanted to take his donut and shove it right up Tippett's ass, in a friendly sort of way, but he was too fucking tired.

The briefing began at seven a.m. with controlled ripples of excitement. Everyone in the room understood that they were about to make history. Tippett was up first. He presented the overview of the buy-bust. Sparshott followed. He ran through his part in the buy using a huge diagram he and Campbell had prepared. He described the rented car he would be driving—red so you can't miss it—and pointed to the exact spot in the White Oak lot where he would park and wait for Carlos Medina. He told them what the takedown signal would be and how he intended to get the fuck out of the lot once he had the dope. He joked with the snipers, hey, remember now, I'm the big white guy with the beard, Carlos is the skinny dark guy with a smooth face. He stressed that Carlos had a radio transmission detector which was good for at least forty feet and that Carlos intended to check him out before the sale—exactly how, Sparshott wasn't sure. Finally, he warned everyone with a radio to stay well away from his car or Medina might pick up a transmission signal. If he did, he might open fire, unlikely—or fly like a bat out of Panama, likely.

Campbell spoke last. He explained the communication system one more time and who was going to arrest whom. He passed out the warrants, then told everyone to be in place by nine-thirty. The buy-bust was scheduled for ten-thirty. There was no turning back.

9:49 A.M.

Campbell is looking out of an apartment window on the sixteenth floor of the highrise across New Hampshire Avenue from White Oak Mall. The snipers are outside on the balcony. From his vantage point, he can watch Carlos drive north or south on New Hampshire. He sees Sparshott's red Firebird parked in the mall lot as close to the street as he can get, the safest for civilians. And he sees the Bureau SWAT van parked in the lot as well. His main job is to give the order over the special administrative channel for all teams to go into action. Silence means the buy is aborted. Sparshott had selected the takedown signal. After he sees the coke, he will remove his Harley hat and, at the same time, Campbell will announce: "The hat's off." The Tabares organization in Washington and in Miami won't know what hit it.

Campbell finally gets the surveillance report he's been waiting for. Roberto Tabares just parked a rented blue Olds Cutlass Ciera between a Safeway Food Store and a Popeye's Chicken Restaurant in a shopping mall five minutes away from White Oak. He then got into a silver Toyota wagon and drove off. Campbell suspects the dope is in the trunk of the blue Cutlass.

Ten minutes later, Campbell gets another surveillance report. Tabares' Toyota just met Medina's Porsche at Bob's Big Boy two miles south of White Oak. Then, the silver Toyota with Tabares still inside returned to Presidential Towers and parked in the underground garage. A few minutes later, Campbell makes the white Porsche driving north on New Hampshire. It passes White Oak Mall, makes a u-turn, then heads back toward Bob's.

The first surprise of the day. Medina is supposed to be driving a rented car, not the Porsche. To Campbell, that means one of two things. Either—Medina is making an intelligence drive-by to see if Terry is in place and if there are any suspicious people hanging around. Or—Medina is scouting White Oak for a ripoff. If it's a ripoff, he merely has to pick up his car phone and tell his gang that Terry Petit is in place and to grab the money and run. But why would Medina take either alternative in his *own* car which he knows Terry will recognize?

The second surprise of the day. Instead of going back to Bob's, Medina turns into the mall, slowly drives by Maxie Waxie, Mrs. Fields, and a pizza joint as if he's cruising for chickies. Then he turns left toward New Hampshire Avenue and heads straight for Sparshott. Campbell doesn't have a clue why and wishes he could discuss the problem with Tracy which, of course, he can't because Sparshott isn't wired and neither is his rented car. So he tells the snipers to get ready, then scans New Hampshire Avenue and the mall lot for any sudden movement. Medina may be pointing Terry out to his gang, like a narc points out the bad guy to the SWAT team, so they won't raid the wrong car or shoot the wrong target.

10:30 A.M.

Sparshott can't tell whether he's more worried or pissed. The Bureau SWAT van, which has its own communication channel, is parked less than forty feet away, well within the range of Carlos' vibrator transmission-detector. He can't move his car because the snipers gave him his position and warned him not to change it. Since he's not wearing a mike, he can't simply say, "Tell the SWAT van to move the fuck away. They're too close." And he can't walk over to it and rap on the window. Carlos might have counters in an apartment across the street watching him as carefully as Billy Campbell is watching Medina. Isn't that just great. The van with the fucking local SWAT team is safely hidden behind a vibrator-proof Sears Automotive Center. The van with the smartassed feds is well within the danger zone.

When he sees the white Porsche enter the lot, circle and drive towards him, Sparshott knows *exactly* what Carlos is up to. He gets a sinking feeling in his gut that it's all over. Medina's $1,700 gadget is about to vibrate the Tabares case to hell unless the SWAT radio in the FBI van parked right on his ass is quiet or the detector doesn't work—fat chance. But just maybe he'll get lucky, like maybe the little fucker was made in North Korea.

14. Carlos arrives to check for a wire

Sparshott is exhausted but doesn't know it, and given the stress of the previous day and the pressure of the moment, he's as wired as a junkie. He wants more than a clean buy-bust. He wants to keep Carlos cool so he doesn't get hinky and spoil the beauty of the takedown. He wants to make the scam run flawlessly, like his $14,000 Rolex, a work of local narc art. He wants to rescue the buy from the feds who'll blow it as surely as greed drives a dealer, then bullets may fly and men may die because there's no fucking way $390,000 is gonna walk. He wants to make the brothers in Montgomery and PG feel proud, and force Tippett and every fucking fed from Washington to Baltimore to eat their own cred shit. And to do all that, he has to cram four and a half years of narc experience into the next ten minutes.

Even if no taxpayer ever hears about or cares about what went down on May 5, 1988, in a little shopping mall in White Oak, Maryland, the brothers will know and their "Atta way to go, Trace, great job" is the only applause he needs. He's every working cop and he feels the weight of the burden. Hey man, only a fucking local can understand.

Carlos pulls up parallel to the Firebird, driver's window to driver's window. The front of the Porsche is facing New Hampshire Avenue and the snipers have Carlos in their sights. Both he and Sparshott roll down their windows.

"Hey, what the fuck's goin' on?" Sparshott demands. He trains ice-water eyes on Carlos. If this is a ripoff, fuck it, he can't afford to watch his back. He has to keep Carlos on edge, guessing, afraid, so if his fucking vibrator goes off, shit, maybe he won't feel it.

"My people aren't comfortable," Carlos says. "We don't want to do it this way."

"What the fuck do you mean, pal?"

Sparshott jumps out of his car and into the Porsche. He's sure the feds in the SWAT van must be jawing on the radio and if Carlos picks up the vibes, fuck, he'd just as soon be sitting right next to the guy so he can watch his face and hands. Carlos explains that Roberto wants the deal to go down in another mall nearby. Fuck, everybody's scared.

"This is bullshit," Sparshott says. He has to take charge, keep Carlos on the defensive, you know, Sparshott's number one rule of undercover work. He's almost on top of Carlos now so he can pin the kid to the seat like a moth if he has to. "Goddamn it, get fuckin' Roberto on the phone . . . right now. I mean it—now! I'm sittin' on a lot of money out here."

Carlos dials Roberto at Presidential Towers. Sparshott coaches him: "Tell him this is bullshit. Tell him no changes." Sparshott watches for a sign that the vibrator has gone off but Carlos seems scared not jumpy. Maybe if he frightens the kid enough he won't feel the fucker tickle. "Tell him I'm out here with my ass on the line. Tell him it fuckin' goes down the way we agreed or not at all! Got it?"

Carlos repeats the message in English, listens to Roberto's answer, then hangs up. "Hey man, I apologize, Terry," he confesses like a kid brother. "Roberto said okay. We do it as planned. I got the keys to the other car. Wait for me, I'll be back in ten minutes."

Sparshott doesn't know whether the vibrator already went off and Carlos was too distracted to know it, whether the vibrator went off and the kid is using the be-back-in-ten as an excuse to run, or whether the gadget doesn't work. Fuck, who has time for bullshit reasons, he's got a bigger problem.

Everyone from the snipers on the balcony across the street to the feds in the van a few feet away are trying to read him and Carlos like a scene in a silent movie. He can almost hear their chipmunk-chatter: "What the fuck's going on? Hey Campbell, you know? Does *anyone* know what the fuck's going on?" The last thing he needs is to have the fucking feds dash to the rescue.

"Okay, buddy," Sparshott says. He needs to get a message to the feds fast. "But no way I'm sittin' here with all that money. I'm outta here. I'll be back in ten."

Sparshott jumps back into the Firebird and races out of the lot past the Bureau SWAT van, then turns onto New Hampshire Avenue and heads north to the staging area at the funeral home. He knows he's just saved the day. He didn't want Carlos to think he was too eager to make the buy. The kid would expect a fed to sit on $390K in an open mall, christ, every bad guy knows how the feds would fuck a lizard to make a deal go down. He's hoping the speed with which he moved will make Terry even more credible and make Carlos even more anxious to please him.

Sparshott is sweating and finally feels his exhaustion. But he fights it like a trench-soldier. When he gets to the funeral home, he grabs a phone and calls Campbell. The poor guy is so relieved to hear the deal's still on he's ready to bungee-jump off the sixteenth floor.

Sparshott says calmly to keep Campbell calm so he'll keep everyone else calm: "Let me know as soon as you see him coming back, Billy. I'm right here, brother."

Sparshott doesn't say a word about the van being too close, Campbell has enough to worry about. Besides, it would be dangerous to have the van move further from the buy site now. Carlos might notice the change and get suspicious. Sparshott's best hope is that Carlos won't be wearing the gadget in case Terry wants to search him . . . or if he is, the vibrator won't tickle him . . . or if it does, he won't notice. Fucking feds . . . you can count on 'em every time.

Sparshott uses the ten minutes between acts to psych

himself up again and stay in the role. The old fear that someone will blow a line and frighten Carlos away begins to nag until Campbell gets back on the radio. The blue Cutlass is entering the mall . . . it's probably Carlos. Then, just as Sparshott is about to pull out of the staging area for the shopping center, Campbell sees a pickup truck with a crew of Hispanic looking painters pull up and park near the Bureau SWAT van. "Hold up, Tracy. It might be a ripoff."

Sparshott sits a very long minute. It's killing him not to be able to see for himself and make his own judgment. To have come this far. To be so close and— "All clear," Campbell says. The strain is gone from his voice. "Just some guys . . . they went into a 7-Eleven."

Carlos is sitting in the Cutlass when Sparshott pulls into his parking spot a few feet away. Both men get out of their cars at the same time. Carlos walks to his trunk and waits. The kid looks like he did at the end of the crazy airplane ride from Harrisburg, pale, shaken, and glad to be on firm ground.

15. Carlos returns with the coke

Sparshott joins him to begin the drug dance they had agreed on in advance: Terry sees the dope, then Carlos sees the money, they exchange car keys, Carlos drives off with the bread, then Terry leaves with the shit.

If Sparshott ever felt confident that the deal would actually go down, it's now. The dope is just a car trunk away. Takedown in two minutes. Even if Carlos gets a last minute hink and tries to run for it, Sparshott can tackle him—not a pretty final curtain—but a sure one.

"I'm really sorry," Carlos says to Terry, his friend. "My people were worried you were a fed."

"Hey, I'm no fed, buddy," Sparshott says. Touched by Carlos' confidence in him, he turns his eyes warm and friendly. "Trust me."

Carlos opens the trunk.

"I'm glad this is almost over," Sparshott says like a drug brother as he peers into the car. The "trust me" line is no bullshit. He has to keep Carlos calm. "I'm glad Marty's gonna do the next one."

Carlos points to a burgundy suitcase. "Fifteen . . . we got nine more for the next delivery. The rest will arrive in two days."

Sparshott unzips the bag. Inside are fifteen beautiful packages, eleven wrapped in white tape and four in yellow. They look like big beanbags. It's all over now. He has what he needs but doesn't feel the peace that comes after a long, difficult, but well-done job. A vague sense of sadness tugs at him. He straightens up. He looks at Carlos, chrissakes, he's not a bad kid, just spoiled and greedy.

"Hey man," Sparshott says, "the shit really looks good."

He takes his Harley hat off, runs his fingers through his hair like it was the most natural thing in the world to do, then puts it back on.

16. Sparshott is shown the cocaine

17. Sparshott's first view inside the trunk showed just an old suitcase

18. When he opened the suitcase, Sparshott felt a rush

19. Sparshott's hat is off – It's a "GO"

Carlos seems relieved and Sparshott knows exactly what he's thinking, hey man, it's half over, all I gotta do is see the money and get the fuck outta here. Carlos slams the trunk-closed and gives the car keys to Sparshott who, in turn, hands him two keys to the Firebird. The kid is trapped. Both keys can open the trunk but neither one will start the engine.

Over Carlos' shoulder, Sparshott sees the van door slide open and the SWAT team jump out with machine guns like paratroopers. "I'm sorry your people think I'm a fed," he tells Carlos as he leads him to the trunk of the Firebird like a hangman to the noose, calmly, surely, firmly. He distracts the kid so he can't see the SWAT team charging or the second SWAT van pulling out from behind Sears to block the exit. He doesn't want Carlos to panic now and make a run for it. Christ, the feds might shoot him like he was bigass Scarface or something.

"I'm not a fed," Sparshott says.

The SWAT team is almost at the Firebird.

"I'm Montgomery County police narcotics."

Carlos' mouth drops to his chest and he looks at his friend, Terry, like he's just been shot with a stun-gun. He's too shocked to run.

The SWAT team is only feet away now aiming machine guns at Carlos' chest.

Sparshott points to them.

"*They're* the feds," he says.

They're on Carlos like wolves on a wounded dog.

They flip him to the ground.

They pin him to the asphalt with polished, booted feet.

They all seem to shout at the same time . . . keep your fucking head down, don't move, hands behind your back. They cuff him before he even feels his bruises.

Carlos doesn't say a word.

FORTY-ONE

Stew Tippett is pacing the office surrounded by wall charts—arrests lists, seizures, searches, who does what to whom. His radio is tuned to the command channel and he's waiting to hear from Campbell. Any fucking thing, brother. His job is to make sure nothing falls through the cracks after the SWAT guys take Carlos down, coordinate all the teams, and troubleshoot. The tension he feels is almost unbearable. A hundred and forty agents and cops in four jurisdictions all poised to go. Talk about budget!

He hears the radio crackle, a comforting sound. Then he hears Billy say loud and clear, "The hat's off." Then he lets out a whoop, grabs the phone, and dials Jeff Favitta and Jerry Macready in Miami. "Everything went down," he says. "Go get em!"

20. Sparshott along with members of the arrest and surveillance team just after the arrest. Shown are members of Montgomery County Police's SWAT team, Special Investigations Division and the FBI

□ □ □

Marty Preston is sitting outside Santiago's house holding the shitty end of the undercover stick. While Tracy Sparshott is about to take down Carlos Medina, he's twenty miles from the action, with two FBI agents he doesn't even know. Just because he's the only member of the team who can positively identify the guy. And he's reduced to learning about the arrest of Carlos over the radio, secondhand, from his supervisor.

Preston's in a lot of pain.

He understands why there was no undercover role for him in the final scenario. But he expected to at least have the satisfaction of watching it. When he got his assignment and realized he wouldn't actually see the takedown, he at least expected the pleasure of hearing Bill Campbell say, "The hat's off." But his radio doesn't get Campbell's command channel so now he'll hear the stale news a minute after the fact. To a cop, that's like reading about it in the paper the next day.

Always reasonable, Preston understands why he has to identify Santiago. After all, the feds have to arrest the right bad guy and no one wants a lawsuit. But what irks him is that with all the Bureau's sophisticated long lenses and night-time photography gadgets, no one had thought of snapping a picture of Santiago for the ID kit. The feds were so worried someone might steal their money, they neglected the important task of the investigator—to create an unbreakable chain of evidence.

He understands why he has to work with two feds he doesn't know. Arresting Santiago—if he's home—is not the most important job of the day, and those who worked on the case get rewarded with a job closer to the action—except him, of course. Only another cop could possibly understand how utterly isolated he feels out there, alone and out of the loop, on Campus Way South in Largo near the Capital Center, on a day as important to him as this one, with no one he can even say "got him" to when the news finally crackles over his radio.

Preston hears a faceless voice filter through the radio static and say, "they gave the signal," then another voice, his supervisor's, "they got fifteen invitations," the signal to all PG cops to go do their thing. He feels no special thrill, just a sense of relief that Carlos and Roberto hadn't backed out of the sale, and that Tippett didn't have to order the feds into Roberto's apartment and the Winnebago in the hopes of finding twenty-five keys of coke there.

Preston gets out of his car as the two special agents ease out of theirs. He hides around the corner of the house in case Santiago himself answers the door. If the guy recognizes Preston and is armed, he might panic and start shooting. A woman lets the two agents in. Preston gives them a minute or two to find Santiago, then enters. He walks up to the guy, grabs his hand, and shakes it. Santiago's face is as white with fear as a light brown face can get. "Hi, Santiago," Preston says. Then in case the guy forgot who he is, "I'm Marty."

Preston savors his single crumb of satisfaction alone as he drives to Presidential Towers to find out what happened to Roberto and whether anyone found the rest of the dope. When he pulls into the lot, drives by the listening post, and parks near the side entrance Roberto liked to use, Tabares is long gone. He learns:

While the FBI SWAT team was taking down Medina in White Oak, Roberto was standing in the parking lot waiting for Carlos to return with the $390,000. With him was Ray Wilhide, a known Tabares-Hernandez distributor who also lived in Presidential Towers. Moments after Campbell had given "the hat's off" signal, an EST team pulled into the lot in an unmarked van. Its job was to raid Wilhide's apartment and the stash pad of Saulo Hernandez who was in Miami at the moment and would soon be in jail. Roberto saw the EST team jump out of the van like terrorists and panicked. If he had a gun, he might have opened fire. Instead, he ran north towards Bob's Big Boy as fast as an out-of-shape fifty-year-old could. Fortunately, the PG vice-squad team which pulled in behind the EST van caught the poor guy before he got a heart attack. Wilhide bolted too but, hey, where was the guy gonna hide. On the beltway?

Preston rides the elevator up to Roberto's apartment on the

twelfth floor. During the early days of the case, he had spent countless hours watching the hallway from behind the fire door in the stairwell hoping to get a make on a Tabares visitor. Now he has an uncontrollable urge to peek inside, a kind of post case catharsis. But the apartment is fed turf and off limits to F.L.'s. Fortunately, Kathy Day, the IRS agent who played Jerry Macready's girlfriend at the Bull on the Mark, is a member of the joint FBI-IRS search team. She understands Preston's need to be close to Roberto one last time and lets him in, another humiliating crumb. She backed Tracy and him for one night and gets a piece of the important action because she's a fed. He worked the case for a solid year and here he is, almost begging to see Roberto's empty room. He learns:

Roberto's apartment door had been a real steel-on-steel bitch. When it finally gave and the feds didn't find anyone inside, they began to hunt for the dope. Naturally, the feds tossed the Wilhide and Hernandez apartment searches to PG locals because they suspected there wouldn't be any camera-worthy dope there and they kept Tabares' pad for themselves. It didn't take an IRS agent long to find a heavy suitcase in Roberto's bedroom. He was about to open it when an FBI agent shouted, "Hey, leave it alone. We're going to do it." But the IRS agent shouted right back, "Fuck you," unzipped the bag and found the nine keys Preston was supposed to buy later that day as part of the Task Force sting. FBI agents all but kissed the IRS agents. "Hey, let's see the DEA top *this* one."

Preston looks at the drugs in the suitcase, thanks Kathy Day, then checks on the brothers searching the other two Presidential Towers apartments. The FBI guessed right for a change, there wasn't much.

Preston gets back into his car and drives north past Bob's Big Boy to the New Hampshire motor lodge to see what happened to the female courier who drove up from Miami with Roberto. She had already checked out and hadn't left so much as a hair behind.

Weary and feeling blue, Preston gets back into his car and heads for the FBI office in Hyattsville where special agents are processing the prisoners before taking them to Baltimore and jail. He rides the elevator up to the fourth floor with two FBI guys he knows. When the elevator door slides open to a large room, Carlos is standing there in cuffs. He hears Marty's voice, turns, and says, "Hi Marty." He wears a sad smile that says, hey man, sorry they got you too.

"Hi Carlos," Preston says. It's a shock to see the kid like this, scared and in cuffs, facing up to life in prison as a drug conspirator and kingpin.

Then Carlos notices that Preston isn't cuffed. Then he hears an FBI agent say, "Good job, Marty." Then he looks so damn hurt that Preston can barely face him.

Without another word, Preston walks to a window at the far end of the room and watches the circus in the parking lot below. Tow trucks hauling seized cars and gently setting them on the asphalt. Television vans, microphones and wires and lights, and reporters everywhere. It was a cruel irony.

The Bureau had managed to forget Santiago's photograph but it sure remembered to invite TV cameras to its post-game show. Minutes after the takedown, it called a hasty press conference in Baltimore for later that afternoon so it wouldn't miss the evening news. But it had taken the Bureau six months to get him an undercover car of his own. The Baltimore SAC would point to twenty-nine white and yellow packages of cocaine lined up on a table and crow into the cameras, "Ladies and Gentlemen . . . if you please . . . in the center ring we have . . . the biggest cocaine seizure in the history of the Washington-Baltimore metropolitan area." This from the same cred who spiked Jerry Macready's IRS money laundering investigation and refused to go for Tabares' supplier, Tomas.

High above the confusion and fear in the lot below, Preston watches bad guys enter the building to be processed and leave it for jail. There is Roberto himself desperately trying to shield his face from the cameras with cuffed hands, and his junkie son Roberto, Jr. . . . At long last, Frank Jones, arrested with coke in his pocket, and his daughter . . . Santiago and Carlos' cousin Pinky . . . Ray

Wilhide and three of his runners . . . and more.

As he watches, Preston cries. The tears are too complicated to understand and he hopes no one sees them.

He had put so much of his career and himself into the case and for a harrowing moment last night in the listening post when Tippett's feet froze, he had thought it was all over. The twelve-month investigation had been filled with painful, humiliating conflict and tension. All through it, a supervisor kept telling him he was wasting county time, the case would never fly, he'd come up empty. There were scary moments along the way when he feared for his job.

In the end, it turned out to be a perfect morning and, in spite of the constant inter-departmental bickering and backstabbing, everyone finally pulled together. He knows it all happened, in no small part, because of him. But a sense of sadness tinges his relief and satisfaction. Another young life is destroyed before it hardly begins. He's seen so many. He got to know Carlos and came to like him, and he often told himself that under different circumstances he'd invite the guy home for dinner. Now the kid is going away for a very long time, and a small piece of Marty Preston is going with him.

□ □ □

Tracy Sparshott shoots out of the White Oak Mall like a Blue Thunder with $390,000 in the trunk of the red Firebird. As he heads for the staging area at the funeral home, all he can think of is:

"I did it, Tippett. Fuck you!"

Frankly, he's a little embarrassed that he allowed the bust to become so personal. But that pin-prick of regret can't stop the high of victory rushing through him like a spoon of blow.

Fuck, he not only did it, man, he did it with style.

Sparshott hands over the rented car and the money to two FBI agents, then gets into his own car and heads for the FBI office in Hyattsville. He may be flying higher than a satellite but he is still thinking about Carlos. On the way, he listens to his radio, a scramble of scratchy voices, pauses, coded messages, license numbers of seized cars, requests for tow trucks, arrests completed, suspects not home. A ringside seat at the greatest show on earth.

The TV cameras are still at work when Sparshott pulls into the lot of the FBI building. Naturally, he avoids the lights.

The last fucking thing he wants is to see his hairy face on the tube. Bad guys watch a lot of television.

Sparshott takes the elevator to the fourth floor and enjoys the "great job, Tracy" he hears on the ride up and in the office. After a few handshakes and pats on the back, he looks around for Carlos and finds him locked in an interview room. The kid looks exhausted, calm, and utterly defeated, like, the party's fucking over, man.

"You okay, Carlos?" Sparshott asks. "Anything I can do for you?"

Carlos looks up from the table at badass Terry whose hulk all but fills the door. There is no anger or bitterness in his face as he shakes his head no. He doesn't say a thing for a moment as if he's deciding whether he should confide in Terry one last time. Then he says:

"Terry, you were fucking good, man. I didn't even know."

"Hey, man," Sparshott says. "Next time trust your instincts."

Sparshott closes the door and walks back to the elevator. His high of an hour ago has suddenly evaporated like dry ice, the void filled with sadness. Like a running back, showered and finally alone, he can't stop replaying the touchdowns he didn't make and dreaming about what *could* have been if the creds weren't such pussies and so cocksure that fucking locals were stupid. Talk about ignorant, hell, bad guys are dealing right around the corner because creds don't fucking understand police work . . . or a cop's gut-need to catch scumbags . . . or what it means to a narc—any narc not just him—to make the *big* play. As the old saying goes: you don't train a hunting dog and then make him sit on his ass and watch the rabbit run by.

Early on in the Tabares case, he wanted to prove that there

isn't a drug battle the good guys can't win if they just work together. Well, if he proved anything it's that the further you get from the trenches, the more the "War on Drugs" becomes, like the eggheads say, the opiate of the masses.

The sad thing is that within weeks, he's gotta rotate out of narcotics, his first love, into another job, one of those dumb regulations bureaucrats make to protect themselves. Yeah, man, big bucks *can* lure a narc over the line and burnout can turn a cop dangerous. But who's tickling whose balls here. As any narc will tell you, compulsory rotation is a chicken-shit reg meant to spare bureaucrats the tummy ache of deciding who stays and who goes. What makes him mad is that he has to go just when he's learned how good he really is, just when he's got a roaring appetite to scam another big dirtball and share what he knows. It's like suddenly becoming a widower after a short, fuck-happy marriage.

And then there's Carlos Medina who won't go away no matter how hard Sparshott tries to push him out of his mind. He lowered his guard for a minute and wouldn't you know, the kid got inside. That scares the polish right off his badge. Hey, he's supposed to be a badass biker with skin as tough as Harley chrome. Fuck all that human-shit that makes narcs weak, hey bro . . . it's just a game, sometimes *you* win, sometimes the bad guys win, bye bye dirtball, hello scumbag. But Carlos exposed the soft underbelly of caring and reminded him that behind all that "fuck you, pal," there's a cop as vulnerable as the next guy. Carlos made him understand that it really isn't just a game after all. It's real, man, not every bad guy is a shithead and not every good guy is Officer Ironballs.

But he's gotta forget Carlos. He's gotta force himself to see it as a game again, reduce all the human stuff to something simple like good guy and bad guy, win or lose. How else is he gonna protect himself from the creds and the courts that fuck lady justice every time you turn your back, and from the public that's either barking at him to do more or dumping on him for doing too much. If Carlos got to him, so can the next guy.

The elevator door slides open. Sparshott steps in. He

knows what he needs to do. Wipe Carlos Medina from his mind like yesterday's weather. Find a way to pass on what he's learned so new local narcs won't become casualties in either the street war on drugs or the other war—the bureaucratic one. Look for another job in the Department where he can survive. Put on a new set of armor so thick that no bad guy and no cred can pierce it.

The elevator door slides closed and begins to take him down to the street. But no matter how hard he tries to think about tomorrow or next week, he still sees the face of Carlos Medina.

Like looking in a mirror, the face is exhausted, calm, and defeated. Like, the party's fucking over, man.

□ □ □

The Task Force made another wave of arrests and seizures a few months later which brought the total number of arrests in the Tabares case to nearly forty and the total amount of assets seized to $8.2 million.

After a grand jury indicted him, Roberto Tabares copped a plea. In exchange for immunity for his daughter Nicky and his wife Nicole, he pleaded guilty to being a drug kingpin, tax evasion, and lying to a grand jury. He was sentenced to twenty years in a federal prison without parole.

Carlos Medina pleaded guilty to kingpin and tax evasion charges. That he and Roberto both received the same sentence, he considers unfair. Although he holds no resentment against Sparshott and Preston—"they did what they had to do and gave an Oscar performance"—he believes they lured him into a crime he would not have otherwise committed. He feels hurt that they didn't encourage him to retire before he got in too deeply.

Tom Roberts didn't have enough evidence to charge Saulo Hernandez, whom they suspected was a bigger dealer than Roberto Tabares, as a kingpin. He pleaded guilty to the lesser charge of conspiracy to distribute cocaine and was sentenced to sixteen years without parole.

Gustavo Rodriguez, Santiago, and Frank Jones all pleaded guilty to cocaine distribution. Rodriguez got seven years without parole. Santiago and Jones got five years each. Both served their time and have been released. Jones is back on the street but Santiago was deported back home to the Dominican Republic since he didn't have American citizenship. Mules and runners like Carlos' cousin "Pinky" Pincus got two to five years with parole.

Roberto, Jr., died of AIDS and his brother Raul is still a quadriplegic in a Florida hospital.

June Boyle is still a Fairfax County cop. When she shot and killed an unarmed suspect in a drug bust, her superiors forced her to resign from narcotics even though Internal Affairs cleared her.

Jerry Macready coordinated the Miami arrests, searches, and seizures for the Task Force. He is still an IRS criminal investigator. A certified instructor, he teaches IRS and DEA agents how bad guys launder money and where they hide assets.

Stew Tippett was so disgusted with narcotics work that he took a transfer to headquarters where he joined the Security detail. He asked the Director for letters of commendation for both Sparshott and Preston.

Bill Campbell left the FBI seven months after the White Oak takedown and became a DEA agent in south Florida.

Marty Preston was soon promoted to sergeant, then to lieutenant after successfully passing the PG County qualifying exams. With Sparshott, he co-won the Medal of Honor of the Maryland Chiefs of Police Association.

For his work on the Tabares case, Detective Tracy Sparshott was voted Narcotic Investigator of the Year by the Metropolitan Council of Governments, Policeman of the Year for Montgomery County, Maryland along with the county's highest honor, the Gold Medal Award of the Montgomery County Police and Fire Departments. Due to a mandatory rotation policy for narcotic investigators, Sparshott was required to transfer immediately after completing this case. He transferred to the K-9 corps. where he and his new partner, Narco, a 73-pound Belgian Malanois, won several awards as a team and apprehended over three-hundred felons during their seven year partnership. Sparshott transferred back to narcotics where he continued to work undercover assignments until he retired in 1999. He now teaches undercover narcotic investigations and drug interdiction classes to law enforcement officers throughout the United States.

Jeff Favitta and Marty Preston kept investigating Tabares leads. Months after the White Oak buy-bust, they learned that Tomas' last name was Betancort-Garcia, Sr., and that he was indeed one of the biggest dealers in Miami with Colombian cartel connections. When they finally got a warrant to search his mansion in Little Havana, he and his cash assets were long gone. The DEA eventually caught Tomas distributing heroin in New York under the alias Guillermo Pena. He died of a heart attack in prison while awaiting trial before the DEA could question him. Based on leads found among Tomas' papers, federal agents were able to eventually arrest Pablo Valdes, a Miami money launderer, who washed cash for Tomas, among others. They also seized $4 million of Valdes' drug assets.

ACKNOWLEDGMENTS

I could not have written this book without the help of many people, some of whose names have been changed to protect their privacy.

In particular, I would like to thank the following members of the Task Force team for their full cooperation in researching and writing this book: William Campbell, Jeff Favitta, Gerard T. Macready, Marty Preston, Tom Roberts, Tracy Sparshott, and Stew Tippett. Their passion to make the Tabares bust story known was a writer's windfall.

Thanks also to the following for sharing their recollections of the Tabares case with me: Robert Bonsib, June Boyle, Penny Campbell, Mike DuMond, Harvey Einsenberg, Scott Hammond, William O'Toole, Bill Tucker, and Robert Wills.

Special thanks to: Richard and Virginia Sparshott for their hospitality during long hours of interviewing; Terry Sparshott for sharing her insights about Panama; Dennis R. "Rick" Gibbins for discussing what it's like to work with Tracy Sparshott; Helen for sharing parts of her life as a former cocaine addict; the Montgomery County SWAT Team for showing me how they work and train, treating me to one hell of a flash-bang, and taking me on a drug raid; PG Police Chief David Mitchell for authorizing Marty Preston to discuss the Tabares case; FBI media specialist Sally Sparks for arranging interviews with special agents familiar with the Tabares case; Marvina Parks for a mountain of material about OCDEFT; Tessa Tilden-Smith for help in researching the town of

Frederick, Maryland; and the anonymous woman who gave me a tour of Roberto Tabares' house in Little Havana which she purchased at a government auction.

Also special thanks to Carlos Medina who allowed me to interview him for hours, some painful; to Bill Melick, Carlos' prison counsel for helping to arrange the interviews; and Mike Kessel of the Federal Correctional Institution in Milan, Michigan, for securing necessary permissions.

Very special thanks to my wife, Paula Kaufmann, for her steady encouragement on an exciting but difficult project and her patient editing.